SECOND EDITION

Daytrips

WASHINGTON D.C.

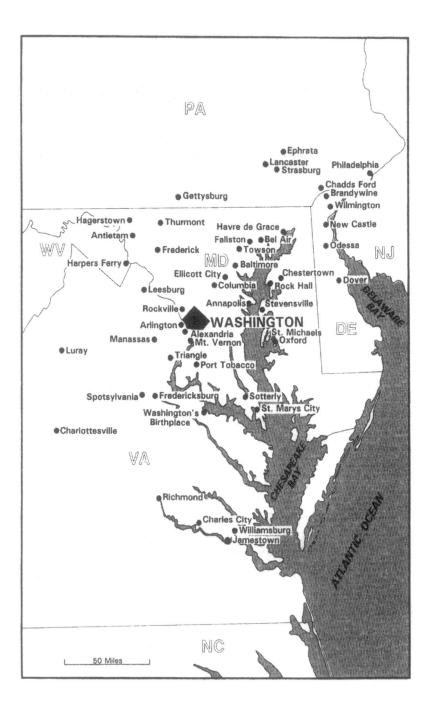

PA

●Ephrata
●Lancaster
Strasburg●

Philadelphia●

●Gettysburg

Chadds Ford●
Brandywine●
●Wilmington

Hagerstown●
Antietam●

●Thurmont

Havre de Grace●

●New Castle

WV

●Frederick

Fallston●
Towson●
●Bel Air

●Odessa

MD

Baltimore●

NJ

Harpers Ferry●

Ellicott City●
●Columbia

Chestertown●

●Rock Hall

●Dover

●Leesburg

Annapolis●

●Stevensville

DELAWARE BAY

Rockville●

WASHINGTON

DE

Arlington●

●Alexandria
●Mt. Vernon

St. Michaels●
●Oxford

Manassas●

●Luray

Triangle●
●Port Tobacco

Spotsylvania●
●Fredericksburg

Sotterly●
●St. Marys City

Washington's●
Birthplace

●Charlottesville

VA

CHESAPEAKE BAY

●Richmond

Charles City●
●Williamsburg
Jamestown●

ATLANTIC OCEAN

NC

50 Miles

SECOND EDITION

Daytrips

WASHINGTON D.C.

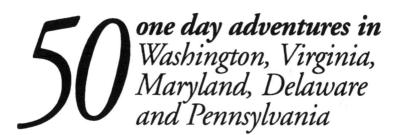

50 **one day adventures in** *Washington, Virginia, Maryland, Delaware and Pennsylvania*

EARL STEINBICKER

HASTINGS HOUSE
Book Publishers
Norwalk, Connecticut

Copyright © 2000 by Earl Steinbicker.
Revised and updated by Sara Southworth Weir.

ISBN: 0-8038-9429-5

Printed in the United States of America
10 9 8 7 6 5 4 3 2 1

Comments?   Ideas?
We'd love to hear from you. Ideas from our readers have resulted in many improvements in the past, and will continue to do so. And, if your suggestions are used, we'll gladly send you a complimentary copy of any book in the series. Please send your thoughts to Hastings House, Book Publishers, 9 Mott St., Norwalk CT 06850, or fax us at (203) 838-4084, or e-mail to Hhousebks@aol.com.

Contents

Introduction

L ucky Washingtonians! Both they and their visitors are within easy striking distance of some of America's greatest attractions, as well as several of its relatively unknown but intriguing byways. Many of these lie within 50 miles of Capitol Hill, and the overwhelming majority are less than 100 miles away. Although it stretches the daytrip concept just a tad, a few destinations are so compelling that they've also been included even though they are located as far as 160 miles from the nation's capital.

For both area residents and visitors alike, daytrips are the ideal way to probe this compact, treasure-filled region. And, if you have a weekend or more at your disposal, why not combine several daytrips into a mini vacation?

Washington is, of course, a fabulous destination in itself. To help you enjoy its wonders, this book opens with six one-day walking tours that explore the most interesting corners of town, ranging from the Mall and Capitol Hill to Kalorama and Georgetown. You won't need a car for these short excursions, as all of them can easily be reached by Metro, bus, cab, or even on foot.

Virginia is next, with 16 daytrip destinations ranging from nearby Arlington to as far away as historic Yorktown. Fully half of these are within 50 miles of Washington, and some can even be reached by public transportation.

Maryland follows, with hikes along the old C&O Canal, a walking tour of Annapolis, four in-depth probes of Baltimore, delightful spots around the Chesapeake Bay and the Eastern Shore, unusual places to the west, and plenty of little-known attractions in the suburban counties near Washington itself. Although it's in West Virginia, Harper's Ferry is close enough to the nation's capital to be included in this section.

Tiny Delaware—America's second-smallest state—is indeed a "small wonder" with its historic villages and elegant estates that rival those of Europe. Here you can also explore the beginnings of American industry, and ride a boat to a restored Civil War fortress.

Finally, the last section deals with southeastern Pennsylvania, whose attractions lie as close as 78 miles from Washington and are yet a world apart in atmosphere. From the battlefield of Gettysburg through the rolling farmland of the Pennsylvania Dutch country; from the civilized treasures of the Brandywine Valley to the urban delights of today's Philadelphia, the Keystone State offers such a wealth of pleasures that you might consider staying for a few days and combining some of the trips.

Wherever practical, the daytrips have been arranged as walking tours following a carefully-tested route on the accompanying map.   This works well in larger towns and cities, and sometimes even in historic villages. In other cases, however, the attractions are just too far apart to see on foot, so their descriptions are arranged in a driving sequence from which you can pick and choose, matching site numbers with those on the trip's road map. A few of the daytrips, such as that to Virginia's Shenandoah National Park, are designed for the sheer pleasure of driving, with just a few attractions that you might want to see along the way.

Dining well is a vital element in any travel experience. For this reason, a selection of particularly enjoyable restaurants has been included for each of the daytrips. These are price-keyed, with an emphasis on the medium-to-low range, regional cooking, and local atmosphere. Their concise location descriptions make them easy to find.

Time and weather considerations are important, and they've been included under the "Practicalities" section of each trip. These let you know, among other things, on which days the sights are closed, when some special events occur, and which places to avoid in bad weather. The location, telephone number, and (when applicable) Internet site of the local tourist information office is also given in case you have questions.

Please remember that places have a way of changing without warning, and that errors do creep into print. If your heart is absolutely set on a particular sight, you should check first to make sure that it's open, and that the times are still valid. Phone numbers and, where applicable, Internet sites for this purpose are given for each of the attractions, or you could contact the local tourist office.

One last thought: It isn't really necessary to see everything at any given destination. Be selective. Your one-day adventures from Washington should be fun, not an endurance test. If they start becoming that, just find your way to the nearest antique shop, gallery, or historic inn and enjoy yourself while soaking up local atmosphere. There will always be another day.

Happy Daytripping!

Section I

DAYTRIP
STRATEGIES

The word "Daytrip" may not have made it into dictionaries yet, but for experienced independent travelers it represents the easiest, most natural, and often the least expensive approach to exploring many of the world's most interesting areas. This strategy, in which you base yourself in a central city (or its suburbs) and probe the surrounding region on a series of one-day excursions, is especially effective in the case of Washington and the nearby states.

ADVANTAGES:
    While not the answer to every travel situation, daytrips have significant advantages over point-to-point touring following a set itinerary. Here are ten good reasons for considering the daytrip approach:

1.   Freedom from the constraints of a fixed itinerary. You can go wherever you feel like going whenever the mood strikes you.
2.   Freedom from the burden of luggage. Your bags remain in your hotel while you run around with only a guidebook and camera.
3.   Freedom from the anxiety of reservation foul-ups. You don't have to worry each day about whether that night's lodging will actually materialize.
4.   The flexibility of making last-minute changes to allow for unexpected weather, serendipitous discoveries, changing interests, new-found passions, and so on.
5.   The flexibility to take breaks from sightseeing whenever you feel tired or bored, without upsetting a planned itinerary. Why not sleep late in your base city for a change?
6.   The opportunity to sample different travel experiences without committing more than a day to them.
7.   The opportunity to become a "temporary resident" of your base city. By staying there for a while you can get to know it in depth,

becoming familiar with the local restaurants, shops, theaters, night life, and other attractions—enjoying them as a native would.

8. The convenience of not having to pack and unpack your bags each day. Your clothes can hang in a closet where they belong, or even be sent out for cleaning.

9. The convenience (and security!) of having a fixed address in your base city, where friends, relatives, and business associates can reach you in an emergency.

10. The economy of staying at one hotel on a discounted longer-term basis, especially in conjunction with package plans. You can make advance reservations for your base city without sacrificing any flexibility at all.

And, of course, for those who actually live in or around Washington, daytrips are the key to discovering one of America's most fascinating regions—one day at a time.

WASHINGTON AS YOUR BASE

GETTING THERE:

By Air: Many of the world's major airlines, along with numerous small carriers, fly in and out of at least one of Washington's three airports. The busy **Ronald Regan Washington National Airport** (DCA) is just across the Potomac River in Arlington, VA, and is very easily reached by Metro, cab, bus, or private car. Its new 35-gate terminal opened in the summer of 1997. The airport primarily serves the East Coast with non-stop domestic flights of 1,240 miles or less, as well as Canada. ☎ (703) 417-8000, Internet: www.Netwashairports.com. Washington **Dulles International Airport** (IAD), about 25 miles west of the city in Virginia, is a modern facility catering to both international and domestic traffic, and is connected to downtown by bus or taxi, a bus/Metro combination, limo, or private car. ☎ (703) 369-1600, Internet: www.netwashairports.com. A third choice, and an especially good one for low-cost flights, is **Baltimore- Washington International Airport** (BWI), about 28 miles northeast of Washington. Offering both international and domestic services, it is conveniently reached via Amtrak or MARC trains from Washington's Union Station, by bus, or by private car. ☎ (800) 435-9294, Internet: www.bwiairport.com.

By Rail: **Amtrak** provides fast, frequent service along the Northeast Corridor to Baltimore, Wilmington, Philadelphia, New York, New Haven, Boston, and points in between. They also offer somewhat more leisurely rides to Canada, the South, and points west. ☎ (800) USA-RAIL,

Internet: www.amtrak.com. Commuter services to Maryland are operated by **MARC** ☎ (800) 325-RAIL, and to Virginia by **Virginia Railway Express**
☎ (800) RIDE-VRE, Internet: www.vre.org. All trains use Washington's
magnificent **Union Station** (see page 49), located near the Capitol and
major hotels, and a stop on the Metro system (see page 20).

By Bus: Greyhound operates out of their terminal at First and L
streets NE, a few blocks north of Union Station. While slower than
planes or trains, intercity bus travel has the decided advantage of being
much cheaper. Direct service is provided to Baltimore, Philadelphia,
New York, Pittsburgh, Richmond, and other cities. For information ☎
(202) 289-5154 or (800) 231-2222, Internet: www.greyhound.com.

By Car: Washington is completely encircled by its notorious **Capital
Beltway**, the eastern part of which is Route I-95 and the western part I-
495. Venturing inside that ring during rush hours exposes you to mon-
ster traffic jams, quirky traffic patterns, and often restrictions on cars
with fewer than three occupants. Try to avoid driving inbound on weekdays from 6:30–9 a.m. and outbound from 4–6:30 p.m. Downtown parking lots are plentiful but very expensive, and free parking spaces are
practically non-existent. You'll certainly need a car for most of the out-
of-town daytrips, but inside the Beltway (and especially downtown)
you're better off sticking to public transportation.

ACCOMMODATIONS:

Unless you live in or around Washington, you'll need a place to
stay. Although the capital has a seemingly infinite number of hotels,
they're often booked solid, making advance **reservations** essential.
Discount **package deals** that combine transportation with hotel rooms
are offered by several airlines as well as by Amtrak. **Hotel** rates are highest in spring and fall, and lowest in the heat of mid-summer. Many
hotels offer deeply discounted **weekend packages**; check your travel
agent about this. The city levies a 13% **room tax** plus a $1.50 per-room-
per-night occupancy tax on all accommodations, which must be figured
into your budget. A convenient source of up-to-the-minute information
on hotels as well as instant reservations is provided by **Washington DC
Accommodations**, ☎ (202) 289-2220 or (800) 554-2220, Internet:
www.dcaccommodations.com. Other web sites include
www.visitdc.com and www.hotelsdc.com.

For adventurous travelers, **Bed & Breakfast** stays in Washington are
becoming an increasingly popular way of cutting costs while enjoying a
much more personalized service. If you'd like to try this alternative,
there are two cooperative booking agencies that can give you information and make arrangements. They are: **Bed & Breakfast
Accommodations, Ltd.**, P.O. Box 12011, Washington, DC 20009, ☎ (202)

328-3510, Internet: www.bnbaccom.com; and **Bed & Breakfast League, Ltd.**, P.O. Box 9490, Washington, DC 20016, ☎ (202) 363-7767.

For the budget traveler, hostels provide dormitory-style accommodations at extremely low rates. A favorite is the **Hostelling International—Washington DC** at 1009 11th St. NW 20001, ☎ (202) 737-2333 or (800)-909-4776, Internet: www.hiayh.org.

NEARBY ALTERNATIVES:

Staying in suburban Virginia or Maryland is a good way to save money, and may actually be more convenient for the out-of-town daytrips. As for visiting Washington itself, you can always drive to the nearest Metrorail station and ride the train in to avoid city traffic. A broad selection of hotels can be found in Arlington VA, Alexandria VA, Bethesda MD, and Silver Spring MD, among other nearby commuter towns. State and local tourist information offices (see page 16) will gladly tell you all about them.

CHOOSING DESTINATIONS

With 50 trips from which to choose, and several attractions for each trip, deciding which are the most enjoyable for you and yours might be problematic. You could, of course, read through the whole book and mark the most appealing spots, but there's an easier way to at least start. Just turn to the index and scan it, looking out for the special-interest categories set in **BOLD FACE** type. These will immediately lead you to choices under such headings as Art Museums, Restored Historic Villages, Civil War Sites, Boat Trips, Children's Activities, Railfan Excursions, and many others.

The elements of one trip can often be combined with another to create a custom itinerary, using the book maps as a rough guide and a good road map for the final routing.

Some of the trips, listed in the index as **SCENIC DRIVES**, are just that—they are primarily designed for the pure pleasure of driving, with just enough attractions along the way to keep things lively. These are especially enjoyable if you are blessed with a car that's fun to drive.

GETTING AROUND

The driving directions for each trip assume that you're leaving from Washington, DC. Chances are, however, that you live (or are staying) elsewhere in suburban Virginia or Maryland, so you'll need to modify the routes a bit.

The route **maps** scattered throughout the book show you approximately where the sites are, and which main roads lead to them. In many cases, however, you'll still need a good, up-to-date road map. An excellent choice for a single-sheet map that covers virtually all of the destinations is the *Delaware/Maryland/Virginia/West Virginia Roadmap* published by Rand McNally. The same publisher's spiral-bound *Northeastern U.S. Road Atlas* covers everything and is exceptionally easy to use while driving. For more detail on the shorter daytrips, an ideal choice would be ADC's *50- mile-Radius Map of Washington, DC*. The free maps distributed by state tourist offices vary greatly in quality, so if the one they give you isn't clear enough, head for your bookstore and look over their selection.

The majority of daytrips in this book are designed to be made by car, and do not really lend themselves to public transportation. If you've arrived in Washington without wheels, you'll have to rent, borrow, buy, or steal a vehicle; or else limit yourself to those 15 trips that can be done easily by **Metro, train or bus**. Besides the six trips within Washington itself, these are: Arlington, Alexandria, Mount Vernon, Baltimore (four trips), Annapolis, and Philadelphia (two trips). Of course, a true public transit fanatic will find ways of getting anywhere by train or bus, but unless you're willing to spend over two hours each way just arriving at a destination, and then walking long distances, it isn't recommended.

Some of the nearby trips can also be done by **bicycle**; Mount Vernon makes a particularly good bike trip at 19 level miles via a special trail.

Specific information about transportation within Washington DC itself will be found in Section II. In addition, each daytrip has a "Getting There" section outlining the most practical routes and, when applicable, public transportation services.

FOOD AND DRINK

Several choice restaurants that make sense for daytrippers are listed for each destination in this book. Most of these are long-time favorites of experienced travelers, are open for lunch, are on or near the suggested tour route, and provide some atmosphere. Many feature regional specialties not generally found elsewhere. Their approximate price range is shown as:

$ — Inexpensive.
$$ — Reasonable.

$$$ — Luxurious and expensive.
X: — Days closed.

If you're really serious about dining you should consult an up-to-date restaurant and hotel guide such as the annual *Mobil Travel Guide—Mid-Atlantic*, or the various *Tour Books* available free to members of the AAA. Strictly for restaurants, the *Zagat Survey* guides for Washington/Baltimore and the Philadelphia area are widely respected and updated yearly.

Fast-food outlets are, of course, nearly everywhere, and have the advantage of not taking up much of your sightseeing time. In warm weather, why not consider a **picnic**? Many of the hotels will make up picnic baskets for you and many of the attractions have picnic facilities that you can use; these are indicated in the practical information for those sites.

PRACTICALITIES

WEATHER:

Washington is notorious for its hot, humid summers, when walking from one air-conditioned interior to another is just about all some people can endure. If heat bothers you, avoid the city during July and August—or plan on making daytrips to the cooler countryside.

Spring and fall are the best seasons for the entire region, and therefore the most crowded. This is a good time to explore the less-famous attractions in the surrounding states.

Winter is at best unpredictable, but rarely severe. Northerners are eternally amused at how little snow it takes to bring this "southern" city to a complete halt. Often a mere dusting will suffice. Still, the attractions remain open and uncrowded, and the temperature seldom gets low enough to inhibit walking tours. Many of the out-of-town destinations sponsor special holiday events that are easily worth a one-day excursion.

OPENING TIMES, FEES, and FACILITIES:

When planning a daytrip, be sure to note carefully the **opening times** of the various sites—these can sometimes be rather quirky. Anything unusual that you should know before starting, such as "don't make this trip on a Monday," is summarized in the "Practicalities" section of each trip.

Entrance fees listed in the text are, naturally, subject to change—and they rarely go down. For the most part, admissions are quite reasonable considering the cost of maintaining the sites. Places with free entry, especially those not operated by governments, are usually staffed with unpaid volunteers and have a donation box to help keep the wolves from the door. Please put something in it.

Any special **facilities** that a site may offer are listed in the italicized information for that site, along with the address and phone number. These often include restaurants or cafeterias, cafés, information counters, gift shops, tours, shows, picnic facilities, and so on.

TELEPHONE NUMBERS:

Telephone numbers are indicated with a ☎; relevant area codes are also indicated. In both Maryland and Pennsylvania the area code must be dialed for all calls, including purely local ones, as several "area codes" sometimes serve the same locale. In these cases it is not necessary to add the prefix numeral "1" for local calls. This 10-digit "overlay" dialing will surely spread to other states as well. Calling ahead, always a good idea, is especially convenient if your car or pocket is equipped with a cell phone.

HANDICAPPED TRAVELERS:

Access varies with each individual's needs and abilities, so no firm statement can be made about any site. Those that are generally accessible without much difficulty are indicated with the symbol ♿, but when in doubt it is always best to phone ahead.

GROUP TRAVEL:

If you're planning a group outing, always call ahead. Most sites require advance reservations and offer special discounts for groups, often at a substantial saving over the regular admission fee. Some sites will open specially or remain open beyond their scheduled hours to accommodate groups; some have tours, demonstrations, lectures, and so on available only to groups; and some have facilities for rental to groups.

SUGGESTED TOURS

Two different methods of organizing daytrips are used in this book, depending on local circumstances. Some are based on **structured itineraries** such as walking tours and scenic drives that follow a suggested route, while others just describe the **local attractions** from which you can choose. In either case, a town or area **map** always shows where things are, so you're not likely to get lost. Numbers (in parentheses) in the text refer to the numbers on the appropriate map.

Major attractions are described in one or more paragraphs each, beginning with practical information for a visit. **Additional sites** are worked into the text, along with some practical information in italics. All are arranged in a logical geographic sequence, although you may want to make changes to suit your preferences.

Walking tours, where used, follow routes shown by heavy broken lines on the accompanying map. You can estimate the amount of time that any segment of a walking tour will take by looking at the scaled map and figuring that the average person covers about 100 yards a minute.

Trying to see everything at any given destination could easily lead to an exhausting marathon. You will certainly enjoy yourself more by being selective and passing up anything that doesn't catch your fancy, and perhaps planning a repeat visit at some other time.

Practical information, such as opening times and admission fees, is as accurate as was possible at the time of writing, but will certainly change. You should always check with the sites themselves if seeing a particular one is crucially important to you.

*OUTSTANDING ATTRACTIONS:
An *asterisk before any attraction, be it an entire daytrip or just one exhibit in a museum, denotes a special treat that in the author's opinion should not be missed.

TOURIST INFORMATION

The addresses, phone numbers, and Internet sites of local and regional tourist offices as well as major sights are given in the text whenever appropriate. These are usually your best source for specific information and current brochures, always bearing in mind that they are often commercial operations intent on getting your business. On a wider scale, state tourist offices offer free "vacation planning kits," maps, and brochures that are often useful. You can contact them at:

Washington, DC Convention & Visitors Association
1212 New York Ave. NW, Ste. 600, Washington, DC 20005
☎ (202) 789-7000, Internet: www.washington.org

Virginia Division of Tourism
901 East Byrd St., Richmond, VA 23219

☎ (800) 932-5827 or (804) 786-4484, Internet: www.virginia.org

Maryland Office of Tourism
217 East Redwood St., Baltimore, MD 21298-6349
☎ (800) 543-1036 or (410) 767-3400, Internet: www.mdisfun.org

West Virginia Division of Tourism
2101 Washington St. East, Bld. 17, Charleston, WV 25305-0317
☎ (800) 225-5982 or (304) 558-2766,
Internet: www.state.wv.us/tourism

Delaware Tourism Office
99 King's Highway, Dover, DE 19903
☎ (800) 441-8846 or (302) 739-4271, Internet: www.state.de.us

Pennsylvania Visitors Bureau
450 Forum Bldg., Harrisburg, PA 17120
☎ (800) 847-4872 or (717) 787-5453, Internet: www.state.pa.us

Section II

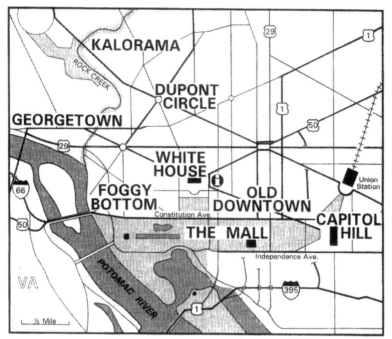

KALORAMA

ROCK CREEK

DUPONT CIRCLE

GEORGETOWN

WHITE HOUSE

FOGGY BOTTOM

OLD DOWNTOWN

Constitution Ave.

THE MALL

Independence Ave.

CAPITOL HILL

Union Station

POTOMAC RIVER

VA

½ Mile

DAYTRIPS WITHIN
WASHINGTON, D.C.

Before heading off on daytrips to Virginia, Maryland, West Virginia, Delaware, or Pennsylvania, you'll probably want to explore some of Washington itself. The six walking tours described in this section can guide you to both the most famous sites and also to some rather obscure attractions—always by way of enjoyable routes. The walks average a bit under four miles in length and should take about four hours or so to complete, assuming that you visit some of the museums and other attractions along the way.

Washington was built on a swamp, on mosquito-infested marshes ceded to the infant nation in a political compromise. That it has since become one of the most beautiful, dynamic, and fascinating cities on Earth is nothing short of a miracle. The decision to locate the federal capital here was made in 1790 when a Southerner, Thomas Jefferson (then Secretary of State) reached a deal with a Northerner, Alexander Hamilton (then Secretary of the Treasury) over repayment of the North's war debts in turn for putting the capital in the South. The site itself was chosen by George Washington and the land taken from Virginia and Maryland.

America's first President appointed a temperamental French army officer and engineer, Pierre Charles L'Enfant, to lay out the new city in a grandiose manner befitting the goals of an idealistic democracy. The design was completed in 1791. Although L'Enfant was soon fired after a brush with wealthy landowners, his plan survived and is still the basic layout of the city.

The development of Washington into a truly urbane capital was a long time in coming, but it has finally happened and the city is now one of the world's most enjoyable places to visit. No longer just a company town with marble monuments and broad avenues, Washington has grown up to become truly civilized, vibrant, cosmopolitan, full of life, and (best of all) full of fun. On top of that, most of its attractions are absolutely free because you've already paid for them in your taxes.

GETTING AROUND WASHINGTON, D.C.

Although all of the tours are designed for walking, you'll still need to use some form of transportation to get to their starting points, and then back home. Here are the options:

METRORAIL:

Washington's **subway system**, which extends well into the Virginia and Maryland suburbs as surface rail, is a revelation to straphangers everywhere. Clean, quiet, safe, comfortable, fast, and convenient, the highly-subsidized **Metro** is what other cities wish they had if only they could dig so deeply into federal coffers. Its only negative aspect is the monotonous "Big Brother" look of the underground stations; a bit of color and human imperfections would surely liven things up.

Five color-coded lines converge on downtown, where transfers can be made at several major stations. Entrances are marked by brown posts bearing a white **M** logo and colored stripes indicating which lines stop there. System maps are prominently displayed in the stations and in each car. To determine which **direction** to travel in, find your destination on the map and trace the line to its end. Not all trains go to the last station on the line; check the markings on the front of the train.

Fares are based on distance and time of day. Each rider must have a magnetically-encoded **Farecard** (or pass), which operates the turnstiles at both the beginning and end of your ride. Don't lose it. The correct fare is automatically subtracted from the card, and its remaining value printed on it at the exit turnstile. When this is all used up, the card is retained. If you owe additional fare, you'll have to go to the **Addfare** machine and pay the difference. Fare cards are offered in denominations of $1.10 to $45, with a 10% bonus if you purchase at least $20 worth of travel on one card. They are sold by vending machines that take both coins and bills ($1 or $5, sometimes also $10 and $20), but often balk at wrinkled, dirty, or worn paper money. The maximum change given is $4.95.

The base fare for one trip within downtown Washington is currently $1.10. For $5 you can purchase a **Metrorail One Day Pass** that allows unlimited travel after 9:30 a.m., or all day on weekends or federal holidays. These are available at the Metro Center station and many other outlets. Two children, age four or under, may travel free with each paying adult. Senior citizens and disabled persons qualify for discounts with a special ID card. **Transfers** to buses are 25¢ provided you get the transfer ticket from a machine as you first board the Metro.

The Metro operates from 5:30 a.m. until midnight on weekdays, and from 8 a.m. until midnight on weekends and holidays. Rush-hour conditions prevail before 9:30 a.m. and from 3 until 8 p.m. on weekdays. The entire system is wheelchair-accessible, with elevators running between street and platform levels. *For further information* ☎ *(202) 637-7000 (TDD 638- 3780), Internet: www.wmata.com.*

BUSES:

The **Metrobus** network serves all of Washington and much of the outlying suburban areas in Virginia and Maryland. Visitors will find it especially useful for trips to Georgetown and any other neighborhoods not reached by Metro subways. Bus stops are indicated by red-white-and-blue signs. Fares follow the same complicated structure as the Metro and must be paid in exact change (unfolded $1 bills and coins accepted), transfers, or passes. Transfers between buses are free but must be requested when first boarding. You can also make transfers for 25¢ to $2.00 from the Metro to a bus, but not the other way around— don't ask why. *For more information* ☎ *(202) 637-7000 (TDD 638- 3780), Internet: www.wmata.com.*

TAXIS:

Cabs are a relatively inexpensive way of getting around

Washington, thanks to a fare structure based on zones rather than on meters. There is a small charge for each additional passenger, for evening rush hours (4–6:30 p.m. weekdays), for snow emergencies, for bulky luggage, and for ordering by phone. Drivers often pick up other passengers going the same way, so be prepared to share. Cabs may be hailed in the street or arranged for by phone. Operating companies include: **Capitol Cab** ☎ (202) 546-2400, **Yellow Cab** ☎ (202) 544-1212, **Diamond Cab** ☎ (202) 387- 6200), and **Liberty Cab** ☎ (202) 636-1600. Always ask what the fare will be before entering; you'll usually be pleasantly surprised. A tip of 20% is expected.

BY CAR:

Avoid driving to destinations in central Washington as much as possible. While the traffic is not particularly horrendous (except during rush hours), the confusing street layout is, and parking is an absolute nightmare. Parking lots are very expensive, but even this is cheap compared to the fines that are swiftly and surely imposed on illegally parked cars. In addition, there is the hazard created by a large diplomatic community, whose members are immune to American laws and can therefore drive as they please. Beware of any vehicle bearing red-white-and-blue license plates; it may be driven by a 12-year-old ambassador's son out for a thrilling spin.

TOURMOBILES:

These narrated sightseeing buses make continuous runs around a circuit that includes all of the Mall, Union Station, Capitol Hill, Kennedy Center, Arlington National Cemetery, and the White House. Since the fare is valid all day long and includes unlimited stops and reboardings, they make a pleasant and convenient (albeit slow) way of getting around those parts of town. Tourmobiles operate every day except Christmas, from 9–6:30 between June 15th and Labor Day, and from 9:30–4:30 the rest of the year. Current fares are: Adults $14, children (3–11) $7. Tickets may be purchased from the driver or at special Tourmobile booths. *For further information* ☎ *(202) 554-7950 or (888) 868-7707, Internet: www.tourmobile.com. ♿ All buses have priority seating and wheelchair storage. Some buses are equipped with a wheelchair lift. Call first.*

BY BICYCLE:

Touring the nation's capital on the miles of trails throughout the city and surrounding areas provides a healthy alternative to motor transportation. Professionally guided tours can be arranged through several companies such as Bike the Sites, Inc., for a moderate price. Ride start times and locations change seasonally. *For further information* ☎ *(202) 966-8662.*

ORIENTATION:

All of Washington is divided into four quadrants: Northwest (NW), Northeast (NE), Southwest (SW), and Southeast (SE)—whose boundaries meet beneath the Capitol dome. The quadrant abbreviation is an essential part of any address; without it you will get hopelessly lost.

Laid out by Pierre L'Enfant in 1791, the streets follow a grid pattern overlaid by avenues radiating out at angles from strategically-placed circles. North-south streets are numbered, and east-west ones named for letters of the alphabet. Beyond "W" Street, the latter are given two-syllable names, then three-syllable names, and finally names of trees and flowers, always in alphabetical order. Avenues are named for states. Discrepancies abound—there is no "J" Street since that letter is missing from the Latin alphabet, "I" Street is usually spelled "Eye," and poor California gets a humble street but no avenue. Address numbers begin at the axes that separate the quadrants, and gain 100 for each full block they pass, more or less. Thus, 1600 Pennsylvania Avenue NW (the White House) is at 16th Street in the northwest quadrant.

The map on page 10 gives a general idea of where things are, while the individual walking-tour maps for each trip show all of the sites and major streets in the relevant neighborhoods.

LOCAL TOURIST INFORMATION

Your best source for all manner of local tourist information is to visit the DC Chamber of Commerce **Visitor Information Center** in the Ronald Reagan Building at 1300 Pennsylvania Avenue NW, close to the National Mall and the White House, Metro stop Federal Triangle. Here you can ask questions, take a virtual tour by computer, get free pamphlets, find out about accommodations and restaurants, purchase tickets, and shop for gifts. *Open Mon.–Sat. 8–6.* ☎ *(202) 328-4748, Internet: www.dcchamber.org.; also visit www.washington.org.*

*The Mall

What better introduction could there possibly be to Washington than to stroll down its Mall? This is the nation's meeting place, its collective backyard, an expression of its very democracy. Here's where millions of people come to take in the sights, to voice their opinions, to picnic, to jog, to celebrate national events, and to just relax and have a good time. It's always an enjoyable place to visit; doubly so since nearly every experience it offers is free.

The Mall is a grassy, tree-shaded esplanade about 800 feet wide, extending nearly two miles from the foot of Capitol Hill west to the Potomac River. Its eastern half is lined with major museums associated with the Smithsonian Institution, while its west end (technically known as West Potomac Park) contains several of the nation's greatest monuments. Although a part of L'Enfant's original 1791 plan for Washington, the Mall remained an unrealized mess until the early 1900s. A fetid canal ran up what is now Constitution Avenue, unsightly railroad yards crossed at 6th Street, and ugly temporary buildings blighted the landscape. Progress was slow, but it was certain; since the 1960s the Mall has finally become what it is today—one of the most satisfying public spaces on Earth.

Among the major highlights of this walking tour is the Smithsonian "Castle," the ever-popular Air and Space Museum, a magnificent view of the Capitol, the two widely-divergent wings of the National Gallery of Art, the Museum of Natural History with its dinosaurs and other beasts, The Museum of American History with its collection of just about everything, the towering Washington Monument, the Holocaust Memorial Museum, the Tidal Basin with its cherry trees and memorial to Jefferson, the stirring Lincoln Memorial, and the deeply moving Vietnam Veterans Memorial.

You won't be able to see it all in a day, of course, so a good plan of attack is to choose perhaps two museums to actually visit, and put off the others that interest you for later. This will allow enough time to stop by most of the monuments, and perhaps enjoy an amble around the Tidal Basin.

GETTING THERE:

By **Metro**, take the Blue or Orange line to the **Smithsonian** station.

By **taxi**, ask for the Smithsonian "Castle" on the Mall.

By **Tourmobile**, get off at the Arts and Industries Building stop. The Tourmobile route pretty much duplicates the walking route (see page 22).

PRACTICALITIES:

Nearly all of the sights along this route are open every day except Christmas. The walk is about five miles long if you follow it all the way. This distance can be substantially reduced by not making the side trip around the Tidal Basin, or by devoting one day to the museums and another to the monuments.

The Japanese **cherry trees** near the Tidal Basin are in bloom from around late March into early April, which is also the best possible time to explore the Mall.

Tourmobiles follow almost the same route, except for some side excursions into neighboring areas. They stop at most of the major sights and may be reboarded all day long for one fare. See page 22 for details.

General information about all of the **Smithsonian** museums along the Mall (and beyond) is available at the Smithsonian Institution Building, commonly known as "The Castle" (2), ☎ (202) 357-2700, TDD (202) 357-1729, Internet: www.si.edu. For other tourist information contact the **Washington Visitor Information Center** in the Ronald Reagan Building, 1331 Pennsylvania Avenue NW, ☎ (202) 789-7000, Internet: www.washington.org.

FOOD AND DRINK:

Having a decent meal near the Mall can be problematical, unless you're willing to settle for cafeteria fare. Some of the restaurants described on Trip 4 (page 63) are close enough to this route to be usable, and there are a number of good establishments south of the Mall, near L'Enfant Plaza and the waterfront, that are described below:

Le Rivage (100 Water St. SW, between Maine Ave. & 9th St.) Fine French cuisine with a view; outdoor deck in summer. Reservations, ☎ (202) 488-8111. $$$

Phillips Flagship (900 Water St. SW, by the waterfront) Eastern shore seafood is the specialty of this enormous waterside restaurant, open to the marina in good weather. ☎ (202) 488-8515. $$

Hogate's (9th & Maine Ave. SW, by the waterfront) Reservations are suggested for this traditional seafood restaurant overlooking the Potomac. ☎ (202) 484-6300. $$

Vie de France Café (600 Maryland Ave. SW, at 7th St. and L'Enfant

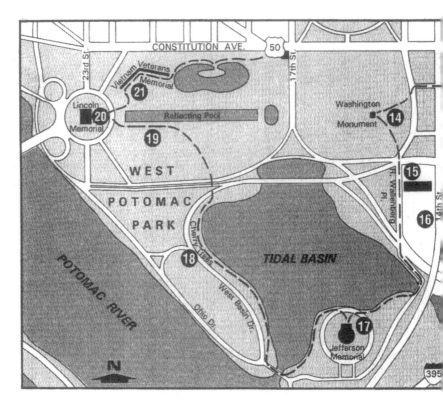

Plaza) Omelets, sandwiches, croissants, and the like are served at this bustling café. ☎ (202) 554-7870. X: Sat., Sun. $

Four of the museums—the Air and Space (8), the National Gallery of Art (11), the Natural History (12), and the American History (13)—have acceptable **cafeterias** that are open to the public and usually crowded. The Air and Space Museum also has a full-service restaurant called **The Wright Place**, and the Hirshhorn Museum has an outdoor café in summer.

Bear in mind that the Mall is a wonderful spot for a **picnic**. If you haven't brought your own food, you'll find several snack bars along the Mall, and street vendors along Constitution and Independence avenues.

SUGGESTED TOUR:

Numbers in parentheses correspond to numbers on the map.

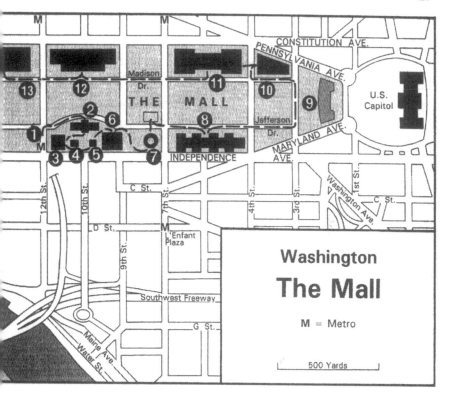

Washington

The Mall

M = Metro

500 Yards

From the **Smithsonian Metro stop** (1), or the Arts and Industries stop on the Tourmobile route (6), it's only a few steps to the:

SMITHSONIAN INSTITUTION BUILDING, a.k.a. **"THE CASTLE"** (2), 100 Jefferson Drive SW, ☎ (202) 357-2700, Internet: www.si.edu (this home page can be used to access all the buildings and museums associated with the Smithsonian). *Open every day except Christmas, 9–5:30. Free. Video show. Gift shop. Info.* &.

Inspired by 12th-century Norman military architecture, the Castle was completed in 1855 as the first home of the Smithsonian Institution. The world's largest museum-and-research complex, holding some 139 million artifacts, has long since spread itself all around the Mall, the rest of Washington, and even into suburban Maryland, New York City, and other places. Its early history is as strange as some of the things it collects.

James Smithson (1765–1829) never visited or had anything to do with America during his lifetime, although he is buried right in this building. The illegitimate son of the British Duke of Northumberland, he was socially snubbed but nonetheless successful as a brilliant scientist. Still, he was not allowed to use the family name until he was nearly 50 years of age. Smithson got his revenge on British snobbery posthumously. When his only heir, a nephew, died without descendants, his will bequeathed the entire fortune "to the United States of America, to found at Washington, under the name of the Smithsonian Institution, an establishment for the increase and diffusion of knowledge," adding that "My name shall live in the memory of man, when the titles of the Northumberlands...are extinct and forgotten." It took Congress some 11 years to decide whether to accept this British money, but in the end they swallowed their pride and the Smithsonian Institution was born.

The Castle now serves as a **Visitor Information Center** for all of the Smithsonian's museums and activities, as well as housing its administrative offices. Just inside the front entrance, to the left, is a crypt containing the body of James Smithson, brought here in 1904. Next to the **Great Hall** are two theaters featuring free 20-minute **video shows** about the organization. Interactive touch-screen terminals answer your questions in seven languages, electronic wall maps guide you around Washington, and scale models help you preview the sights.

Directly behind the Castle is the four-acre **Enid A. Haupt Garden**, which sits atop a vast, mostly underground complex of museum, research, and educational facilities, opened in 1987 as the **Smithsonian Quadrangle**. Along the west side of this stands the:

FREER GALLERY OF ART (3), Jefferson Drive at 12th St. SW, ☎ (202) 357-2700, Internet: www.si.edu. *Open daily except Christmas, 10–5:30. Free. Gift shop. ♿, use Independence Ave. entrance.*

The Freer Gallery features a magnificent collection of Asian art dating from Neolithic times to the 20th century, along with 19th- and early 20th-century American art including the world's best assemblage of works by James McNeill Whistler. It was donated to the Smithsonian in 1906 by a rags-to-riches Detroit industrialist named Charles Freer (1856–1919), who made an early fortune in railroad cars and spent the rest of his life collecting art. Freer also paid for the building and worked closely with the architect on its design. Don't miss the famous ***Peacock Room**, a luxurious London dining room of 1876 that was decorated by Whistler. The gallery connects both internally and through the garden with the:

ARTHUR M. SACKLER GALLERY (4), 1050 Independence Ave. SW, ☎ (202) 357-2700, Internet: www.si.edu. *Open daily except Christmas, 10–5:30. Free. Gift shop. ஃ, use elevator from the street-level pavilion in the garden.*

Space along the Mall was already at a premium when the Sackler Gallery was first proposed in 1982, so both it and two other new Smithsonian galleries were placed underground, beneath the garden adjacent to the Castle.

Dr. Arthur M. Sackler (1913–87) was a noted medical researcher and publisher who began collecting art after graduating from medical school. In the 1950s his interests changed from Western art to that of China, Southeast Asia, and the Near East. The collections, ranging in age from Neolithic times to the present, were donated to Harvard University, New York's Metropolitan Museum of Art, and the Smithsonian. Those shown here have been augmented with additional private collections of art from ancient Persia, Japan, and other Asian civilizations, as well as with rotating loan exhibitions. Among the most notable treasures are the ancient **Chinese jade carvings** and **bronzes, Iranian silver and gold** from 3000 BC, and **Persian Islamic manuscripts**.

While you're underground, you might want to see what's currently showing at the **International Gallery** of the S. Dillon Ripley Center, reached via the third level or by a separate entrance kiosk in the garden. The exhibitions here are widely eclectic, but always interesting.

Also underground, and connected via the third level as well as through its own pavilion in the garden, is the:

NATIONAL MUSEUM OF AFRICAN ART (5), 950 Independence Ave. SW, ☎ (202) 357-2700, Internet: www.si.edu. *Open daily except Christmas, 10–5:30. Free. Gift shop. ஃ, use elevator from the garden pavilion.*

This is the only museum in the United States to be devoted entirely to the traditional arts of sub-Saharan Africa. Founded in 1964 in a historic row house on Capitol Hill, it became part of the Smithsonian in 1979 and moved into these new subterranean quarters in 1987. More than just a gallery, it also serves as a research and reference center as well as an educational facility.

Some 900 distinct cultures are represented in the permanent collection of over 6,000 pieces in wood, metal, ivory, clay, and fiber. Not all of these can be displayed at once, of course, but the rotating exhibits always demonstrate the unique relationship of art to daily life among the peoples of Africa. Some of the highlights include the magnificent collection of 15th- to 19th-century **Royal Benin Art** from the former Kingdom of Benin (today's Nigeria), **masks** from Zaire, and **grave figures** from Cameroon.

Return to street level. Immediately east of the Castle stands the:

ARTS AND INDUSTRIES BUILDING (6), 900 Jefferson Drive SW, ☎ (202) 357-2700, Internet: www.si.edu. *Open daily except Christmas, 10–5:30. Free. Gift shop. Special events. ♿, use ramp on Mall side.*

This marvelously Victorian structure was the Smithsonian's first expansion, and was completed in 1881 to display remnants of the 1876 Centennial Exhibition in Philadelphia. After a checkered career, it was restored in 1976 and is now home to changing exhibitions from various Smithsonian organizations. Another feature of the building is the **Discovery Theater** where live performances are aimed at young audiences. ☎ *(202) 357-1500 for theater information and ticket reservations.*

Kids—and adults too—will enjoy a ride on the delightful **Carousel** on the Mall in front of the Arts and Industries Building. *Daily in warm weather, 10–5:30. Nominal charge.*

Only yards away from all this Victoriana, but a world apart, is the:

HIRSHHORN MUSEUM AND SCULPTURE GARDEN (7), Independence Ave. at 7th St. SW, ☎ (202) 357-2700, Internet: www.si.edu. *Open daily except Christmas, 10–5:30. Sculpture Garden 7:30–dusk. Tours daily at noon, Sat. and Sun. at 12 and 2. Tours of the Sculpture Garden 12:15 Mon.-Sat. (May and Oct. only) Free. Special events. Gift shop. Café in summer. ♿.*

It may look like a concrete doughnut on legs, but it's really an art museum. When Joseph Hirshhorn (1899–1981) gave his vast collection of contemporary works to the Smithsonian in 1966, he exposed a bit of that venerable institution to the avant-garde. Both the building and the collection it houses carry the stamp of a strong-willed individual who knew what he liked, even when his ideas were controversial or out of fashion. Since then, the museum has continued in the same vein, acquiring new works by today's artists and hosting exhibitions of the latest trends.

Begin your visit on the third floor, working your way clockwise through the galleries. Along the way you'll come to a **balcony** with a superb view across the Mall. This is the only opening in the otherwise windowless exterior wall, although there is plenty of glass facing the interior courtyard. The most modern paintings are on the second floor, while the lower level features temporary exhibitions and an introductory film.

On the Mall side of Jefferson Drive is the sunken ***Sculpture Garden**, a gorgeous outdoor collection of works by Auguste Rodin, David Smith, Henri Matisse, Henry Moore, and others.

Continue down the Mall to the:

*NATIONAL AIR AND SPACE MUSEUM (8), Independence Ave. at 6th St. SW, ☎ (202) 357-2700, Internet: www.nasm.edu. *Open daily except Christmas, 10–5:30, closing at 6:30 in summer. Free. Guided tours at 10:15 and 1. Interactive audio tours in 7 languages. IMAX Theater: Adults $5 to $5.50; seniors, students, children $3.75 to $4.50. Planetarium: Adults $5; seniors, students, children $3.75. Gift shops. Flight Line Cafeteria on ground floor at east end, Wright Place full-service restaurant above it. ᕃ, use ramp on Mall side.*

You'll quickly discover why this is the most popular museum in the world, attracting over ten million visitors annually. That's 30,000 a day! Where else can ordinary mortals touch a piece of the Moon, walk through the Skylab space station, or see in one glance the actual aircraft that make up the history of flight?

Experiencing most of the museum requires at least a full day, and is best done in several shorter visits. Since admission is free, why not just pop in and take a quick look around? You can always come back later.

As you stroll through this immense facility, you'll see such *mile-stones* as the Wright Brothers' 1903 *Flyer*, a Fokker T-2 that made the first non-stop coast-to-coast flight in 1923, a Ford Tri-Motor of 1926, Charles Lindbergh's *Spirit of St. Louis*, Amelia Earhart's Lockheed Vega, a DC-3, Chuck Yeager's *Bell X-1*, John Glenn's *Friendship 7* spacecraft of 1962, the Apollo II Command Module *Columbia* that returned the first astronauts from the Moon in 1969, and the ultra-lightweight *Voyager* that flew non-stop around the world without refueling in 1986. That's just for starters. There are dozens and dozens of more aircraft on display, along with thousands of flight artifacts dating from the 17th century right up to the present. All of the aircraft—and most of the spacecraft—are the actual ones that made history, as are most of the other items exhibited.

Another major attraction of the museum is its *Samuel P. Langley Theater*, which uses the IMAX system of enveloping an audience in a five-story-high screen. The specially-made films all concern flight or space, and will have you hanging onto your theater seat for dear life. Choose which film you want, and purchase tickets for that particular performance from the box office on the ground floor. It's best to do this as soon as you enter the museum.

The **Albert Einstein Planetarium** on the second floor has regularly scheduled sky shows that simulate the heavens on a 70-foot overhead dome. There is a nominal charge for these.

If all this is not enough and you'd like to see more, you can make reservations to tour the **Paul E. Garber Preservation, Restoration, and Storage Facility** in suburban Maryland. Here's where the rest of the Smithsonian's aerospace collection resides, and where you can watch it being restored. Be aware that this is a maintenance facility, not a museum, so don't expect heat or air-conditioning. *3904 Old Silver Hill Rd., Suitland, MD, ☎ (202) 357-1400. Tours Mon.–Fri. at 10, weekends and hol-*

idays at 10 and 1, closed Christmas. Free. Phone for reservations at least 3 weeks in advance. This facility will be moving into the new Air and Space Museum Dulles Center expansion facility at Dulles International Airport in northern Virginia, scheduled to open sometime after 2001 — hopefully before the 100th anniversary of the Wright Brothers' first flight on December 17, 2003. Over 180 aircraft and 100 spacecraft will be on display there.

The vacant lot just east of the Air and Space Museum is the last undeveloped land along the Mall, but not for long. The Smithsonian's **National Museum of the American Indian**, with a branch in New York City, is scheduled to move into its new quarters here in 2001.

Turn left on 3rd Street. From here you'll have a wonderful *view of the Capitol, perched atop its low hill and mirrored in its **Reflecting Pool** (9). Make another left on Madison Drive and amble west to the:

EAST BUILDING—NATIONAL GALLERY OF ART (10), Constitution Ave. and 4th St. NW, ☎ (202) 737-4215, TDD 842-6176, Internet: www.nga.gov. *Open Mon.–Sat. 10–5, Sun. 11–6, closed Christmas and New Year's Day. Free. Tours. Lectures. Films. Gift shop. Restaurant on upper level, cafeteria in lower concourse.* ⬥.

It's been called a triumph of architecture over art, but whether that's a fair assessment depends on your point of view. I.M. Pei's 1978 addition to the National Gallery calls so much attention to its angular self that the art it contains must really be special to be noticed at all. Fortunately, it is. One of the world's foremost collections of 20th-century art, this gallery concentrates on the major European and American movements and masters in that field, rather than on current trends. Seeing it properly will take well over an hour, so you may want to plan on coming back later. In any case, at least drop in for a quick look at the spectacular interior *atrium, which can be enjoyed even if you don't care for modern art.

Given the odd trapezoidal lot that he had to work with, and the surrounding structures to harmonize with, architect I.M. Pei did a superb job of reconciling difficult choices. The spacious interior is amazingly flexible, and can be arranged to suit anything from blockbuster exhibitions to the most intimate of shows. The pieces on display are changed frequently, since the museum's holdings are far greater than could ever be shown at one time. You can, however, expect to see major works by Picasso, Van Gogh, Matisse, Kandinsky, Brancusi, Georgia O'Keefe, Joan Miró, Max Ernst, Henry Moore, Mark Rothko, Giacometti, Alexander Calder, Anthony Caro, Warhol, Lichtenstein, Rauschenberg, and many, many others.

While affiliated with the Smithsonian, the National Gallery is not actually a part of that institution. Its real heritage can be best appreciated in its main West Building, easily reached from the East Building via an underground concourse with a moving sidewalk. Along the way you'll pass a cafeteria and a café, both bathed in sunlight by glass tetrahedrons in the plaza above. At the end of the concourse, step into the:

WEST BUILDING—NATIONAL GALLERY OF ART (11), Constitution Ave. and 6th St. NW, ☎ (202) 737-4215, TDD 842-6176, Internet: www.nga.gov. *Open Mon.–Sat. 10–5, Sun. 11–6, closed Christmas and New Year's Day. Free. Tours. Concerts. Gift shop. Restaurant on ground floor, cafeteria and café in lower concourse. &.*

Opened in 1941, this massive neoclassical museum building looks much older than it is. It was the last major work by the famed architect John Russell Pope (1874–1937), who also designed the National Archives and the Jefferson Memorial. This is a traditional museum in every sense of the word, and houses one of the most distinguished collections of serious art to be found anywhere.

The National Gallery is largely the creation of one man. Andrew Mellon (1855–1937) made his fortune in banking, then moved to Washington as Secretary of the Treasury and later as ambassador to Great Britain. Between his many activities he managed to find time to scour the art world for all the treasures his wealth could acquire, all with the intended purpose of creating a truly national art gallery for the American people. During the 1930s he even purchased part of the vast holdings of the Soviet Union, who needed the cash to buy tractors. Since the museum's opening, several other great collections have been donated to it by wealthy patrons.

From Rembrandt to Renoir, the artists represented here are far too numerous to list, but rest assured that they constitute a comprehensive survey of art history from medieval times until the dawn of the 20th century. A diagram of the museum layout is available free at the information desk.

Continue west on Madison Drive to the:

NATIONAL MUSEUM OF NATURAL HISTORY (12), Constitution Ave. and 10th St. NW, ☎ (202) 357-2700, Internet: www.si.edu. *Open daily except Christmas, 10–5:30, remaining open until 6:30 in summer. Free. Self-guided touchscreen tours $4.75 and free highlight tours Mon.–Thurs. 10:30 and 1:30, Fri. 10:30. Films. Gift shop. Atrium Café cafeteria. &, use Constitution Ave. entrance.*

Even if you don't have time for a proper visit to one of America's best natural history museums, at least step into the rotunda to say hello to the great *African bush elephant. You might be tempted to see more, either now or later, of the marvels that lurk within the halls of this neoclassical structure. Built in 1911, this was the Smithsonians's third building and is today one of the three most popular museums operated by them.

Immediately east of the stuffed pachyderm is the *Dinosaur Hall with its enormous, scary flying pterosaur and other prehistoric creatures. Kids love these fantastic bones, as they do the great blue whale, the ferocious Indian tiger springing right out at them, and the creepy, crawly Insect Zoo. More mundane exhibits include the ubiquitous dioramas, without which no natural history museum is complete, and the extensive collection of anthropological artifacts from vastly different times and cultures throughout the world. The latter is officially known as the Museum of Man, although some of its displays include women, too. There's also a stunning exhibit of minerals and gems in the newly renovated Gem and Mineral Hall that features the fabulous *Hope Diamond, a 45.5-karat rock said to carry a curse. The Discovery Room allows visitors, especially kids, to handle all sorts of specimens, but it has limited hours and capacity, so you'll need to get a free pass to enter it. *Open Tues.–Fri., noon–2:30; weekends 10:30–3:30.* Amateur researchers can make their own discoveries in the Naturalist Center, provided they're at least 12 years of age. Finally, there are always special exhibitions to hold your interest before continuing west to the:

*NATIONAL MUSEUM OF AMERICAN HISTORY (13), Constitution Ave. and 14th St. NW, ☎ (202) 357-2700, Internet: www.si.edu. *Open daily except Christmas, 10–5:30, remaining open until 6:30 in summer. Free. Tours. Gift shops. Cafeteria on lower level, café on first floor.* &.

This is the Smithsonian's famous Museum of Practically Everything, and it takes hours to explore. However, since it's free, why not pop in and glimpse a few of the sights before coming back for a more thorough visit?

Once centered around history and technology, the museum now focuses more on the nation's social and cultural side. Its monumental but hopelessly dull building of 1964 houses millions of pieces of what in any other context would be considered junk, but here add up to a fascinating mosaic of American life, past and present. Amid such treasures as Archie Bunker's chair, Muhammed Ali's boxing gloves, and plastic radios of the 1940s are several items worth a visit in themselves. Don't miss (how can you?) the *Foucault Pendulum directly inside the Mall entrance, the original *Star-Spangled Banner that flew over Fort McHenry during the War of 1812 and is now briefly unveiled every hour on the half-hour, and the slightly-hilarious, larger-than-life **statue of George Washington** wearing a toga and nothing else, that was removed from the Capitol in 1843 amid much embarrassment. Then there's the **First Ladies Hall** devoted to the wives of presidents, the gunboat *Philadelphia* of 1776, a marvelous collection of early automobiles in the **Road Transportation Hall**, and a **Railroad Hall** full of steam locomotives and rolling stock. There's really something here for everyone, so pick up a free guide map at the information desk near the entrance before probing all the hidden nooks and crannies.

Now follow the map into the western part of the Mall to visit the:

*WASHINGTON MONUMENT (14), The Mall and 15th St. SW, ☎ (202) 426-6841, Internet: www.nps.gov/wamo/index2.htm. *Ascents by elevator daily except Christmas; Apr.–Sept., 8 a.m.–11:45 p.m.; Sept.–Mar., 9–4:45. Free tickets for timed admission available at the kiosk at the base. Expect long lines in summer. To reserve passes in advance (for $1.50 fee)* ☎ *TicketMaster, (800) 505-5040. Tours down the steps on some weekends, call for details. Snack bar at base.* ♿, *disabled persons may bypass lines.*

Take a good look at this elegant, simple obelisk and then try to imagine what it might have been like had the original plans been completed. Instead of a dignified memorial to the first president, you'd witness a "shamelessly eclectic" heap of an "Egyptian shaft emerging from a Babylonian base ringed by a Greek temple," with a statue of Washington in a toga riding a "chariot drawn by Arabian steeds driven by an Etruscan Winged Victory"—to paraphrase the famous 1937 *Washington: City and Capital* guide by the W.P.A. It's a good thing they ran out of money.

The monument's slightly off-center location, in violation of L'Enfant's orderly plan, is due to unstable earth at the exact axis of the Mall. Somehow it's more comforting this way; to realize that imperfections are possible even here. Rising some 555 feet, the monument is still the tallest masonry structure on Earth, and a landmark for many miles around.

Construction, funded by a private group soliciting small donations from citizens, began in 1848 but stopped during the Civil War at a height of only 150 feet. In 1876 the truncated shaft was given to the federal government, and construction resumed by the Army Corps of Engineers. After a defective base that nearly made it the Leaning Tower of Washington was corrected, it was finally completed and opened to the public in 1888. The slight change in the color of the stone, about a quarter of the way up, was due to the interruption, during which the same Maryland quarry had reached a lower level with darker marble.

The elevator ride, once you get to it, takes only 70 seconds to reach

the top. Initially, only men were allowed to ride this newfangled contraption. Women and children had to walk up until elevators were made
safer. Hopefully they found the *view as breathtaking as do the tourists
of today. It's best after twilight, as the lights of Washington come on. You
might want to come back then, especially if the lines are long that day.

From here you can make a **side trip** around the Tidal Basin, passing
by the **Sylvan Theater** where open-air dramatic, musical, and dance performances are staged in summer. Although it adds nearly a mile to the
total distance, this extension is highly worthwhile; doubly so in cherry
blossom time. Just follow the map to the:

UNITED STATES HOLOCAUST MEMORIAL MUSEUM (15), 100 Raoul
Wallenberg Place (15th St.) SW, ☎ (202) 488-0400, Internet:
www.ushmm.org. *Open daily except Yom Kippur and Christmas, 10–
5:30, closing at 8 on Thurs. from Apr.–Sept. Free same-day tickets available at 14th St. entrance from 10 on, first-come, first-served. Advance
tickets from ProTix ☎ (800) 400-9373. Expect crowds. Tickets are only
required for the Permanent Exhibition, not for the other exhibitions,
memorials, resources and facilities. Gift shop. Café.* &.

Visiting this museum is a deeply disturbing experience, as it was
intended to be. By design it makes you feel, if only in a small way, as
though you are actually living through the nightmare of the Holocaust
in Nazi Europe.

The museum raises interesting questions. Why here? Why in
Washington? Why so near the joys of the Mall? After all, the unspeakable events so graphically displayed happened long ago, in a far-off
land. The whole point of the memorial is that the lessons are universal;
that they apply to everyone, everywhere. This is not just the story of one
persecuted group, but of intolerance, bigotry, and hate in general. It is
especially relevant today as mankind stumbles through wrenching
changes around the globe.

Upon entering the museum you will be given a new identity appropriate to your age and gender, with a computer-generated card bearing
the name and story of one of the victims. Visitors then take an elevator
to the top floor and begin a dark descent into hell as they relive the
experiences of that person. Only, at the end, your fate is different—you
are still alive and free to leave.

A **Hall of Remembrance** provides a quiet place for reflection before
continuing on to the:

BUREAU OF ENGRAVING AND PRINTING (16), 14th and C streets SW, ☎
(202) 874-3019, Internet: www.bep.treas.gov. *Open Mon.–Fri., 9–2 (also*

5–6:40 June–Aug.); closed Federal holidays and Dec. 23–Jan.2. Expect long lines in summer. Free. 35-minute tours are offered 9–2 Mon.–Fri. Tickets are required for all general tours and can be picked up the same day as the tour at the ticket booth on Raoul Wallenberg Place. ♿.

Here's where the green stuff is printed, along with postage stamps, bonds, and other valuable bits of paper. And here's where millions of tourists come to witness the process. Major renovations have greatly enhanced the visitor's experience from the gallery. If you'd like to join them, you'll see a film and displays on the history of money, followed by a walk along glassed-in galleries overlooking the actual production of paper bills. Don't look for coins, however; they're minted in Philadelphia (see page 346). At the end, you can purchase souvenir shreddings of what was once of value.

Now stroll over to the **Tidal Basin**, a part of the Potomac River until 1882. The basin was created to improve navigation and reclaim land for parks. It fills up during high tide; much of the water is then released at low tide to flush out the adjacent Washington Channel down by the waterfront.

Thousands of visitors and Washingtonians alike flock to the basin when the celebrated *Japanese cherry trees are in blossom, usually from late March into early April. They were a gift from the Japanese people in 1912, and were supplemented in 1958 by additional gifts of a 17th-century stone lantern and a stone pagoda, both in the western reaches of the basin.

You can rent **paddleboats** for a modest charge at the kiosk just across from the Bureau of Engraving. This is a particularly nice diversion in Cherry Blossom Time, and is good exercise anytime.

Following the water's edge, you'll soon come to the:

JEFFERSON MEMORIAL (17), West Potomac Park SW, ☎ (202) 426-6841, Internet: www.nps.gov. *Open daily except Christmas, 8–midnight. Free. Tours given by request.* ♿.

Thomas Jefferson, no mean architect himself, would probably have approved of his classical memorial based on the Pantheon in Rome. Or at least of its concept. Completed in 1943 to a design by John Russell Pope, it was considered by many to be outmoded at the time, but has since become one of the most beloved sights in Washington. Its location at the south end of an axis formed by the Mall, the Lincoln Memorial, and the White House could hardly be more perfect, even if this is more apparent on a map than on the ground. There is something serene, something deeply satisfying about this place to the many visitors who stroll around the Tidal Basin to see it.

Follow the map along the water's edge to the:

*FRANKLIN DELANO ROOSEVELT MEMORIAL (18), West Basin Drive at the Tidal Basin NW, ☎ (202) 619-7222, Internet: www.nps.gov. *Open daily at all times, rangers on duty 8 a.m. to midnight. Free.* ♿.

Four outdoor areas honor the four terms that F.D.R. served as President, from the depths of the Great Depression to victory in World War II. Numerous sculptures depict the history of that momentous era, with quotations from his famous speeches carved into the walls. There is also a statue of Eleanor Roosevelt, the only First Lady to be so honored in a national memorial.

Continue on to the:

KOREAN WAR VETERANS MEMORIAL (19), West Potomac Park at 21st St. NW, ☎ (202) 619-7222, Internet: www.nps.gov. *Open daily 8 a.m. to midnight. Free.* ♿.

Images of the "forgotten war" of 1950–53 are etched into the long granite wall behind statues of combat soldiers on patrol in that distant land.

Nearby is the:

*LINCOLN MEMORIAL (20), West Potomac Park at 23rd St. NW, ☎ (202) 426-6841, Internet: www.nps.gov. *Open daily except Christmas, 8–midnight. Accessible anytime. Free.* ♿.

Facing straight up the center of the Mall stands one of the most recognizable structures in Washington. In fact, you probably have a few pictures of it in your pocket right now as it's on the back of every penny and five-dollar bill. More than a memorial to the "Great Emancipator," the 16th president, it is a revered symbol of conscience to a nation "of the people, by the people, and for the people."

Appropriately, this has been the setting for several milestones in America's long, unfinished struggle towards civil rights.   When the renowned African-American opera singer, Marian Anderson, was denied permission to perform in the D.A.R.'s Constitution Hall in 1939, she brought her concert to these steps for an audience of over 75,000 people. It was here that Martin Luther King Jr. gave his immortal "I have a dream" speech in 1963, and it was also here that President Richard Nixon had his strange, impromptu, middle-of-the-night encounter with Vietnam War protesters. The place has a certain mystique about it, and the power to unleash deep emotions.

A decision to build a monument in memory of Abraham Lincoln was made as early as 1867, but nothing came of it until 1911 when the present site, then a swampy landfill, was selected. The memorial was completed in 1922. Despite much criticism of its being a "cold Greek temple," it has always been warmly received by the public and remains one of the most-visited sights in Washington.

Inside, the enormous *statue of a contemplative Lincoln is made of 20 blocks of crystalline Georgia marble so perfectly joined together that the seams are nearly invisible. To the sides are inscribed the words of Lincoln's Second Inaugural Address along with his unforgettable Gettysburg Address.

The memorial looks its very best at dawn or at dusk. Some, however, prefer to visit it late at night, especially in bad weather, when they can be alone with their thoughts.

From here it is only steps to another poignant sight, the:

*VIETNAM VETERANS MEMORIAL (21), Constitution Ave. at 22nd St. NW, ☎ (202) 634-1568, Internet: www.nps.gov. *Open daily 24 hours. Free.* ᕃ.

Surely the subtlest and most successful of Washington's monuments, this simple rift in the earth arouses the most complex emotions while totally avoiding the political controversies surrounding that traumatic conflict. Over 58,000 names of those killed or missing in action are inscribed on two shiny black granite walls pointing to and reflecting both the Lincoln Memorial and the Washington Monument, with the first and the last entries—the beginning and the end of the nightmare— meeting at the junction of the walls. Directories at either end show the location of each of the names, which are arranged chronologically. Many visitors make rubbings of the inscriptions of loved ones who perished, and often leave flowers or personal mementos behind that are then collected and stored by the National Park Service in perpetual remembrance.

The Vietnam Memorial was initiated by veterans troubled by America's sad indifference to those who served in an unpopular war, and was completely funded by private donations. After gaining congressional approval for the site, a design competition was held in 1981. The winner was Maya Yin Lin of Athens, Ohio, a then-21-year-old architectural student at Yale. Some veterans, however, felt that her concept was too abstract and funereal, and so a more conventional sculpture of three combatants was added a short distance away, overlooking the Wall. Another addition is a memorial honoring the many women who served in the Armed Forces during the Vietnam War.

Continue on through **Constitution Gardens**, a quiet, sylvan spot with a small lake and an island, and pass the **Lock Keeper's House** at the corner of 17th Street and Constitution Avenue. This is all that remains of the former canal that once ran from the Potomac River to the foot of Capitol Hill and beyond. From here you can wander back to your hotel, or the nearest Metro, bus, or Tourmobile stop.

Capitol Hill

W hen Pierre L'Enfant first planned the new city of Washington in 1791, he thought that it would be a dandy idea to crown Jenkins Hill with something special, as this none-too-spectacular rise seemed to him to be "a pedestal waiting for a monument." What he placed there was the U.S. Capitol, around which developed the legislative and judicial branches of the Federal Government, safely distancing themselves from the executive branch.

Capitol Hill—as it has long been called—is home to many of Washington's most interesting sights, enough to easily keep you busy for an entire day. The U.S. Capitol itself is, of course, a "must" for every visitor. Then there is the Supreme Court, the Library of Congress, the Folger Shakespeare Library, the historic Sewall-Belmont House, the U.S. Botanic Garden, the Smithsonian's Postal Museum, and the magnificently-restored Union Station. Also restored are the many blocks of a delightful residential area, bordered by inviting shops, restaurants, and cafés. If you have abundant energy, you might want to make side trips to the bustling Eastern Market for fresh treats, to the Government Printing Office for anything they publish, or to the Capital Children's Museum just for fun.

GETTING THERE:
By Metro, take the Red Line to **Union Station** and walk a few blocks south.

By taxi, ask for the Capitol.

By Tourmobile, get off at the U.S. Capitol stop. At the end of the walk, you can reboard the Tourmobile in front of Union Station.

PRACTICALITIES:
Most of the major sights along this tour are open daily except for a few federal holidays. The Supreme Court and the Government Printing

Office are also closed on weekends, and the Folger Shakespeare Library on Sundays. The Sewall-Belmont House closes on Sundays and Mondays.

If you'd like to watch Congress in action (or inaction), you'd do best to contact your elected Representative or Senators in advance for a pass to the galleries, or visit their office for possible same-day arrangements. Foreigners may request a pass from the Office of the House Doorkeeper or the Senate Sergeant-at-Arms.

The total walk is nearly four miles long, not including any side trips, so wear comfortable shoes. Expect stringent **security checks** at the Capitol, Supreme Court, Library of Congress, and possibly other sites as well.

For current tourist information, contact the **Washington Visitor Information Center** in the Ronald Reagan Building, 1331 Pennsylvania Avenue NW, ☎ (202) 789-7000, Internet: www.washington.org.

FOOD AND DRINK:

Capitol Hill abounds in good restaurants. Here are a few of the better choices:

The Monocle (107 D St. NE, north of the Senate office buildings) Traditional American food for Senate powerbrokers and those who like to watch them. Specializes in steaks and seafood. ☎ (202) 546-4488 for reservations. X: weekends. $$$

Café Berlin (322 Massachusetts Ave. NE, 2 blocks northeast of the Senate office buildings) Hearty German fare in pleasant surroundings, inside or alfresco. ☎ (202) 543-7656. X: weekend lunches. $$

Taverna—The Greek Islands (307 Pennsylvania Ave. SE, near the Library of Congress) Greek specialties in an appropriate setting. ☎ (202) 547-8360. X: Sun. lunch. $$

White Tiger (301 Massachusetts Ave. NE, at 3rd St.) Tasty Indian cuisine in a delightful setting. ☎ (202) 546- 5900. $$

Capitol City Brewing (Postal Sq., 2 Massachusetts Ave. at 1st St.) A popular, lively pub with seasonal microbrews. ☎ (202) 842-2337. $$

Hawk and Dove (329 Pennsylvania Ave. SE, near the Library of Congress) The intriguing clientele alone makes this '60s throwback worth a visit; the "menu" features sandwiches, burgers, and lots of beer. ☎ (202) 543-3300. $

Le Bon Café (210 2nd St. SE, near the Library of Congress) Great sandwiches, salads, pastries, and especially coffee makes this a popular spot with Hill insiders. ☎ (202) 547-7200. X: Sun. $

Madison Building Cafeteria (in the Library of Congress, Madison Building, 6th floor) Open to the public after 12:30, this might be the best of the government cafeterias and features excellent, healthy foods along with a view of the city. ☎ (202) 707-8300. X: weekends. $

Burrito Brothers (205 Pennsylvania Ave. SE at 2nd St., near the Library of Congress) A great variety of overstuffed burritos and other Mexican treats at low prices. ☎ (202) 543-6835. $

SUGGESTED TOUR:

Numbers in parentheses correspond to numbers on the map. Begin your walk at the East Front of the:

*U.S. CAPITOL (1), Capitol Hill, ☎ (202) 225-6827, handicapped services (202) 224-4048, TDD (202) 224-4049, Internet: www.aoc.gov. *Open daily March through August 9:30–8; Sept. through Feb. 9–4:30. Closed Thanksgiving, Christmas, New Year's Day. Free. Tours every 15 minutes 9–3:45. Gift shops. Special events. Cafeteria and dining room. ♿, use ground-floor entrances with ramps.*

There's a lot that is unusual about the U.S. Capitol, but what is perhaps most amazing is the simple fact that just about everyone is welcome to step inside and pay a visit. Think about that—in how many nations can ordinary mortals just stroll into the halls of power unannounced?

George Washington laid the cornerstone of the Capitol on September 18, 1793, although just where remains a mystery. The original plans were made by a physician and amateur architect named William Thornton, who won a design competition. In 1800 the wandering Congress, having previously met in Philadelphia, Lancaster, York, Baltimore, Princeton, Annapolis, Trenton, and New York City, finally settled into its permanent, albeit unfinished, home. But not for long.

During the War of 1812 the building was set ablaze by the invading British, completely destroying its interior. Fortunately, a providential downpour that night saved the basic structure. By the end of 1819 the damage was repaired and the building enlarged under two successive architects, Benjamin Henry Latrobe and Charles Bulfinch. The latter completed the Capitol in 1829, although two large wings and the dome were added during the 1850s and 60s, and the East Front extended in 1958-62. With all of its enlargements and modifications, it remains a truly majestic building, surely one of the grandest on Earth.

Unique among places in Washington, the Capitol is not in any one of the city's four quadrants; rather it is in all four, as their boundaries meet beneath its dome.

Enter the Capitol via the center steps of the **East Front**, or use the adjacent ground-level entrance and take the elevator up. *Those taking the free tours should wait in the line outside.* Until recently, virtually all

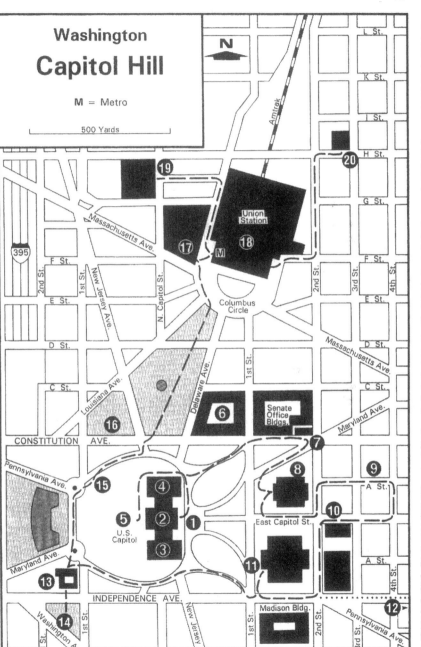

Washington
Capitol Hill

M = Metro

500 Yards

presidential inaugurations took place here (they are now sometimes held on the West Front). William Henry Harrison delivered the longest inaugural speech ever in 1841, in a rainstorm no less, and promptly died of pneumonia a few weeks later. It was here, too, that Franklin D. Roosevelt insisted that "...the only thing we have to fear is fear itself," and John F. Kennedy said "Ask not what your country can do for you, but what you can do for your country." At the top of the steps are the bronze **Columbus Doors** of 1858, depicting events in the life of Christopher Columbus in high relief.

Step into the Rotunda, where you can join the line for a free **guided tour** that usually includes the Crypt, Statuary Hall, and possibly one of the congressional chambers, depending on whether it's in use at the moment. You can also just wander around on your own, or do both.

The ***Rotunda** (2), where such national heroes as Abraham Lincoln and John F. Kennedy have lain in state, is the center of the Capitol and a repository of national beliefs. Look up into the immense ***dome** some 180 feet above your head, and examine the fresco in its eye. Painted by Constantino Brumidi in 1865, **The Apotheosis of Washington* depicts the first president in a mythological setting, surrounded by a host of allegorical virtues. Brumidi also began the *grisaille* **fresco** circling the base of the dome, but slipped from the scaffolding and sustained injuries that led to his death. Another Italian, Filippo Costaggini, continued the work, which was completed by Allyn Cox in 1953. Over 400 years of American history are celebrated on its panels, from the landing of Columbus to the takeoff of the Wright brothers.

The eight large paintings on the walls present idealized versions of events in the nation's history. Four of these are by John Trumbull, who served with Washington in the Revolution. His *Signing of the Declaration of Independence* graced the unloved two-dollar bill of 1976. Between the paintings are statues of American leaders from George Washington to Martin Luther King Jr.

Beneath the Rotunda is the **Crypt**, built as a tomb for President Washington but never used as such. Today it houses displays on the history of the Capitol. While you're down at the ground-floor level, stroll a few steps north to the **Old Supreme Court Chamber**, where the first joint session of Congress was held in 1800, and where the Supreme Court deliberated from 1810 until 1860. After that, the court moved upstairs to the Old Senate Chamber, remaining there until 1935. The room was restored to its 1860 appearance in time for the 1976 celebrations.

Continuing north along the ground-floor corridor brings you to the **Brumidi Corridor** with its interesting paintings, including a recent one honoring the crew of the doomed space shuttle *Challenger*.

Return to the main floor and head south from the Rotunda into **Statuary Hall**. For 50 years, from 1807 to 1857, this was home to the House of Representatives, which then moved into its present chamber. John

Quincy Adams, serving as a congressman after having been president, is often credited with the discovery of a peculiar quirk to this room—its **strange acoustics**. Whispered conversations in one part of the chamber can be clearly heard in another, but not in between, allowing for all sorts of political intrigue. Adams, incidentally, collapsed here in 1848 and died in the adjoining Speaker's Office. When the House moved out, the Congress in 1864 allowed each state to place statues of two of its most prominent dead citizens in the hall. Eventually, the sheer weight of accumulated greatness became more than the foundations could bear, so some of the sculptures were moved elsewhere. Still, enough of the highly eclectic collection remains to make this a most worthwhile stop.

South of Statuary Hall stands the **House Chamber** (3), an addition completed in 1865 but in use since 1857. The 435 members of the House of Representatives sit in a semi-circle, Democrats to the right of the Speaker, and Republicans to the left. This large room is also used for joint sessions such as the President's annual State of the Union Address. Other than a brief possible visit on a guided tour, you'll have to get a pass from your elected Representative to enter the chamber, and even then you can only go to the upstairs gallery overlooking the room. Foreigners can get passes from the Doorkeeper's office.

Return to the Rotunda and continue north to the ***Old Senate Chamber**, restored to the way it looked when occupied by the Senate from 1810 until 1859. From 1860 until 1935, this room was home to the Supreme Court. Beyond it is the present **Senate Chamber** (4), where the nation's 100 senators have assigned desks arranged in order of seniority. To visit its gallery and watch the goings-on, you'll have to obtain a pass from one of your Senators' offices or, if you're not a U.S. citizen, from the Sergeant-at-Arms.

Leave the Capitol and walk around to its **West Front** (5). From its terraces you'll have a sweeping ***panoramic view** up the Mall and down Pennsylvania Avenue, surely one of the finest urban vistas anywhere.

From here you can walk or, with luck, ride the tiny **Capitol Subway** from the basement of the Capitol to the **Senate Office Buildings** (6). This strange underground conveyance shuttles congresspersons, staffers, and even tourists back and forth from the Capitol to the Senate and House office buildings. It generally runs from 9 a.m. to 4:30 p.m. on weekdays and 9 a.m. to noon on Saturdays, but continues as long as sessions last. The Senate's offices are located in the Russell Building of 1909, the Dirksen Building of 1958, and the Hart Building of 1982, all grouped together along Constitution Avenue. Here you can visit the offices of your senators; perhaps getting passes for the gallery, hearings, or other events; or at least having your opinions heard. To locate any particular senator's office, phone (202) 224-3121, or ask at the appointments desk on the crypt level of the Capitol.

Oddly stuck into a corner of the office buildings is the **Sewall-Belmont House** (7) of 1800, an elegant Federal-style residence incorporating an earlier structure from around 1680. Between 1801 and 1813 it was the home of Secretary of the Treasury Albert Gallatin (1761-1849), who reportedly negotiated financial details of the Louisiana Purchase here. During the War of 1812 the house was the only place in Washington that resisted the British, and was consequently damaged by fire. Parts of the Treaty of Ghent, ending that war, may also have been worked out within these walls. Since 1929, the Sewall-Belmont House has been the headquarters of the National Woman's Party, and is now mostly a **museum** honoring the women's movement in America. Among the things you can see here are the living quarters of Alice Paul, who founded the party in 1913 and fought for passage of the Nineteenth Amendment, which doubled the number of U.S. voters in 1920. Also on view is the desk of Susan B. Anthony, suffragettes' banners, and a statue of Joan of Arc. *144 Constitution Ave. NE, ☎ (202) 546-3989. Open Tues.–Fri. 11–3, Sat. and holidays noon–4. Donation. Tours.*

Just a few steps south is the:

SUPREME COURT (8), 1st St. and Maryland Ave. NE, ☎ (202) 479-3000. *Open Mon.–Fri. 9–4:30, closed weekends and holidays. Free. Lectures. Film. Gift shop. Cafeteria and snack bar. ♿, use ramp on north side.*

"Equal Justice Under Law" reads the inscription above the august Corinthian columns of this 1935 temple to American ideals. Before that, the highest court in the land met inside the Capitol building, but a growing caseload as well as an evolving independence from any form of politics necessitated the move. The sole function of the court is to interpret the Constitution and rule on the constitutionality of laws, be they federal, state, or local. Its decisions set precedents that affect the lives of all Americans, and sometimes alter the nature of society.

If at all possible, try to get at least a glimpse of the judicial process. The court is in session, usually on Mondays through Wednesdays in two-week intervals, from October through April (it continues to sit through the end of June to announce decisions). Visitors may either watch about five minutes of the proceedings from a gallery, or be seated for an entire session. To do the latter, you'll have to show up as early as possible, say 8:30 a.m., and wait in line. Seats are allocated on a first-come, first-served basis. During miscellaneous court recesses and over the summer months, when the court is not in session, you can attend free lectures in the courtroom. These are held from 9:30 a.m. to 3:30 p.m., every hour on the half-hour. A small theater offers a free continuous film about the court, and there are displays on its history. If you hunger for the justice of a cheap lunch, the cafeteria will treat your wallet with leniency.

Now follow the map through an old residential neighborhood that has become quite fashionable in recent years. Once rather seedy, the area east of the Capitol was almost torn down in the 1950s to make room for yet more government offices, but the insensitive plan was successfully thwarted by preservationists. Frederick Douglass (1817–95), the noted abolitionist and author, lived in the **house** (9) at number 316 A Street NE from 1871 until 1877. Between 1964 and 1987 it housed the Museum of African Art, which has since moved to the Mall (see page 29).

Continue around the block to the:

FOLGER SHAKESPEARE LIBRARY (10), 201 East Capitol St. SE, ☎ (202) 544-4600, Internet: www.folger.edu. *Open Mon.–Sat. 10–4, closed Sun. and Federal holidays. Free, contributions welcome. Tours at 11, also at 1 on Sat. Gift shop. Special events. &, call 544-4600 for assistance.*

The world's largest collection of Shakespeariana is not in Stratford-upon-Avon; it's right here in Washington. Although most of the holdings are accessible only to scholars, casual visitors can examine the treasures on display in the **Great Hall**. Besides the works of Shakespeare, the collection includes a great deal of other material from Renaissance Europe, including early maps, rare books, musical instruments, and works of art. The intimate **Elizabethan Theater** is an adaptation of the type of outdoor theaters common during Shakespeare's time, and is used for special performances.

Nearby are the three main buildings of the:

LIBRARY OF CONGRESS (11), 10 First St. SE, ☎ (202) 707-8000, Internet: www.loc.gov. *Open Mon.–Sat. 10–5:30, closed on federal holidays. Free. Tours at 11:30, 1, 2:30 and 4. Gift shop. Special events. Cafeteria, 6th floor of Madison Bldg., open to public after 12:30. &, ramps at main entrances.*

What began in 1800 as a reference source for Congress has grown into the largest library on Earth. Holding some 30 million books (and 60 million other items), it is open to the public at large, and its special facilities to anyone over the age of 18 who is pursuing legitimate research.

For tourists, however, the library's main attraction is not its endless stacks of books, but its fascinating **special exhibitions** as well as the extravagant architecture of its main **Jefferson Building**. If you still haven't

had lunch, the **cafeteria** in the Madison Building is highly recommended. The best way to acquaint yourself with the library is to watch the 12-
minute film shown in the Visitors Center in the Jefferson Building, then
take the free **guided tour** at 11:30, 1, 2:30 and 4 from there. If this is not
possible, at least pop in for an eyeful of splendor and possibly a look at
some fabulous treasures, such as the *Gutenberg Bible* of 1455 and the
Great Bible of Mainz from 1452. Be sure to get at least a glimpse of the
extremely ornate **Main Reading Room**, which can be entered if you have
research to do. Ask at the information desk in the Visitors Center about
this.

From here, ambitious walkers can make a little **side trip** to the
Eastern Market (12). Established in 1873, this genuine old farmers' market
is at its liveliest on Saturday mornings. On Sundays the site becomes a
flea market. *7th and C streets SE. Open Tues.–Sat. 7 a.m.–6 p.m., Sun. 9–4.*
    Now follow the map west on Independence Avenue and descend
Capitol Hill through a park to the:

U.S. BOTANIC GARDEN (13), Maryland Ave. and First St. SW, ☎ (202)
225-8333, Internet: www.aoc.gov. *Open daily 9–5. Free.* ♿. *NOTE: The
greenhouse is closed for renovation until late 2000.*
    An oasis of exotic flora in the middle of official Washington, this
Victorian-style greenhouse complex contains an amazing variety of
plants in a delightful setting. It's a great escape for weary bureaucrats
and tourists alike.

Just across the street, in a small park administered by the Botanic
Garden, stands the big bronze **Bartholdi Fountain** (14), a leftover from
the Philadelphia Centennial Exhibition of 1876. Designed by Frédéric-
Auguste Bartholdi, who also created the Statue of Liberty in New York
Harbor, the aquatic fantasy represents water and light.
    Follow the map north on First Street SW, passing the **James Garfield
Monument**. It honors the 20th President of the United States, who was
assassinated only months after taking office in 1881. Beyond, on the left,
is the **Capitol Reflecting Pool** of 1970. The serene waters here belie the
fact that they are right above busy, buried Interstate Highway 395.
Directly in front of this stands the 252-foot-long **Grant Memorial**, the
largest sculptural group in Washington. A bronze General (and later
President) Ulysses S. Grant, on horseback, is flanked by an extraordi-
narily realistic group of Union cavalry and artillery in action, whose
expressions reveal the true horror of warfare.

Beyond the nearby **Peace Monument**, an 1877 memorial to the sailors who perished during the Civil War, is the marvelous little **Spring Grotto** (15). Designed in 1875 by Frederick Law Olmsted, the creator of New York's Central Park, this well-hidden oasis was originally a source of cool spring water, but is today connected to the municipal water supply. Stop by for a drink.

Just across Constitution Avenue rises the **Taft Memorial** (16), a concrete monolith of 1959 built to honor Senator Robert A. Taft (1889–1953) of Ohio, a.k.a. "Mr. Republican," the son of President William Howard Taft. Its 27 bells chime every 15 minutes.

Stroll through the park towards Union Station, then bear left to the:

NATIONAL POSTAL MUSEUM (17), Massachusetts Ave. at 1st St. NW, ☎ (202) 357-2700, Internet: www.si.edu/postal. *Open daily except Christmas, 10–5:30. Free. Gift shop. Stamp store.* ᶜ.

The Smithsonian's Postal Museum occupies Washington's former City Post Office, a grandiose Beaux-Arts structure of 1914. Much more than just a collection of stamps, the museum graphically recalls the entire history of getting the mail through, despite rain, snow, sleet, gloom of night, etc. At points it becomes rather adventurous, and even humorous.

From the museum's ***Central Atrium**, stuffed with airplanes, mail trucks, a train, and a stagecoach, you enter a "time tunnel" leading down a dirt road as a simulated storm gathers. You then walk through the history of mail service in America, gradually working your way up to the present—and that vast collection of some 16 million stamps, a few of which are for sale.

Directly across the street is **Union Station** (18), once the largest rail terminal in the world. Built in 1908 in the monumental Beaux-Arts style, it served as Washington's main point of arrival and departure until the near-demise of rail travel in the 1950s. Although a few decrepit trains continued to chug their way in, the station became seedier and seedier as the holes in its roof got bigger. Then came the Bicentennial of 1976 and an ill-fated plan to convert the station into a "national visitors center." Unfortunately, there were few visitors. Trains, by now run by Amtrak, were shunted to a miserable depot stuck well behind the station. By 1981 the situation had become so bad that the powers-that-be finally realized their mistake and corrected it. In view of America's rail renaissance, it was decided to restore the station—at a cost of 160 million dollars—to its original splendor, circa 1908. Finally they got it right; what you see today is a fabulous interior well worth exploring thoroughly. In addition to once again being a busy station, it is also something of a grand shopping mall, complete with interesting shops, restaurants, and cafés. ☎ *(202) 371-9441, Internet: www.lasalle.com/union.*

If you have any time (and energy) left, you might want to make a short little **side trip** to either of two nearby attractions. Two blocks to the northwest is the **Government Printing Office** (19), where you can purchase what the government prints. There are some real bargains here, especially in manuals dealing with unbelievably esoteric subjects. *North Capitol and H streets NW,* ☎ *(202) 512-0132. Open Mon.–Fri. 8–4.* ♿.

To the northeast is the **Capital Children's Museum** (20), where visitors can touch and handle every exhibit. Designed as a "hands-on" discovery center for children aged 2 to 12, it can also be a lot of fun for grown-ups, especially if they have a kid in tow. Be sure to see the **Mexican Marketplace** in the International Hall, the **Ice Age Cave**, and the **City Room.** *800 3rd St. NE,* ☎ *(202) 675-4120. Open daily 10–5, closing at 6 from Easter to Labor Day; closed Thanksgiving, Christmas, and New Year's Day. Admission $6, seniors $4, children under 3 free.   Special events. Toy shop.* ♿.

From the White House
to Foggy Bottom

W hen the White House was first occupied in 1800, its only neigh-
bor was a small farm owned by the Pierce family since 1685.
This presidential isolation did not last for long, however. By
1815 or so, town houses of the rich and influential began popping up
nearby, several of which still survive around Lafayette Square and its
precincts. Today, the neighborhood offers a wide range of first-rate
attractions, with more than a little something for every taste.

Immediately to the west lies Foggy Bottom, once a desolate tract
known as Funkstown, whose history predates that of Washington itself.
Now home to the State Department, Kennedy Center, the Watergate
complex, and George Washington University, it still retains much of its
colorful past in its little lanes and mews lined with tiny (and newly chic!)
19th-century dwellings.

Along this walking route you'll have a chance to visit the White
House, tour the interiors of several old mansions, look over one of the
nation's foremost art collections, glimpse the insides of one or two government agencies, explore a vast cultural center, and get a fabulous view
from its roof. Nearly all of the streets along the way are exceptionally
pleasant to stroll along, and offer a nice variety of architectural styles
from the 18th century to the present.

GETTING THERE:

By Metro, take the Blue or Orange line to the **McPherson Square** station, using the Vermont Avenue exit. At the end of the walk you can
return from the Foggy Bottom stop on the same lines.

By taxi, ask for Lafayette Square.

PRACTICALITIES:

Be sure to get off to an early start if you intend to tour the White
House—the lines begin forming as early as 7 a.m. in summer, although
it doesn't open until 10.

The White House, Decatur House, and the Octagon are closed on Mondays and a few major holidays. The White House is also closed on Sundays, while the Corcoran Gallery closes on Tuesdays. Some of the other sites are closed on weekends and holidays. The D.A.R. Museum closes on Saturdays and most of April.

By planning in advance, you might avoid the waiting lines to enter the White House *and* get a better VIP tour by contacting one of your elected Congresspersons several months in advance to arrange for a special early-morning tour.

Taken all the way, the suggested walking tour is about three-and-a-half miles long, with no steep hills.

For current tourist information, phone the sites directly or contact the **Washington Visitor Information Center** in the Ronald Reagan Building, 1331 Pennsylvania Avenue NW, ☎ (202) 789-7000, Internet: www.washington.org.

FOOD AND DRINK:

There's not a lot to choose from along this route, but here are a few reliable places for lunch:

Roof Terrace Restaurant (in Kennedy Center) Reservations are urged for this luxurious restaurant featuring regional American cuisine with a view. ☎ (202) 416- 8555. X: lunch on non-matinee days. $$$

Zuki Moon (824 New Hampshire Ave. NW near Washington Circle) Contemporary light Japanese and Southeast Asian cuisine. ☎ (202) 333-3312. $$

Café at the Corcoran (in the Corcoran Gallery) A museum admission is not necessary to enjoy the light lunches or Sunday brunches in the elegant atrium café. Reservations are possible, ☎ (202) 639-1786. X: Tues. $

Cup A' Cup A' (in the Watergate complex, near F St.) Light lunches in a café with a view. $

SUGGESTED TOUR:

Numbers in parentheses correspond to numbers on the map.

Leave the McPherson Square Metro Station and stroll a block south on Vermont Avenue to **Lafayette Square** (1), a public park ever since Thomas Jefferson separated it from the White House grounds in the early 19th century. The square has long been a popular venue for political demonstrations, some of which seem to be permanently encamped. Scattered among those enjoying their freedom of speech are five hero-

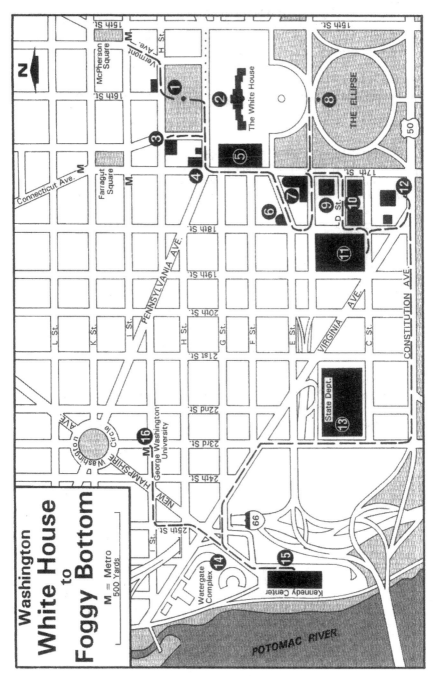

ic **statues**, the largest of which, in the center, depicts President Andrew Jackson astride his rearing horse. One of the earliest equestrian statues in America, it was cast in 1853 from bronze cannon captured by Jackson during the War of 1812. As for the Marquis de Lafayette himself, his statue has stood in the southeast corner since 1891, although the park was named for him as early as 1824. The other sculptures are of Jean-Baptiste Rochambeau (southwest corner), Thaddeus Kosciuszko (northeast corner), and Baron Von Steuben (northwest corner)—all foreign heroes of the American Revolution.

Opposite the north side of the park, at 16th and H streets NW, stands **St. John's Episcopal Church**, built in 1816 and long renowned as the "Church of Presidents." Step inside to see **Pew 54**, which has been used by every President since Madison, whether they were Episcopalian or not. Originally designed by the noted architect Benjamin Latrobe, who also worked on the Capitol and the White House, the church was enlarged in 1822 and later renovated by another great architect, James Renwick, in 1883. ☎ *(202) 347-8766. Open daily 9–3, closed during Federal holidays and during services.* よ.

The elegant **Hay-Adams Hotel**, on the northwest corner, was erected in 1927 on the site of the homes of John Hay and Henry Adams, both famous historians.

Facing the south side of the park is one of the world's best-known buildings, the:

*WHITE HOUSE (2), 1600 Pennsylvania Ave. NW, ☎ (202) 456-7041 (recording) or (202) 472-3669, TDD (202) 456-6213, Internet: www.white house.gov. *Open Tues.–Sat. 10–noon; closed Sun., Mon., holidays, and for official functions. Tickets may be obtained on a first-come, first-served basis after 7:30 a.m. from the White House Visitors Center at E and 15th streets. Expect long lines, especially in summer.   "VIP" tours arranged in advance through Members of Congress are held Tues.–Sat. 8–10. Free. Special events. よ, disabled people do not have to wait in line, and should go directly to the northeast gate on Pennsylvania Ave.*

Contrary to myth, the President's House has been popularly known as the "White House" since at least 1808, and was in fact covered with whitewash as early as 1798. It is the world's only official residence for a head of state that is regularly open to the public without charge.

The first public building to be erected in the nation's new capital was designed by James Hoban, a Dublin-trained architect who won a nationwide competition in 1792 with his plan for an elegant-yet-unpretentious mansion based on traditional Irish and English country houses. Construction began in 1793 but advanced slowly due to a shortage of both skilled labor and money. President Washington agreed to cut expenses by reducing the size of the building, but even so it was not ready for occupancy during his term of office. The next President, John Adams, was able to move into the uncompleted house in 1800, just a few months before his term ended. His family, unfortunately, had to put up with such inconveniences as hanging their laundry in the East Room and trying to keep warm around a few scanty fireplaces.

The first President to spend a full term in the White House was Thomas Jefferson, who added the east and west terraces, and began the tradition of opening the house to visitors in the mornings.

On August 24, 1814, the White House was set ablaze by invading British forces, but fortuitously saved from total destruction by a sudden shower. Reconstruction began the next year and was completed by 1817. As the nation grew, so did the President's House, acquiring north and south porticoes by 1829, indoor plumbing by 1833, gas lighting in 1848, central heating in 1853, and electricity in 1891. A major renovation and enlargement was completed during the administration of Theodore Roosevelt, and the Oval Office added in 1909. In 1948, after nearly 150 years of use, the entire structure was found to be dangerously unstable. President Truman moved across the street to Blair House for three years while the White House was completely gutted and a new steel structure erected inside the old exterior walls. Succeeding administrations have concentrated on restoration and preservation of the house as a showcase of American history.

Tourist **visits** to the White House (other than VIP tours) begin at the East Wing entrance, where a security check is made. These are not guided tours—you walk through on your own following a marked route—but there are guards on hand to answer your questions. Portraits of past Presidents and First Ladies adorn the corridors and hallways, and you can look out through a glassed-in colonnade into the intimate **Jacqueline Kennedy Garden**, arranged in the 18th-century style. The ground- floor corridor leads into the **Library**, which is decorated in the Late Federal style and which contains some 2,700 volumes by American authors. Across the hall is the **Vermeil Room**, once used to play billiards. It now houses an extensive collection of antique French and English gilded silver. Closeby is the **China Room**, where pieces of china and glass used by the First Family are displayed, and the **Diplomatic Reception Room**, from which F.D.R. broadcast his famous fireside chats. The latter rooms are normally shown only on the VIP tours.

Stairs lead up to the **State Floor**, where you step into the **East Room**, the largest in the White House. No longer used for drying the presidential laundry or for Theodore Roosevelt's boxing matches, this splendid chamber is now the setting for ceremonies, receptions, concerts, press conferences, and the like. On its east wall hangs Gilbert Stuart's renowned 1797 portrait, *George Washington*, which was saved from destruction by First Lady Dolley Madison when the British burned the White House in 1814. It is reputed to be the sole surviving object from the original mansion of 1800.

Continue into the **Green Room**, a reception parlor that once served as Thomas Jefferson's dining room. Most of the furniture here dates from the early 19th century, with many pieces by the acclaimed cabinetmaker Duncan Phyfe. Next to it is the magnificent ***Blue Room**, often considered to be the most beautiful room in the White House. Oval in shape, it is handsomely decorated with French Empire furniture ordered from Paris by James Monroe in 1817. Among the various presidential portraits on the walls is Rembrandt Peale's familiar painting of *Thomas Jefferson*. The White House Christmas tree is placed here each year.

The route leads through the **Red Room**, furnished in the American Empire style of 1810-30. Primarily used for small receptions, the room contains several notable paintings, including Albert Bierstadt's *The Rocky Mountains* of 1870.

At the end of the tour is the **State Dining Room**, where up to 140 guests can be accommodated for luncheons and dinners. Note the quotation from a letter by John Adams carved into the fireplace mantel, and the contemplative portrait of *Abraham Lincoln* by G.P.A. Healy above it. From here you will exit through the Entrance and Cross halls, and the North Portico.

Several of the old houses along Jackson Place, the west side of Lafayette Square, are interesting and worth examining. Most of these restored town houses are now used by various presidential commissions as identified by their plaques, but the one on the corner of H Street NW remains in private hands and may be visited. Known as the **Decatur House** (3), it was built in 1818 as the first private residence in the vicinity. Commodore Stephen Decatur (1779–1820) was an American naval hero who became immensely popular for his victories against the British in the War of 1812 and for his suppression of the Barbary pirates of Algeria in 1815. He is also remembered for his famous toast that ended, "...our country, right or wrong!" Decatur selected the noted architect Benjamin Latrobe, who had worked on both the White House and the Capitol, to design his three-story town house, which he occupied in 1819. Sadly, the commodore was killed in a duel the very next year. After his widow moved to Georgetown, the house was rented to a succession of notables including Henry Clay and Martin Van Buren, then Secretary of State. In 1871 it was purchased by a colorful Western adventurer named Edward Fitzgerald Beale, whose descendants bequeathed it to the National Trust, which operates it today. The first floor is restored to its original condition and furnished with pieces of that period, while the delightful upper floor represents the rather eclectic Victorian tastes of the Beales. ☎ *(202) 842-0920, Internet: decatur house.com. Open Tues.–Fri. 10–3, weekends noon–4. Tours are given*

*every half hour. Adults $4, students with ID and seniors $2.50, under 12
free. National Trust members free. Gift shop.* ♿, *advance notice preferred.*

Return to Pennsylvania Avenue. The **Blair House** at number 1651,
built in 1824, was the residence of President Truman while the White
House was being rebuilt. It is now used as a guest house for foreign dignitaries and heads of state, and may not be visited. At the end of the
block stands the:

RENWICK GALLERY (4), Pennsylvania Ave. at 17th St. NW, ☎ (202) 357-
2531, Internet: www.si.edu. *Open daily except Christmas, 10–5:30. Free.
Gift shop. Special events.* ♿.

Operated by the Smithsonian Institution as part of the National
Museum of American Art (see page 70), the Renwick features marvelous
exhibitions of American crafts and decorative arts, past and present.
Many of these, especially contemporary pieces, transcend the genre
and would be at home in just about any major art museum. Don't miss
the ***Grand Salon** and the **Octagon Room**, both on the second floor and
both fabulously decorated in an opulent Victorian style. The building
itself, designed by James Renwick (of Smithsonian Castle fame) in 1859,
was originally the home of the Corcoran Gallery (see page 58), which
outgrew it by 1897.

Across Pennsylvania Avenue, just west of the White House, is a
structure that you can't help but notice. The **Old Executive Office
Building** (5), a ponderous pile that stretches on for two long blocks, is
amazingly hideous in all of its overblown French Second Empire detail,
but lovable all the same. Built between 1871 and 1888 to house the State,
War, and Navy departments, it was already out of style upon completion
and several times threatened with demolition. Fortunately, there were
never funds to do this, and after 1947 the then-vacant building was
appropriated by the Executive Office of the President as an annex of the
White House. Thoroughly renovated, the structure now houses various
Executive Branch functions, including the Office of the Vice-President.
By making advance reservations, you can tour the sumptuous interior
on Saturdays between 9 and noon. Arrangements should be made at
least four weeks ahead, and must include the birth date of every person
in your group. ☎ *(202) 395-5895. Free.* ♿.

Head down New York Avenue for a block to the **Octagon House** (6)
of 1801, and decide for yourself whether it actually has eight sides. This
strangely-shaped mansion was built by a friend of George Washington's,
Colonel John Tayloe III, and served as a temporary residence for
President Madison after the White House was burned by the British in
1814. It was here that the Treaty of Ghent, ending the War of 1812, was

signed by Madison in 1815. The Tayloe family continued to live in it until 1855, after which it became a seedy tenement. Around the turn of the century, the American Institute of Architects (AIA) acquired the run-down structure and refurbished it as their headquarters, which was later moved into the massive (and somewhat uninspired) office building that nearly engulfs it today. Allegedly haunted by the ghosts of Dolley Madison and others, the house has been beautifully restored to its orig-inal elegance by the AIA, and may be visited. ☎ *(202) 638-3105, Internet: www.amerarchfoundation.com. Open Tues.–Sun. 10–4. Closed Mon. and major holidays. Adults $3, seniors and students with ID $1.50. Tours. Bookshop. ৬, partial access via ramp in rear.*

Turn east on E Street, following it a block to 17th Street and the entrance of the:

*CORCORAN GALLERY OF ART (7), 500 17th St. and New York Ave. NW, ☎ (202) 639-1700, Internet: www.corcoran.org. *Open Wed.–Mon. 10-5, until 9 on Thurs. Closed Tues., Christmas, and New Year's Day. Donation: Adults $3, seniors and students with ID $1, families $5, chil-dren under 12 free. Tours daily (except Tues.) at noon and 7:30 p.m. on Thurs. On Sat. and Sun. tours are at 10:30, noon and 2:30. Museum shop. Special events. Restaurant. ৬, mostly accessible.*

Best known for its stunning collection of 19th-century American art, the Corcoran also has a substantial number of European master-pieces, and puts on some of the most exciting exhibitions of contem-porary works by today's young artists. The museum was founded in 1869, ranking it among the three oldest art museums in the United States. Quickly outgrowing its first home, which now houses the Renwick Gallery (see above), the Corcoran opened its present Beaux-Arts structure in 1897. Unlike most Washington museums, it is privately funded and not a part of the Smithsonian complex. In addition to its gal-leries, the Corcoran is also an accredited art school offering full-time courses leading to a BFA degree, along with part-time art education pro-grams.

Among the treasures to look for are Frederic E. Church's lumines-cent 1857 painting of *Niagara Falls, Albert Bierstadt's 1875 rendering of the non-existent *Mount Corcoran,* obviously titled to curry favor, *The Old House of Representatives* (1822) by Samuel F.B. Morse of telegraph fame, and the statue of *The Greek Slave* (1846) by Hiram Powers. The lat-ter scandalized Victorian society when it was first shown—to adults only, with separate times for men and women!

From here you can make a very short side trip to **The Ellipse** (8), a lovely, animated park facing the south side of the White House. In the center of its north side is the **Zero Milestone** from which all distances in Washington are measured. Just below that is the **National Christmas Tree**, illuminated each year by the President. From here you'll enjoy great views in all directions.

Return to 17th Street and pass the national headquarters of the **American Red Cross** (9), which has some interesting historical exhibitions in the lobbies of its three floors. Don't miss the ***stained-glass windows** by Louis Tiffany on the second floor, depicting characters from Edmund Spenser's allegorical *The Faerie Queene* of 1590. ☎ *(202) 737-8300. Open Mon.–Fri. 9–4. Free.*

Turn west on D Street to the:

DAUGHTERS OF THE AMERICAN REVOLUTION MUSEUM (10), *1776 D St. NW,* ☎ *(202) 879-3241, Internet: www.dar.org. Open Mon.–Fri. 8:30–4, Sun. 1-5. Closed most of April and major holidays. Free. Tours. Gift shop. ♿, use ramp at 1775 C St.*

Founded in 1890 by female descendants of Revolutionary War patriots, the DAR is a nationwide organization devoted to the ideals of American independence. Its national headquarters, occupying an entire block of connected buildings, contains two galleries and some 33 **period rooms** furnished and maintained by individual DAR state chapters. Among these is an 1820 parlor filled with furniture from the Monroe White House, an early Oklahoma kitchen, a Georgia tavern, and a 1775 Massachusetts bedroom. In the main gallery, a permanent rotating collection of antique quilts is on display. Be sure to see the ***New Hampshire attic** with its 18th- and 19th-century toys, dolls, and games. The Yochim Gallery highlights important American paintings and furniture of note. A small exhibition of Presidential objects is also on display. There is also a noted **library** of genealogical material.

At the west end of the complex stands the DAR's **Constitution Hall**. Built in 1905 it is the headquarters oldest section and is still a popular spot for concerts, conferences, and cultural events.

Turn south on 18th Street and west on C Street to the:

DEPARTMENT OF THE INTERIOR MUSEUM (11), *C St. between 18th and 19th streets NW,* ☎ *(202) 208-4743. Open Mon.–Fri. 8–5, closed weekends and Federal holidays. Free. Adults must show a photo ID, such as a driver's license. Indian craft shop (room 1023). National Parks Information Office. ♿, use E St. entrance.*

Take a step back in time by visiting this wonderfully old-fashioned museum, whose displays seem to have hardly changed since 1937, when it opened. Canoes hang from the ceiling, stuffed animal heads abound, and dioramas depict your National Park Service at work. There are excellent displays of **Native American crafts**, original land patents, mineral specimens, and on such diverse subjects as mining, mapping, and the Fish and Wildlife Service. Some concessions to the present age, such as videos, are beginning to creep in, but so far they have not detracted from the earthy charm found here. With so many slick shows at other museums, it would be a sin to overly "modernize" this one.

The museum is housed in a monumental building, erected in the late 1930s to house a growing bureaucracy. Though starkly plain in design, it was years ahead of its time with the incorporation of central air conditioning, banks of escalators, and many employee amenities. When President Franklin D. Roosevelt laid the cornerstone in 1936, he used the same trowel that George Washington employed at the Capitol in 1793. Not unexpectedly, the interior of Interior is heavily decorated with heroic murals on appropriate themes, a few of which you'll see.

Just a block south, facing 18th Street, is a complex of interesting buildings belonging to the **Organization of American States** (OAS) (12). Founded in 1890 and formerly known as the Pan American Union, the organization represents some 35 sovereign nations in both North and South America as well as the Caribbean. Its primary function is to promote political and economic cooperation among the member countries, and to further their joint interests. The **Headquarters Building**, a Beaux-Arts hacienda of 1910 built on international territory donated by the United States, opens onto 17th Street and may usually be visited. Step inside to see the lush, covered **Tropical Patio** featuring Aztec motifs, the **Art Gallery** and, on the second floor, the ornate **Hall of the Americas** with its Tiffany chandeliers and stained-glass windows. ☎ *(202) 458-3000, Open Mon.–Fri. 9:30–3:30, closed holidays. Guided tours by advance appointment. Free.* &.

Behind the Headquarters Building, and reached by a garden path or through its 18th Street entrance, is the organization's **Art Museum of the Americas**, housed in the former residence of the Secretary-General. This small gallery hosts changing exhibitions of works by contemporary artists, mostly from Latin America, along with selections from the permanent collection. ☎ *(202) 458-6016. Open Tues.–Sat. 10–5. Free.*

Continue west on Constitution Avenue, passing the **Federal Reserve Building**, and the **National Academy of Sciences** with its marvelous statue of Albert Einstein lurking in the bushes just off the sidewalk. Turn right on 23rd Street to the massive-but-nondescript **Department of State Building** (13) between C and D streets. Although it is not normally open to the public, by making arrangements well in advance you can take a free guided tour of the stunning ***Diplomatic Reception Rooms**, where the very best examples of early American decorative arts have been gathered for the benefit of visiting dignitaries. Donations, not taxes, have changed the eighth floor of a dull office building into a showcase of American crafts, circa 1750 to 1825. *Tours by advance reservation only, Mon.–Fri. at 9:30, 10:30, and 2:45. Free.* ☎ *(202) 647-3241.* ঙ.

Keep heading north on 23rd Street and turn left onto Virginia Avenue. Ahead of you, at New Hampshire Avenue, is the infamous **Watergate Complex** (14). Built in the 1960s, this strikingly curvaceous group of buildings houses apartments, boutiques, restaurants, a luxury hotel, and (of course) the office building in which a botched 1972 burglary led to the resignation of President Nixon—and the addition of a new suffix, "...gate," to the English language. Despite its notoriety, the Watergate is still one of Washington's most affluent addresses.

A short walk south on New Hampshire Avenue brings you to the:

*JOHN F. KENNEDY CENTER FOR THE PERFORMING ARTS (15), New Hampshire Ave. at Rock Creek Parkway NW, ☎ (202) 467-4600, TDD (202) 416-8524, Internet: www.kennedy-center.org. *Box office open Mon.–Sat. 10–9, Sun. and holidays noon–9. Free entry. Free tours daily 10–5. Gift shop. Restaurant.* ঙ, *to reserve wheelchairs* ☎ *(202) 416-8340.*

Whatever its architectural merits, the Kennedy Center has a great deal going for it inside, and offers fabulous views from its rooftop terraces. Most people come here to attend performances in its six theaters, but this vast complex is a great attraction in itself, and can be explored free of charge.

Plans for a national cultural center were already well underway at the time of President Kennedy's tragic assassination in 1963; funding, however, was insufficient until Congress voted to make it a living memorial to the slain leader. More than 40 nations contributed to its opulent decor. Designed by the prominent architect Edward Durrell Stone, Kennedy Center first opened its doors in 1971.

Begin your visit at the **Information Desk** on the ground floor of the **Hall of States**, just inside the first entrance you come to. Here you can ask about the free guided tours (the best way to see Kennedy Center as they take you inside the theaters) and pick up a diagram and guide sheet to the complex.

If you decide to explore on your own, be sure to take an elevator to the Roof Terrace level and stroll outside for a grand ***view** of Washington, Georgetown, and across the Potomac.

This is the end of the walking tour. To get to the nearest Metro station, head north on New Hampshire Avenue as far as Virginia Avenue, then continue north on 25th Street. This will take you through a historic residential area of tiny old houses that have been gentrified into highly-desirable homes in recent years. Turn right on I (Eye) Street to the **Foggy Bottom—GWU Metro Station** (16) on the Campus of George Washington University.

The Old Downtown

The first three walking tours have taken you through the most touristed parts of Washington; with this one you'll begin getting off the beaten path to visit some of the capital's less-familiar sights. Once a rather elegant district, the old downtown had deteriorated badly as both its prosperous citizenry and their businesses fled to the suburbs. Beginning with the Kennedy administration in the early 1960s, however, a rejuvenation effort brought the area back to life—especially along Pennsylvania Avenue. Similarly, the area north of this has been greatly invigorated by the MCI Center, a massive sports and entertainment complex. Several architectural gems of the 19th century, such as the Old Post Office, the former Patent Office, and the utterly fantastic Pension Building (now The National Building Museum), have been successfully recycled as shopping malls and museums, while others like the once-derelict Willard Hotel have never looked better than they do today.

Along the way you'll be able to see the actual Declaration of Independence and the Constitution, snub your nose at the IRS, visit some fish, get the best bird's-eye view of the city, watch the FBI at work, see the theater box where President Lincoln was shot and the bed that he died on, enjoy real Chinese food, try your hand at interactive sports, and explore no less than three superb art museums.

GETTING THERE:

By Metro, take the Yellow or Green line to the **Archives/Navy Memorial** station. At the end of the walk, return from the Judiciary Square stop on the Red line.

By taxi, ask for the corner of 7th St. NW and Pennsylvania Ave., by the Navy Memorial.

PRACTICALITIES:

Nearly all of the sights along this route are open daily, except for Christmas and sometimes New Year's and Thanksgiving. The FBI tour does not operate on weekends or holidays. If you follow it all the way, the walk is about four miles long.

The **Washington Visitor Information Center** in the Ronald Reagan Building, 1331 Pennsylvania Avenue NW, ☎ (202) 789-7000, Internet: www.washington.org, provides free advice, brochures, and maps on a walk-in basis. They are open Mondays through Fridays, 9–5.

FOOD AND DRINK:

You'll find a multitude of good places to eat along this walking tour, including:

Café Mozart (1331 H St. NW, near the Museum for Women in the Arts) Classic German and Austrian cuisine. ☎ (202) 347-5732. $$

A.V. Ristorante Italiano (607 New York Ave. NW, 3 blocks northeast of the Convention Center) A really old-fashioned Italian restaurant, complete with Chianti bottles. ☎ (202) 737-0550. X: Sun. $$

Tony Cheng's Mongolian (619 H St. NW, in the heart of Chinatown) Have a Mongolian barbecue or prepare your own dish in a hot pot. ☎ (202) 842-8669. $$

Szechuan Gallery (617 H St. NW) Szechuanese, Hunanese, and Taiwanese dishes in the center of Chinatown. ☎ (202) 898-1180. $$

District Chop House & Brewery (509 7th St. NW, between E & F streets) Close to MCI Center, with a wide menu and great beers. ☎ (202) 347-3434. $$

Fadó Irish Pub (808 7th St. NW, between H & I streets) Modern versions of Irish dishes in a setting right out of the old country. ☎ (202) 789-0066. $$

Capitol City Brewing Co. (1100 New York Ave. at 11th St.) Burgers and such with a variety of microbrews. ☎ (202) 628-2222. $$

Planet Hollywood (1101 Pennsylvania Ave. NW at 11th St.) Go for the experience as much as for the burgers, salads and the like. ☎ (202) 783-7827. $ and $$

Hard Rock Café (999 E St. NW, across from the FBI Bldg.) Join the line of teenagers (and their parents) waiting to enter this local branch of a world-wide phenomenon. Good burgers. ☎ (202) 737-7625. $

Dean & DeLuca Café (1299 Pennsylvania Ave. NW at Freedom Plaza) Light lunches and snacks in a self-service café. ☎ (202) 628-8155. $

Austin Grill (750 E St. NW, between 7th & 8th streets) Tex-Mex food in a fun atmosphere. ☎ (202) 393-3776. $

Burma Restaurant (740 6th St. NW at Gallery Place) This upstairs Chinatown restaurant serves unusual Burmese specialties. ☎ (202) 638-1280. $

Mr. Yung's Restaurant (740 6th St. NW, in Chinatown) A favorite place for both Dim Sum and regular Cantonese dishes. ☎ (202) 628-1098. $

In addition, the **National Museum of American Art** has an excellent cafeteria called the "Patent Pending" that serves lunch daily from 11-3, both indoors and outdoors. The Pavilion in the **Old Post Office Building** features a number of sometimes-unusual fast-food restaurants around a common atrium, as does the nearby Ronald Reagan Building.

SUGGESTED TOUR:

Numbers in parentheses correspond to numbers on the map.

Begin your walk at the **Navy Memorial** (1), where a statue of the *Lone Sailor* overlooks the largest grid map of the world anywhere — a full 100 feet in diameter. Nautical flags wave from the posts while fountains splash merrily away. Concerts by the Navy Band are held here on Tuesday evenings from Memorial Day until Labor Day. Adjacent to this is the **Naval Heritage Center** with its interactive videos, a stunning film about the U.S. Navy, a video record of Navy veterans, and more. *Memorial open daily. Free. Heritage Center open March–Oct., Mon.–Sat. 9:30–5:30; rest of year Tues.–Sat. 10:30–4. Adults $3.75, seniors & students $3.* ☎ *(202) 737-2300 or (800) 821-8892, Internet: www.lonesailor.org.*

The nearby **Temperance Fountain**, just across 7th Street, runs dry these days, having long since proven to be a lost cause. Its history is interesting. A teetotaling California dentist named Henry Cogswell put it there in the late 19th century in the hopes that its cool water would attract the multitudes away from Pennsylvania Avenue's notorious saloons. That didn't work, but the bars eventually fell victim to the unstoppable power of encroaching bureaucracy.

Take a look down Pennsylvania Avenue to the **Canadian Embassy** at the corner of 5th Street, a triumph of monumental Postmodern architecture that serves to soften the conflict between the two wings of the National Gallery of Art, just across the street. The embassy has its own museum of Canadian culture, which can be visited. *501 Pennsylvania Ave. NW,* ☎ *(202) 682-1740. Open weekdays 10-5. Free.*

Stroll around to Constitution Avenue to visit the:

*NATIONAL ARCHIVES (2), Constitution Avenue between 7th and 9th streets NW, ☎ (202) 501-5000, TDD (202) 501-5404, Internet: www.nara.gov. *Rotunda and Exhibition Hall open daily except Christmas, 10–5:30, closing at 9 from Apr. through Labor Day. Free. Gift shop.* ♿, *use Pennsylvania Ave. entrance. Guided tours Mon.–Fri. at 10:15 and 1:15, by advance appointment only,* ☎ *(202) 501-5205 for arrangements, use*

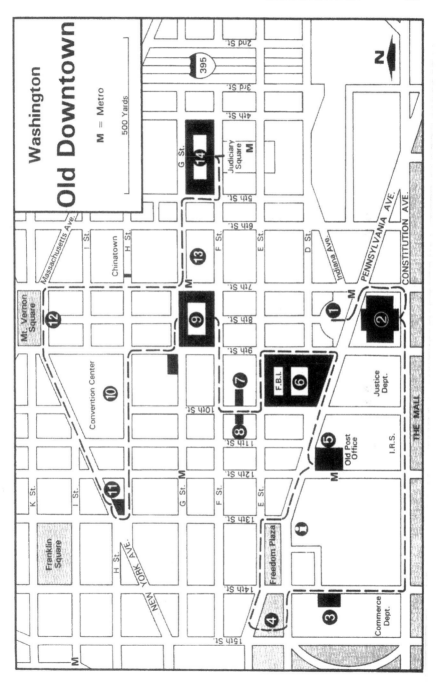

Washington
Old Downtown

M = Metro

500 Yards

Pennsylvania Ave. entrance.

As the central repository of the nation's documents, the National Archives has its hands full protecting literally billions of treaties, proclamations, deeds, written laws, photographs, maps, sound recordings, motion picture films, and other evidence of America's past. They are not all stored here, of course, but mostly in regional centers and Presidential libraries across the country. What *is* kept here is the nucleus of the collection, the documents that establish and protect American democracy—along with other historic records of enduring value. Inside the Rotunda you can view the original Declaration of Independence, the Constitution, the Bill of Rights, and even a 1297 version of England's Magna Carta.

The massive building itself is of considerable interest. Designed in the Classical Revival style by John Russell Pope, who also created the National Gallery of Art and the Jefferson Memorial, it was completed in 1937. Its monumental flight of steps, august Corinthian columns, and colossal bronze doors certainly inspire confidence in the safety and security of the documents stored within.

Climb the steps on the Constitution Avenue side and enter the portico. A line usually forms here to go through the security check, but this moves quickly so you won't have a long wait. In the ***Rotunda** are displayed the "Charters of Freedom," an official collective name for the ***Declaration of Independence**, the ***Constitution**, and the ***Bill of Rights**. These are sealed in green-filtered glass-and-bronze cases, filled with inert helium gas, and lowered every night into a vault some 22 feet beneath the floor. Also on display in the Rotunda is a 1297 version of England's ***Magna Carta**, the forerunner of the American Bill of Rights. This forced revision was signed by King Edward I and is the first document to grant Parliament—not the king—the sole right to control taxation. Discovered in England in 1974, it is on indefinite loan from its owner, the Texas billionaire and sometimes presidential candidate H. Ross Perot.

The **Circular Gallery** behind the Rotunda displays changing exhibitions from the Archive's collections. Free **guided tours** of the Archive's inner workings, including glimpses of some unusual items, may be arranged by phoning them well in advance. The facilities are also open to the public for historical and genealogical research purposes.

Stroll west on Constitution Avenue and get a good grip on your wallet as you pass the headquarters of the **Internal Revenue Service** around number 1040 (and you wondered where that infamous form number came from?). Turn right on 14th Street. On your left is the **Commerce Department Building**, opened in 1932 as the then-largest government office building on Earth. It was the first completed structure in what is known as the **Federal Triangle**, a mass of huge neoclassical government office buildings wedged between Constitution Avenue, Pennsylvania

Avenue, and 15th Street. Prior to 1929, this area had been a notorious slum, which at least had the virtue of being more interesting than the present bureaucratic facelessness. Secreted away in the Commerce Department's basement is a rather unusual attraction that might interest you, the:

NATIONAL AQUARIUM (3), 14th St. NW between Constitution and Pennsylvania avenues on the lower level of the Dept. of Commerce building, ☎ (202) 482-2825. *Open daily except Christmas, 9–5. Shark feedings on Mon., Wed., Sat. at 2; piranha feedings Tues., Thurs., Sun. at 2. Adults $2, seniors & children (2–10) 75¢. Gift shop. Café.* ♿.

Established in 1873 as America's first public aquarium, this institution settled into its present subterranean home in 1932. Since 1982 it has been a private, non-profit organization no longer connected to the government. By modern standards, it is a very old-fashioned aquarium—but an interesting one nonetheless. Besides the requisite tanks filled with exotic creatures from the deep, it features a **Touch Tank** where visitors may actually handle some of the more gentle live specimens, and a **video theater** with aquatic shows.

Continue up 14th Street and turn left into **Pershing Park** (4), a delightful oasis in the midst of pompous government offices. In its center is a pool that becomes an skating rink in winter, overlooked by a statue of General John "Black Jack" Pershing of World War I fame. An outdoor café adds to its considerable charms. Just north of the greenery is the magnificent **Willard Hotel**, built in 1901 on the site of an earlier Willard. Legend has it that the term "lobbyist" was first coined here during the hotel's previous incarnation, when favor-seekers would waylay President Grant in the lobby. The present hotel closed in the late 1960s as the neighborhood sank into decrepitude. Following the 1970's revival of Pennsylvania Avenue, the Willard was fully restored to its previous splendor, and since 1986 has been once again catering to the rich and powerful. Take a look at its lobby, then stroll along "Peacock Alley," the grand hallway running north to F Street.

Walk around **Freedom Plaza**, a large open space used mostly by skateboarders, and head down **Pennsylvania Avenue** past the enormous new Ronald Reagan Building. Meant to provide a direct line from the White House to the Capitol, the broad avenue was badly compromised in the mid-19th century by the construction of the **Treasury Building** (*guided tours by advance reservation,* ☎ *(202) 622-0896*), which blocks the view at the western end and snarls traffic. Although used for inaugural parades, the "Avenue of Presidents" has been plagued by seediness since at least the Civil War. Only in recent years has it begun to reach its potential. One of the more interesting sights along its length is the:

OLD POST OFFICE (5), 1100 Pennsylvania Ave. NW, ☎ (202) 289-4224, Internet: www.oldpostofficedc.com. *Shops and food court open Mon.–Sat. 10–9, Sun. noon–8. Tower open mid-Apr. to mid-Sept. daily 8–10:45, 10–6 during the rest of the year. Closed holidays. Free. ๖.*

For many decades the city planners have yearned to tear down this alleged monstrosity; then suddenly everyone recognized its true beauty and the landmark building was saved. Stylistically outmoded even when it was built in 1899, this heavy Victorian-Romanesque castle was the largest government building in Washington at the time. It served as the headquarters of the Postal Service until 1934. Then slated for the wrecking ball to make way for the ever-growing Internal Revenue Service, it was given a reprieve by budget cuts during the Great Depression.

A death warrant for its demolition was finally issued in 1971, but this time salvation came at the hands of concerned citizens and passage of the Cooperative Use Act, which allows free enterprise to operate within certain federal buildings. After a thorough restoration, the upper floors were taken over by the National Endowment for the Arts and related agencies, and the lower section converted into—what else?—a shopping mall. Not just any shopping mall, but possibly the fanciest one you'll ever see. Besides the stores, it has entertainment, lots of restaurants, a multi-ethnic food court, and even an indoor miniature golf course.

Towering above the Old Post Office is its 315-foot **Clock Tower**, which offers the best possible *****view** of downtown Washington. Free tours operated by the National Park Service leave frequently from the glass elevators by the courtyard. Near the top are the **Congress Bells**, a set of ten replicas of the bells in London's Westminster Abbey. A Bicentennial gift from the British, they are used for ceremonial occasions.

Continuing down Pennsylvania Avenue, you cannot help noticing a looming hulk of brutal concrete on the left. Further investigation reveals this to be the:

FBI HEADQUARTERS (6), J. Edgar Hoover Bldg., 10th St. at Pennsylvania Ave. NW, ☎ (202) 324-3447, TDD (202) 324-1016, Internet: www.fbi.gov/yourfbi/tour. *Guided one-hour tours Mon.–Fri. except federal holidays, 8:45–4. Free. Tour entrance on E St. Expect long waiting lines during peak summer season, or make reservations at least three months in advance through your Congressperson or Senator.* ♿.

Tastes in architecture change, but it's doubtful that this pile will ever be regarded as anything other than hideous. Inside, though, you can get a fascinating look at the inner workings of the secretive **Federal Bureau of Investigation**. Tracing its ancestry to 1908, this arm of the Justice Department came into national prominence after 1924, the year that a young attorney named J. Edgar Hoover (1895–1972) was made its director. The sometimes dictatorial Hoover stayed in that post for an incredible 48 years despite the efforts of several presidents to remove him. Whichever way the political winds may blow, however, the agency has always remained true to its mission of combating crime at the federal level.

You cannot just wander around the interior on your own—visitors must take an hour-long guided tour that departs every 15–20 minutes. The tour includes an introductory video, artifacts from past crimes, a visit to a forensic laboratory, and mug shots of the current ten most-wanted fugitives. A spectacular finale is provided by a live **firearms demonstration**.

Just around the corner from the FBI is the scene of one of America's most heinous crimes:

FORD'S THEATRE (7), 511 10th St. NW, ☎ (202) 426-6924, Internet: www.nps.gov/foth. *Open daily except Christmas, 9–5. Theater portion closed during rehearsals or matinees. Free. Museum and shop.* ♿*, limited access.*

President Abraham Lincoln was assassinated here on April 14, 1865, while seated in his box, enjoying a performance of the popular comedy *Our American Cousin*. Both the President and the entire capital were no doubt in a festive mood that evening, as the long, bitter Civil War had effectively come to an end just five days earlier with Lee's surrender at Appomattox. A disgruntled actor with Confederate sympathies named John Wilkes Booth was not so happy, however, and he conceived a plan to avenge the South. Easily gaining entry to the boxes, he shot the President and then leaped 12 feet to the stage, injuring his leg, as he shouted *"Sic semper tyrannis!"* (Thus always with tyrants). Oddly, the audience at first thought it was part of the play. Booth escaped, but was later trapped in Virginia and shot. President Lincoln, still alive, was taken to a house across the street, where he died the next morning.

Ford's Theatre first opened in 1863 as one of the grandest auditoriums in the nation. Lavishly decorated, it could accommodate an audience of about 2,500. After the assassination, the theater was closed and later purchased by the government for use as offices. Tragically, in 1893 the floors collapsed, killing 22 employees. Until 1932 the building was just used for storage; then a small museum of Lincoln's life opened on the ground floor. Full restoration to its 1865 appearance began in the mid-1960s, and it is today both a memorial and a working theater, administered by the National Park Service. The *Presidential Box has been authentically re-created with its original sofa, although Lincoln's rocking chair is a reproduction.

Be sure to visit the **Lincoln Museum** in the basement, which traces the history of the assassination and the political tensions that led to it. The Derringer pistol used by Booth is on display along with his diary and related items.

Now cross the street to visit the house where Lincoln died.

PETERSEN HOUSE (8), 516 10th St. NW, ☎ (202) 426-6830. *Open daily except Christmas, 9–5. Free.*

Built in 1850, this modest boardinghouse was owned by a tailor named William Petersen. The unconscious President was brought here as he was too severely wounded to be moved back to the White House or even to a hospital. Being six feet, four inches in height, Lincoln had to be laid diagonally across the bed. A doctor, who had been in the audience that evening, attempted treatment but realized that there would be no recovery. President Lincoln died at 7:22 the following morning.

The federal government purchased the Petersen House in 1896 for use as a small museum of Lincoln artifacts, now shown in the basement of Ford's Theatre. The house has since been restored with period furnishings, although the only original object from that fateful night is the blood-stained pillow.

Continue up 10th Street and turn right on F Street to the:

NATIONAL MUSEUM OF AMERICAN ART and the **NATIONAL POR-TRAIT GALLERY** (9), F St. to G St., between 7th and 9th streets NW, ☎ (202) 357-2700, Internet: www.nmaa.si.edu. *Open daily except Christmas, 10–5:30. Free. Gift shops. Restaurant, cafeteria. ⅙, use ramp at 9th and G streets.*

The marvelous **Old Patent Office Building**, like many of

Washington's historic structures, barely escaped becoming a parking lot in the 1950s. Fortunately, it was instead chosen by the Smithsonian Institution to house two of their major art museums. Begun in 1836 as a "Temple of the Useful Arts," this Greek Revival edifice was the largest building in the country when it was finally completed in 1867. During the Civil War it served as a hospital for Union soldiers; among those who cared for the wounded here were Clara Barton and the poet Walt Whitman. Lincoln's second inaugural reception was held under this roof in 1865.

The entrance on F Street opens directly into the **National Portrait Gallery**, which connects internally with the other museum. Noted Americans from every walk of life are portrayed here, both reverentially and critically, and sometimes even humorously. Ranging from the familiar paintings of George Washington by Gilbert Stuart and the Civil War photographs of Matthew Brady to *Time* magazine covers and illustrations from the *Rolling Stone*, the works here cover the entire scope of American history, past and present. Be sure to visit the **Great Hall** on the third floor, once the largest room in America. Reached via a grand staircase in the south wing, it formerly displayed thousands of patent models and is now part of the portrait gallery.

Stroll through the East Wing or the courtyard and you'll soon be in the **National Museum of American Art**, also a part of the Smithsonian. The "Patent Pending" cafeteria on the first floor of the East Wing is a great place for a light lunch or refreshments.

Only about 1,000 out of a collection of some 35,000 paintings, sculptures, graphics, photos, and other objects are on display at any given time. These range from works of the earliest Colonial period to the very latest trends in American art. Perhaps the most unusual—and unforgettable—highlight is the creation of a mid-20th-century Washington janitor named James Hampton, whose **Throne of the Third Heaven of the Nations' Millennium General Assembly** occupies an entire room with found objects sheathed in aluminum foil, a strangely-moving piece of visionary religious art.

You'll also find a refreshing selection of folk art, art of the West, monumental American landscapes, American Impressionists such as Mary Cassatt and Childe Hassam, and an enormous gallery of contemporary works by today's artists on the third floor. Free tours of the museum are conducted at noon on Mondays through Fridays, and at 2 p.m. on weekends.

Exit onto G Street and turn left. At the corner of 9th Street, catercorner to the museums, is the **Martin Luther King Jr. Memorial Library**. Completed in 1972, it is Washington's central library and the only structure in the city designed by Mies van der Rohe — perhaps the most influential architect of the 20th century. Step inside to see a mural depicting events in the life of Dr. King. ☎ *(202) 727-0321, Internet: www. dclibrary.org.*

Continue north on 9th Street and turn left on H Street. To your left is the imposing **Washington Convention Center** (10), which has brought new life (and dollars) to the rejuvenated downtown area ever since its opening in 1983.

At this point you might prefer to skip the next attraction and take a shortcut directly to Chinatown by heading east on H Street. Otherwise, continue west to the:

NATIONAL MUSEUM OF WOMEN IN THE ARTS (11), 1250 New York Ave. at 13th St. NW, ☎ (202) 783-5000, Internet: www.nmwa.org. *Open Mon.–Sat. 10–5, Sun. noon–5. Suggested donation: Adults $3, seniors and children $2. Gift shop. Café.* ♿.

Once the exclusive province of males, this former Masonic temple today houses the world's leading collection of works by women artists. Although they have long been denied much recognition, women artists have quite a history of major achievements. The earliest works on display here are by Lavinia Fontana (1552–1614), a Bolognese painter of the Italian Renaissance who managed to support a large family with her many portrait commissions. Seventeenth-century Flemish still lifes are followed by court paintings and illustrations of nature from the 18th and 19th centuries, leading to Impressionist works by such talents as Mary Cassatt. The 20th-century galleries include creations by Georgia O'Keeffe, Helen Frankenthaler, Kathe Kollwitz, and others.

Begin your visit by taking the elevator to the third floor, where the **permanent collection** starts, following more-or-less in chronological sequence. **Temporary exhibitions** are shown on the second floor, along with parts of the permanent collection. A new and expanded gift shop, along with several new galleries is located in the museum's new Kasser wing.

Turn east on New York Avenue and go as far as **Mt. Vernon Square** (12). From here head south on 7th Street into **Chinatown**, one of Washington's more colorful neighborhoods. You'll know you're there when you see the pagoda-roofed **Archway** across H Street, erected in 1986 with funds from Washington's sister city, Beijing. If you haven't had lunch yet, this is a great place to sample the tasty cuisines of Szechuan, Hunan, Canton, or even Mongolia.

Now continue a block south to the enormous:

MCI CENTER (13), 601 F St. NW, ☎ (202) 628-3200, Internet: www.mci center.com. *Guided tours daily 10–4, adults $7.50, seniors and under 13 $5. National Sports Gallery opens daily at noon, closing after events, admission $5, under 5 free. Extra charge for interactive sports games. Discovery Channel Destination Store* ☎ *(202) 783-5751, Internet: www.flagship.discovery.com. Open daily 10–10. Restaurants. Sporting goods store.* ♿.

Home to the Washington Wizards (NBA), Capitals (NHL), and Mystics (WNBA), as well as the Georgetown Hoyas (NCAA), the stunning MCI Center also hosts other sporting events, shows, and concerts. For the purpose of this walking tour, however, the focus is on its ***National Sports Gallery**—a 25,000-square-foot attraction on the third floor (take the elevator at 601 F St.). Here you will be treated to some of the most significant sports memorabilia anywhere, allowed to actually touch Babe Ruth's bat, learn about the history of sports, and test your athletic abilities at some 40 interactive sites. For an extra charge, you can even try your hand at sportscasting, reading from a script and getting at VHS tape of the results. The **Discovery Channel Destination Store** is a major attraction in itself, filled with many wonders and even things you can buy.

Continue east for a block to the:

NATIONAL BUILDING MUSEUM (14), 401 F St. NW, ☎ (202) 272-2448, Internet: www.nbm.org. *Open Mon.–Sat. 10–4, Sun. noon–4, closed Thanksgiving, Christmas, New Year's. Free. Tours available weekdays at 12:30, weekends at 12:30 and 1:30. Gift shop.* ♿, *use ramp on 5th St.*

The National Building Museum, the old Pension Building of 1887, is recognized as a major achievement of the building arts, and appropriately houses an important museum devoted to design, architecture, and building. Its astonishing Great Hall is one of the grandest interior spaces anywhere, used as the site of inaugural balls for over a century.

Before entering, take a look at the 1,200-foot-long terra-cotta ***frieze** that encircles the building just above the first-floor window level. It depicts an endless parade of Union soldiers, representing all those who have served their country. Designed by U.S. Army General Montgomery Meigs (1816–92), who was also partly responsible for the Capitol dome and some other Washington landmarks, this structure was a pioneer in providing adequate ventilation and lighting for the workers it housed.

Step inside and enter the ***Great Hall.** Over 300 feet long by 116 feet wide, it is some 15 stories high and contains the eight largest Corinthian columns in the world. Surrounding it are elegant galleries with Doric and Ionic columns, as in the courtyards of Renaissance palaces. To get a good view of this *really big* space, take an elevator to the second or third level and look out from the balcony. Numerous exhibitions on the building arts occupy rooms flanking the Great Hall on the first and second levels.

Facing the National Building Museum is **Judiciary Square**, a handsome city park containing the **National Law Enforcement Officers Memorial**. Two elliptical marble walls here are engraved with the names of over 14,000 law enforcement officers killed in the line of duty from 1794 until the present. A visitors center features interactive exhibits on the lives of the slain officers. *Memorial open at all times, visitors center Mon.–Fri. 9–5, Sat. 10–5, Sun. noon–5. Free.* ☎ *(202) 737-3400, Internet: www.1nleomf.com.*

From the Metro stop here you can get a subway back to anywhere in Washington.

Dupont Circle and Kalorama

Relatively few visitors to Washington venture beyond Dupont Circle, if they get that far at all. Those who do are in for a pleasant treat, especially if they continue on through Kalorama. These relaxed neighborhoods are dotted with the kind of unexpected sights that make a leisurely stroll so rewarding.

With elegant residences lining its streets, Dupont Circle was the most affluent corner of Washington from the 1890s through the 1920s. After that, it slowly deteriorated and by the 60s had become the capital's counterculture center. Today the neighborhood is once again fashionable as a younger, trendier, professional set has moved in, renovating and preserving the fine old houses.

Embassy Row (Massachusetts Avenue) connects Dupont Circle with the rarefied precincts of Kalorama, an enclave of wealth and power overlooking Rock Creek Park. It is the perfect place for an unhurried walk.

Along the route you can see what the National Geographic Society is up to, traipse through some fabulous mansions, enjoy one of the world's best collections of modern art, tour the preserved home of President Woodrow Wilson, visit a magnificent mosque, and observe Washington's elite in their natural habitat.

GETTING THERE:

By Metro, take the Red line to the **Farragut North** station and exit onto L Street. At the end of the walk, you can return by boarding any southbound bus along Connecticut Avenue, or walk a half-mile south to the Dupont Circle Metro station.

By taxi, just ask for the Mayflower Hotel.

PRACTICALITIES:

Several of the attractions along this walk are closed on Sundays and/or Mondays; the B'nai B'rith Klutznick Museum on Saturdays, legal and Jewish holidays; and the Historical Society on Sundays through Tuesdays. If you follow it all the way, the walk is about three miles long.

For current tourist information, contact the **Washington Visitor Information Center** in the Ronald Reagan Building, 1331 Pennsylvania Avenue NW, ☎ (202) 789-7000, Internet: www.washington.org.

FOOD AND DRINK:

The streets around Dupont Circle are chock-a-block with interesting and inexpensive restaurants, so you won't go hungry. Beyond that, however, the pickings are slim. Some good choices are:

Skewers (1633 P St. NW, between 16th & 17th streets) Middle Eastern delicacies in an upstairs restaurant. ☎ (202) 387-7400. $$

Sala Thai (2016 P St. NW, a block west of Dupont Circle) Subtle Thai dishes served in crisp modern surroundings. ☎ (202) 872-1144. X: Sun. lunch. $$

Raku (1900 Q St. NW at Dupont Circle) Asian noodles, skewers, snacks, and dumplings in a delightful café. ☎ (202) 265-7258. $$

Pizzeria Paradiso (2029 P St. NW, a block west of Dupont Circle) Light Italian dishes in a lively setting. ☎ (202) 223-1245. $ and $$

Pan Asian Noodles & Grill (2020 P St. NW, a block west of Dupont Circle) A popular spot for all kinds of noodles from all around the Orient. ☎ (202) 872-8889. $

Zorba's Café (1612 20th St. NW, 2 blocks northwest of Dupont Circle) This self-service café features tasty Greek dishes plus pizza and sandwiches, to eat inside or out. ☎ (202) 387-8555. $

Food for Thought (1738 Connecticut Ave., 3 blocks northwest of Dupont Circle) The Age of Aquarius lives on in this vegetarian hangout. ☎ (202) 797-1095. X: Sun. lunch. $

C.F. Folks (1225 19th St., between M & N streets) Great lunches at low, low prices—at the counter or to take out. ☎ (202) 293-0162. X: evenings. $

SUGGESTED TOUR:

Numbers in parentheses correspond to numbers on the map.

Begin your walk in front of the **Mayflower Hotel** (1) on Connecticut Avenue at L Street, just north of Farragut Square and the Metro station. This *grande dame* of Washington hotels opened in 1925, just in time for Calvin Coolidge's inaugural ball. Its sumptuous interior has been renovated, and since the marble lobby extends all the way through to 17th

Street you might as well use it as an elegant shortcut to the first major attraction:

*NATIONAL GEOGRAPHIC SOCIETY / EXPLORERS HALL (2), 17th and M streets NW, ☎ (202) 857-7588, Internet: www.nationalgeographic.com/ explorer. *Open Mon.–Sat. and holidays 9–5, Sun. 10–5, closed Christmas. Free. Gift shop.* ♿, *use ramp at M St.*

Explorers Hall occupies the entire first floor of the society's marble-and-glass headquarters building, a 1965 structure by the famed architect Edward Durrell Stone. Like the Air and Space Museum, this exhibition is a popular favorite with visiting groups of school kids, and rightly so. Through the use of the most modern interactive technology they—and you—can have lots of fun while learning about the Earth and beyond.

Don't miss the show at ***Earth Station One**, a 72-seat amphitheater in which orbital flight is simulated around the world's largest unmounted globe. The program lasts about 15 minutes and runs several times an hour. There is a computerized photo booth that for a fee puts a picture of you on a facsimile cover of the *National Geographic*, and exhibitions of works by that renowned magazine's crack photographers. The rest of the hall is occupied by changing exhibitions and by a gift shop where you can buy current and back issues of the society's publications, maps, videos, and more.

Continue up 17th Street to Rhode Island Avenue and the **B'nai B'rith Klutznick National Jewish Museum** (3). Celebrating several thousand years of Jewish history, the collections here include ancient coins from Biblical times, a 16th-century Torah cover, artifacts from the Holocaust, modern Israeli art, a copy of a letter from George Washington to a synagogue in Rhode Island, and many more objects relating to Jewish life and culture. *1640 Rhode Island Ave. NW,* ☎ *(202) 857-6583. Open Sun.–Fri. 10–4:30, closed Sat., legal and Jewish holidays. Suggested donation: Adults $2, children $1. Gift shop.* ♿.

Turn right to **Scott Circle** (4), where you can get a view of the White House by looking down 16th Street. The equestrian statue of "Old Fuss and Feathers," General Winfield Scott (1786–1866), was cast from a cannon captured in the Mexican War of 1847. In the northwest corner, at 1601 Massachusetts Avenue, is the **Australian Embassy**, whose art gallery mounts free shows from Down Under. *Open Mon.–Fri. 9-4:30,* ☎ *(202) 797-3255.*

Turn left and head west up Massachusetts Avenue, passing the **Brookings Institution**, a liberal think tank at number 1775. At the corner of 18th Street stands the former **McCormick Apartments** (5), a lavish

Beaux-Arts building of 1917 that once housed such notables as Andrew Mellon and Perle Mesta. Perfectly maintained, it is now the headquarters of the National Trust for Historic Preservation. Although the landmark structure is not open to the public, you might be able to get a good look at its opulent lobby.

Amble up 18th Street and make a left onto P Street. This takes you to **Dupont Circle** (6). Three broad avenues and two streets flow into this busy hub, with their traffic circling around a shady park. In its center is a marble fountain designed in 1921 by Daniel Chester French, the sculptor of Lincoln's statue in the Lincoln Memorial. The three allegorical figures represent the wind, the sea, and the stars in honor of Civil War hero Admiral Samuel F. DuPont. Today, Washingtonians of all kinds frequent the park, from bureaucrats to counterculture types, making it the best place in town for casual people-watching.

Of the several great mansions that once graced Dupont Circle, only two remain. One of these is the flamboyant **Patterson House** on the northeast corner of P Street, built in 1903 for the publisher of the *Washington Times-Herald*. President Calvin Coolidge stayed here in 1927 while the White House was being renovated, and it was here that he played host to the young aviator Charles Lindbergh. The house is now occupied by a social club.

Stroll southwest on New Hampshire Avenue to the:

HISTORICAL SOCIETY OF WASHINGTON, D.C. / HEURICH MANSION (7), 1307 New Hampshire Ave. NW, ☎ (202) 785-2068, Internet: www.hswdc.org. *Open Wed.–Sat., 10–4. Adults $3, seniors and students under 18 $1.50. Tours. Bookshop.* ᐒ.

Beer baron Christian Heurich completed his unique Romanesque-Revival castle in 1896 and lived in it until his death in 1945. His heirs donated it to the Historical Society in 1956 after his third wife passed away the previous year. The ornate interior is filled to overflowing with all of the trappings of late-19th-century wealth. Downstairs is the German Breakfast Room or *Alt Deutsche Bierstube* (old German tavern), where the family ate breakfast every morning and by day's end let their hair down while enjoying products of the Heurich Brewery. *Herr* Heurich, a native of Germany, considered beer to be good for the health and drank it every day. He lived to be 102.

One of Washington's first poured-concrete structures, the building was designed to be fireproof as a result of several disastrous conflagrations at the brewery. The Historical Society has preserved the mansion pretty much as the Heurichs left it, but have added an impressive third floor library dedicated to Washington D.C.'s economic, political, social and physical development. In conjunction with the Pleasant Company, the society also runs a two-hour long American Girls Museum Program, popular with the 7- to 12-year-old set.

Now turn north on 20th Street and left onto Massachusetts Avenue, a.k.a. **Embassy Row**. In that wonderful world before income taxes, the country's nouveau riche built their mansions here as they climbed the social ladder. After the Great Depression, when these white elephants could no longer be maintained, they were sold off to foreign countries for tax-free use by the diplomatic corps. You will soon pass the magnificent **Indonesian Embassy** (8) at the southeast corner of 21st street. One of the grandest residences in Washington, it was built in 1903 by an Irish immigrant named Thomas Walsh who struck gold in Colorado. His daughter Evalyn Walsh McLean was the last private owner of the famous Hope Diamond, now on view at the National Museum of Natural History. She sold the house to the Indonesian government in 1951.

Pass by the exclusive Ritz-Carlton Hotel to the **Anderson House** (9) of 1905, once the residence of the wealthy diplomat Larz Anderson III. Since 1937 it has been occupied by the **Society of the Cincinnati**, a patriotic organization founded in 1783 by officers of the Revolution. Its present members are direct male descendants of the founders who made George Washington their first President-General. The society took its name from the Roman general Lucius Quinctius Cincinnatus (6th century BC); a name later bestowed by a member upon a town in Ohio. Much of the mansion's lavishly decorated interior is furnished as it was when the Andersons lived there, and is open to the public. *2118 Massachusetts Ave. NW, ☎ (202) 785-2040. Open Tues.–Sat. 1–4, closed legal holidays, call ahead. Group tours by appointment. Free. ໕ by prior arrangement.*

Now cross the avenue for a real treat:

*THE PHILLIPS COLLECTION (10), 1600 21st St. NW, ☎ (202) 387- 2151. *Open Tues.–Sat. 10–5, Thurs. until 8:30, Sun. noon–7. Closed New Year's Day, July 4, Thanksgiving and Christmas. Weekend admission charge and weekday suggested contribution: Adults $6.50, students with ID and seniors over 62 $3.25, children under 18 free. Gift Shop. Café. ໕.*

Washington boasts other world-class art museums, but none that present their treasures in so intimate a manner as does the Phillips. A private institution, it retains much of the atmosphere of the home it once was. This is America's pioneering gallery of modern art, established long before contemporary styles became popular. Going to the Phillips is like visiting an old friend—it's so comfortable that you'll probably want to linger.

Duncan Phillips (1886–1966), grandson of a founder of the Jones and Laughlin Steel Company, began his art collection after graduating from Yale in 1908. Following the untimely deaths of both his father and brother, he decided to transform the collection into a museum in their memory. This opened to the public in 1921 — the same year that he married the painter Marjorie Acker — and occupied two rooms of the family home on 21st Street. The collection grew so rapidly that by 1930 it took over the entire house and the family had to move. In 1960 an extensive new wing was added, but the original relaxed ambiance was successfully preserved. There are no guards visible. Instead, art students are employed to assist visitors in their understanding of the works.

You might be surprised at the richness of this collection, which includes Renoir's *Luncheon of the Boating Party*—surely one of the most memorable images of the entire Impressionist school. Major works by Van Gogh, Cézanne, Degas, Klee, Braque, Rothko, Bonnard, O'Keeffe, and others are enhanced by the presence of earlier paintings by past masters such as El Greco, Manet, and Daumier. The museum is kept lively with the acquisition of new works by today's emerging talents, and by frequent special exhibitions. Enjoy your visit!

Continue north on 21st Street and turn left onto R Street. The **Fondo del Sol Visual Arts Center** (11) at number 2112 celebrates the creative heritage of the Americas with changing exhibitions. Besides a permanent collection of delightful *Santos*, pre-Columbian art, and folk art, there are works by contemporary Hispanic, Caribbean, African-American, and Native-American artists. Founded in 1973 by a group of artists and writers, the non-profit organization also sponsors a wide variety of cultural programs. ☎ *(202) 483-2777. Open Wed.–Sat. 12:30–5:30. Tues. by appointment. Closed major holidays. Adults $3, students $1.*

R Street soon runs into **Sheridan Circle**, named for Union General Philip H. Sheridan (1831–88), who forced Lee's surrender to Grant at Appomattox. The equestrian statue of him was designed by Gutzon Borglum, better known as the sculptor of Mount Rushmore. Although thick with foreign embassies, this neighborhood retains much of its elegant residential character. It's certainly a great place to test your knowledge of national flags!

Along the southwestern edge of Sheridan Circle stands the charming **Barney Studio House** (12) of 1903, once an informal center of Washington's cultural life. It is now maintained by the Smithsonian's National Museum of American Art and may be visited by advance arrangement only. Alice Pike Barney (1857–1931) was a wealthy widow with a strong bohemian streak (and loads of talent) who gathered a circle of friends into activities aimed at filling Washington's notorious cultural vacuum. Her Mediterranean-style studio-home was her stage, and it is still filled with the original dramatic furnishings, mementos, and art. *2306 Massachusetts Ave. NW, ☎ (202) 357-3111. Open for tours by reservation only, Oct.–June, Wed. & Thurs. at 11 and 1, plus the second and fourth Sun. of each month from Oct.–June. Free.*

Continue northwest on Massachusetts Avenue, passing several striking embassies along the way, and turn right on S Street to visit the:

WOODROW WILSON HOUSE (13), 2340 S St. NW, ☎ (202) 387-4062, Internet: www.nthp.org/main/sites/wilsonhouse.htm. *Open Tues.– Sun. 10–4. Closed Mon. and major holidays. Adults $5, seniors over 62 $4 and students with ID (ages 7–18) $2.50, National Trust members and children under 7 free. Tours. Gift shop. ᵭ call in advance.*

Woodrow Wilson was the only U.S. President to have retired in Washington right after leaving the White House. He purchased this comfortable home in 1920 and remained there until his death in 1924, after which his widow continued to live in it until passing away in 1961. Truly a time capsule of a bygone era, the house offers a special glimpse into the private life of a visionary statesman. Among the highlights shown on the tour are the ***Drawing Room** with its Gobelins tapestry, the Library, the former President's bedroom, and the large 1920's kitchen.

Next door to the Wilson House is the **Textile Museum** (14), where extremely rare textiles and rugs from all over the world are displayed. More interesting than you might think, the museum occupies two elegant townhouses designed by leading architects, and features such exotic items as pre-Columbian fabrics from the Peru of 600 BC, rug and curtain fragments from ancient Egypt, and Classical carpets from India and Iran. *☎ (202) 667-0441, Internet: www.textilemuseum.org. Open Mon.–Sat. 10–5, Sun. 1–5. Closed Federal holidays and Dec. 24. Suggested donation $5. Gift shop. ᵭ by prior arrangement.*

You are now entering the heart of **Kalorama**, a gorgeous enclave of quiet urbanity whose name is Greek for "beautiful view." Once a large Colonial estate, Kalorama has been a prime residential area for Washington's wealthy elite since the early 20th century. Today's tax structures are responsible for the conversion of many of its mansions into foreign embassies, but that only makes the neighborhood more interesting. Continue up Massachusetts Avenue to the:

ISLAMIC CENTER (15), 2551 Massachusetts Ave. NW, ☎ (202) 332-8343. *Open Sat.–Thurs. 10–5, Fri. 10–noon and 3–5. Donation requested.*

Proper attire required: no shorts, women's heads and arms must be covered, shoes removed to enter mosque. Tours are available by advance arrangement. Bookstore.

Looking like a scene right out of the Middle East, the Islamic Center is one of Washington's most fascinating—and unexpected—sights. Its slender white minaret rises some 162 feet above Massachusetts Avenue and overlooks the heavily-wooded Rock Creek Park. Below it, and set at an angle to face Mecca, is the **mosque** where prayers are held five times daily—before sunrise, after noon, late in the afternoon, after sunset, and in the late evening. The structure is richly decorated with geometric and floral designs as well as with calligraphy, as Islamic law forbids the representation of human or animal forms.

Built between 1949 and 1957 with funds and materials from Muslim nations all around the globe, the center serves Washington's large Islamic population and promotes a better understanding of Islam among non-Muslim Americans. You'll find that a visit here is both friendly and informative.

Head northeast on Belmont Road to **Kalorama Circle**, where the seductive charms of this secluded enclave are strongest. Along the way you'll have great *views of Rock Creek Park. At 2401 Kalorama Road stands a lovely old house called **The Lindens** (16), which didn't always stand here. Built in 1754 in Danvers, Massachusetts, it was the home of the last royal governor of that colony. In 1936 it was moved to Washington by an architect and workmen from Colonial Williamsburg—who knew something about reassembling old houses!

Continue past the **French Embassy** at number 2221 and turn left onto Wyoming Avenue. This soon brings you to Connecticut Avenue, where you can board a bus south to Dupont Circle or just walk the half-mile distance.

*Georgetown

Whatever you may think of Georgetown, you'll have to admit that it's the most colorful corner of Washington, D.C., and a whole lot of fun to explore. Most visitors enjoy its cosmopolitan ambiance, although some may find it a bit too trendy. Home to many of Washington's most affluent citizens, Georgetown is also a bustling university town, a fashionable shopping center, and a beautifully-preserved repository of historic sites. Thanks largely to the deep gorge cut by Rock Creek, this neighborhood has always remained separate from the rest of Washington, and flaunts its own very distinct personality.

First settled around 1703, Georgetown was officially established in 1751 but did not become a part of upstart Washington until 1871. It was supposedly named in honor of King George II, although this is unproven and it could just as well have been for two of its earliest landowners, George Gordon and George Beall. The town's strategic location at the farthest point inland that the Potomac River remained navigable determined its future for many years to come. During the 18th and early 19th centuries it was a thriving port for the developing western reaches of Maryland and the Ohio Valley, especially for the export of tobacco. At that time its wharves extended all the way from Rock Creek to the present site of Key Bridge. The coming of steamships, however, made deeper ports such as Alexandria (see page 101) more practical, and commerce in Georgetown declined. Construction of the Chesapeake and Ohio Canal, begun in 1828, temporarily revived the local economy. Ironically, on the very same day that President John Quincy Adams dug the first shovelful of earth for this project, building also began on the vastly more efficient Baltimore and Ohio Railroad linking the rival port of Baltimore with the same hinterlands served by the waterway. Nevertheless, the 184-mile-long canal remained more-or-less active until 1924, and has since been preserved as a National Historical Park.

Georgetown's fortunes declined toward the end of the 19th century, although its proximity to downtown Washington kept it alive as a residential area for the burgeoning number of civil servants. While its university prospered and its wealthy citizens remained in the northern reaches, some sections below M Street had become virtual slums. The Old Georgetown Act of 1950 helped reverse matters by declaring the area a National Historic District, subject to strict zoning regulations. Rediscovered by Washington's elite, preserved and gentrified, for many people Georgetown is now the capital's most desirable neighborhood.

GETTING THERE:

By Metro, take the Blue or Orange line to the **Foggy Bottom—GWU** station and walk a bit over a half-mile northwest, following Pennsylvania Avenue across a bridge.

By bus, take routes 30, 32, 34, or 36 west along Pennsylvania Avenue, getting off shortly after crossing the bridge.

By taxi, ask for M and 30th streets NW.

By car, you'll have a difficult time finding a parking place, even in an expensive lot. Good luck!

PRACTICALITIES:

The best time to visit Georgetown is on Wednesdays through Sundays during the summer, when the colorful canal boats operate. There is also limited service in April, May, September, and October. Outdoor cafés, mostly near the canal, flourish in warm weather. Dumbarton Oaks, a major sight, is closed on Mondays and national holidays, although its gardens are open daily except holidays. The totally separate Dumbarton House is open mornings only, and closes on Sundays, Mondays, and holidays. The Old Stone House closes on Mondays, Tuesdays, Thanksgiving, Christmas, and New Year's. Tudor Place requires advance reservations. Overall, your best bet is to come on any day (except major holidays) from Wednesdays through Saturday, preferably between late spring and early fall.

The total walk is about four miles long, not including any side trips, and involves a few mild hills plus one short, steep climb. Some of it is on unpaved paths, so wear comfortable shoes.

For current tourist information, contact the **Washington Visitor Information Center** in the Ronald Reagan Building, 1331 Pennsylvania Avenue NW, ☎ (202) 789-7000, Internet: www.washington.org.

FOOD AND DRINK:

Georgetown has a vast selection of good restaurants, few of which are cheap. Here are some sensible choices for lunch:

Aditi (3299 M St. NW, between Wisconsin Ave. and 33rd St.) One of the best Indian restaurants in town, and a bargain at that. ☎ (202) 625-6825. $$

Zed's Ethiopian (3318 M St. NW, between 33rd and 34th streets) Dip your *injera* bread into authentic Ethiopian dishes, both meaty and vegetarian. ☎ (202) 333-4710. $$

Martin's Tavern (1264 Wisconsin Ave. NW, at N St.) A favorite Georgetown fixture since the repeal of prohibition, Martin's is the place for substantial Irish/American meals. ☎ (202) 333-7370. $$

Paolo's (1303 Wisconsin Ave. NW, between N and Dumbarton streets) Inventive pizzas and other modern Italian dishes in a contemporary setting. ☎ (202) 333-7353. $$ and $

Dean and Deluca (by the Old Market at M and Potomac streets NW) Light lunches and snacks in a self-service café with indoor/outdoor tables, near the canal. ☎ (202) 342-2500. $

Booeymonger (3265 Prospect St. NW, near Potomac St.) Hearty sandwiches to eat in or take out are the specialty of this neighborhood favorite. ☎ (202) 333-4810. $

La Madeleine (3000 M St. NW at 30th St.) French-inspired dishes served cafeteria-style, in a stylish setting. ☎ (202) 337-6975. $

Wrap Works (1079 Wisconsin Ave., between K & M streets) Trendy and healthy wraps and smoothies. ☎ (202) 333-0220. $

SUGGESTED TOUR:

Numbers in parentheses correspond to numbers on the map.

Start your walk at Washington's oldest existing building, the:

OLD STONE HOUSE (1), 3051 M St. NW, between 30th and 31st streets, ☎ (202) 426-6851, TDD 426-0125, Internet: www.nps.gov/rocr/ oldstonehouse/walk.htm. *Open Wed.–Sun. 9–5. Closed Mon., Tues., Federal holidays. Free. ♿, partial access.*

Step off busy M Street and into a tranquil **garden**, arranged in the 18th-century manner with fruit trees and seasonal plantings. Adjacent to this stands the old house, begun around 1764 by a cabinetmaker named Christopher Layman, who used it as both a dwelling and a workshop. Later additions were made by the next owner during the 1770s, after which the building sheltered a variety of trades. An old tradition suggests that it was the headquarters of Pierre L'Enfant as he planned the Federal City, or was even used by George Washington himself. With this in mind, Congress in 1950 authorized its purchase and restoration by the National Park Service, which maintains it today. The interior reflects the tastes of middle-class America in Colonial times, and cos-

tumed guides are often on hand to demonstrate 18th-century crafts.

Stroll east on M Street, turning south on 30th to the towpath of the
*Chesapeake and Ohio Canal (2). Georgetown is situated as far up the
Potomac River as ships can go; beyond this lies a series of forbidding
waterfalls. A canal link from here to the Ohio Valley was proposed as
early as the mid-18th century, and was promoted by George Washington
and his Potomack Company in 1785. Some sections skirting the falls
were actually built, but the scheme was largely unsuccessful and ceased
operations around 1820. Still, the idea had merit at the time, and in 1828
construction began on a continuous canal running the entire 364 miles
from Georgetown to Pittsburgh. By the time it reached Cumberland,
MD, in 1850, a distance of 184.5 miles, the rival B&O Railroad (see page
218) had already been there for eight years. Further construction on the
canal ceased, but it remained in commercial operation until 1924, when
a disastrous flood seriously damaged the waterway. The derelict canal
was purchased by the Interior Department in 1938 and some restorations begun. In 1971 it was designated a National Historical Park.

Head west along the ascending locks, passing a bust of Supreme
Court Justice William O. Douglas (1898–1980), who did so much to preserve the canal. Today, its towpath is popular with joggers, hikers, and
bicyclists. Beyond the picturesque 19th-century row houses is the
Visitor Center of the National Park Service, where you can board a mule-
drawn barge for a wonderful 90-minute ***boat ride** into America's past.
1057 Thomas Jefferson St. NW, ☎ *(202) 653-5190, Internet:
www.nps.gov/choh/. Operates from mid-March until early Nov.,
Wed.–Sun. Ask for current schedule. Adults $5.50, seniors $4.50, children
$3.50.* ♿. For more about the canal, see Trip 23.

Cross the canal at 31st Street and head south into the old waterfront district, passing under the elevated Whitehurst Freeway above K
Street. The impressive **Washington Harbor Development** (3) makes imaginative use of the river's edge, and offers magnificent ***views**. In 1748, a
ferry service to the Virginia shore was begun from around here. Stroll
west through a park and turn north on Wisconsin Avenue. On your left
are the old **Dodge Warehouse Buildings** from about 1813, reminders of
Georgetown's past as an inland port. Continue uphill past the **Grace
Episcopal Church**, built in 1866 as a mission church for boatmen. Beyond
this, a 19th-century bridge spans the canal without access, after which
you pass an obelisk commemorating the building of the waterway. The
1840 **Vigilant Firehouse** at 1066 Wisconsin Avenue displays a memorial
plaque to an old fire dog who was poisoned in 1869.

Turn left on M Street, the bustling Main Street of Georgetown, then
left again into **Georgetown Park** (4), which is not a park at all but rather a

kind of indoor playpen for affluent adults. Behind the old exterior façade lurks what could only be described as a neo-Victorian shopping mall, a multi-level skylit extravaganza of truly "upscale" emporiums, cafés, and restaurants. A doorway in its southeast corner leads to waterside cafés, and an upper-level walkway bridges the canal to more shops on the south side. Even if you detest malls, you'll probably enjoy exploring this place.

Exit onto M Street and turn left. On the south side, opposite Potomac Street, is the **Old Public Market** (5) of 1865. An enclosed market place has stood on this site since 1795, and has always been a center for social exchange as well as shopping for food. The present market closed in 1935 and the building was later used as an auto-parts store. Now fully restored, the historic structure is presently an outpost of a fashionable New York food store, and sports an indoor/outdoor café along its side.

Continue west on M Street to **Francis Scott Key Park** (6), otherwise known as The Star-Spangled Banner Monument. Key lived in a house near here when he was sent to Baltimore in 1814 on a rescue mission that ultimately resulted in the famous words of the national anthem. From here you will have good views and access to another part of the canal. If you're burning with energy, you might want to stroll across the adjacent **Key Bridge** to Rosslyn, VA, for a superb panoramic *view of Georgetown and Washington.

Now it's uphill to the next several sights. You can either walk up 35th Street or, if you can face it, climb the very steep outdoor staircase opposite the old carbarn at 36th Street. These steps were the locale of the climatic last scene in that scariest of movies, *The Exorcist*. Once at the top, turn left to the campus of **Georgetown University** (7). America's oldest Catholic college was founded in 1789 by Archbishop John Carroll of Baltimore, who selected this magnificent site overlooking the river. Its most prominent structure and main administration building, visible for miles around, is **Healy Hall**, a Victorian Gothic monstrosity of 1879 noted for its clock tower. Behind this is Old North, erected in 1795 and now the oldest building on campus. *Tours by advance arrangement,* ☎ *(202) 687-3600.*

Follow the map east on N Street, passing a group of five houses (numbers 3339-3327) from 1817 known as **Cox's Row**, built by a former mayor of Georgetown. The Marquis de Lafayette was entertained at number 3337 in 1824. A bit farther down the block, at number 3307, stands a modest 1811 town house that was purchased in 1957 by Senator John F. Kennedy. The Kennedy family continued to live in it until January 20, 1961, when they moved into larger quarters on Pennsylvania Avenue following his inauguration as President.

Turn north on Potomac Street to **St. John's Episcopal Church** (8), built in 1809 and attributed to William Thornton, the first architect of the Capitol. Renovations around 1870 have dramatically changed its appearance. At the corner of the lot is a tablet commemorating Ninian Beall (1625–1717), the first owner of the land that is now Georgetown. Beall, a Scotsman, commanded forces loyal to King Charles I during the English Civil War. When Charles lost his head to Oliver Cromwell, Beall was shipped off to Maryland as a political prisoner, and after the restoration of the monarchy was granted land there.

Turn left on O Street, which still has its brick surface and streetcar tracks, although (alas!) the trolley cars no longer run. Now follow the route on the map to:

TUDOR PLACE (9), 1644 31st St. NW, ☎ (202) 965-0400, Internet: www.tudorplace.org. *Reservations suggested, tours Tues.–Fri. at 10, 11:30, 1, and 2:30; and on Sat. every hour on the hour from 10–3. Suggested donation $6 adults, $5 seniors and $3 for students.*

Six generations of a prominent Washington family have maintained this Federal-period mansion and stately grounds for about 180 years before it was opened to the public in 1988. Martha Custis Peter, granddaughter of Martha Washington (from a previous marriage), inherited $8,000 from her step-grandfather George Washington, with which she and her husband purchased the Georgetown Heights land overlooking the Federal City in 1805. Two wings of the house predate this, having been built in 1796, but the main section was completed in 1816. It was designed by William Thornton, the first architect of the U.S. Capitol. With continuous occupation by the same family, the house reflects a remarkable unity in its furnishings. Several of the pieces had originally come from Mount Vernon itself. The period **gardens** are especially lovely and should not be missed.

Return to Q Street and head east past **Cooke's Row** (numbers 3007-3029), an unusually elaborate set of Victorian houses built in 1868. Continue south on 30th Street and east on P Street. Fronting numbers 2803-2805 and extending around the corner is the famous **Daw's Fence**, a perfectly ordinary looking iron fence whose stakes are actually musket barrels that the thrifty Mr. Daw had purchased cheaply as Mexican War surplus. It takes close examination to discover this, as he imbedded the stock ends in a low wall and added spikes into the muzzles.

Turn north on 28th Street. A short distance east on Q Street is the:

DUMBARTON HOUSE (10), 2715 Q St. NW, ☎ 337-2288. *Open Sept.– July, Tues.–Sat. 10–12:15. Afternoon tours by appointment. Closed Sun. and Federal holidays. Adults $3, seniors over 60 $2, children under 12 and students with ID free.* ♿.

Operated by the Colonial Dames of America as their national headquarters, Dumbarton House is a Federal-style brick mansion dating from about 1798. In 1915 it was moved 100 yards north to accommodate the extension of Q Street, a feat accomplished with rollers and one very strong horse! The house was acquired by its present owners in 1928 and renamed for the original Rock of Dumbarton tract that is now Georgetown. Restored to its original appearance, it is furnished with period antiques, mostly dating from 1790 to 1830. Several of the items originally came from Mount Vernon. The Museum Room is especially interesting with its carefully-preserved clothing that once belonged to such famous people as Martha Washington and Dolley Madison.

Continue up 28th Street, bearing left onto R Street and passing **Oak Hill Cemetery** (11), where many notables have been going to their final rest since 1849. Its Gothic Revival chapel, reminiscent of medieval England, was designed by James Renwick, the architect of the Smithsonian Castle and the original Corcoran Gallery. Just west of the cemetery is **Montrose Park**, a public park with delightful paths leading down, down, down to Rock Creek Park.

Finally, what for many is the star attraction of Georgetown, an estate that's well worth the trip by itself:

*DUMBARTON OAKS (12), 1703 32nd St. NW, ☎ (202) 339-6401 (recording) or (202) 339-6409, Internet: www.doaks.org. *Gardens open daily 2–6, closing at 5 from Nov.–March. Collections open Tues.–Sun. 2–5, Rare Book Room on weekends only. Both closed on national holidays and Christmas eve. Garden admission: Adults $4, seniors and children $3. Free to all from Nov.-March. Donations accepted at museum. Museum shop.* ♿, *partial access, hillside gardens difficult.*

Although the names are similar, Dumbarton Oaks is a completely different kind of place from Dumbarton *House*, described previously. This 16-acre estate reflects the highly sophisticated tastes of Ambassador and Mrs. Robert Woods Bliss, who bought the property in 1920 and developed it into the remarkable institution that it is today. In 1940 they donated the mansion, gardens, and world-class art collections to Harvard University for use as a research library and museum, and provided it with an endowment. Living nearby, they continued their support of Dumbarton Oaks and its activities for the rest of their lives. In 1944 the mansion was used for two international conferences that set the stage for the creation of the United Nations. Ambassador Bliss died in 1962, and Mrs. Bliss in 1969.

The estate is actually two separate entities, with different entrances.

Strolling west on R Street, you'll first come to the incredible ***Gardens**, easily among the best in the country. Step through the gateway and pick up a map for the self-guided tour, available from the kiosk to the right of the entrance. A nominal admission is charged here from April through October. Tumbling steeply down a spectacular hillside, a series of broad terraces make the transition from studied formality to a refreshing simplicity. Romantic paths lead to secluded spots, such as **Lovers' Lane Pool**. Don't miss the lovely **Rose Garden**, along whose west wall were placed the ashes of Mr. and Mrs. Bliss, or the **Pebble Garden** with its shallow pool and mosaics. Remarkably, the gardens are almost as beautiful in winter as in the growing season.

The **Mansion**, housing the ***Art Collections**, is entered from 32nd Street. Begin with the ***Byzantine Collection** of works from the Greek and Roman eras, as well as from the Byzantine and Post-Byzantine periods (4th to 18th centuries). The Blisses started their collection in 1931 after viewing an exhibition in Paris, and over the years it has grown into one of the finest in the world. From here you can walk into the stunning ***Pre-Columbian Museum**, a complex of eight small circular glass pavilions arranged around a central fountain, designed in 1963 by the noted architect Philip Johnson. The objects are displayed in transparent and translucent cases, making them appear to almost float in the natural wooded environment. Ambassador Bliss began this collection in 1914 and turned it over to Dumbarton Oaks in 1962. It covers much of the cultural history of Central and South America, from prehistoric times until the Spanish conquest.

The **Music Room**, a 1929 addition to the mansion, is furnished with European furniture and fittings from the 15th to the 17th centuries. Its works of art include *The Visitation* by El Greco and a *Madonna and Child* by Tilman Riemenschneider. Jan Paderewski, the Polish pianist and statesman, gave concerts here, as did other leading musicians. Several works by the composer Igor Stravinsky were first performed in this room, including his *Concerto in E Flat*, a.k.a. the "Dumbarton Oaks Concerto." Finally, it was in this chamber that the proposals for the United Nations charter were developed in 1944.

Walk a block west on R Street to Wisconsin Avenue, where you can catch a southbound bus back through Georgetown and into Washington proper via Pennsylvania Avenue.

Section III

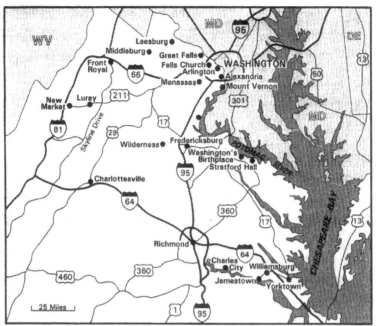

DAYTRIPS TO
VIRGINIA

The Old Dominion begins just across the Potomac from Washington, with some of its best attractions only a subway ride away. By car, you can easily reach the very origins of English settlement in America; beautifully-preserved places where the nation's heritage is kept alive for future generations. Here you can also experience gracious reminders of the Old South, and explore the battlefields of the Civil War that so profoundly changed it. And if you tire of the past, there's plenty of natural beauty as well, especially in the Shenandoah Valley.

More than half of the destinations are less than 100 miles from downtown Washington, with others not much farther. Although slightly more than 150 miles away, Williamsburg and the Jamestown/Yorktown area are so compelling that they've also been included.

If you have the time, several of the excursions could be connected to form a touring itinerary lasting from a long weekend to two weeks.

Arlington

You could easily walk from Washington to Arlington, but you probably won't want to stroll around too far within the town. This sprawling mess of tangled highways, malls, and office complexes stretches on for mile after mile with little relief. Yet, it contains some of the capital region's most memorable sights. Fortunately, the Metro connects its three major areas, so you can avoid most of the traffic congestion as you explore.

Visiting the Arlington National Cemetery is the main reason for coming this way, but there is also Robert E. Lee's Arlington House mansion, the Marine's Iwo Jima Memorial, the Newseum, the Netherlands Carillon, the unspoiled wilderness preserve on Theodore Roosevelt Island and, to end your day with a bang, a tour through the Pentagon.

One nice aspect of this trip is that all of the sights are free, so your only expense will be transportation and meals. Elements of it could be combined in the same day with Alexandria, described on pages 101-109, which is on the same Metro line.

GETTING THERE:

By car, cross the Arlington Memorial Bridge and park in the pay lot at the entrance of the cemetery. From there you can walk or take a Tourmobile through the cemetery. To reach Theodore Roosevelt Island, take the northbound lane of the George Washington Memorial Parkway to the parking-lot turnoff. A pedestrian bridge leads from there to the island. Visitor parking at the Pentagon is possible but limited.

By Metro, take the Blue Line to the **Arlington Cemetery** stop, next to the entrance. From here you can walk or take a Tourmobile. Theodore Roosevelt Island can be reached on foot from the **Rosslyn** Metro stop on the Blue and Orange lines, and the **Pentagon** has its own stop on the Blue and Yellow lines.

By Tourmobile, get off at the Arlington Cemetery stop (see page 000). A *separate* Tourmobile route starts here, with stops at the Kennedy grave site, Tomb of the Unknowns, and Arlington House.

PRACTICALITIES:

This tour can be taken on any day, bearing in mind that the

Pentagon is closed to visitors on weekends and Federal holidays. If you plan to visit there, make sure that you're carrying a photo ID, such as a driver's license or passport.

For further information, contact the sites directly or the **Arlington Visitors Center** at 735 18th St., Arlington, VA 22202, ☎ (703) 228-5720 or (800) 677-6267, Internet: www.stayarlington.com.

FOOD AND DRINK:

There are no places to eat near the sites, but it isn't too far north to nearby Rosslyn, which is loaded with mostly ethnic restaurants, including:

Kabul Caravan (Colonial Village Ctr., 1725 Wilson Blvd.) The exotic atmosphere matches the unusual cuisine in this marvelous Afghani restaurant. ☎ (703) 522-8394. X: weekend lunch. $$

Mezza 9 (1325 Wilson Blvd., in the Hyatt Hotel) Creative Mediterranean cuisine. ☎ (703) 276-8999. $$

Ireland's Four Courts (2051 Wilson Blvd. at N. Courthouse Rd., Rosslyn) An Irish pub with Irish food. ☎ (703) 525-3600. $$

Red Hot & Blue (1600 Wilson Blvd., near Pierce St.) Expect crowds at this Memphis-style barbecue pit, where you can wallow in smoked pork ribs or a "pulled pig sandwich." ☎ (703) 276-7427. $

Pho 75 (1711 Wilson Blvd., near Quinn St.) *Pho* is a Vietnamese soup that makes an entire meal, concocted of beef, noodles, and various veggies. The decor here is minimal, but you'll enjoy slurping this bargain repast. ☎ (703) 525-7355. $

Hard Times Café (3028 Wilson Blvd. at Highland St.) Huge selections of chili as you like it—Texas, Cincinnati, or vegetarian. ☎ (703) 528-2233. $

Alternatively, you could enjoy an alfresco picnic on Theodore Roosevelt Island in the middle of the Potomac.

LOCAL ATTRACTIONS:

Numbers in parentheses correspond to numbers on the map.

*ARLINGTON NATIONAL CEMETERY (1–4), Arlington, VA 22211, ☎ (703) 697-2131, Internet: www.mdw.army.mil/cemetery.htm. *Open daily; Apr.–Sept. 8–7; Oct.–Mar. 8–5. Free. Paid parking off Memorial Drive. Cars are not permitted within the cemetery grounds except for handicapped persons and relatives of those interred. Visiting the main sites on foot involves at least two miles of walking on somewhat hilly terrain. Tourmobile rides with on/off privileges: Adults $4.75, children 3–11 $2.25.* ♿.

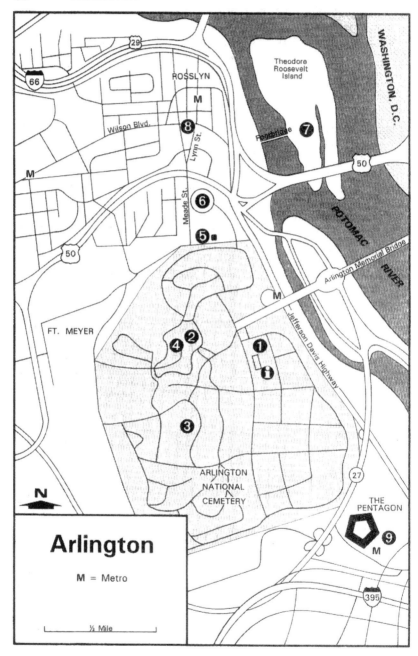

Established during the Civil War and still in active use, the nation's most revered burial ground is the final resting place for over 200,000 veterans and their dependents. More than that, it is a shrine honoring their courage and sacrifice in defending the ideals of freedom around the world. Two U.S. presidents are buried here, William Howard Taft and John F. Kennedy, along with numerous other persons who served their nation with distinction.

The 612-acre cemetery is on the former estate of Confederate General Robert E. Lee, whose Arlington House mansion may be visited. The land was confiscated by the Federal government after the outbreak of hostilities, initially used as a Union Army headquarters, and after 1864 as a military cemetery. It now holds veterans of every armed conflict in which the U.S. has ever participated, from the Revolutionary War to the present.

Begin at the Visitors Center (1), close to the Metro stop and parking lot. Here you can get a map and guide to the grave sites, and obtain information about the location of any specific grave. This is also the departure point for Tourmobile rides through the cemetery, and for a separate Tourmobile route back to Washington. Nearby is the **Women in Military Service for America Memorial**, honoring women who served in the armed forces and featuring a gallery filled with artifacts along with a computerized database.

The ***Kennedy grave sites** (2), just below Arlington House, center around the grave of President John F. Kennedy (1917–63), which is marked by an eternal flame. Nearby are interred two of his children who died in infancy. His brother, Attorney General Robert F. Kennedy (1925–68), rests a few yards away, under a simple white cross.

Probably the most poignant sight at Arlington is the ***Tomb of the Unknowns** (3), watched over 24 hours a day by sentries from the U.S. Army's Third Infantry. On November 11, 1921, an unknown soldier from World War I was entombed here, joined in 1958 by an unidentified warrior of World War II and another from the Korean conflict. In 1984, an unknown soldier from the Vietnam conflict was added, but later identified and disinterred. This may be the last, as modern science has made identification of remains almost certain. The memorial, erected in 1932, reads "Here Rests in Honored Glory an American Soldier Known But to God." An impressive **changing-of-the-guard ceremony** is performed every half-hour from April through September, and every hour the rest of the year.

Adjoining the tomb is the **Memorial Amphitheater**, where ceremonies are held on Easter, Memorial Day, and Veterans Day. Close to this are memorials to the astronauts killed in the space shuttle *Challenger* disaster, the aborted Iran rescue mission of 1980, and the sinking of the U.S.S. *Maine* in 1898. Near the top of the hill stands the **Confederate Memorial**, erected in 1912 as an act of reconciliation.

Continue on to **Arlington House** (4), for many years the home of Robert E. Lee (see page 107). The mansion was begun in 1802 by George Washington Parke Custis (1781–1857), the grandson of Martha Washington by a previous marriage, who had inherited the 1,100-acre tract right across the Potomac from the new capital city. Having also inherited many of the Washingtons' personal possessions from Mount Vernon, which he expanded by purchases, young George Custis wanted to make the house into what he called a "Washington Treasury" in honor of the first president. He later married a distant cousin of the Lee family, producing a daughter who married Lieutenant Robert E. Lee (1807–70) in 1831. From then until the outbreak of the Civil War 30 years later, the Lee family made this their permanent homestead. When Virginia seceded from the Union in 1861, then-Colonel Lee resigned from the U.S. Army and joined the Confederacy as a general, never again to return to Arlington House.

Mrs. Lee fled south as the estate was taken over by advancing Union forces. The mansion became a Federal military headquarters and its vast collection of Washington family memorabilia was moved to the capital city for safekeeping. Through some questionable legalities, the U.S. Government confiscated the property and began burying its Civil War dead on the grounds in an apparent attempt to make certain that the Lees would never again want to live there. General Lee's son sued in 1882 and recovered the estate, but sold it back to the government for $150,000. The mansion was used as an administration center for the cemetery until 1925, when a full restoration to its pre-Civil War appearance began.

Now a memorial to General Lee, the house contains original items that belonged to the family, filled out by other period pieces and careful reproductions. Pick up a descriptive brochure before beginning your self-guided tour of the interior. Outside, you can't help but notice the extraordinary *view of Washington, DC. This is the perfect setting for the grave of Pierre L'Enfant, the unappreciated genius who planned the city in 1791 and died penniless for his efforts. His bones were moved here in 1909. ☎ *(703) 557-0613, Internet: www.nps.gov/arho. Open Apr.–Sept. 9:30–6, Oct.–March 9:30–4:30. Closed Christmas and New Year's. Free. Bookstore. ⑁, first floor accessible.*

Just north of the cemetery is the **Netherlands Carillon** (5), a thank-you gift from the Dutch people for America's help during and after World War II. The rectilinear metal tower, which you can climb for another great view, contains 49 bells that are played at various times from May through September. ☎ *(703) 289-2550, Internet: www.nps.gov/gwmp/carillon.htm. Open daily, dawn to dusk. Free.*

Continue north a few more steps to the **Iwo Jima Memorial** (6), officially known as the Marine Corps War Memorial. Joe Rosenthal's world-famous, Pulitzer Prize-winning photograph of six U.S. servicemen raising the flag on Iwo Jima's Mount Suribachi after one of the bloodiest, most decisive battles of World War II, has been re-created into the largest cast-bronze statue in the world by sculptor Felix W. de Weldon. Measuring some 78 feet high, it is topped by a real flag that flies 24 hours a day. Marine Corps parades are held here on Tuesday evenings at 7 from June through August, with free transportation provided from the Arlington Cemetery Visitors Center. *Internet: www.nps.gov/gwmp/ usmc.htm.*

Another nearby attraction, reachable by foot, car, or from the Metro stop in Rosslyn, is:

THEODORE ROOSEVELT ISLAND (7), ☎ (703) 285-2598, Internet: nps.gov/gwmp/tri.htm. *Accessible via a footbridge from the Virginia side. Open daily 7–sunset. Free. Hiking trails. Guided tours.*

It is only fitting that America's 26th President is remembered by an 88-acre nature preserve, left virtually unspoiled by civilization. Here, in the middle of the Potomac River, visitors can momentarily escape the pressures of Washington in a setting marred only by the sounds of jets landing at Ronald Reagan National Airport. Those wandering along the 22 miles of nature trails will eventually come across the 17-foot bronze statue of Roosevelt.

Just a few blocks to the west is the:

THE NEWSEUM (8), 1101 Wilson Blvd., ☎ (888) NEWSEUM or (703) 284-3544, Internet: www.newseum.org. *Open Wed.–Sun. 10–5. Free.* ♿.

The only interactive museum of news opened in April of 1997. It takes visitors behind the scenes to see and experience how and why news is made. The $50 million, 72,000-square-foot museum is funded by the Freedom Forum, a non-partisan international foundation dedicated to free press, speech and free spirit for all people. Highlights include a 126-foot long Video News Wall displaying dozens of satellite television news feeds, plus a display of daily front pages from around the world; a News History Wall showing the evolution of news from the early days of spoken news to today's global village; a domed 220-seat theater featuring the Newseum's signature film; a state-of-the-art broadcast studio producing television and radio programs; a Newseum store and a News Café offering on-line access to the Internet, magazines and newspapers, as well as refreshments.

The **Rosslyn Metro Station** is nearby, in an area filled with good, cheap ethnic restaurants. From there you can get a subway train back to

Washington, or south to:

THE PENTAGON (9), I-395 at Washington Blvd., ☎ (703) 695-1776, Internet: www.defenselink.mil/pubs/pentagon. *Open to visitors Mon.–Fri. 9–3. Closed weekends and Federal holidays. Mandatory tours every hour, depart from tour sign-up window near the Metro entrance. Free. Photo ID required. Non-citizens require passport. Groups over 15 persons require reservations. ♿, reserve two weeks in advance for special tour.*

The world's largest office building, built in just 16 months during World War II, is home to the U.S. Department of Defense and a five-sided symbol of America's military might. Its 172 miles of corridors cover 29 acres, but are so cunningly arranged that no place is more than a seven-minute walk from any other. Some 23,000 people work here, about half of whom are military.

Naturally, you cannot just wander around loose here. Guided tours lasting about 90 minutes begin with an introductory film, and are then led by a guide who walks backwards to make sure that no one slips off into secret areas.

You can return to Washington from the adjacent Pentagon Metro stop.

*Alexandria

O ne of the easiest daytrips that you can possibly make from Washington is also one of the most enjoyable. Alexandria is only a few minutes from downtown DC by Metro or car, but a world apart in atmosphere. This magnificently-restored Colonial seaport offers such attractions as centuries-old mansions, houses, and public buildings that you can tour with guides in period costume, waterfront activities including boat rides on the Potomac, a lively visual-arts center where you can watch artists and archaeologists at work, unusual shopping opportunities, and a wide choice of intriguing restaurants. More than a cultural experience, a visit to Alexandria can be a lot of fun.

First settled by Scottish merchants sometime in the early 1700s, Alexandria became a town in 1749 and was surveyed, in part, by a young George Washington. Having a fine, natural port, and situated on the King's Highway from Williamsburg to New England, the town prospered on the tobacco trade as well as on other imports and exports.

Alexandria was ceded to the new District of Columbia in 1791, but given back to Virginia in 1846. During the Civil War, it was occupied by Union troops and totally escaped the devastation suffered by other Southern towns. Declining as a port, Alexandria's proximity to a growing Washington made its charming old streets irresistible to commuters, especially after Washington's Metro reached right into the heart of town. Restoration of the Old Town during the 1980s has made it a major tourist attraction, as well.

GETTING THERE:

By car, take the George Washington Memorial Parkway (VA- 400) south past Ronald Regan National Airport, turning left (east) on King Street. Alexandria is about 6 miles south of the Washington Monument.

By Metro, take the Blue or Yellow line to the **King Street** station; then DASH bus 2 or 5, or a three-quarter-mile walk, east to the Visitors Center.

By train, take Amtrak (1-800-USA-RAIL) or Virginia Railway Express (703-684-0400) to the Alexandria station; then DASH bus 2 or 5, or a three-quarter-mile walk, east to the Visitors Center.

By bicycle, take the Mount Vernon Bike Trail along the Potomac River.

PRACTICALITIES:

Several of Alexandria's prime attractions are closed on Mondays, and do not open until noon on Sundays. The total walking distance, nearly level all the way, is under three miles. This does not include the three-quarter-mile stroll from the Metro station, which can be done by bus. For further information, contact the **Alexandria Convention & Visitors Association** (Visitors Center) at 221 King St., Alexandria, VA 22314-3209, ☎ (800) 388-9119 or (703) 838-4200, Internet: www.FunSide.com. Ask them about the many **special events** held throughout the year.

FOOD AND DRINK:

If anything, Alexandria has just too many good restaurants. Out of a vast offering, here are a few prime selections:

Gadsby's Tavern (138 N. Royal St., adjacent to Gadsby's Tavern Museum) George Washington was a regular customer here, and the menu hasn't changed much since those days. Strolling minstrels, Colonial cuisine, and period costumes make the experience seem authentic. Reservations recommended, ☎ (703) 548-1288. $$

Union Street Public House (121 S. Union St., between King and Prince streets) This popular pub offers something for everyone, including micro-brewed beers. ☎ (703) 548-1785. $$

Le Gaulois (1106 King St., between Henry and Fayette streets) A provincial French bistro with such treats as *pot-au-feu* and *cassoulet* at eminently fair prices. ☎ (703) 739-9494. X: Sun. $$

King Street Blues (112 N. St. Asaph St., near King St.) A fun place for southern comfort food, with a funky atmosphere to match. ☎ (703) 836-8800. $$

Ecco Café (220 N. Lee St. at Cameron St.) Enjoy innovative Italian pizzas and dishes in this local favorite. ☎ (703) 684-0321. $ and $$

Hard Times Café (1404 King St., at West St.) Huge selections of chili as you like it—Texas, Cincinnati, or vegetarian style. ☎ (703) 683-5340. $

South Austin Grill (801 King St., at Washington St.) Serious Tex-Mex fare in a friendly-but-crowded saloon. ☎ (703) 684-8969. $

SUGGESTED TOUR:

Numbers in parentheses correspond to numbers on the map.

What better place to start your visit than at the friendly **Visitors Center** (1) in the heart of the Old Town? Here you can find out about the

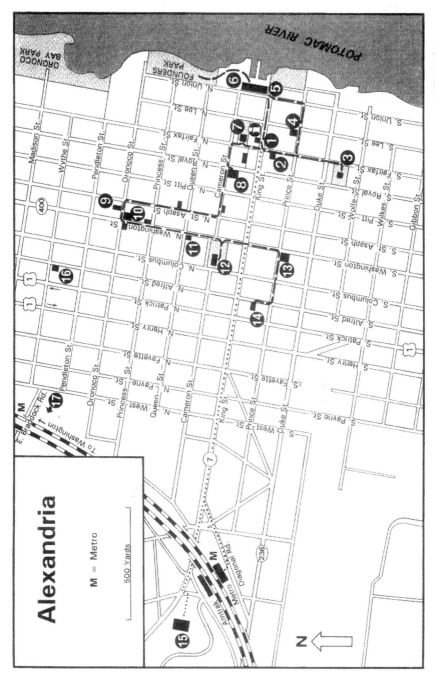

frequent special events that keep this town lively and pick up brochures about all of its sights. The center is housed in Alexandria's oldest dwelling, the **Ramsay House**, which was built around 1724. Curiously, it was most likely moved here by barge from the early Scottish settlement at Dumfries, about 30 miles to the southwest. William Ramsay, a close friend of George Washington's, served the town in various capacities, including that of postmaster. In later years the house was used as a tavern, a cigar factory, and for other purposes before being restored in the early 1950s as a historic site. ☎ *(703) 838-4200. Open daily 9–5, except Thanksgiving, Christmas, and New Year's.*

Head south on Fairfax Street to the:

STABLER-LEADBEATER APOTHECARY SHOP (2), 105 S. Fairfax St., ☎ (703) 836-3713. Open Mon.–Sat. 10-4, Sun. 1–5, closed Wed. from Jan.–March. Adults $2.50, ages 11–17 $2. Gift shop.

Both George Washington and Robert E. Lee were customers of America's second-oldest drugstore, as were Daniel Webster, Henry Clay, and John Calhoun. Lee, in fact, was here when he received orders to put down John Brown's insurrection at Harpers Ferry in 1859. Established in 1792, the apothecary remained in continuous operation by the same family until 1933, and had hardly changed since the 1850s. Fully restored and stocked with original wares, some of which were excavated from its wells, the shop is now run as a museum.

Continue along South Fairfax Street, perhaps as far as the **Old Presbyterian Meeting House** (3) just below Duke Street. Built by the Scottish founders of Alexandria in 1774, this meeting house was a gathering place for patriots during the Revolution. George Washington's funeral service was held here in 1799 as weather conditions did not permit travel to the Episcopal church. In the adjacent graveyard is the Tomb of the Unknown Soldier of the American Revolution. ☎ *(703) 549-6670. Open Mon.–Fri. 9-5, Sunday services at 8:30 and 11. Free.* ♿.

Turn east on Prince Street, passing a block of fine 18th-century houses known as **Gentry Row**. On the corner of South Lee Street is **The Athenaeum** (4), a former bank in the Greek Revival style that was built in 1851. It now houses a gallery featuring contemporary art shows. ☎ *(703) 548-0035. Open Wed.–Sat. 11-4, Sun. 1–4. Donations accepted.* Farther along the street is **Captain's Row**, an early-19th-century neighborhood that once fronted on the Potomac and still retains some of its nautical ambiance.

Turn left on Union Street, crossing King Street to the:

*TORPEDO FACTORY ART CENTER (5), 105 N. Union St., ☎ (703) 838-4565, Internet: www.torpedofactory.org. *Open daily 10–5. Closed New Year's Day, Easter, July 4, Thanksgiving and Dec. 25. Free. Galleries. Museum.* ♿.

This industrial complex of 1918 manufactured naval torpedo shell cases until the end of World War II, and was then used by the Federal Government to store records. In 1969 it was bought by the City of Alexandria, who converted it into an art center in 1974. Here you can watch some 150 professional artists busily working in all sorts of visual media, each in their own studio provided at reasonable rent in return for public access and education. While the works are for sale, there is no sense of commercialization here, and absolutely no pressure to buy anything. Take the elevator to the third floor, where you'll also find the intriguing, city-owned **Alexandria Archaeology Museum** in unit 327. Volunteers and professional archaeologists are at work here piecing together bits of the town's history, some of which are displayed along with a simulated dig site. ☎ *(703) 838-4399, Internet: http://ci.alexan dria.va.us/oha/archaeology/index.html. Open Tues.–Fri. 10–3, Sat. 10–5, Sun. 1–5. Free, donation accepted.* ♿.

Just beyond the art center is the colorful **Waterfront** (6), once the busiest port on the Potomac River. Now it's a marina, where a variety of **boat rides** are offered in season. There's also an indoor/outdoor food court and, to the north, **Founders Park** on the site of the earliest tobacco warehouses of 1730.

Return to King Street and head west, passing the Visitors Center (1) and turning right at the **Market Square**, where an outdoor market is still held on Saturday mornings. Facing this is the Victorian **City Hall** of 1873 and, across North Fairfax Street, the:

*CARLYLE HOUSE (7), 121 N. Fairfax St., ☎ (703) 549-2997. *Open Tues.–Sat. 10–4:30, Sun. noon–4:30. Adults $3, children $2. Tours. Gift shop.* ♿, *partial access.*

John Carlyle, a wealthy Scottish merchant, built this Georgian mansion in 1753. At that time its rear garden nearly touched the river, affording him a good view of the coming and going of ships. In 1755 the house was used as the headquarters of General Braddock as he and five Colonial governors planned the early campaigns of the French and Indian War, but failed to reach accord on just *who* would pay for the conflict. It was this disagreement over future tax increases that helped bring about the Revolutionary War.

By the mid-19th century the house had passed into other hands, becoming a hotel, a hospital, and eventually a wreck. Six years of restoration work brought it back to its original condition, opening to the public in time for the Bicentennial of 1976. Today it is decorated with period furnishings approximating an inventory taken in 1780, but only a few of the objects actually belonged to Carlyle. After your tour, be sure to visit the lovely **formal gardens** behind the house.

Turn left on Cameron Street to the:

*GADSBY'S TAVERN MUSEUM (8), 134 N. Royal St., ☎ (703) 838-4242, Internet: http://ci.alexandria.va.us/oha/gadsby/index.html. *Open Apr.–Sept., Tues.–Sat. 10–5 and Sun. 1–5; Oct.–March, Tues.–Sat. 11–4 and Sun. 1–4. Tours at quarter before and quarter past the hour, last tour begins 45 minutes before closing. Adults $4, students 11–17 $2, under 11 free. Restaurant. ಈ, partial access.*

George Washington was a regular customer at this historic tavern of 1770, long a gathering place for Alexandria's residents and traveling merchants alike. Other notables who were entertained here include Thomas Jefferson, John Adams, James Madison, and the Marquis de Lafayette. Like other inns of its time, the budget sleeping accommodations were none too comfortable, but the public rooms are quite appealing. An adjoining building was added in 1792 as the City Tavern and Hotel, with both structures remaining in use until the late 19th century. Rescued from demolition by the American Legion in 1929, they were thoroughly restored by the City of Alexandria for the 1976 Bicentennial celebrations. Your tour will take you through the **Tap Room**, **Dining Room**, **Assembly Room**, third-floor communal **bedrooms**, and into the rather elegant **Ballroom** of the 1792 building. A functioning restaurant beneath this re-creates Colonial life with costumed personnel and 18th-century dishes.

Continue down Cameron Street past a reconstruction of **George Washington's Town House** at number 508, a modest dwelling that he used whenever he was in Alexandria. It is not open to the public.

Turn right on North Saint Asaph Street, noting the odd **flounder-style house** at number 311, a shape that was fairly common in the early 19th century and seems to have derived from loopholes in the property-tax laws. As you pass Princess Street, take a close look at its original cobblestone paving. A left turn on Oronoco Street leads to the:

BOYHOOD HOME OF ROBERT E. LEE (9), 607 Oronoco St., ☎ (703) 548-8454. *Open Mon.–Sat. 10–4, Sun. 1–4. Closed mid-Dec. through Jan.,*

Easter, Thanksgiving, and for special occasions. Adults $4, students 11–17 $2.

Revolutionary War hero General "Light-Horse Harry" Lee (1756–1818), a friend of George Washington's, moved his family into this 1795 mansion in 1812. His youngest son, Robert E. Lee (1807–70)(see page 98), continued to live in the house with his widowed mother until enrolling in West Point in 1825, except for a four-year hiatus from 1816 until 1820. Prior to the Lee occupancy, George Washington had been a frequent guest as the house was owned, at different times, by two of his closest friends. Martha Washington's grandson, George Washington Parke Custis, married a distant Lee here in 1804.

Completely restored to its original condition, the mansion is furnished with period pieces, including portraits of Robert E. Lee made over a 40-year period, and other Lee family memorabilia. One of the bedrooms is decorated as it would have been in young Robert's time.

The Lee story continues around the corner when you visit the:

LEE-FENDALL HOUSE (10), 614 Oronoco St. (entrance on Washington St.), ☎ (703) 548-1789. Open Tues. and Thurs.–Sat. 10–4, Wed. and Sun. 1–4. Closed holidays. Adults $4, students 11–17 $2.

Thirty-seven different Lees lived in this house since its construction in 1785 until 1903, and it was here that "Light-Horse Harry" Lee penned his famous funeral oration for George Washington that contains the familiar words, "First in war, first in peace, and first in the hearts of his countrymen." More recently, it was the home of labor leader John L. Lewis from 1937 to 1969. Restored to its mid-19th-century condition, the large clapboard house is filled with Lee memorabilia, furnishings, and documentation concerning this remarkable family.

Yet another Lee, Edmund J., brother of Light-Horse Harry and mayor of Alexandria from 1815 to 1818, lived across the street at 428 North Washington Street. No wonder this intersection is known as "Lee Corner!" To further complicate matters, the nearby house at 407 North Washington Street was built by another brother and occupied by young Robert E. Lee and his mother from 1817 to 1820. Continue south on Washington Street to the **Lloyd House** (11), a late Georgian structure of 1797. It was purchased in 1832 by John Lloyd, whose wife was a first cousin of Robert E. Lee, and remained in the family until 1918. In 1976 it was restored and decorated in the Federal style, and as part of the town's library now houses a collection of rare books and material on Virginia's history. *220 N. Washington St., ☎ (703) 838-4577. Mon.–Sat. 9–5, closed major holidays. Free.*

A block farther down Washington Street stands the magnificent **Christ Church** (12) of 1773, where both George Washington and Robert E. Lee had their own pews. Set in a quiet churchyard, it strongly resembles a typical Georgian country church in England. If it's open, step into the simple, luminous interior to see the unusual pulpit as well as pews 46 and 60. Most American presidents have attended services here, usually on the Sunday closest to Washington's birthday (February 22). *Corner of Cameron and N. Washington streets.* ☎ *(703) 549-1450.* ♿.

Cross King Street on busy Washington Street, continuing south to the **Confederate Statue** at the corner of Prince Street. Although Alexandria was occupied by Union troops throughout the entire Civil War, its own men fought on the Confederate side. Those who died are honored by this statue, erected in 1889. Close by is:

THE LYCEUM (13), 201 S. Washington St., ☎ (703) 838-4994, Internet: http://ci.alexandria.va.us/oha/lyceum/index.html. *Open Mon.–Sat. 10–5, Sun. 1–5. Closed Thanksgiving, Christmas, and New Year's Day. Free. Gift shop.* ♿, *use ramp at rear.*

Alexandria's history museum is housed in a handsome Greek Revival structure of 1839, originally built as a cultural center by the Lyceum Company, an organization founded by Robert E. Lee's tutor. Restored in 1974, the building now contains a permanent collection of artifacts, furnishings, documents, photographs, and Civil War memorabilia relating to Alexandria and Northern Virginia. If you want to find out more about the sites along the walking tour, this is the place to look.

Turn west on Prince Street, then north on South Alfred Street to the:

FRIENDSHIP FIREHOUSE (14), 107 S. Alfred St., ☎ (703) 838-3891, Internet: http://ci.alexandria.va.us/oha/friendship/index.html. *Open Fri.–Sat. 10–4, Sun. 1–4. Closed major holidays. Free.* ♿.

Traditionally associated with George Washington, who may have been a founder and benefactor, Alexandria's first firehouse was established in 1774. The present building dates from 1855 and was completely restored in 1992. All sorts of early fire-fighting apparatus are on display, along with uniforms, regalia, and the like. Upstairs, the Meeting Room features elaborate Victorian furnishings of the period.

This is the end of the walking tour, but Alexandria has several other sights outside of the Old Town, some of which might interest you:

GEORGE WASHINGTON MASONIC NATIONAL MEMORIAL (15), King St. and Callahan Drive, just west of the train station. ☎ (703) 683- 2007. *Open daily 9–5, tower tours at 9;30, 10:30, 11:30, 1, 2, 3, and 4. Closed New Year's Day, Thanksgiving and Dec. 25. Free.*

Overlooking Alexandria and the nation's capital from its perch atop Shooter's Hill, the massive tower and its base contain many personal effects and other materials pertaining to George Washington—Patriot, President, and Mason.

BLACK HISTORY RESOURCE CENTER (16), 638 N. Alfred St., ☎ (703) 838-4356, Internet: http://ci.alexandria.va.us/oha/bhrc/index.html. *Open Tues.–Sat. 10–4. Free.* ♿.

The history and achievements of African-Americans in Alexandria and Virginia from 1749 to the present are celebrated in this museum and interpretive center.

FORT WARD MUSEUM & HISTORIC SITE (17), 4301 W. Braddock Rd., 22 miles northwest of the Old Town. ☎ (703) 838-4848, Internet: http://ci.alexandria.va.us/oha/fortward/index.html. *Open Tues.–Sat. 9–5, Sun. noon–5. Site open daily 9–sunset. Free. Picnic facilities.* ♿, *partial access.*

During the Civil War, the Union troops occupying Alexandria built several forts to defend Washington against Confederate attack. One of the largest of these was Fort Ward, which has been restored as a living-history museum of that tragic conflict. Visitors can take a self-guided tour lasting about 45 minutes.

Mount Vernon and Beyond

A merican independence had some of its earliest roots in the gorgeous countryside just south of Alexandria and going into Fairfax County, where men like George Mason and George Washington first considered the idea of leaving the mother country, and of establishing a universal bill of rights. Besides their remarkable political achievements, these wealthy Virginia gentlemen also left behind several magnificent estates for everyone to enjoy today. Three of the restored plantations, all near the Potomac River, can be visited on this easy one-day excursion. Along the way, you can also explore an historic gristmill once owned by George Washington, a country church associated with him, a delightful park and, back in the 20th century, a visionary small home by Frank Lloyd Wright.

GETTING THERE:

By car, leave Washington via **US-1** and head south on the George Washington Memorial Parkway to Mount Vernon, a distance of 16 miles.

Continue west on **VA-235** for about three miles to the Gristmill, Woodlawn Plantation, and the Pope-Leighey House.

Take US-1 west through Fort Belvoir, then **VA-242** southeast to Gunston Hall. This adds about 11 miles to the trip.

By Metro and bus, take the Yellow Line of the Metro south to the Huntington stop, then the number 101 bus (in the direction of Ft. Hunt) to Mount Vernon. The other sites cannot be easily reached by bus.

By Tourmobile from downtown Washington, make a reservation at the Lincoln Memorial or Washington Monument ticket booth for the 10 a.m., noon, or 2 p.m. departure. ☎ *(888) 868-7707 or (202) 554-7950, Internet: www.tourmobile.com. Fares include admission to Mount Vernon: Adults $22, children 3-11 $11. Tour visits Alexandria and Mount Vernon, but not the other sites.*

By boat, Mount Vernon is served Tues.-Sun. by Spirit Cruise Lines and the Potomac Riverboat Company, from mid-March until October. ☎ *(202) 554-8000. Leaves from Pier 4, 6th and Water streets SW, Washington,* *and from the docks in Old Town, Alexandria. Ticket prices are $26.50 per adult and $18 per child from Washington; a bit less from Alexandria. Admission to Mt. Vernon is included.*

By bicycle, take the Mount Vernon Trail south from the Arlington Memorial Bridge to Mount Vernon, a distance of 18 miles.

PRACTICALITIES:

This trip can be taken on any day, noting only that many attractions are closed on Thanksgiving, Christmas, and New Year's Day. Woodlawn and the Pope-Leighey House are closed in January and February. You can expect hordes of visitors at Mount Vernon during the peak summer months, although the other sites remain comfortably uncrowded. Getting off to an early start will help.

While Mount Vernon is accessible by public transportation, you'll need a car (or bicycle and strong legs) to visit the other sites.

For further information contact the **Fairfax County Visitors Center**, 8180-A Silverbrook Rd., Lorton, VA 22079, ☎ (703) 550- 2450 or (800) 7-FAIRFAX, Internet: www.visitfairfax.org.

FOOD AND DRINK:

There's a wonderful selection of restaurants in nearby Alexandria, eight miles to the north, as described on page 102. At Mount Vernon itself, you can have lunch at the:

Mount Vernon Inn (on the estate) Both light and full meals served in an elegant Colonial atmosphere. Reservations accepted, ☎ (703) 780-0011. $$

Quick Bite To Eat (on the estate) This cafeteria offers burgers, salads, and other light lunch fare. ☎ (703) 780-0011. $

LOCAL ATTRACTIONS:

Numbers in parentheses correspond to numbers on the maps.

*GEORGE WASHINGTON'S MOUNT VERNON: ESTATE & GARDENS (1–4), Mount Vernon, VA 22121, ☎ (703) 780-2000, TDD 799-8121, Internet: www.mountvernon.org. *Open daily; Nov.–Feb. 9–4, March 9–5, Apr.–Aug. 8–5, Sept.–Oct. 9–5. Adults $8, seniors $7.50, children 6–11 (when accompanied by an adult) $4. Gift shops. Restaurant and cafeteria. &, first floor and grounds.*

George Washington (1732–99) slept here, on and off, for some 45 years, and it is here that you can best get to know the private man. The land had been in his family since 1674, when great-grandfather John

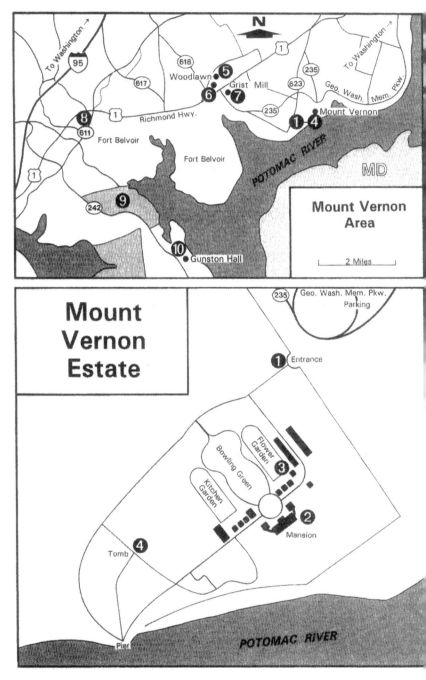

Washington obtained a grant from Lord Culpeper. George's elder half-brother Lawrence inherited the property in 1740 and named it Mount Vernon in honor of a British admiral under whom he had served. In 1754, after Lawrence died, George leased the property from his sister-in-law, acquiring it on her death in 1761.

Although he spent much time away from home as an aide to General Braddock and as commander of the Virginia militia (and later as commander-in-chief of the Continental Army and as President), George was happiest when playing the role of gentleman farmer. He increased the size of the estate from about 2,000 acres to some 8,000, divided into five farms worked by some 200 slaves. The simple farmhouse of 1735 was expanded several times, throughout the rest of his life, into the elegant mansion that you see today.

After his death, Mount Vernon remained in the Washington family until it was no longer profitable as a farm. Attempts after 1850 to sell it to the Federal government or to Virginia were unsuccessful, but a private organization called the Mount Vernon Ladies' Association raised the necessary funds through a public campaign, and has owned and operated the 500-acre estate since 1858.

Enter through the **North Gate** (1), close to which is a gift shop and restaurant. To hopefully keep one jump ahead of the crowds, go directly to the ***Mansion** (2) and tour it as early in the morning as possible. Beautifully and authentically restored, the interior may surprise you with its bold colors and attention to stylish detail. Many of the furnishings are original, while others are genuine period pieces from the late 18th century.

Outside, the large porch known as the "piazza" offers cool breezes and a stunning ***view** across the Potomac, a panorama that remains much the same today as it was when Washington entertained guests here.

Adjacent to the house are over a dozen outbuildings that can be visited, including the **kitchen**, the **stable**, the **greenhouse and slave quarters**, and two **museums** (3) where collections of Washington memorabilia are on display. To the north of the Bowling Green are **flower gardens**, and to the south is the **kitchen garden** where fruits and vegetables are grown. Before leaving, be sure to stroll down to the **tomb** (4) where George and Martha Washington are buried along with dozens of other family members. Close to this is the old slave burial ground with its unmarked graves, now identified by a simple memorial.

About three miles west on VA-235 is the:

WOODLAWN PLANTATION (5), 900 Richmond Hwy., Mt. Vernon, VA 22121, ☎ (703) 780-4000. *Open daily 10–4 in March; Mon.–Sat. 10–4 and Sun. noon–4 in Apr.–Dec. Closed Thanksgiving and Christmas. Adults $6,* *seniors and students $4, children under 5 free. Combination ticket with Pope-Leighey House: Adults $10, seniors and students $8. Guided tours. Gift shop. Special events. &, limited access, call ahead.*

Once part of the Mount Vernon estate, Woodlawn is in some ways more impressive, and much less visited. George Washington bequeathed the 2,000-acre property to his adopted daughter Eleanor Parke Custis and his favorite nephew, Lawrence Lewis, who were married in 1799. The couple commissioned William Thornton, the original architect of the U.S. Capitol, to design an elegant Georgian mansion for the estate. Furnished with inherited pieces from Mount Vernon, the house was completed in 1806. Following Lewis' death in 1839, Woodlawn was eventually sold to a group of businessmen who converted it into a Quaker community of small farms, a Friends meetinghouse, and the first integrated free school in Virginia. The mansion and surrounding grounds have been the property of the National Trust for Historic Preservation since 1957.

Inside, a guide will take you through a large hall used as a ballroom, a cozy **Family Parlor** with several heirlooms from Mount Vernon, the master bedroom, center hall, and music room. The **Dining Room** has original pieces, some of which belonged to George Washington. A curving staircase leads to the second floor, where you'll see the children's' bedrooms and a guest room used by the Marquis de Lafayette in 1824.

Visitors can also wander around the grounds with their extensive lawns and boxwood plantings. The 19th-century **gardens**, featuring over three dozen beds of roses, has been restored to their original condition.

On the same estate is the:

POPE-LEIGHEY HOUSE (6), 900 Richmond Hwy., Mount Vernon, VA 22121, ☎ (703) 780-4000. *Open daily 10–4 in March; Mon.–Sat. 10–4 and Sun, noon–4 from Apr.–Dec. Closed Thanksgiving and Christmas. Adults $5, seniors and students $3. Combination ticket with Woodlawn: Adults $10, seniors and students $8. Guided tours. Gift shop. &, partial access, call ahead.*

The great American architect, Frank Lloyd Wright (1867–1959), created his "Usonian" houses to meet a special need—a well-designed home for people of moderate means. Costing only around $7,000 to build back in 1940, this modest 1,200-square-foot L-shaped dwelling pioneered many architectural features that are common today but at the time were found only in expensive avant-garde residences. Its organic unity, built-in furniture, and large windows give it a sense of spaciousness the belies the relatively small size.

Strangely, the house was not originally built on this site, but in Falls Church, near Arlington. About to become yet another victim of highway

construction in 1964, the cypress, brick, and glass structure was donated to the National Trust for Historic Preservation and moved to this site,
which closely resembles the original setting.

Just south of US-1, along VA-235, is the **Grist Mill Historical State
Park** (7). Here you'll find a 1930's reconstruction of George Washington's
pre-Revolutionary gristmill, which he owned for some 30 years as part of
the Mount Vernon plantation. Never very profitable, the mill on Dogue
Creek fell to ruin after his death, with only the foundations remaining
intact. It was rebuilt in time for the bicentennial of his birth by the
Civilian Conservation Corps, and fitted with period machinery dating
from 1770. ☎ *(703) 339-7265. Open Thurs.–Mon. in summer, 9–5. Adults
$1.25, children $1.*
Take US-1 west through the Fort Belvoir Military Reservation to the
hamlet of Pohick, where you'll find the **Pohick Episcopal Church** (8).
Completed in 1774 from plans drawn by George Washington himself,
this was the parish church of the local gentry including Mason,
Washington, and Fairfax. Heavily damaged during the Civil War, it has
been renovated several times and is still home to an active parish. ☎
*(703) 550-9449. 9301 Richmond Hwy. (US-1) at Telegraph Rd. Open daily
9–4:30. Free.*
Head southeast on Gunston Road (VA-242), passing **Pohick Bay
Regional Park** (9). A wide variety of recreational facilities can be enjoyed
here, including sailboat and pedalboat rentals, swimming, miniature
golf, 18-hole golf, nature trails, equestrian trails, picnic tables, and camp-
sites. ☎ *(703) 339-6104. Open daily 8-dusk. Admission $4 per vehicle.
Fees for swimming, golf, activities.* ᕦ.
Continue along Gunston Road to:

GUNSTON HALL (10), 10709 Gunston Rd., Lorton, VA 22079, ☎ (703) 550-
9220, Internet: www.Visit.GunstonHall.org. *Open daily 9:30–5, last tour at
4:30. Closed Thanksgiving, Christmas, and New Year's Day. Adults $5,
seniors $4, children $1.50.* ᕦ, *limited access.*

Gunston Hall was the home of George Mason (1725–92), father of
the Bill of Rights and champion of individual liberty. The eloquent
words he penned in his Virginia Declaration of Rights, "That all men are
by nature equally free and independent and have certain inherent
rights...namely, the enjoyment of life and liberty, with the means of
acquiring and possessing property, and pursuing and obtaining happi-
ness and safety," found an echo in his friend Thomas Jefferson's draft of
the Declaration of Independence later in 1776. Once unleashed, these
subversive ideas found their way into other declarations in both

America and Europe, and eventually into the United Nations Declaration of Human Rights.

A member of the Constitutional Convention that met in Philadelphia (see page 336) in 1787, Mason strongly opposed the document that emerged as it lacked a bill of rights and did not abolish slavery. It was his criticism that was largely responsible for the adoption of the first ten amendments to the Constitution in 1791, known to all as the Bill of Rights.

Mason, a wealthy plantation owner, began construction on Gunston Hall in 1755. Its beautifully-restored interior is noted for its outstanding *carved woodwork created by William Buckland, a renowned English carpenter. The rooms are unusually graceful, and filled with period furniture, some of which actually belonged to the Mason family. Outside are several dependencies including a schoolhouse, beyond which is the formal boxwood garden planted in part by George Mason. Visitors can also hike the nature trail to the river, view the deer park, and look at the exhibits in the Visitors' Center.

Suburban Fairfax County

You don't have to go far from Washington, DC, to enjoy real bucol-ic pleasures. Although Virginia's Fairfax County is solidly subur-ban, it boasts numerous enclaves of preserved Colonial tranquili-ty ranging from old-time farms to a small 18th-century town. Other sites in the county, including Mount Vernon, were described in the previous chapter. Along this route you can stop at the Great Falls of the Potomac, a working gristmill from around 1820, and a restored plantation of 1794. And, returning to the present, there's one of the most successfully planned "new towns" anywhere in America, along with some of the best shopping opportunities in the region.

GETTING THERE:

While some of the individual sites could be reached by public transportation, if you're visiting more than one you'll need wheels.

By car, head towards the Claude Moore Colonial Farm just above McLean, about eight miles northwest of the Washington Monument. Take the **George Washington Memorial Parkway**, then go west on **VA-123** to its intersection with **VA-193**.

Continuing northwest another eight miles brings you to Great Falls Park.

Colvin Run and the Pet Farm are about another three miles south-west of here on local roads, and Reston another five miles.

A bit out of the Way, Sully Plantation is a few miles to the southwest, on **US-50** near Chantilly.

Wolf Trap and Tysons Corner are easily reached via **VA-123** and/or **VA-7**. Continuing southeast on VA-7 brings you to Falls Church.

PRACTICALITIES:

The Claude Moore Colonial farm is closed on Mondays, Tuesdays, Thanksgiving, and from mid-December through March. Colvin Run closes on Tuesdays. The Reston Animal Park shuts up completely from

November through mid-March, while the Sully Plantation is closed on Tuesdays, Thanksgiving, Christmas, and New Year's. In general, you should avoid making this trip on a Monday or Tuesday.

As nearly everything is out of doors, you'll need to dress appropriately.

For further information, contact the **Fairfax County Visitors Center**, 8180-A Silverbrook Rd., Lorton, VA 22079, ☎ (703) 550- 2450 or (800) 7-FAIRFAX, Internet: www.visitfairfax.org.

FOOD AND DRINK:

Suburban Fairfax County overflows with restaurants, many of which are branches of popular Washington eateries. Among the best choices for casual travelers are:

Evans Farm Inn (1696 Chain Bridge Rd, VA-123, just inside the Beltway at McLean) A Colonial-style farm with good home cooking, traditional Virginia specialties, and entertaining diversions. Reservations needed on weekends. ☎ (703) 356-8000. $$

Charley's Place (6903 Rt. 123 in McClean) A friendly, casual spot for American dishes. ☎ (703) 893-1034. $$

Paolo's (11898 Market St. at Fountain in Reston Town Center) Contemporary Italian dishes with a California touch. ☎ (703) 318-8920. $$

Clyde's (8332 Leesburg Pike, Tysons Corner, near Wolf Trap) This outpost of Georgetown features seafood, burgers, pasta, and the like. ☎ (703) 934-1901. $$

Da Domenico (1992 Rt. 123, junction of Rt. 7) A traditional, warm Italian eatery. X: Sat. lunch, Sun. ☎ (703) 790-9000. $ and $$

Panjshir (224 W. Maple Ave., VA-123, Vienna, a mile south of Wolf Trap) Exotic Afghani cuisine including kebabs and vegetarian dishes; comfortable surroundings. ☎ (703) 281-4183. $

Or, if the weather's nice, why not pack a **picnic lunch** to enjoy at the Claude Moore Colonial Farm or in Great Falls Park?

LOCAL ATTRACTIONS:

There are more worthwhile attractions here than can be seen in one day, so you'll have to pick and choose. *Numbers in parentheses correspond to numbers on the map.*

CLAUDE MOORE COLONIAL FARM at TURKEY RUN (1), 6310 Georgetown Pike, McLean, VA 22101, ☎ (703) 442-7557, Internet: www.nps.gov/gwmp/clmo.htm. *Open Apr.–mid-Dec., Wed.–Sun., 10–4:30. Closed Thanksgiving, mid-Dec.-Mar. Adults $2, seniors and children 3-12 $1, higher for special events. Demonstrations. Picnic facilities. ᕼ, call in advance.*

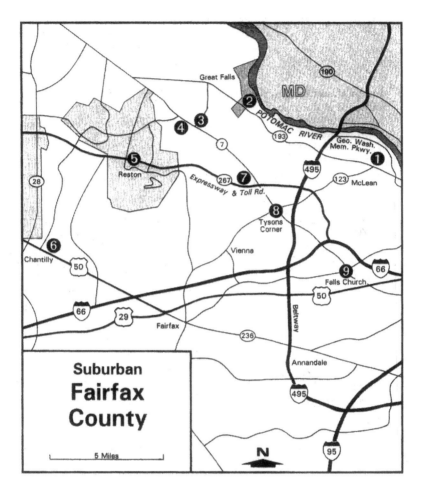

Restored Colonial farms tend to reflect the life of country gentlemen, or at least prosperous farmers. No so at Turkey Run. Here, costumed staff members re-create the day-to-day existence of a low-income 1770's tenant farm family. There are no tours to distract from the atmosphere, but you can watch as they go through the various chores, plant and harvest crops, and tend livestock. They'll be only too happy to take a break from the drudgery to answer your questions and chat a bit. A rather unusual experience, the Claude Moore Farm is operated by a non-profit group in cooperation with the National Park Service.

Farther up VA-193 is the:

GREAT FALLS PARK (2), 9200 Old Dominion Drive, Great Falls, VA 22066, ☎ (703) 285-2965, Internet: www.nps.gov/gwmp/grfa. *Park open daily 7 to dark, Visitor Center 9–5. Closed Christmas. Admission: $4 per vehicle; pedestrians, joggers, or bicycles $1. Hiking trails. Picnic facilities. Equestrian trails. Fishing (license required). Cross-country skiing. Rock climbing (dangerous, prior registration required). Snack bar. &, limited access.*

The Potomac River makes a spectacular 76-foot drop into a deep gorge at Great Falls, sometimes even surpassing Niagara Falls in volume. George Washington built one of America's first canals, the Potomack Company of 1785, to skirt the falls and open lands to the west to water-borne trade. Although commercially unsuccessful, sections of this ditch were later incorporated into the Chesapeake and Ohio Canal of 1828 (see pages 88 and 183). The stretches here on the Virginia side are in ruin, but can still be seen along with remnants of Matildaville, an abandoned town founded by General "Light-Horse" Harry Lee around 1790.

Along with magnificent *vistas, visitors can enjoy nature walks, picnics, and a variety of outdoor activities. Stop first at the Visitors Center for a map and more information. Wherever you wander in this National Park, be sure to keep your distance from the river as several people drown here each year in the deceptively swift currents.

About three miles to the southwest is the:

COLVIN RUN MILL HISTORIC SITE (3), 10017 Colvin Run Rd. off VA-7, McLean, VA, ☎ (703) 759-2771, Internet: www.virginia.org/Destinations. *Open daily (except Tues.) March–Dec. 11–5; Jan.–Feb. 11–4. Last tour at 4. Adults $4, students 16 and up $3, seniors and children $2. Special events. Gift shop. &, call ahead.*

Dating from about 1820, this old mill was quite revolutionary for its time. Its 20-foot waterwheel drives an amazing array of mostly-wooden gears and machinery, a sort of vertical mass-production line that allowed one miller to do all of the jobs that previously took several hands. Visitors can watch as grain becomes flour, samples of which are for sale in the general store. You can also tour the Miller's House and the 19th-century dairy barn.

Just up the road is the:

RESTON ANIMAL PARK (4), 1228 Hunter Mill Rd., Routes 7 and 606, Vienna, VA 22182, ☎ (703) 759-3637, Internet: www.virginia.org/Destinations. *Open mid-March through Oct., daily 10–5, closing earlier in spring and fall. Admission: Adults $9.95, seniors and children 2–12 $6.95.*

As the name suggests, you can pet the animals here, both domestic and exotic, and feed them as well. This is a great place for kids, who can watch an egg hatch or ride a pony or elephant. Hayrides are included in the admission.

While you're in the area, why not take a look at **Reston** (5), a well-engineered "new town" begun in 1962 to the applause of civic planners everywhere. Covering nearly 12 square miles, it is expected to eventually have a population of over 65,000 people. The homes are arranged in small clusters separated by open spaces, including several lakes, with many recreational facilities and several flourishing business complexes. **Reston Town Center**, adjacent to Exit 3 of the Dulles Airport Access Road (VA-267), covers 20 pedestrians-only acres with nearly 70 upscale shops and indoor/outdoor restaurants centered around a public green.

From here, you can make an interesting little side trip to the:

SULLY PLANTATION (6), 3601 Sully Rd., off VA-28, Chantilly, VA, ☎ (703) 437-1794. *Open year-round: March through Dec., tours are offered every hour and half-hour (average length 45 minutes) Wed.–Mon., 11–4; Jan. and Feb. Wed.–Mon. 11–3:30 p.m. Closed Tuesdays, Thanksgiving, Christmas, and New Year's Day. Adults $4, students 16 and over with ID $3, seniors (60+) and children (5–15) $2. Special events. Gift shop. &, partial access first floor of Big House and outbuildings.*

Another branch of Virginia's famous Lee family built this unusual plantation house in 1794. Richard Bland Lee, brother of "Light-Horse" Harry Lee and uncle of Robert E. Lee, was northern Virginia's first congressman, serving in Philadelphia where he became familiar with that city's style of architecture. At Sully, he combined this with the typical Georgian plantation style. Threatened by the construction of nearby Dulles Airport, the house and its various outbuildings were saved by citizen action and restored to original condition during the 1970s. Besides the main house, the estate includes a kitchen/laundry, smokehouse, stone dairy, formal gardens, and schoolhouse.

Six miles east of Reston lies:

WOLF TRAP FARM PARK for the PERFORMING ARTS (7), 1551 Trap Rd., Vienna, VA 22182, ☎ (703) 255-1860, Internet: www.wolf-trap.org. *Park open daily 7–dusk, closed Christmas. Filene Center open-air theater operates June–Labor Day. Tickets required for performances, otherwise the park is free. Picnic facilities. Tours. Restaurant, open for performances. &, call for details.*

The nation's sole national park for the performing arts was established by an act of Congress in 1966. The only real way to appreciate it is to attend a performance of anything from ballet to rock, but if you're passing by you might want to stop for a look at the facilities anyway. Of special note are the two 18th-century barns brought here from upstate New York in 1981, and used for more intimate performances.

About three miles east on VA-7 is the shopper's paradise of **Tysons Corner** (8), a wonderland of megamalls, strip malls, and just plain shops. Tysons Corner Center aims at middle-income folk, Galleria at Tysons II is more upscale, while Fairfax Square caters to those with money to burn.

If shopping makes you weary, you can replenish the soul at **Falls Church** (9), a lovely little town dating from Colonial times. Its famous **Falls Episcopal Church** was originally built in 1732, and replaced with the present structure in 1769. Used as a recruiting station during the Revolutionary War, it also served as a hospital and stable in the Civil War. Now fully restored, the church also houses a small museum of historical artifacts. *115 E. Fairfax St. at Washington St. on US-29.* ☎ *(703) 532-7600. Open Mon.–Fri. 9–4, Sat. 9–1, services Sun. Free.*

Prince William County

Military history buffs, and indeed anyone interested in American history, will find much to ponder over on this excursion. Two major battles of the Civil War were fought near Manassas, both decisively won by the South. Today they are remembered in a National Battlefield Park, where you can tour the scene of the conflicts and gain an understanding in the Visitor Center. The beautifully-preserved Victorian-era town of Manassas has an outstanding regional museum that you won't want to miss.

Lovers of the great outdoors get a special treat at the Prince William Forest Park, a nearly unspoiled wilderness area of some 17,000 acres. Among its many features is a paved forest trail that is suitable for strollers and wheelchairs.

You can learn a lot about more recent military history at the Marine Corps Air-Ground Museum at Quantico.

To finish off the day, why not explore an old Colonial town that's become a bit of an art colony, with many galleries and boutiques, or perhaps save bundles at one of the nation's largest factory outlet malls?

GETTING THERE:

By car, head southwest from Washington on **I-66** for 26 miles to Exit 47 (old 11), then north a short distance on **VA-234** to the Manassas National Battlefield Park Visitor Center.

Take VA-234 southeast to the town of Manassas, a distance of five miles.

Continue southeast on VA-234, then take **VA-619** southeast to the Prince William Forest Park entrance. The Marine Corps Air-Ground Museum is on the same road, just south of I-95 and US-1, about 16 miles from Manassas.

To reach Potomac Mills or Occoquan, head north on **I-95** to exits 156 (old 52) or 160 (old 53). I-95 will return you to the Beltway and Washington.

PRACTICALITIES:

Avoid making this trip on a Monday, when both the Manassas

Museum and the Marine Corps Air-Ground Museum are closed. The latter also closes from mid-November through March. Except for the museums, this is largely an outdoor excursion, so decent weather is necessary.

For further information, contact the **Prince William Manassas Conference and Visitors Bureau,** 14420 Bristow Road, Manassas, VA 20112-3932, ☎ (703) 792-4254 or (800) 432-1792, Internet: www.visitpwc.com.

FOOD AND DRINK:

Some choice restaurants are:

Carmello's Ristorante (9108 Center St., at Battle St., Manassas) Offers a full range of Northern Italian specialties. ☎ (703) 368-5522. X: weekend lunch. $$

Pargo's (10651 Balls Ford Rd., Rt. 234 near junction of I-66, Manassas) Contemporary American cuisine in a lively setting. ☎ (703) 369-5800. $$

The Globe and Laurel (18418 Jefferson Davis Hwy, Triangle) A restaurant steeped in Marine Corps history, near the Air-Ground Museum. ☎ (703) 221-5763. $$

Garden Kitchen (404 Mill St. in historic Occoquan) Light lunches, with garden terrace seating in season. ☎ (703) 494-2848. X: evenings. $

Alternatively, there are **picnic areas** at Manassas National Battlefield Park and at Prince William Forest Park.

LOCAL ATTRACTIONS:

Numbers in parentheses correspond to numbers on the map.

MANASSAS NATIONAL BATTLEFIELD PARK (1), 12521 Lee Hwy., Manassas, VA 22110, ☎ (703) 361-1339, Internet: www.nps.gov/mana. *Open daily dawn to dusk. Visitor Center open daily 8:30–5, 6 in summer. Closed Thanksgiving and Christmas. Admission $2. Tours. Hiking trails. Equestrian trails. Picnic area.* ₲.

The two battles of Manassas, also called Bull Run, were fought over control of a vital railroad junction nearby. The Confederacy won both, facilitating their invasion of Maryland at a combined cost of over 26,000 casualties. General Thomas J. "Stonewall" Jackson (1824–63) earned his nickname during the First Battle of Manassas in July, 1861, when he routed Union troops and put to rest any illusions of a short war. In the Second Battle of Manassas, fought in August, 1862, General Robert E. Lee defeated Northern forces and brought the South to the height of its military power.

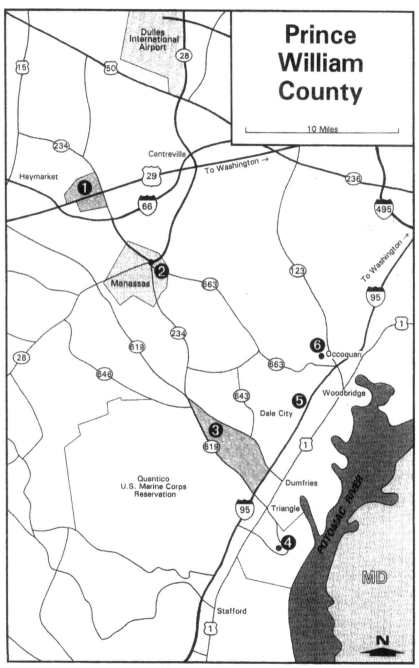

Prince William County

10 Miles

Begin at the **Visitor Center**, where a museum offers exhibits and an audiovisual outline of the battles. Here you can get maps and background information for a self-guided walking tour of First Manassas, and a driving tour of Second Manassas.

Drive five miles southeast on VA-234 to the center of **Manassas**, a town that hardly existed until after the Civil War. Its Old Town section offers well-preserved buildings from the Victorian era, along with the:

MANASSAS MUSEUM (2), 9101 Prince William St., Manassas, VA 20110, ☎ (703) 368-1873. *Open Tues.–Sun. 10–5. Closed Mon. except on Federal holidays, Thanksgiving, Christmas, and New Year's. Adults $2.50, seniors and children 6–17 $1.50. Gift shop.* ⅃.

Both the history and the culture of the Northern Virginia Piedmont region are thoroughly explored in this modern museum, with outstanding exhibits on the Civil War, railroads, and Victoriana. In addition to artifacts and memorabilia, there are videos to watch and a vast collection of old photographs to examine.

Continue southeast on VA-234 and VA-619 to the entrance of the:

PRINCE WILLIAM FOREST PARK (3), 18100 Park HQ Rd., Triangle, VA 22172, ☎ (703) 221-7181, Internet: www.nps.gov/prwi. *Open daily, dawn to dusk. Admission $4 per vehicle, pedestrians and bicycles $2. Nature trails. Picnic areas. Biking. Camping. Fishing (license required).* ⅃.

A part of the National Park system since 1939, this forested park of some 17,000 acres offers over 35 hiking trails, campgrounds, and ranger-guided programs year-round. Wildlife thrives in this setting, including many native species of plants and animals. One of the several trails you can follow is paved, making it accessible by stroller or wheelchair.

Just south of highways I-95 and US-1 is the:

MARINE CORPS AIR-GROUND MUSEUM (4), Marine Corps Development and Education Command, Quantico, VA 22134-5001, ☎ (703) 784-2606. *Open Apr.–Nov. 15, Tues.–Sat. 10–5 and Sun. noon–5. Free.* ⅃.

Housed in pre-World War II hangars, artifacts of the Marine Corps' long involvement in air-ground operations are arranged in chronological order. These include aircraft from World War I onwards, armor, artillery, small arms, and uniforms; along with graphic materials and dioramas.

Heading north on I-95 to Exit 156 brings you to one of America's largest factory-outlet malls, the famous **Potomac Mills** (5). Good shoppers who really know their prices can save from 20 to 60 percent on all kinds of name-brand merchandise here, and have fun doing it. More than 220 merchants operate shops and eateries in this vast emporium. *Internet: www.potomac-mills.com.*

Another nice place to shop, or at least stroll around in, is the historic waterfront village of **Occoquan** (6), located just north of Exit 160 on I-95. Dating from Colonial times, it was a milling center and tobacco trading town in the early 18th century. Today, arts and crafts have taken over, with some 120 shops, galleries, boutiques, and restaurants filling the four square blocks. *Visitor Center at 200 Mill St.,* ☎ *(703) 491-4045, Internet: www.pwcweb.com/gov/occoquan.*

Loudoun County

H istoric Loudoun County may be less than an hour from Washington, and actually a bit north of it, but its heart is very definitely in the South. This is Virginia's Hunt Country, where fox hunting and steeplechase races are still part of the gracious lifestyle. Visitors can join the horsey set in appreciating two magnificent old estates, an entire town that's now a National Historic Landmark, beautifully-restored neighborhoods, and a museum. To end the day, several vineyards offer tours and tastings of their wine-making facilities.

GETTING THERE:
By car, Leesburg is about 35 miles northwest of Washington via routes **VA-193** and **VA-7**, or the faster **Dulles Toll Road**.

Leave Leesburg on Old Waterford Road, heading northwest about one mile to Morven Park.

For Waterford, drive west on VA-7 and turn right onto **VA-9**. In a short while turn right again onto **VA-662**, heading north about five miles to Waterford.

Oatlands is six miles south of Leesburg on **US-15**.

Continue south another six miles, then go west six miles on **US-50** to Middleburg.

PRACTICALITIES:
Don't make this trip in the dead of winter, when practically everything hibernates. Morven is closed on Mondays and also from November through March; while Oatlands closes from late December through March, and also on Thanksgiving.

For further information, contact the **Loudoun Tourism Council**, 108-D South St. S.E., Leesburg, VA 22075, ☎ (703) 777-0519 or (800) 752-6118, Internet: www.visitloudoun.org.

FOOD AND DRINK:
Some good restaurants in Leesburg and Middleburg are:

Red Fox Inn (2 E. Washington St., US-50, Middleburg) Regional American and Continental cuisine in a cozy inn dating from 1728.

Reservations recommended, ☎ (540) 587-6301. $$ and $$$

Tuscarora Mill Restaurant (203 Harrison St. S.E., just south of VA-7 in central Leesburg) Imaginative American cuisine in a century-old mill. Reservations suggested, ☎ (703) 771-9300. $$

Lightfoot (13 N. King St., US-15, in central Leesburg) Seasonal American dishes served with style. X: Mon. ☎ (703) 771-2233. $$

Hidden Horse Tavern (7 W. Washington St. on US-50, Middleburg) An historic tavern noted for its seafood. ☎ (540) 687-3828. $$

LOCAL ATTRACTIONS:
Numbers in parentheses correspond to numbers on the map.

Once called Georgetown in honor of England's King George II, **Leesburg** (1) switched its allegiance as early as 1758, renaming itself after Virginia's prominent Lee family. It became the county seat in 1761, was the acting U.S. capital for a few days during the War of 1812, totally escaped Civil War devastation, and is today one of the most picturesque communities in the state. Before wandering around the small town, make a stop at the **Loudoun Museum** for a look at the area's history. Ask the folks there for a Leesburg walking tour map. *16 W. Loudoun St. S.W., Leesburg, VA 20175, ☎ (703) 777-7427. Open Mon.–Sat. 10–5, Sun. 1–5. Closed Thanksgiving, Christmas, New Year's Day, and last two weeks of Jan. Adults $1, children 50¢.*

One mile north of town is:

MORVEN PARK (2), Old Waterford Rd., Leesburg, VA 20178, ☎ (703) 777-2414, Internet: www.morvenpark,com. *Open Apr.–Oct., Tues.–Fri. noon–4:30, Sat. 10–4:30, Sun. 1–4:30; Sat. and Sun. noon–5 in Nov. Holiday tours available in Dec. Adults $6, seniors over 55 $5, children ages 6–12 $3. Partially ♿.*

Set in a 1,200-acre estate, this 1781 Greek Revival mansion more than slightly resembles the White House. Inside, you can visit some 16 rooms filled mostly with European antiques collected by Westmoreland Davis, the second of two state governors who lived here. The admission charge also includes the **Windmill Carriage Collection** with over 100 horse-drawn conveyances including landaus, phaetons, sulkies, and sleighs, and the **Museum of Hounds and Hunting**, where fox hunting is brought to life through artifacts, videos, and the like. There is also a formal **boxwood garden** and two **nature trails** for you to explore.

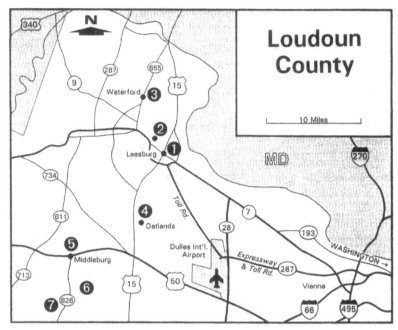

Continue northwest a few miles to **Waterford** (3), one of the few villages in the nation to be designated a National Historic Landmark. Founded in 1733 by Quakers, it was bypassed by the railroad and seems to have missed out on both the 19th and 20th centuries. Other Colonial hamlets have been restored or re-created; Waterford has survived intact, with a large number of its structures dating from the 18th century. It was the only Virginia town to organize a military force on the side of the North during the Civil War.

If you can, try to visit Waterford over the first weekend in October, when its popular **Home Tours and Crafts Exhibit** draws thousands to explore the town's private homes, try their hands at old-time crafts, and witness the re-enactment of a Civil War battle. This is the oldest such fair in Virginia. Whenever you come, check with the **Waterford Foundation** to find out what's going on. *Box 142, Waterford, VA 22190,* ☎ *(703) 882-3018, Internet: www.waterfordva.org.*

Driving south from Leesburg, you'll soon come to:

OATLANDS (4), Rte. 2, Box 352, Leesburg, VA 22075, ☎ (703) 777-3174. *Open Apr. to late Dec., Mon.–Sat. 10–4:30, Sun. 1–4:30. Closed Thanksgiving and late Dec. through March. Adults $8, seniors over 60*

*and students ages 12–18 $7, children under 12 $1. Gift shop. Equestrian
events. ♿, partial access.*

Built in 1803, this Georgian mansion was once the center of a vast
plantation that belonged to the famous Carter family since early
Colonial times. Noted for its fine façade and interior plasterwork, the
restored house now reflects the sophisticated European tastes of Mr.
and Mrs. William Corcoran Eustis, prominent Washingtonians who lived
here from 1897 to 1965. The formal **boxwood gardens** are among the best
in the country. With luck, you might run into a race or horse show, several of which are held between spring and fall.

If time permits, continue on to **Middleburg** (5), originally called
Chinn's Crossroads. Home to wealthy horse breeders, this is Virginia's
center of fox hunting, polo, and steeplechase racing. Ask at the Visitors
Center on North Madison Street for a walking-tour map.

Another attraction of the Middleburg area is its **vineyards**, several of
which offer free tours and tastings. The best-known of these is **Meredyth
Vineyards** (6) on VA-628, just south of Middleburg. ☎ *(540) 687-6277 for
directions. Open daily 11–5, closed Thanksgiving, Christmas, and New
Year's.* Also nearby is **Piedmont Vineyards** (7) on VA-626. ☎ *(540) 687-5528.
Open daily except Mon., 10–4. Closed Thanksgiving, Christmas, and
New Year's.*

Fredericksburg

The idea of establishing a port here on the protected banks of the Rappahannock River first came to Captain John Smith in 1608 as he led an expedition probing the Chesapeake Bay region. In 1728 thought became reality when a town named for Frederick, Prince of Wales, was founded to handle the shipping of tobacco from inland plantations back to Mother England. Profits from the weed brought great prosperity, and the town flourished.

George Washington grew up on a farm just across the river, where he allegedly chopped down the famous cherry tree. His younger brother owned a tavern in town, and his only sister and her husband built an elegant mansion here. To keep the family safely together, George purchased a home for his mother in the same neighborhood, and there she spent the rest of her life. All of these sites have been lovingly preserved and may be visited on this trip.

Fredericksburg is closely associated with another president, as well. James Monroe began his career as a lawyer here, and his former office is now a museum devoted to the life of the fifth president.

Prosperity continued until the Civil War, when strategically located Fredericksburg changed hands seven times during some of the most brutal battles of the conflict. Utterly devastated, the town somehow survived and today features a National Historic District with over 350 original, restored 18th- and 19th-century buildings. It is a compact place best explored on foot.

By staying overnight, you could easily combine this trip with the one to nearby Spotsylvania (page 139) or Virginia's Northern Neck (page 144). Fredericksburg also makes a fine stopover en route to Richmond, Williamsburg, and other Virginia attractions.

GETTING THERE:

By car, Fredericksburg is about 50 miles southwest of Washington via Route **I-95**. Get off at Exit 130 and take **VA-3** (William Street) east into town, heading south on Caroline Street to the Visitor Center. Parking passes are available there.

By train, Fredericksburg is about an hour south of Washington's

Union Station via **Amtrak**, ☎ (800) USA-RAIL for schedules and fares. The Fredericksburg station is only three blocks from the Visitor Center. **Virginia Railway Express**, ☎ 703-684-0400, offers low-cost commuter service on the same route, although not at times convenient for daytrippers.

PRACTICALITIES:

All of the major sites are open daily except Thanksgiving, Christmas, and New Year's Day. The total walking distance is less than a mile.

Money-saving joint admission tickets are available for the seven most important sights, sold at the Visitor Center or at the participating attractions. The **Hospitality Pass** is valid for all seven, while the **Pick Four Pass** lets you choose any four.

For further information, contact the **Fredericksburg Visitor Center**, 706 Caroline St., Fredericksburg, VA 22401, ☎ (540) 373-1776 or (800) 678-4748, Internet: www.fredericksburgva.com.

FOOD AND DRINK:

Considering its relatively small size, Fredericksburg is just loaded with good restaurants. Among them are:

Smythe's Cottage (303 Fauquier St., at Princess Anne St.) Colonial and contemporary American dishes are served in an early 19th-century cottage. ☎ (540) 373-1645. $$

La Petite Auberge (311 William St., between Princess Anne and Charles streets) Reservations are needed for this popular French country restaurant, which also features contemporary American dishes. ☎ (540) 371-2727. X: Sun., holidays. $$

Ristorante Renato (422 William St., west of Prince Edward St.) Traditional Northern Italian cuisine in a Colonial setting. ☎ (540) 371-8228. X: weekend lunch, holidays. $$

Merriman's (715 Caroline St., near the Visitor Center) Contemporary American cuisine; vegetarian dishes available. Reservations suggested, ☎ (540) 371-7723. $$

Sammy T's (801 Caroline St., a block north of the Visitor Center) Homemade soups, salads, sandwiches and the like, plus vegetarian specialties. ☎ (540) 371- 2008. $

SUGGESTED TOUR:

Numbers in parentheses correspond to numbers on the map.

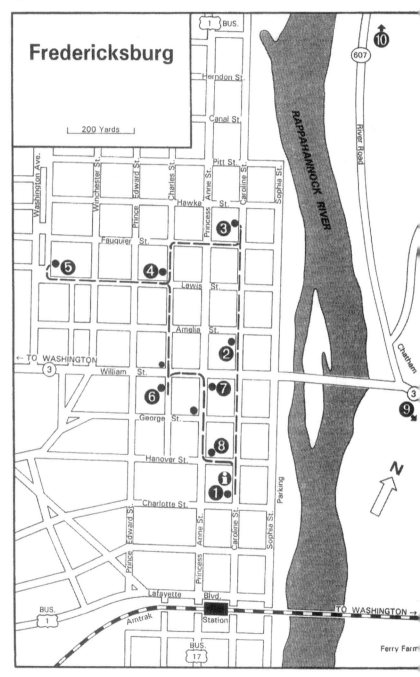

Fredericksburg

200 Yards

Begin your walk at the **Visitor Center** (1), where you can watch a 14-minute orientation video and get current information on the sights, restaurants, and lodging. Maps, joint admission tickets, and parking passes are also available here. *706 Caroline St.,* ☎ *(540) 373-1776 or (800) 678-4748, Internet: www.fredericksburgva.com. Open daily 9–5, extended hours in summer. Closed Thanksgiving, Christmas, and New Year's. Free.*

Stroll north on Caroline Street to the:

HUGH MERCER APOTHECARY SHOP (2), 1020 Caroline St., ☎ (540) 373-3362. *Open March–Nov., daily 9–5; Dec.–Feb., daily 10–4. Closed Thanksgiving, Dec. 24, 25, 31, New Year's Day. Adults $4, students 6–18 $1.50. Joint admission ticket applies.*

Doctor Mercer practiced medicine, dispensed prescriptions, fixed teeth, and even powdered wigs in this shop from 1771 until 1776. After that, he left to fight in the Revolution as a brigadier-general. A friend of George Washington's, he perished during the Battle of Princeton.

However good a doctor he may have been, needing medical care in Colonial times was a nightmare—as this restored office makes perfectly plain. The gruesome instruments and revolting "cures" are enough to make anyone cringe. Take a look at this preserved bit of American history, then be thankful you're living in the present.

Continue north to the:

RISING SUN TAVERN (3), 1304 Caroline St., ☎ (540) 371-1494. *Open March–Nov., daily 9–5; Dec.–Feb., daily 10–4. Closed Thanksgiving, Dec. 24, 25, 31, New Year's. Adults $4, students 6-18 $1.50. Joint admission ticket applies.*

A costumed tavern wench will show you around this 18th-century watering hole where the likes of George Washington, Thomas Jefferson, the Marquis de Lafayette, and other Colonial luminaries were entertained. The building, in fact, was erected in 1760 by Washington's youngest brother, Charles, as his residence. It served as a tavern from 1775 until about 1825, and has survived intact with some of its original furnishings. Visitors get to sample spiced tea in the tap room.

Amble west on Fauquier Street, turning south on Charles Street to the:

MARY WASHINGTON HOUSE (4), 1200 Charles St., ☎ (540) 373-1569. *Open March–Nov., daily 9–5; Dec.–Feb., daily 10–4. Closed Thanksgiving, Dec. 24, 25, 31 and New Year's Day. Adults $4, students 6–18 $1.50. Joint* *admission ticket applies.*

George Washington purchased this home for his mother, Mary, in 1772, and this is where she spent the remaining 17 years of her life. Her daughter, Betty, lived in the adjoining estate, while some other members of the Washington family resided nearby. Mary's lovely **boxwood garden** continues to flourish today, as it did when she greeted the visiting Marquis de Lafayette there. Inside, several of the period furnishings are original and actually belonged to the Washington family.

Follow Lewis Street west to:

*KENMORE (5), 1201 Washington Ave., ☎ (540) 373-3381, Internet: www.kenmore.org. *Open March–Nov., daily 9–5; Dec.–Feb., daily 10–4. Closed Thanksgiving, Dec. 24, 25, 31 and New Year's Day. Adults $6, students 6–18 $3, family rate $12.50. Rates include tea and ginger cookies. Joint admission tickets apply. Gift shop. ᴅ, limited access.*

From the outside, this Georgian manor house looks rather ordinary, but its interior is among the most elegant in America. Colonel Fielding Lewis and his wife, Betty, the only sister of George Washington, built the mansion in 1752 on their 861-acre plantation near the northwest corner of Fredericksburg. Washington was, of course, a frequent visitor, and according to tradition helped design the extremely ornate room settings.

Visits begin in a gallery with historical exhibits and a diorama, followed by a guided tour of the house. At the end, you'll be served tea and gingerbread made to Mary Washington's very own recipe. Don't miss the restored gardens.

Return to Charles Street and turn south. On the northwest corner of Charles and William streets is the **Old Slave Block**, a large circular stone from which slaves were auctioned before the Civil War put an end to that unspeakable practice. Just below this is the:

JAMES MONROE MUSEUM AND MEMORIAL LIBRARY (6), 908 Charles St., ☎ (540) 654-1043. *Open March–Nov., daily 9–5; Dec.–Feb. 10–4. Closed Thanksgiving, Dec. 24, 25, 31, New Year's. Adults $4, students 6-18 $1. Joint admission tickets apply. Gift shop. ᴅ.*

James Monroe (1758–1831), the fifth president of the United States, practiced law in Fredericksburg from 1786 through 1789, after which he had a brilliant political career ending in the Presidency (1817–25). Now restored, his small office contains many of his personal possessions, including the Louis XVI desk on which he signed the Monroe Doctrine in 1823. The library contains books and historical manuscripts, most relating to the president and the period during which he lived.

Take William Street east to Princess Anne Street and turn south to the:

FREDERICKSBURG AREA MUSEUM AND CULTURAL CENTER (7), 905 Princess Anne St., ☎ (540) 371-3037. *Open Mon.–Sat. 9–5, Sun. 1–5, closing at 4 from Dec.–Feb. Adults $4, students 6–18 $1. Joint admission tickets valid.* ♿.

The history of the Fredericksburg region from pre-historic times to the present is explored through permanent and changing exhibitions.

Continue south, passing **St. George's Episcopal Church** at the northeast corner of George and Anne streets. Mary Washington belonged to the first church on this site; the present structure dates from 1849. Inside are three stained-glass windows by Louis Tiffany, installed by the D.A.R. in honor of George Washington's mother. ☎ *(540) 373-4133. Open daily 8–5. Free.*

Across the street is the **National Bank Museum**, where almost two centuries of American banking history are displayed in one of the nation's oldest bank buildings. ☎ *(540) 899-3243. Open Mon.–Fri. 10–1. Free.*

On the southwest corner of the same intersection is the **Presbyterian Church.** Civil War cannonballs are still stuck in its left front pillar, and the belfry retains scars of an 1862 bombardment. Clara Barton, founder of the American Red Cross, is supposed to have nursed Union soldiers here.

A block farther down Princess Anne street stands the **George Washington Masonic Museum** (8), one of the oldest Masonic lodges in America. Young George Washington was initiated as a Mason here in 1752, and memorabilia pertaining to his membership are on display, along with a Gilbert Stuart portrait of him. ☎ *(540) 373-5885. Open Mon.–Sat. 9–4, Sun. 1–4. Closed Thanksgiving and Christmas. Adults $2, students 8–18 $1.*

Return to the nearby Visitor Center. From here you might want to drive across the river to:

FERRY FARM (9), Rte. 3 East at Ferry Rd., Falmouth, VA, ☎ (540) 373-3381. *Open Mon.–Sat. 10–5, Sun. noon–5. Free.*

George Washington lived here from the age of 6 until he was 20, and inherited the property when he was 11. His mother continued to live on the farm until George bought her the house in Fredericksburg. Legend has it that a certain cherry tree got chopped down here, and a coin tossed across the Rappahannock River. Whatever the truth of those stories, this is where he received his education and taught himself surveying.

If you continue up River Road for about six miles, you'll come to:

BELMONT—THE GARI MELCHERS ESTATE AND MEMORIAL GALLERY (10), 224 Washington St., Falmouth, VA, ☎ (540) 654-1015. *Open Mon.–Sat. 10–5, Sun. 1–5, closing at 4 from Oct.–Mar. and on Thanksgiving, Dec. 24, 25 and 31, and New Year's Day. Adults $4, seniors $3, students 6–18 $1. Joint admission tickets valid.*

Relax. None of the Founding Fathers lived, ate, or slept here, although it is an 18th-century estate. After several previous owners, this became the home of the famous American artist Gari Melchers (1860–1932) in 1916. His stone studio of 1924 is now a gallery devoted to his paintings, and the rest of the house is filled with European antiques and works of art by Breughel, Rodin, Childe Hassam, and others.

Spotsylvania

Memories of the Civil War still haunt the countryside surrounding Fredericksburg, where you can trace the movements of armies at four battlefields, chronologically following the ebb and flow of the conflict. This is an ideal daytrip for history buffs, who can follow each attack and counterattack from information provided right at the sites. For others, it can be a pleasurable day spent exploring the peaceful farmland and taking short walks in the woods to sites where so much of the nation's history was decided.

By staying overnight, you could easily combine this excursion with the one to Fredericksburg, described previously, or to Virginia's Northern Neck (see page 144). It also makes a nice stopover en route to Richmond, Williamsburg, and other destinations in Virginia.

GETTING THERE:

By car, Fredericksburg is about 50 miles southwest of Washington via Route I-95. Get off at Exit 130 and take **VA-3** east to **US-1** (Sunken Road), turning right and heading south to the Battlefield Visitor Center on the left at Lafayette Boulevard.

After touring the Fredericksburg Battlefield sites, drive west on VA-3 past Old Salem Church. In about 10 miles you'll reach the Chancellorsville Battlefield Visitor Center.

Wilderness is another five miles west on VA-3.

VA-613 leads southeast to Spotsylvania Court House, a distance of about 12 miles.

To reach Chatham Manor, take **VA-208** northeast into Fredericksburg, then VA-3 east across the river, turning north on Chatham Lane in Falmouth. This stretch is about 12 miles.

PRACTICALITIES:

All of the battlefield sites are free, and open every day except Christmas and New Year's. The walking trails are unpaved, so wear appropriate shoes.

A complete tour of every site involves about 75 miles of driving, but you can substantially reduce that by seeing only the highlights.

For further information contact the **Spotsylvania County Visitor Center**, 4704 Southpoint Parkway, Fredericksburg, VA 22407, ☎ (540) 891-8687 or (800) 654-4118. This is on US-1, just south of I-95 Exit 126. Alternatively, you can get battlefield information from the **Fredericksburg and Spotsylvania County Battlefield Memorial National Military Park**, 120 Chatham Lane, Fredericksburg, VA 22405, ☎ (540) 373-4461, Internet: www.nps.gov/frsp.

FOOD AND DRINK:

Although the battlefield area has a fair selection of chain restaurants and fast-food emporiums, your best bet is to have lunch in the Old Town part of Fredericksburg. Several good choices for this are described on page 133.

On the other hand, why not pack a picnic lunch to enjoy outdoors at one of the battlefield sites, where facilities are available?

SUGGESTED TOUR:

Numbers in parentheses correspond to numbers on the map. Begin your auto tour at the:

FREDERICKSBURG BATTLEFIELD VISITOR CENTER (1), 1013 Lafayette Blvd. at Sunken Rd., Fredericksburg, VA 22401, ☎ (540) 373-6122. *Open daily, 9–5, usually closing at 6 in summer. Closed Christmas and New Year's. Admission $3. Museum. Picnic sites. Audiotape tour cassette rentals/sales. ৬, limited access.*

Free information, maps, and brochures are available here for exploring all of the **Fredericksburg and Spotsylvania National Military Park** sites. Before setting off, however, you can get a good background orientation by watching the slide show and seeing the museum exhibits.

The **Battle of Fredericksburg,** fought on December 13, 1862, is remembered as General Robert E. Lee's most one-sided victory. Union forces, commanded by General Ambrose E. Burnside, had successfully crossed the Rappahannock River and were on their way to Richmond, capital of the Confederacy. At first, things went well for the North, but Lee's skillful use of the terrain enabled his smaller force, entrenched behind a stone wall, to send the invaders back across the river, where they spent the rest of the winter licking their considerable wounds.

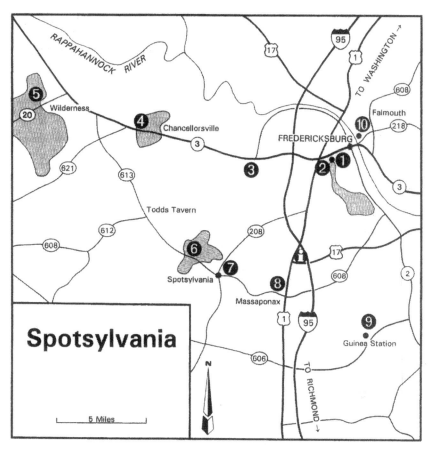

Explore the battlefield using a map from the Visitor Center, then cross Sunken Road to the **Fredericksburg National Cemetery** (2). Over 15,000 Union soldiers are buried here; three-quarters of whom remain unknown.

Drive west on VA-3 to **Old Salem Church** (3), around which another battle raged on May 3–4, 1863. Built in 1844, the church itself was used as a military hospital during the conflict.

Continue west on VA-3 to the:

CHANCELLORSVILLE BATTLEFIELD VISITOR CENTER (4), Rte. 3, 7 miles west of I-95, ☎ (540) 786-2880. *Open daily, 9–5, usually closing at 6 in summer. Closed Christmas and New Year's. Museum. Picnic sites.*

Audiotape tour cassette rentals/sales. &.

General Lee won the greatest victory of his career at the **Battle of Chancellorsville**, April 27–May 6, 1863, this time assisted by Stonewall Jackson. The strategies used were so brilliant that they are studied by military commanders to this day. Union forces commanded by General Joseph Hooker, again headed for Richmond and then retreated across the Rappahannock. The Confederacy, however, suffered the loss of Stonewall Jackson, who was accidentally shot by his own men. It was this decisive triumph that sent Lee marching north toward Gettysburg (see page 296).

Using the audiovisual show and exhibits as an orientation, you can easily follow the map from the Visitor Center to explore as much of the battlefield as desired.

Those not weary of war can continue west for another five miles on VA-3 to the **Wilderness Battlefield** (5). It was here, a year later (May 5–6, 1864), that Lee first encountered Union forces led by their new commander, General Ulysses S. Grant. Although the Confederate side more or less won this battle, its losses both here and at Spotsylvania were so great, and Grant's resolve so tenacious, that the conflict became a irreversible grinding war of annihilation with no hope of a Southern victory.

Tour the battlefield with the aid of the map you obtained at one of the previous visitor centers, then drive southeast on VA-613 to the **Spotsylvania Court House Battlefield** (6). From May 8–21, 1864, armies under Lee and Grant once again fought a bloody duel with no clear-cut victory. On-site exhibits outline the two-week-long battle, which included the most intense hand-to-hand combat of the war at the Bloody Angle. Despite grievous losses, Grant's forces survived and pushed ever onward towards Richmond.

The little village of **Spotsylvania** (7) has an interesting Historic District, whose war-damaged **Court House** was reconstructed in the early 1900s with its original Doric columns. Local artifacts are shown in the **Spotsylvania County Museum**, located in the Old Berea Church of 1856. ☎ *(540) 582-7167, open mid-May–Oct., Mon.–Sat. 10–4 and Sun. 1–4; and Nov.–mid-May, Mon.–Fri. 10–3.* Take a look at the **Old Jail** of 1781, which was moved to its present site in 1839. Six hundred of the men who perished in the battle have found their final resting place in the **Confederate Cemetery**.

If time permits, you could head east on VA-608 to **Massaponax Church** (8) near US-1, where General Grant stopped after the battle. Beyond, east on VA-607, is the **Stonewall Jackson Shrine** (9) at Guinea Station in Caroline County. It was in the plantation office here that the legendary Confederate hero died while murmuring the words, "Let us cross over the river, and rest under the shade of the trees." ☎ *(804) 633-6076. Open daily in summer, 9–5, reduced days in other seasons.*

Return to Fredericksburg and cross the Rappahannock River on VA-3 (William Street). Turning north in Falmouth, Stafford County, brings you to:

CHATHAM MANOR (10), 120 Chatham Lane, Fredericksburg, VA 22405, ☎ (540) 373-0802. *Open daily 9–5. Closed Christmas and New Year's Day.* ♿. *Picnic facilities.*

Although this Georgian mansion was built in 1768 and was frequently visited by several presidents, it is best remembered for its Civil War associations. This was one of the Union headquarters during the Battle of Fredericksburg, and a place where President Lincoln met with his generals. Later, both Clara Barton and Walt Whitman nursed the wounded here when it served as a field hospital for the North. Restored, it is now operated by the National Park Service.

Virginia's Northern Neck

T wo of America's most celebrated families—the Washingtons and
the Lees—had their ancestral homes only a few miles apart on a
watery peninsula between the Potomac and Rappahannock estu-
aries. Visitors coming this way can explore George Washington's birthplace, a "living" Colonial farm complete with a representational plantation house that re-creates the lifestyle of the early Washingtons. They
can also walk the scenic trails, enjoy bucolic views across Pope's Creek,
and perhaps have a picnic. More waterside hiking trails and a wide variety of outdoor activities are featured at nearby Westmoreland State
Park.

The grand manor house in which Robert E. Lee was born is just minutes down the road, surrounded by a vast plantation still worked today.
Here you can tour one of the greatest Colonial mansions in America,
visit an operating gristmill, stroll along lovely nature trails, and even
have lunch in a log cabin.

GETTING THERE:

By car, take MD-5 and US-301 south from the I-95 Beltway, crossing
the Potomac into Virginia. Head east on VA-3, then turn north on VA-204
to Washington's Birthplace. The total distance is about 75 miles southeast of Washington.

To reach Westmoreland Park, go east 5 miles on VA-3, then north a
mile on VA-347.

Stratford Hall is another two miles east on VA-214, and Montross
about five miles southeast on VA-3.

PRACTICALITIES:

This trip can be made on any day of the year except Christmas and
New Year's Day, but it's best from mid-spring through mid-fall.

For further information, contact the Northern Neck Tourism Council,
P.O. Box 452, Reedville, VA 22539, ☎ (800) 453-6167, Internet: www.north
ernneck.org; or the Westmoreland County Council for Travel, Historic

Courthouse Square, Montross, VA 22520, ☎ (804) 493-8440 or (888) 733-9282.

FOOD AND DRINK:

There's not much to choose from in this remote neck of the woods, but you can have an enjoyable lunch at:

The Inn at Montross (21 Polk Street) First opened in 1683, this small inn serves meals to the public as well as guests. Please call ahead. ☎ (804) 493-0573. X: Wed. and Thurs. lunch. $$

Stratford Hall Dining Room (on the Stratford Hall Plantation) A "plantation lunch" is served daily in a rustic log cabin in the woods. ☎ (804) 493-8038. $

Alternatively, there are free picnic facilities at both Washington's Birthplace and Westmoreland Park. The latter also has a snack bar in season.

LOCAL ATTRACTIONS:

Numbers in parentheses correspond to numbers on the map.

GEORGE WASHINGTON BIRTHPLACE NATIONAL MONUMENT (1), 1732 Popes Creek Rd., Washington's Birthplace, VA 22443, ☎ (804) 224-1732, Internet: www.nps.gov/gewa. *Open daily 9–5. Closed Christmas and New Year's. Admission $2, under 17 free. Visitor Center. Orientation film. Tours. Exhibits. Picnic facilities. Nature trails.* ♿.

George Washington was born here at **Pope's Creek Plantation** on February 11, 1732 (February 22 by the Gregorian calendar adopted in 1752). Three years later, in 1735, the family moved to what became known as Mount Vernon, and in 1738 to Ferry Farm near Fredericksburg (see page 137).

Although the original farm house burned down on Christmas Day, 1779, and was never replaced, the National Park Service has re-created the plantation pretty much as it was at the time of Washington's birth. The **Memorial House**, a modern composite of what the original structure might have looked like, is furnished with authentic period pieces similar to those probably owned by the Washingtons. Archaeological digs on the site have yielded a few small items that most likely belonged to the family. The **Colonial Farm** today grows the same crops, using 18th-century methods. Occasional demonstrations are made of farm chores and rural crafts. A trail leads to the **Family Burial Ground**, where the 1664 home of great-grandfather Colonel John Washington, the first Washington in Virginia, once stood, and where the First President's ancestors are buried.

WESTMORELAND STATE PARK (2), State Route 347, Montross, VA 22520, ☎ (804) 493-8821, Internet: www.state.va.us/~dcr/parks,westmore.htm. *Open daily. Nominal use fees. Visitor Center. Boat rentals. Swimming. Camping. Cabins. Picnic facilities. Hiking trails. Groceries. ♿, limited access.*

The swimming pool, beach, hiking trails, and other outdoor activities here make a nice break from sightseeing, especially on a hot summer day.

*STRATFORD HALL PLANTATION (3), Stratford, VA 22558, ☎ (804) 493-8038, Internet: www.stratfordhall.org. *Open daily except Thanksgiving, Christmas and New Year's Day, 9–4:30. Adults $7, seniors $6, children 6–18 $3, military $6. Tours. Museum. Gift shop. Restaurant. ♿.*

Built in the 1730s, Stratford is a most unusual mansion, and surely one of the greatest of the Colonial era. It began as the home of Thomas Lee (1690–1750), a leading Virginia planter and acting governor of the colony, who begat six sons, two of whom were signers of the Declaration of Independence. Their cousin, Revolutionary War hero "Light-Horse Harry" Lee, a friend of George Washington's, lived here for over 20 years. His famous offspring, General Robert E. Lee, was born in this house in 1807.

The ***Great House** is noted for its unique clusters of chimneys, and for having its major rooms on the second floor, in the style of the Italian Renaissance. Inside, you'll see the **Great Hall**, a magnificently paneled room some 29 feet square. Out buildings include a kitchen, where you can sample ginger cookies, a plantation office, and a gardener's house. The **East Garden** is outlined in boxwood, while the **West Garden** has 18th-century varieties of vegetables, herbs, and flowers.

Another major attraction here is the working **Gristmill**, reconstructed on its original foundations, where wheat, oats and corn are ground as they were over two centuries ago. It operates, weather permitting, from 1:30 to 3:30 p.m. on the second and fourth Mondays from March through October, and on Saturdays from May through October.

You might want to head down the road about five miles to the village of **Montross** (4), where you'll find an old inn on the historic Courthouse Square. Near this is the **Westmoreland County Museum and Information Center**, with small exhibits of local history. ☎ *(804) 493-8440. Open Apr.–Oct., Mon.–Sat. 9–5, Sun. 10–5; Nov.–Mar., daily 10–3. Free.*

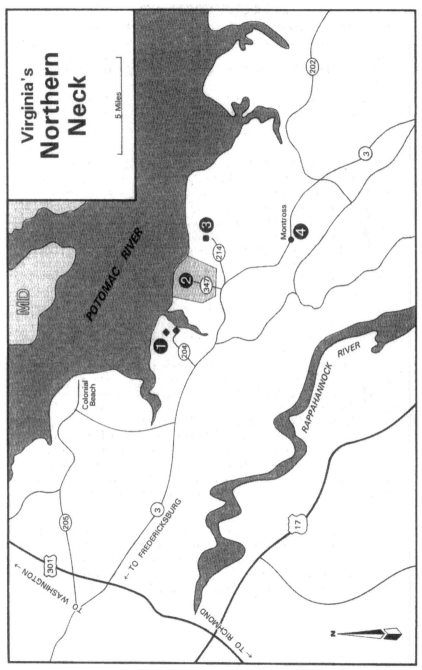

Downtown Richmond

Although its history dates back to the early 17th century and figures prominently in the events leading to American independence, Virginia's state capital is best known for the major role it played in the Civil War. From 1861 to 1865 it was the capital of the Confederacy and the constant target of Union attack.

Evacuated and partially destroyed in the final moments of that tragic conflict, Richmond bounced back to become one of the most prosperous cities of a reborn South. Its historic core thankfully escaped the urban renewal mania of the 1950s, saving much of its old downtown area for today's more enlightened restorations.

Today the city's $500 million riverfront development project is underway. Expected to take up to 15 years, this multi-phased project will include bringing back to life the original canal system chartered by George Washington in 1784, plans for pedestrian-friendly walkways, plaza hotels, shops and boutiques.

Beginning with Thomas Jefferson's classic State Capitol of 1785, visitors can tour many historic buildings, homes of famous people, numerous museums, and beautifully-preserved neighborhoods. The walk described here will keep you busy all day, but as you'll discover, there's much more to Richmond than just its downtown. Other attractions both in town and nearby are covered in the following chapters, so why not consider staying over for a few days?

GETTING THERE:

By car, Richmond is about 105 miles south of Washington via Route I-95. Get off at Exit 74B and head west three blocks to the State Capitol.

PRACTICALITIES:

While the State Capitol Building is open daily, the City Hall building is closed on weekends. A few of the other sights close on weekends or Mondays, but most of the attractions are open daily except, of course, on Thanksgiving, Christmas, or New Year's. Ideally, the best time to come is on a Tuesday, Wednesday, Thursday, or Friday; preferably in spring or fall. There are more sights here than can be comfortably enjoyed in a single day, so you'll have to pick and choose.

Taken all the way and going to all the sights, this walk is about four miles in length, but that can be cut in half without too much loss. Those preferring to drive will find that parking is not particularly difficult, although the route will have to be modified a bit because of the many one-way streets.

Richmond operates a free trackless "trolley" service on several downtown routes, serving roughly the same area as the walking tour. You can get a free route map from the tourist office. Visitors may purchase a Historic Downtown Block ticket for $15 allowing them entrance into over three dozen museums, houses, churches and buildings all linked via trolley. Children under 7 are admitted free.

For further information, contact the **Metro Richmond Convention and Visitors Bureau**, 550 East Marshall St., Richmond, VA 23219, ☎ (804) 782-2777 or (888) RICHMOND, Internet: www.richmondva.org. Their **Visitor Center** is located in Capitol Square at the Bell Tower. Alternatively, contact the **Virginia Tourism Corp.**, 901 E. Byrd. St., Richmond, VA 23219, ☎ (804) 786-2051.

FOOD AND DRINK:

There are plenty of good places to eat along this walking tour, including:

Mr. Patrick Henry's Inn (2300-2302 E. Broad St., near St. John's Church) Filled with antiques, this 1850's inn has a delightful dining room, pub, and garden café, all serving Continental cuisine. ☎ (804) 644-1322. X: Sat. lunch and Sun. $$

Sam Miller's Warehouse (1210 E. Cary St., near Shockoe Slip) Seafood is the specialty here, although there's also beef for landlubbers. ☎ (804) 644-5465. $$

Tobacco Company (1201 E. Cary St., near Shockoe Slip) A colorful place in a 19th-century tobacco warehouse, with an indoor atrium and lots of antiques. Meat and fish dishes. ☎ (804) 782-9431. $$

Peiking Pavilion (1302 E. Cary St., Shockoe Slip) An elegant Chinese restaurant with good-value lunches ☎ (804) 649-8888. X: Sat. lunch. $ and $$

Winnie's Caribbean Cuisine (200 E. Main St. at 2nd St.) West Indian dishes served at appropriate surroundings, with reggae music. ☎ (804) 649-4974. X; Sat. lunch, Sun. $ and $$

Bottoms Up Pizza (1700 Dock St. at 17th St., south of E. Main) Creative pizzas and light Italian fare. ☎ (804) 644-4400. $

SUGGESTED TOUR:
Numbers in parentheses correspond to numbers on the map. Begin your walk at the:

VIRGINIA STATE CAPITOL (1), 9th and Grace streets, ☎ (804) 786-4344. *Open Apr.–Nov., daily 9–5; rest of year Mon.–Sat. 9–5 and Sun. 1–5. Closed Thanksgiving, Christmas, New Year's. Free. Tours.* よ.

Thomas Jefferson, clearly inspired by the Maison Carrée, a Roman temple of 20 BC in Nîmes, France, designed the central portion of this magnificent structure in 1785. Completed three years later, it is still home to the oldest English-speaking legislature in America. In its **Rotunda** stands Jean-Antoine Houdon's famous ***statue of George Washington**, commissioned in 1785 on the recommendation of Benjamin Franklin. The Rotunda also contains busts of the seven other Virginians who made it to the White House. Beyond, the old **Hall of the House of Delegates** has seen much history in the making: Aaron Burr's trial for treason in 1807, Virginia's ratification of the Articles of Secession, and Robert E. Lee's acceptance of command of the forces of Virginia in 1861 being the most memorable events. Throughout the Civil War, the building was also the meeting place of the Confederate Congress.

Take the free half-hour tour, then stroll outside onto the Capitol Grounds to admire the **Governor's Mansion** of 1813 and the old **Bell Tower** of 1824, which houses Richmond's Visitor Center. You might want to stop here for some free information.

Head north on 9th Street to Richmond's:

CITY HALL (2), 9th and Broad streets, ☎ (804) 780-7000. *Open Mon.-Fri. Free.*

The 18th-floor **Observation Deck** offers a fabulous ***view** of the city in all directions, and it's free. Practically adjacent to it is the **Old City Hall** of 1886, a Victorian Gothic beauty with an elaborate cast-iron interior that can be seen at the same times. Continue up 9th Street to the:

JOHN MARSHALL HOUSE (3), 818 E. Marshall St., ☎ (804) 648-7998, Internet: www.apva.org. *Open Tues.–Sat. 10–5 Apr.–Sept., closing 30 min. earlier from Oct.–Dec. Open Jan.–March by appointment. Adults $3, seniors $2.50, children 7–12 $1.25. Discounted combo ticket with other attractions available.*

John Marshall (1755–1835), Chief Justice of the Supreme Court from 1801 to 1835, built this house in 1790 while a member of the Virginia Executive Council and a practicing lawyer. The restored interior, with its original woodwork, contains a mixture of period pieces and original

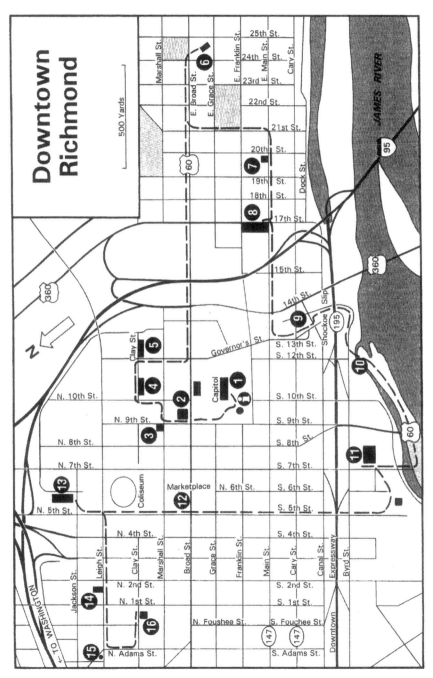

family heirlooms.

Follow the map to the:

VALENTINE MUSEUM (4), 1015 E. Clay St., ☎ (804) 649-0711, Internet: www.valentinemuseum.com. *Open Mon.–Sat. 10–5, Sun. noon–5. Adults $5, seniors and students $4, children 7–12 $3 (6 and under free). Tours.* ♿.

Richmond's long history is told through artifacts, costumes, toys, furnishings, and all sorts of mementos from the 17th century to the present. Admission includes a tour of the adjacent Wickham House of 1812, and the garden.

Stroll down the block to the:

MUSEUM and WHITE HOUSE OF THE CONFEDERACY (5), 1201 E. Clay St., ☎ (804) 649-1861, Internet: www.moc.org. *Open Mon.–Sat. 10–5, Sun. noon–5. Closed Thanksgiving, Christmas, New Year's. White House tours Mon., Wed., Fri., Sat. 10:30–4:30; Tues., Thurs. 11:30–4:30; Sun. 1:15–4:30. Adults $8, seniors $7, students $5, children $3.50 (7 and under free). Gift shop.* ♿.

Civil War buffs can revel in the world's largest known collection of Confederate memorabilia, covering virtually every aspect of the conflict. Among the items on display is the sword worn by General Lee as he surrendered at Appomattox, and the suit worn by Jefferson Davis the day he was captured. There are also weapons, flags, uniforms, photos, maps, and various documents detailing the entire scope of the Civil War experience.

Next to this is the **White House of the Confederacy**, shown on tours starting in the museum. Built in the Classical Revival style in 1818 (and never actually painted white), it was the official residence of Jefferson Davis (1808–89), President of the Confederate States of America throughout its short existence. Davis was indicted for treason after the war, but never prosecuted. Now restored to its antebellum appearance, the house has many of its original furnishings.

Follow the route shown on the map to:

ST. JOHN'S EPISCOPAL CHURCH (6), 2401 E. Broad St., ☎ (804) 648-5015. *Open Mon.–Sat. 10–4, Sun. 1–4, last tour at 3:30. Adults $3, seniors $2, children over 7 $1. Tours. Gift shop.* ♿, *partial access.*

"Give me liberty or give me death" cried Patrick Henry (1736–99) here on March 20th, 1775, while addressing the revolutionary Second Virginia Convention. His words have echoed ever since, and still do every summer Sunday at 2 p.m., when the scene is re-enacted. Tours of the 1741 church show visitors the original fittings, a prayerbook that belonged to Queen Anne, the font where Pocahontas was baptized, the pews where Patrick Henry, George Washington, George Mason, Thomas Jefferson, and other rebels sat, and the graveyard where several notables are buried.

Retrace your steps on Broad Street, turning south on 21st Street and west on Main to the:

EDGAR ALLAN POE MUSEUM (7), 1914 E. Main St., ☎ (804) 648-5523 or (888) 21-EAPOE, Internet: www.poemuseum.org. *Open Tues.–Sat. 10–4:30, Sun.–Mon. noon–4:30. Last tour at 4. Closed Christmas. Adults $6, seniors and students $5. Gift shop.*

This stone house of 1737 may be the oldest building still standing within the original boundaries of Richmond, but Poe never lived in it. However, it is a fitting place to display the vast collection of memorabilia concerning his life and works. There are actually five buildings here, grouped around an "Enchanted Garden" planted with flowers mentioned in his writings. Poe's life in Richmond is well documented with an audiovisual show and personal possessions, but the highlight of the museum is the ***Raven Room** with its eerie illustrations of that most evocative of poems.

Head west on Main Street, turning north a few steps on 17th Street to the colorful **Farmers' Market** (8), where fresh produce has been sold for over three centuries on the site of an Indian trading village. *Open daily.*

Continue west on Main and turn south on 13th Street, strolling into the historic **Shockoe Slip District** (9). Old warehouses here, near the James River, have been adapted to such modern uses as upscale shopping, dining, lodging, and nightlife. The streets, of course, are cobbled and lit with gas.

Follow the map south to the restored **Kanawha Canal Locks** (10) of 1790. North America's first commercial canal system was initiated by George Washington, and skirted the falls of the James River between Richmond and Westham. ☎ *(804) 281-2000. Daily, 9–5. Free.*

Canal Walk leads across a footbridge and through a park. Nearby, on Byrd Street, is the:

FEDERAL RESERVE BANK MONEY MUSEUM (11), 701 E. Byrd St., ☎ (804) 697-8108. *Open Mon.–Fri., 9:30–3:30. Closed weekends, holidays. Free.*

You can learn all about money here, courtesy of the "Fed," and it won't cost you a cent. Exhibits include rare bills and gold bars.

Turn north on Fifth Street, perhaps detouring to the **6th Street Marketplace** (12) between Grace Street and the Coliseum. Built by the same folks who gave Baltimore its Harborplace, this assembly of restored historic buildings is now a vast shopping mall.

If you happen to have a kid in tow, you might want to head a few blocks north to the:

CHILDREN'S MUSEUM OF RICHMOND (13), 740 N. 6th St., ☎ (804) 788-4949. *Open Tues.–Sun.; daily in July and Aug. Closed holidays. Moderate admission fee. Adults must be accompanied by a child 2–12.*

Young kids will love the hands-on activities here, where they can explore a simulated cave with stalactites and stalagmites, pretend to be policemen or a host of other professions, and in general experience the world around them.

West of 7th Street is the historic **Jackson Ward** neighborhood, birthplace of many noted African-Americans. Among its classical and Victorian houses festooned with ornamental ironwork stands the:

MAGGIE L. WALKER NATIONAL HISTORIC SITE (14), 1102 E. Leigh St., ☎ (804) 780-1380. *Open Wed.–Sun. 9–5. Closed Mon., Tues., Thanksgiving, Christmas, New Year's. Free. &, partial access.*

Maggie Walker, the daughter of an ex-slave, in 1903 became the first American woman to establish a bank. Despite physical handicaps, she was successful in both business and in her advocacy of civil rights. This large Victorian house, home to her family from 1904 until 1934, is now a museum celebrating her achievements.

Amble west on Leigh Street to Adams Street, where you'll see the **Bill "Bojangles" Robinson Statue** (15) memorializing the famous tap dancer who was born nearby in 1878. Turn south on Adams and east on Clay Street to the:

BLACK HISTORY MUSEUM and CULTURAL CENTER OF VIRGINIA (16), 00 E. Clay St., near 1st St., ☎ (804) 780-9093. *Open Tues.–Sat., 11–4. Adults $2, seniors and children $1. Partially &.*

Black life in Virginia from the early days of the 17th century until today are explored in this 1832 house that later served as a school.

The Rest of Richmond

S ome of Richmond's best attractions are scattered around the outer reaches of the city, a bit too remote to be included in the downtown walking tour but much too enticing to miss. All are easily reached by car. Let your interests be your guide as you pick and choose from the destinations described in this chapter.

By staying overnight, the trip can easily be combined with the previous one, and also with the next.

GETTING THERE:

By car, Richmond is about 105 miles south of Washington via Route **I-95**. For Agecroft and Wilton, take Exit 79 and turn south onto **I-195**, getting off at the Cary Street exit. Follow Cary Street west to the vicinity of the sites.

The Art Museum, Science Museum, and Maymont are closer to downtown, about three miles east via Cary and other local streets. To reach them directly from I-95, use Exit 78 and go south on Boulevard (VA-161), then local streets.

The Aviation Museum is east of downtown, following East Broad Street and Williamsburg Road. To reach it directly from I-95, take Exit 74C.

PRACTICALITIES:

Avoid making this trip on a Monday or major holiday, when most of the sites are closed.

For further information, contact the **Metro Richmond Convention and Visitors Bureau**, 550 East Marshall St., Richmond, VA 23219, ☎ (804) 782-2777 or (888) RICHMOND, Internet: www.richmondva.org. Their convenient **Visitor Center** is located in Capitol Square at the Bell Tower where you can get local maps, brochures, and advice on visiting Richmond, and even arrange for overnight accommodations if you decide to stay.

Alternatively, you can contact the **Virginia Tourism Corporation**, 901 E. Byrd St., Richmond, VA 23219, ☎ (804) 786-2051, Internet: www. virginia.org.

FOOD AND DRINK:

A few choices for lunch are:

Strawberry Street Café (421 N. Strawberry St., between Park and Stuart avenues, near the Art Museum) Well-known for its great salad bar, this Fan District favorite also features fancy burgers and similar dishes. ☎ (804) 353-6860. $$

Texas-Wisconsin Border Café (1501 W. Main St., at Plum St. in The Fan) Tex-Mex with a fierce chili, plus Wisconsin ethnic dishes. ☎ (804) 355-2907. X: weekend lunch. $

Coppola's (2900 W. Cary St., near Wilton House) Italian deli dishes; sandwiches to spaghetti. X: Sun. ☎ (804) 359-6969. $

Farouk's House of India (3033 W. Cary St., at Belmont Ave.) Traditional Indian cuisine, with a lunch buffet. X: Sun. lunch. ☎ (804) 355-0378. $

LOCAL ATTRACTIONS:

Numbers in parentheses correspond to numbers on the map.

*AGECROFT HALL (1), 4305 Sulgrave Rd., ☎ (804) 353-4241, Internet: www.agecrofthall.com. *Open Tues.–Sat. 10–4, Sun. 12:30–5. Closed Mon. and major holidays. Adults $5, seniors $4.50, students $3.* ♿.

You might wonder what a 15th-century half-timbered English Tudor manor house, built a decade before Columbus discovered America, is doing here on the banks of the James River. Well, back in the 1920s a Virginia couple discovered it in Lancashire, England, and decided to save it from impending destruction. Purchasing the threatened mansion, they had it carefully disassembled and brought to the New World in pieces for reconstruction in an appropriate setting. At first a private residence, it is now a showcase of life among Britain's landed gentry at the time when the earliest colonists were first settling Jamestown, Virginia. Your visit begins with an audiovisual show, after which you are taken on a tour through the ***Great Hall** and other rooms, all richly filled with 16th- and 17th-century furnishings and art. Outside, the **Sunken Garden** is copied from the one at Hampton Court near London, while the Elizabethan **Knot Garden** is planted with flowers and herbs authentic to the period.

WILTON HOUSE (2), 215 S. Wilton Rd., ☎ (804) 282-5936. *Open Mar.–Jan., Tues.–Sat. 10–4:30, Sun. 1–4:30. Last tour begins at 3:45. Closed Mon. and*

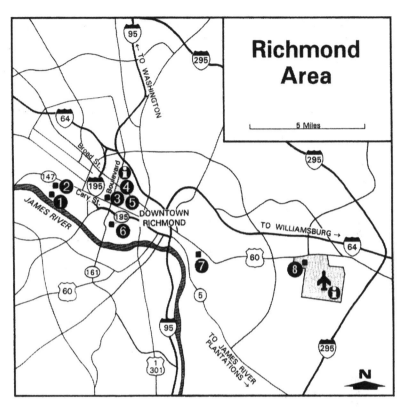

Richmond
Area

5 Miles

*holidays. Adults $5, seniors and students ages 6–college (with ID) $4. ♿,
partial access.*

    Colonial Virginia lives on at this 1750's Georgian mansion. Visited by
George Washington and the Marquis de Lafayette, it was the home of an
aristocratic plantation owner named William Randolph III. The house
now serves as headquarters of the National Society of Colonial Dames
in Virginia. Step inside to admire the extraordinary paneling, English
and American period furnishings, and exquisite decorative arts.

*VIRGINIA MUSEUM OF FINE ARTS (3), 2800 Grove Ave. at Boulevard, ☎
(804) 367-0844, Internet: www.vmfa.state.va.us. *Open Tues.–Sun. 11–5,
closing at 8 on Thurs. Closed Mon., July 4, Thanksgiving, Christmas, and
New Year's. Admission $4. Gift shop. ♿.*

Five thousand years of art, from ancient Egypt to a Manhattan SoHo loft of today, fill the spacious galleries of one of the nation's most varied and interesting art museums. Among its treasures is a priceless collection of *Fabergé jewelry and Easter eggs made for the czars of Russia; ancient icons from India, Nepal, and Tibet; *Impressionist paintings by Monet, Renoir, van Gogh, and others; African masks; marvelous pieces of Art Nouveau and Art Deco; and contemporary works by 20th-century artists. If you like art, you'll love this place. Nearby is the:

VIRGINIA HISTORICAL SOCIETY: MUSEUM OF VIRGINIA HISTORY (4), 428 N. Boulevard, ☎ (804) 358-4901, Internet: www.vahistorical.org. *Open Mon.–Sat. 10–5, Sun. 1–5. Closed July 4, Thanksgiving, Christmas, New Year's. Adults $4, seniors $3, students and children $2. Gift shop.* ♿.
The whole sweeping history of Virginia, from the earliest times to the present, is covered in many wonderful displays and re-creations.
Turn right on Broad street to the:

SCIENCE MUSEUM OF VIRGINIA (5), 2500 W. Broad St., 3 blocks east of Boulevard, ☎ (804) 367-6552 or (800) 659-1727, Internet: www.smv.mus.va.us. *Open Mon.–Sat. 9:30–5, Sun. noon–5, remains open till 7 on Fri. and Sat. in summer. Museum admission: Adults $5.50 exhibit only, $4 film only, $8.50 both. Seniors 60 and over $5 exhibit only, $4 film only, $8 both. Youth 4–12 $4.50 exhibit only, $4 film only, $7.50 both. Gift shop.* ♿.
Housed in a wonderful old railroad station that is no longer used, the Science Museum has all sorts of interactive, hands-on exhibits where you (and zillions of schoolchildren) can learn how the modern world works. This is a fun place to visit if you enjoy the mysteries of nature and technology; especially if you have a kid in tow. As a special treat, there is also an **IMAX** theater with spectacular sight and sound from every direction, and a **planetarium** with multi-media sky shows.
About two miles to the south is:

MAYMONT (6), 1700 Hampton St. at Pennsylvania Ave., ☎ (804) 358-7166. *Mansion open June–Aug., Tues.–Sat. 10–5, Sun. noon–5; rest of year Tues.–Sun. noon–5. Donations accepted. Grounds open daily, 10–7, closing at 5 in winter.*
Built in the 1890s, Maymont is everything a grand Victorian mansion should be. The 33-room house is filled with exotic art and artifacts from all around the globe. On top of that, it sits on an extensive 100-acre estate complete with pastoral grounds in the English style, a delightful **Italian Garden** with hidden features, a **Japanese Garden** with cherry trees,

a nature center, and a **Children's Farm** with tame animals. These can be enjoyed on foot or, weather permitting, on an old-fashioned **carriage ride**.

There are a few sights to the east of downtown Richmond, namely:

RICHMOND NATIONAL BATTLEFIELD PARK (7), Chimborazo Visitor Center, 3215 E. Broad St., ☎ (804) 226-1981, Internet: www.nps.gov.rich. *Visitor Center open daily 9–5. Closed Christmas and New Year's. Free. Picnic facilities. Hiking trails.* ౬.

Numerous Civil War battles were fought around Richmond, some won by the Confederacy and some by the North. Visible remains of these are preserved at ten different sites spread over a rather large area, mostly north and east of the city. You probably won't want to drive the entire 97-mile route connecting them, but you can get a good introduction to the battles here and decide just which to visit. Built on the site of one of the Confederacy's largest military hospitals, the **Chimborazo Visitor Center** is operated by the National Park Service and offers audio-visual shows, museum exhibits, and free brochure/maps to guide you. In the summer of 1999, park officials are planning to move the visitors center to a much larger space in downtown Richmond (the old Tredegar Iron Works building) right on the James River. The current visitors center on Broad St. will be maintained as administrative offices, as well as a museum focusing on the Confederacy military hospital. Continue on to the:

VIRGINIA AVIATION MUSEUM (8), Richmond International Airport, 5701 Huntsman Rd., Sandston, VA 23150-1946, ☎ (804) 236-3622. *Open daily 9:30–5, closed Thanksgiving and Christmas. Adults $5, seniors $4, ages 4–12 $3. Gift shop.* ౬.

Aircraft and artifacts from the Golden Age of Aviation, 1914 to World War II, fill the halls of this modern facility operated by the Science Museum of Virginia. Visitors can also watch vintage aircraft being renovated, and view a film on the history of aviation.

James River Plantations

Travelers headed south towards the Williamsburg area usually take Interstate Route 64, which gets them there in a hurry but shows them nothing. Instead, why not enjoy the drive and spend a day meandering down old Virginia Route 5? The attractions along this largely ignored road are certainly worth the journey, and make a fine daytrip in themselves.

Six gracious plantations, one dating as far back as 1613, follow the road along the James River as it flows east from Richmond into Chesapeake Bay and the Atlantic. Here, in the Tidewater region near America's first permanent English settlement, history lives on in a quietly unassuming way. All six sites may be visited; several offer house tours, gardens, a good look at a working plantation, and even a place to have lunch or spend the night.

If you can spare more than a day, you'll find that this excursion combines very well with those to Richmond and the Williamsburg area.

GETTING THERE:

By car, the first of the plantations is about 125 miles south of Washington. Take Route I-95 south to Richmond Exit 74A, then **VA-5** southeast to Shirley, on the right.

Edgewood is about four miles down the road, on the left.

The other four plantations, all on the right, are just a short distance down the same road.

PRACTICALITIES:

All of the plantations are open daily all year round, except for Sherwood, whose house tours are not held from January through March. The sites are, of course, closed on Christmas and in some cases also on Thanksgiving and New Year's Day. Visits are best made in the spring or fall, avoiding the heat and humidity of summer. A combined ticket is available for Berkeley, Evelynton, Sherwood Forest, and Shirley.

For further information, contact the **Williamsburg Area Convention &**

Visitors Bureau, P.O. Box 3585, Williamsburg, VA 23187, ☎ (757) 253-0192 or (800) 368-6511, Internet: www.williamsburg.com.

FOOD AND DRINK:

Some choice restaurants along the way are:

Coach House Tavern (at Berkeley Plantation) Reservations are advised for lunch and necessary for dinner in the popular coach house of historic Berkeley Plantation. ☎ (804) 829-6003. X: dinner on Mon. and Tues. $ and $$

Indian Fields Tavern (9220 John Tyler Memorial Hwy, Charles City, between Evelynton and Sherwood) Guests can enjoy local specialties on the porch of this old farmhouse-turned-tavern. ☎ (804) 829-5004. X: major holidays, Mon. in Jan. and Feb. $ and $$.

LOCAL ATTRACTIONS:

Numbers in parentheses correspond to numbers on the map.

*SHIRLEY PLANTATION (1), 501 Shirley Plantation Rd., Charles City, VA 23030, ☎ (804) 829-5121 or (800) 232-1613, Internet: shirleyplantation.com. *Open daily 9–5. Closed Thanksgiving, Christmas, weekdays from mid-Jan. to mid-Feb.. Adults $8.50, seniors over 60 $7.50, youths 13–21 $5.50, children 6–12 $4.50. Gift shop. ♿, partial access.*

First settled around 1613, Shirley is still home to the same family after 11 generations. The present mansion was begun in 1723, completed in 1738, and visited by such notables as George Washington, Thomas Jefferson, John Tyler, and Theodore Roosevelt. Robert E. Lee's mother was born here. Prospering through the Revolution and surviving the Civil War, the plantation was unusually well run and so managed the difficult transition to slaveless labor. Today's visitors can tour the elegant Georgian manor with its famous hanging staircase, explore the dependencies, and get a taste of life on a plantation that is still being worked.

EDGEWOOD PLANTATION (2), 4800 John Tyler Memorial Hwy., Charles City, VA 23030, ☎ (804) 829-2962. *Tours Tues.–Sun. 11–4. Adults $8, youths 7–10 $3. Overnight accommodation available, luncheon by appointment.*

Operated today as an inn, this Gothic Revival plantation house is also shown on tours for non-guests. It was built in 1849 and is still filled with Victorian antiques, old charm, and even a resident ghost.

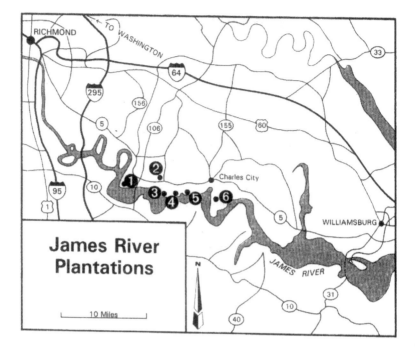

James River
Plantations

10 Miles

*BERKELEY PLANTATION (3), Box 390, Charles City, VA 23030, ☎ (804) 829-6018. *Open daily 9–5. Closed Christmas. Adults $8.50, over 65 $7.95, children 13–16 $6.50, 4–12 $4. Restaurant. ᠔, partial access.*

Regardless of Yankee propaganda, Virginians maintain that the first Thanksgiving was celebrated here on December 4, 1619, and not in Massachusetts. That's when the earliest settlers arrived. The present Georgian mansion dates from 1726 and was the birthplace of Benjamin Harrison (1726–91), a signer of the Declaration of Independence and Governor of Virginia. It is also the ancestral home of two American presidents, William Henry Harrison (1773–1841) and Benjamin Harrison (1833–1901). Every U.S. president from George Washington to James Buchanan was entertained here; Lincoln for obvious reasons was not. Honest Abe, however, did come to confer with Union General George McClellan during the Civil War, when Berkeley was a headquarters for the invading Federal forces.

After the Civil War, the now-slaveless plantation became uneconomical to run and fell into ruin. In 1907, what was left of it was purchased by a former drummer boy in McClellan's army. His son began a long period of restoration in 1927, resulting in the magnificent estate of today.

WESTOVER GARDENS (4), 7000 Westover Rd., Charles City, VA 23030, ☎ (804) 829-2882. *Grounds open daily 9–6. Adults $2, children 50¢.*

Westover's plantation house of 1735 is open to visitors during April Garden Week only, but the marvelous gardens and grounds may be explored on any day.

EVELYNTON PLANTATION (5), 6701 John Tyler Memorial Hwy., Charles City, VA 23030, ☎ (804) 829-5075 or (800) 473-5075. *Open daily 9–5. Closed Tues.–Thurs. in Jan. and Feb., Thanksgiving and Christmas. Adults $7.50, seniors and active military personnel with ID $6.50, students $5.50, children 6–12 $3.50. Gift shop. 占.*

Originally part of the Westover Plantation (above), Evelynton has been home to the Ruffin family since 1847. It was their patriarch, Edmund Ruffin (1794–1865), who fired the first shot of the Civil War at Fort Sumter in 1861. Fierce fighting during that conflict destroyed the original mansion, whose 250-year-old bricks were salvaged and used again to build the present manor house in 1935. Looking as though it had been there all the time, this Colonial Revival structure is filled with authentic 18th- and 19th-century furnishings, and is noted for its fabulous flower arrangements. Still in the family, and still a working plantation, Evelynton is also renowned for its lush grounds and exquisite formal gardens.

SHERWOOD FOREST PLANTATION (6), Box 8, Charles City, VA 23030, ☎ (804) 829-5377, Internet: www.sherwoodforest.org. *Open daily 9–5. Entrance fee: Adult $8.50, seniors $8, students (K–college) $5.50, under 5 free. Military discounts. Guided house tour and self-guided grounds tour are available.*

Built in 1730, this 300-foot-long, 44-room wooden house was owned in the 1790s by President William Henry Harrison (see Berkeley, above), the Tippecanoe of "Tippecanoe and Tyler Too." When Harrison died in office, his succeeding vice-president, John Tyler (1790–1862) bought the property as a retirement home. Upon President Tyler's leaving office in 1845, his arch-foe Henry Clay commented that "Like Robin Hood, he is going off to his Sherwood Forest." The name stuck, and the plantation has been called that ever since. It is still in the Tyler family.

Fully restored, the mansion is furnished with family heirlooms as well as period pieces. It is the only James River plantation to have a ballroom, and is thought to be the longest frame house in America. The 1,600-acre grounds feature several dependencies that can be seen, including a tobacco barn, slave quarters, and an elegant three-hole privy.

*Colonial Williamsburg

Can you really see Colonial Williamsburg in just a day? Of course not, but you can sure enjoy yourself trying. A one-day sampling of its many offerings might tempt you to come back for a stay of several days, possibly including other nearby attractions such as the James River Plantations (page 000), the Jamestown and Yorktown historic sites (page 000), or the Busch Gardens theme park.

Originally known as Middle Plantation, Williamsburg was settled in 1633 as a defensive outpost of Jamestown. Its College of William and Mary, the second-oldest in the nation, was founded in 1693, and in 1699 the growing town became the capital of a Virginia colony that extended west to the Mississippi and north to the Great Lakes. During the Revolution, however, the government fled to the more easily defended Richmond, where it remains to this day. From 1780 until the 1920s, Williamsburg prospered as a college town and market center. Then, in 1926, the Reverend W.A.R. Goodwin, rector of the Bruton Parish Church, persuaded John D. Rockefeller Jr. to lead a long-term project to restore the town's historic core to its 18th-century splendor. Today, America's largest outdoor living-history museum covers some 173 acres with about 500 buildings, of which 88 are original.

Not only did the Colonial Williamsburg Foundation revive the Historic Area physically, but it also populated it with people in 18th-century costume going about daily 18th-century life. That's what makes Williamsburg such a fascinating place. Visitors can really immerse themselves in an authentic Colonial past as they chat with tradesmen, housewives, aristocrats, and all manner of locals going about their business, and even join in the activities. Of course, life here is somewhat sanitized—there is now well-concealed indoor plumbing, the streets are no longer a mess, and slavery no longer provides the labor.

GETTING THERE:

By car, Williamsburg is 153 miles southeast of Washington via Interstate routes **I-95, I-295,** and **I-64.** Get off at Exit 238 of the latter and follow signs to the Visitor Center, where parking is free. A bus will take you from there to the edge of the Historic Area.

Trains operated by Amtrak connect Williamsburg with Washington and the Northeast Corridor. The schedule hardly allows enough time for a daytrip, but this is a viable option if you're staying overnight. All trains are reserved, ☎ (800) USA-RAIL for details. Williamsburg's station is within walking distance of the historic sites.

PRACTICALITIES:

Any time is a good time to visit Colonial Williamsburg, but it's most enjoyable in the spring or fall—when you can avoid summer's heat, humidity, and crowds. Carter's Grove is closed on Mondays, and from January until mid-March. The Visitors Center is open Mon.–Fri. 9–5, Sat.–Sun. 8:30–6, with extended hours during peak seasons.

While it costs nothing to just stroll the streets (all of which are closed to automobiles), tickets are required to enter restored buildings and ride the shuttles or buses. Your best bet is to purchase a comprehensive pass, which includes an orientation film at the Visitor Center, use of the transportation system, and an introductory guided tour. The most versatile arrangement is the **Patriot's Pass**, admitting the bearer to everything run by the foundation as well as shopping and entertainment discounts, and valid for one full year. *Adults $34, children 6–12 $19.50.* The **Colonist's Pass**, good for two consecutive days, includes admission into almost all of the area's buildings and shops and two of its three museums. *Adults $30, children 6–12 $17.* The one-day or half-day **Basic Pass** includes the orientation film and admission into most of the area's buildings. *Adults $26, children 6–12 $15.* All are sold at the Visitor Center and elsewhere.

The **basic walk** through the Historic Area is about 2.5 miles in length. Two continuous shuttles and a circuit bus take visitors to and from the Visitor Center and selected points in the Historic Area from 8:50 a.m.–10 p.m.

Because of the authenticity of the restorations, **wheelchair access** varies with each building. Advance arrangements can be made to have temporary ramps put in place, to rent wheelchairs, or for other special needs including those for the hearing or sight impaired, ☎ (757) 220-7644.

Frequent **special events** are held all year round. Ask at the Visitor Center about these, or call ahead for a free printed schedule.

For further information, contact the **Colonial Williamsburg Foundation**, P.O. Box 1776, Williamsburg, VA 23187, ☎ (757) 220-7645 or (800) HISTORY, Internet: www.colonialwilliamsburg.org.

FOOD AND DRINK:
Colonial Williamsburg has plenty of atmospheric restaurants catering to tourists; among the best of which are:

Trellis (Merchant's Square, west end on Duke of Gloucester St.)
Take a break from Colonialism at this California-style restaurant, which
offers imaginative contemporary cuisine and a large selection of wines.
Indoor/outdoor dining. Reservations preferred, ☎ (757) 229-8610. $$ and
$$$

King's Arms Tavern (Duke of Gloucester St., a block west of the
Capitol) Colonial-style specialties in a re-created 18th-century tavern.
Reservations advised, ☎ (757) 229-1000. $$

Cascades (near the Visitors Center) A popular, modern place for
good dining within view of quiet woods and a waterfall. ☎ (757) 229-
1000. $$

Chowning's Tavern (Duke of Gloucester St., at Queen St.) This reconstructed alehouse of 1766 features lighter fare with a Colonial touch,
such as Brunswick stew and Welsh Rabbit. ☎ (757) 229-1000. $ & $$

SUGGESTED TOUR:
Numbers in parentheses correspond to numbers on the map.

The best place to begin is at the **Visitor Center** (1), where you can
park free, purchase a pass, get any necessary information or help, and
watch a half-hour **orientation film.**

Board one of the frequent buses or shuttles to the eastern end of
the **Historic Area** and visit the *****Capitol** (2). First built in 1704, it was
destroyed by fire and rebuilt in 1753. A second Capitol building also
succumbed to flames in 1832. What you see today is a re-creation of the
original structure, a rather ornate affair reflecting the aristocratic
lifestyles of Colonial Virginia's ruling class. Step inside and take a 30-
minute guided tour that explains the evolution of American democracy
from its English roots. It was here that Patrick Henry (1736–99) opposed
the Stamp Act with his fiery 1765 speech ending in the words: "Caesar
had his Brutus; Charles the First, his Cromwell; and George the Third—
may profit by their example."

Such treasonous thoughts could bring the perpetrator before the
General Court in the same building, where today's visitors can participate in mock "trials," and then to the **Public Gaol** (3) just north of it. Life
in this 1704 jail was no picnic, but then neither were the hangings held
here. The lockup remained in use until 1910, and is now restored to its
Colonial appearance.

Stroll over to the **Raleigh Tavern** (4), a major social center where
Washington, Jefferson, Henry, and other influential citizens met in pre-
Revolutionary times. Named in honor of Sir Walter Raleigh, it burned
down in 1859 and was reconstructed from historical records in 1932.

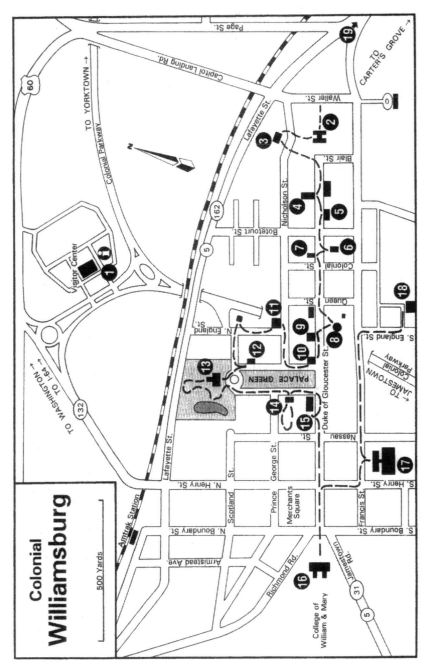

Colonial
Williamsburg

Tours are given of both the tavern and its outbuildings.

*Duke of Gloucester Street is the wide, mile-long main thoroughfare of Colonial Williamsburg, running from the Capitol west to the College of William and Mary. Turn right on it for a few steps to Wetherburn's Tavern (5), an authentic survivor from the early 18th century. First built as a private house, it became an inn around 1743. A precise inventory from 1790, as well as excavations of the site, have made this possibly the most accurate restoration in the Historic Area. Although political bigwigs made occasional pit stops here, it was never as important a social center as the Raleigh. The inn's authenticity, however, compels a visit. Guided tours of the property are given frequently.

Continuing down the main street takes you past several shops representing a variety of Colonial trades. Two particularly interesting ones to pause at are the Blacksmith's (6), where you can watch iron being forged, and the Printer's and Bookbinder's (7). A costumed printer here will show you how it was done in the 18th century.

Amble on to the Market Square, an area opening on either side of Duke of Gloucester Street. On its south extension is the Magazine (8), an original octagonal structure built of brick in 1715 to store arms and ammunition. Used by the British to defend the colonies, it also saw service in both the Revolution and the Civil War. After serving more peaceful purposes, this arsenal has been restored and now displays a collection of period firearms. The Guardhouse, almost adjacent to it, dates from the French and Indian War.

Cross the main street to the restored Court House of 1770 (9). Visitors who've been naughty lately can try the outdoor stocks on for size. Step inside to see a courtroom where civil and criminal trials continued to be held until 1932, and where you can participate in today's re-enactments.

On the corner, by the Palace Green, stands the James Geddy House (10) of 1750. The home and shop of a silversmith, it's a relatively simple place where you can watch a skilled craftsman at work.

Turn down Nicholson Street to the Peyton Randolph House (11). This was the residence of the first President of the Continental Congress, a wealthy Williamsburg lawyer who sided with the colonists. The Comte de Rochambeau planned his siege of Yorktown here in 1781, and another Frenchman, the Marquis de Lafayette, visited in 1824. North of the house stands a windmill that operates in good weather, and an area where various Colonial trades are demonstrated.

Facing the Palace Green, the Brush-Everard House (12) was built in 1717 by a gunsmith and later served as the home of a two-time mayor of Williamsburg. Remaining in continuous use until 1946, the house is among the oldest surviving buildings in town. Its boxwood gardens are particularly attractive.

Now for the star attraction. The *Governor's Palace (13), Colonial

Williamsburg's most lavish building, is a complete re-creation of a 1720 original that burned down in 1781. The royal authority of the British Crown is made manifestly clear by the sumptuous appointments, a rare bit of luxury in the colonies. After the last royal governor fled in 1775, the mansion was used by Virginia's first two elected governors, Patrick Henry and Thomas Jefferson. Although some of the furnishings are original, most are either period pieces or careful reproductions conforming to an inventory of 1770. Today's reconstructed building sits on the original foundations.

Visitors are greeted by a liveried lackey and given a tour by a costumed guide, after which they can enjoy the magnificent **gardens**, complete with a **maze** inspired by that of Hampton Court near London.

Stroll south along the Palace Green, perhaps stopping at the **George Wythe House** (14). Thomas Jefferson's law professor and Virginia's first signer of the Declaration of Independence, George Wythe (1726–1806) also taught law to John Marshall and Henry Clay. George Washington used this house as his headquarters just before the Siege of Yorktown, and Rochambeau afterward.

A visit to the **Bruton Parish Church** (15) of 1715 is appropriate as one of its 20th-century pastors, W.A.R. Goodwin, was instrumental in the restoration of Colonial Williamsburg. One of America's oldest Episcopal churches, Bruton remains in continuous use to this day. Visitors are welcome to step inside to admire the simple, graceful interior with its white box pews.

At the far end of Duke of Gloucester Street, past Merchant's Square, is the handsome **Wren Building** (16) of 1695. Its design was inspired by the works of Sir Christopher Wren (1632–1723), perhaps the greatest English architect of all time. Located just west of the Historic Area, it is a part of the **College of William and Mary**. America's second-oldest college (after Harvard) was founded in 1693 and named for the joint sovereigns of England, King William III and Queen Mary II. Regular guided tours are conducted by undergraduates. ☎ *(757) 221-1540. Free.*

Follow the map back into the Historic Area, stopping at the **Public Hospital of 1773** and **The DeWitt Wallace Gallery** (17). The first part of this combined structure is a re-creation of America's earliest insane asylum, originally built in 1773, which serves as a cover for the modern museum of 1985. In the latter you'll find a vast collection of English and American decorative arts from the 17th to early 19th centuries, including paintings, tapestries, china, musical instruments, porcelains, furniture, weapons, and the like.

The route now leads east to the **Abby Aldrich Rockefeller Folk Art Center** (18), where you can see one of the best collections of folk art in the country. These sometimes-naïve works were created not by trained artists, but by naturally gifted persons who expressed the world around them in a variety of media.

You'll have to drive to get to ***Carter's Grove** (19), a part of Colonial Williamsburg that lies some eight miles to the southeast. This early plantation was founded by settlers in 1619 as Wolstenholme Towne, but wiped out by an Indian uprising in 1622 and later divided into farmsteads. Eventually consolidated by the most powerful of Virginia's 18th-century planters, Robert "King" Carter, it acquired an elegant brick mansion in 1755. The site, now reduced to 790 acres, has been thoroughly restored after intensive archaeological discoveries. Among the sights to see are the ***mansion**, the slave quarters, the town site, and the Winthrop Rockefeller Archaeology Museum. A short orientation is given in the Visitor Reception Center. ☎ *(757) 229-1000. Open mid-March–Dec., Tues.–Sun., 9–4 (open one hour later during summer months). Adults $17, children 6–12 $10, free to Patriot's Pass holders.*

Jamestown and Yorktown

nglish rule in what is now the United States began at Jamestown in
1607 and effectively ended just a few miles down the road at
Yorktown in 1781. Both sites have a lot of history to offer, and both
can be seen on a longish daytrip, although an overnight stay would be
more enjoyable. For those with a few days to spend, this excursion combines very nicely with Williamsburg (page 164), the James River
Plantations (page 160), or with the nearby Busch Gardens theme park.

On May 13, 1607, some 100 men and boys stepped ashore onto a
marshy peninsula now known as Jamestown Island, and there founded
the first permanent English settlement in the New World. After several
years of terrible hardships, the colony began to prosper on the tobacco
trade and Jamestown became the first capital of Virginia.
Representational government, the first in the New World, flourished
since 1619, but in 1699 it moved to a more desirable location at
Williamsburg. After that Jamestown declined and was soon abandoned,
with nothing left above ground but the church tower. Archaeological
digs and historical research have provided information about the original settlement, but the search for knowledge continues. The actual site
itself is now a national park. Nearby is the Jamestown Settlement
Museum. Operated by the State of Virginia, it provides a re-creation of
the original fort, an Indian village and replica ships.

Yorktown is where the last major battle of the Revolution was
fought and independence won. The battlefield site, surrounding the
present town, is part of Colonial National Historical Park, with its own
self-guided tour. Also within the town is the Yorktown Victory Center, a
living history museum with costumed soldiers, a military camp and an
18th-century farm. The Yorktown Victory Center is a state-run museum.

GETTING THERE:

By car, Jamestown is about 160 miles southeast of Washington via
Interstate routes **I-95, I-295,** and **I-64.** Get off at the **Colonial Parkway** exit
and follow the parkway southwest to Jamestown and the Jamestown

Settlement Museum.

The Colonial Parkway connects Jamestown with Yorktown and the Yorktown Victory Center, a distance of about 23 miles.

PRACTICALITIES:

All of the sites are open daily except on Christmas and New Year's Day. A few minor attractions are closed in winter.

For further information contact **Colonial National Historic Park**, P.O. Box 210, Yorktown, VA 23690, ☎ (757) 229-1733, Internet: www.nps.gov/cdo, or the **Jamestown-Yorktown Foundation**, P.O. Box 1607, Williamsburg, VA 23187, ☎ (757) 253-4838, Internet: www.historyisfun.org.

FOOD AND DRINK:

Both sites are located close to Williamsburg, which has an extensive selection of restaurants. Besides those in the Historic Area described on page 166, you might consider:

Le Yaca (1915 Pocahontas Trail, US-60E in Kingsmill Village shopping center) A charming country restaurant with superb Southern French cuisine. ☎ (757) 220-3616. X: Sun., major holidays. $$ and $$$

Old Chickahominy House (1211 Jamestown Rd., at routes 199 and 315) Authentic Southern home cooking in a Colonial setting, very popular with the locals. ☎ (757) 229-4689. X: evenings, major holidays. $

In addition, there are picnic facilities in Jamestown and Yorktown. There is also a seasonal restaurant at Jamestown Settlement.

LOCAL ATTRACTIONS:

Numbers in parentheses correspond to numbers on the map.

*JAMESTOWN SETTLEMENT (1), VA-31 and Colonial Parkway, P.O. Box 1607, Williamsburg, VA 23187, ☎ (757) 253-4838 or (888) JYF-IN-VA, TDD (757) 253-7236, Internet: www.historyisfun.org. *Open daily 9–5. Closed Christmas and New Year's. Adults $10.25, children (6–12) $5. Combination ticket with Yorktown Victory Center: Adults $14, children $6.75. Gift shop. Restaurant in season.* ♿.

Early 17th-century life in America's first permanent English settlement is faithfully re-created at Jamestown Settlement, a living history museum located near the original site. Visits begin with a 20-minute introductory film, followed by three exhibition galleries. The first of these deals with the political and social conditions in 16th-century England that led to overseas colonization; the second with life among the Powhatan Indians at the time; and the third with the earliest history of the Virginia colony.

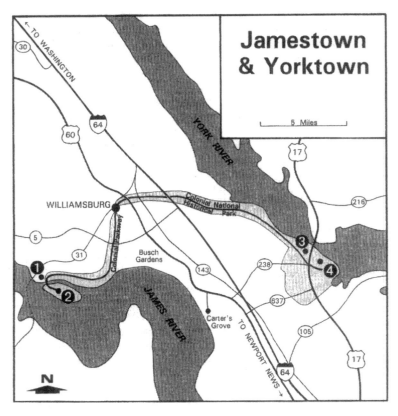

Step outdoors and see for yourself what it was like. At the re-creat-ed **Powhatan Indian Village** you can experience Native American life, then stroll down a path to the James River to see full-size replicas of the **three small ships** that brought the original settlers here in 1607. A cos-tumed "sailor" will lead you on board one of these, where you can wit-ness demonstrations of life at sea. The palisaded **James Fort**, a re-cre-ation of the settlers' first home, takes visitors back in time to watch "colonists" in appropriate attire go about their daily life.

Just down the road is:

JAMESTOWN ISLAND, (2), Colonial National Historical Park, P.O. Box 210, Yorktown, VA 23690, ☎ (757) 229-1733, Internet: www.nps.gov/cdo. *Open daily 8:30–5, later in summer. Closed Christmas. Entrance fee: $5 per adult or child over 16. Gift shop. Rental of audio tour cassette tapes.* &, *partial access.*

This is the actual site of the original Jamestown, of which precious little remains. The church tower dates from 1639, and the reconstructed foundations of "New Towne" evoke the past. Begin at the Visitors Center, where a short film and museum exhibits set the stage for a guided walking tour. You might also want to enjoy the five-mile nature drive around the island, visit the archeological excavation, and watch glassmaking demonstrations.

Head back on the Colonial Parkway, passing Williamsburg, and continue on to Yorktown and the:

***YORKTOWN VICTORY CENTER** (3), Old Route 238 at Colonial Pkwy., P.O. Box 1607 Williamsburg, VA 23187, ☎ (757) 253-4838 or (888) 593-4682, Internet: www.historyisfun.org. *Open daily 9–5. Closed Christmas and New Year's. Adults $7.25, children (6–12) $3.50. Combination ticket with Jamestown Settlement: Adults $14, children $6.75. Gift shop. Picnic facilities.* ♿.

Britain's adventures in what is now the United States came to an end here in 1781 as General Cornwallis surrendered to the combined American and French armies. The story of the American Revolution, from Colonial unrest to ultimate victory at Yorktown, unfolds in this magnificent, living re-creation of history operated by the Commonwealth of Virginia.

Visits begin on the "Road to Revolution" walkway, where the events that led up to the Declaration of Independence unfold before entering a **museum** of Yorktown's role in the struggle. Here, life-size figures tell their stories, and a dramatic film brings the final major battle to life.

Outdoors, costumed soldiers go about their daily drill in a re-created **Continental Army Camp**, and "farmers" tend their crops in a simulated 18th-century farm.

Close by, and surrounding today's village of Yorktown, is the:

YORKTOWN BATTLEFIELD (4), Colonial National Historical Park, P.O. Box 210, Yorktown, VA 23690, ☎ (757) 898-3400, Internet: www.nps.gov/cdo. *Open daily 9–5, later in summer. Closed Christmas. Entrance Fee: $4 per person over 16. Bookstore. Rental of audio tour cassette tapes. Picnic facilities.* ♿, *partial access.*

Stop first at the Visitor Center to watch a thoughtful orientation film, look at museum displays including George Washington's original field tent, and obtain a free map of the battlefield. You can get your bearings on the rooftop overlook, then take a self-guided tour of the battlefield that includes earthworks, Washington's Headquarters, the Surrender Field, and other highlights.

If time permits, you might want to wander around the delightful village of **Yorktown**, settled in 1691 and once a prosperous tobacco port. Several buildings from the Colonial era survive, including a church of 1697.

*Charlottesville and Monticello

harlottesville is the heart of "Mr. Jefferson's Country"—where America's third president was born in 1743, where he lived most of his life, where he founded the University of Virginia in 1819, where he died in 1826, and where he is buried. In those days it took four days to make the journey from Washington. Today you can do it in just over two hours, a bit long for a daytrip perhaps, but the visit to Monticello alone makes it highly rewarding. While there, you can also drop in on the home of another president, James Monroe, explore an historic tavern, and tour the magnificent grounds of the University of Virginia.

Located in the foothills of the Blue Ridge Mountains, Charlottesville was first settled in the 1730s and made a town in 1762. It is named for Queen Charlotte, the wife of King George III. Always a delightful place, Charlottesville has in recent years become a favorite hideaway for celebrities and creative types who appreciate its low-key, yet fashionable, and somewhat intellectual lifestyle. The university is the largest employer.

By staying overnight, you can easily combine this trip with the Shenandoah National Park, described in the next chapter.

GETTING THERE:

By car, Charlottesville is about 120 miles southwest of Washington via Route **US-29.** For the Visitors Center, Monticello, Ash Lawn-Highland, or Michie Tavern, continue south on the 29 Bypass, then east on **I-64** to Exit 121 and south a short distance on **VA-20.**

PRACTICALITIES:

All of the sites are open daily except on Christmas and New Year's Day, while the University of Virginia tours close for three weeks around Christmas. Try to avoid summer weekends, when Monticello can be overrun with tourists.

For further information contact the **Charlottesville/Albemarle**

Convention & Visitors Bureau, P.O. Box 178, Charlottesville, VA 22902, ☎ (804) 977-1783, Internet: www.charlottesvilletourism.org. Their Visitors Center is located on VA-20, just south of I-64 Exit 121, and is open daily.

FOOD AND DRINK:

Some good places for lunch are:

C&O Restaurant (515 E. Water St., near the downtown Mall) The downstairs bistro of this fancy French restaurant offers modern American and French cuisine at affordable prices. ☎ (804) 971-7044. $$

The Hardware Store (316 E. Main St., at the downtown Mall) This antiques-filled 1890s hardware emporium now dishes up an eclectic variety of light meals. ☎ (804) 977-1518. $

Northern Exposure Bar and Grill (1202 Main St. SW, near the University) Extensive vegetarian selections. ☎ (804) 977-6002. $

The Ordinary (at the Michie Tavern) The buffet luncheon in this 200-year-old log cabin features fried chicken with veggies, salad, cornbread, and apple cobbler. Outdoor tables are available. ☎ (804) 977-1235. $

LOCAL ATTRACTIONS:

Numbers in parentheses correspond to numbers on the map.

MONTICELLO VISITORS CENTER (1), VA-20 just south of I-64, ☎ (804) 977-1783, Internet: www.charlottesvilletourism.org. *Open daily 9–5, until 5:30 from March–Oct. Closed Thanksgiving, Christmas, and New Year's. Free.*

This friendly center features an unusually informative permanent exhibition on Jefferson's life at Monticello, with artifacts discovered in recent digs. Additionally, you can get free travel information, maps, brochures, and assistance in finding local lodging. A discounted combination ticket for Monticello, Ash Lawn-Highland and Michie Tavern is offered.

Turn east on VA-53 for about two miles to:

*MONTICELLO (2), P.O. Box 316, Charlottesville, VA 22902, ☎ (804) 984-9800, Internet: www.monticello.org. *Open daily March–Oct., 8–5; Nov.–Feb., 9–4:30. Closed Christmas. Adults $9, children (6–11) $5. Year-round guided tours. Daily family tours June–Aug. Gift shop.* &.

You probably have a picture of Monticello in your pocket right now; it's on the reverse side of every nickel. Flip the coin over and you'll see Thomas Jefferson, who spent much of his life "putting up and pulling down" this astounding residence until he had it just the way he wanted

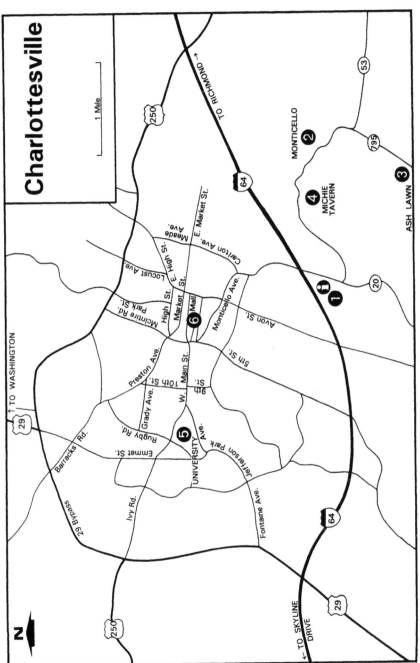

Charlottesville

1 Mile

N

it. Unlike so many homes of the great, Monticello has a lived-in quality that endears it to ordinary mortals. Still, this is an architectural masterpiece of the highest order; perhaps the first such in the nation.

Inspired by the works of the 16th-century Italian Renaissance architect, Andrea Palladio, Monticello sits atop a small mountain; thus its name. Jefferson began building his ever-evolving house in 1769 and tinkered with its design for the next 40 years. In a sense, it was always a work in progress, a sort of permanent construction site, remaining that way until he retired in 1809. What you see today is much neater, of course, but it still conveys the personality of its owner more clearly than just about any other restored historical house in America.

The interior is shown on guided tours, where you'll get to see some of the quirky innovations designed by Mr. Jefferson for his own comfort and pleasure. Among these is the bed installed between two rooms (so he could get up on whichever side he felt like), a "polygraph" writing contraption that made duplicates of his letters, a revolving table, and a dumbwaiter that brought wine up from the cellar.

Be sure to take a walk around the grounds, where you can appreciate Jefferson not only as a statesman, but as a progressive farmer deeply devoted to the land. There are several outbuildings to visit, including a kitchen and a wine cellar. The Thomas Jefferson Center for Historic Plants features interpretive gardens and exhibits. Here, visitors can purchase the offsprings of original Monticello plantings before strolling back to the entrance.

Continue down the road, then turn right onto Route 795 to nearby:

ASH LAWN–HIGHLAND (3), County Route 795, Charlottesville, VA 22902, ☎ (804) 293-9539, Internet: www.avenue.org/ashlawn. *Open daily; March–Oct. 9–6; Nov.–Feb. 10–5. Closed Thanksgiving, Christmas, and New Year's. Adults $7, seniors (60+) $6.50, children (6–11) $4. Special events. Music festival. Gift shop. Picnic facilities.* &.

Jefferson was not the only president to live in these parts. His close friend James Monroe (1758–1831) moved here in 1799, staying, on and off, until 1823. The site was selected by T.J. himself, who also helped with the design. Like Monticello, it strongly reflects the character of its owner, a man of the people who enjoyed a rather simple, cozy life. Although a later proprietor enlarged the modest house (and changed its name from Highland to Ash Lawn), it is today furnished with some original pieces along with appropriate antiques and memorabilia. Owned by Monroe's alma mater, the College of William and Mary, this working plantation also features crafts demonstrations, a summer music festival, old boxwood gardens, and its famous strolling peacocks.

Return along the same road, passing Monticello, and stop at the:

HISTORIC MICHIE TAVERN (4), Thomas Jefferson Parkway, Charlottesville, VA 22902, ☎ (804) 977-1234. *Open daily 9–5. Closed Christmas and New Year's. Adults $6, seniors (60+), students and military $5.50, children (6–11) $2. Tours. Wine museum. Gift shop. Restaurant with buffet lunch.*

William Michie built his inn in 1784, not here but on a well-traveled stagecoach route some 17 miles to the northwest. In 1927 it was moved, stick by stick, to the present location after a century and a half of operation. Today it's a museum filled with exceptional 18th-century artifacts, and surrounded with interesting outbuildings. The Virginia Wine Museum occupies the old wine cellar, while the grist mill houses a gift shop.

Return to Charlottesville, where you can tour the:

*UNIVERSITY OF VIRGINIA (5), University Ave. at Rugby Rd., ☎ (804) 924-7969, Internet: www.virginia.edu. *Tours daily at 10, 11, 2, 3, and 4. Closes for three weeks at Christmas time. Free.*

Thomas Jefferson's final achievement, after a lifetime of public service, was his founding in 1819 of the University of Virginia. Typically, he not only wrote the charter and raised the money, but also designed the buildings. And that is what makes a visit here so special. Tours begin at the **Rotunda**, the design of which he based on the Pantheon of ancient Rome. On either side of this are the original buildings of his "academical village," each in a different style to serve as architectural specimens. Between them spreads the **Lawn**, and beyond that the famous brick serpentine walls. In the student dormitories, in Room 13 no less, you can visit the quarters occupied by Edgar Allan Poe as a student in 1826.

If time permits, you might want to stroll around Charlottesville's **Downtown Historic District** (6), centering around Court Square and the shady, brick-paved **Pedestrian Mall** near the east end of Main Street.

Shenandoah National Park

One of America's classic scenic drives can be enjoyed on this rather long—but magnificent—excursion. Virginia's famous Skyline Drive, running the length of the Shenandoah National Park, offers stunning views and many opportunities for outdoor adventures along its 105 miles of mountaintop wilderness.

The park's facilities were largely created by the Civilian Conservation Corps as a work program during the Great Depression. From its long, high perch atop the Blue Ridge Mountains it overlooks the distant Alleghenies and the adjacent Shenandoah Valley, whose name means "Daughter of the Stars" in the Native American language.

It isn't necessary to drive the full length to get great pleasure from this trip; turnoffs can be made much earlier to such nearby attractions as the world-famous Luray Caverns, or the Civil War museums at New Market. If you do go the whole way, however, you might consider staying overnight and combining this excursion with the previous one to Charlottesville.

GETTING THERE:

By car, the northern entrance to the Park is at Front Royal, 71 miles west of Washington via Route **I-66** to Exit 6, then **US-340** south to the Skyline Drive.

The **Skyline Drive** extends 105 miles south, with intermediary exits at US-211 and US-33. Luray Caverns is nine miles west on US-211, and New Market another 12 miles.

Count on a total round-trip distance of at least 210 miles from Washington, D.C. (including a side trip to Luray Caverns), and about 365 miles if you drive the entire length.

PRACTICALITIES:

Such easily-accessible wilderness comes at a price, of course. Everyone knows about the drive, and it sometimes seems that everyone takes it at the same time. Avoid holidays, or weekends in spring or fall.

If you can manage it, the loveliest time to come is on a weekday during the fall foliage season.

Be prepared for cool weather, even in summer, and bring a sweater or light jacket for visiting the caves. Suitable footwear is essential if you plan to traipse over any of the 500 miles of trails, including portions of the Appalachian Trail.

The park is open daily all year round, but stretches of the drive might be closed during severe weather conditions. Restaurants along the way tend to be closed in winter.

For further information about the park and its Skyline Drive, contact the **Shenandoah National Park**, 3655 US Hwy. 211 East, Luray, VA 22835, ☎ (540) 999-3500, Internet: www.shenandoah.org. The **Shenandoah Valley Travel Association**, P.O. Box 1040, New Market, VA 22844, ☎ (540) 740-3132, Internet: www.svta.org., can help you with all of the other sights.

FOOD AND DRINK:

Restaurants along the Skyline Drive are concessionaire-operated, offering decent food at moderate prices. All are handicapped-accessible. You will also find a selection of eateries around Luray and New Market. Some choices are:

Skyland Lodge (Mile 41.7 of Skyline Drive) This large mountain inn was founded in 1894, and offers suitably rustic meals. ☎ (540) 999-2211. X: Dec.–March. $ and $$

Big Meadows Lodge (Mile 51.2 of Skyline Drive) Dining with a rustic mountain atmosphere, cuisine to match. ☎ (540) 999-2221. X: Nov.–mid-May. $ and $$

Panorama Restaurant (Mile 31.5 of Skyline Drive) Both light and full meals, served with a view. X: mid-Nov.–Apr. $

Brookside Restaurant (US-211, 4.5 miles east of Luray) The extensive menu here includes steak, seafood, and a salad bar ☎ (540) 743-5698. X: mid-Dec.–early Jan. $

Picnics are a great idea in the park, with seven picnic areas provided along the entire length.

SUGGESTED TOUR:

Numbers in parentheses correspond to numbers on the map.

Enter the park at **Front Royal** (1), paying the use fee. *$10 per car, $5 motorcycle, bicycle, or pedestrian. Valid 7 days.* All distances along the Skyline Drive are measured from here. Head south 4.5 miles to the **Dickey Ridge Visitor Center** (2), where you can get free maps, current information about the various amenities along the way, and advice

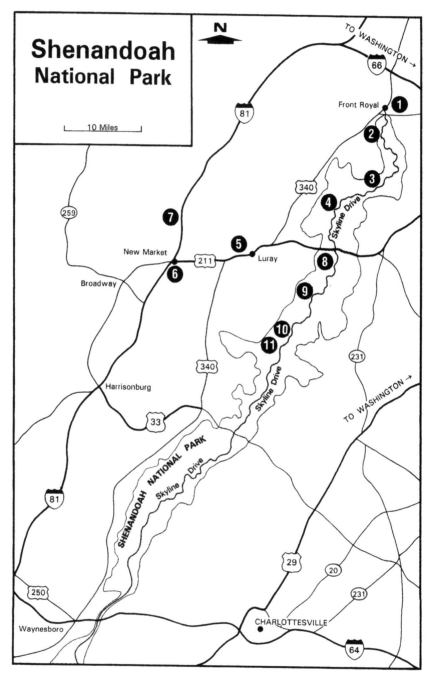

about short hikes that can be taken from points along the drive. ☎ *(540) 635-3566. Open daily, Apr.–Oct. Bookstore. Picnic facilities.* &.

Near Mile 21 is the **Hogback Overlook** (3) with its spectacular panoramic views. Several short trails lead off from here. There's another rest stop at **Elkwallow Wayside** (4), at Mile 24, offering supplies, food, and picnic tables. *Open daily, May–Oct.*

Coming up in a few miles is the intersection with Route **US- 211**, where you can exit the park for the moment to visit one of the area's premier attractions:

*LURAY CAVERNS (5), US-211 Bypass, 9 miles west of Skyline Drive, P.O. Box 748, Luray, VA 22835, ☎ (540) 743-6551, Internet: www.luray caverns.com. *Open daily, 9–4, 5, 6, or 7 depending on season. Adults $14, seniors and active military $12, children (7–13) $6. Admission includes tour plus Historic Car & Carriage Caravan. Interior temperature is 54°F. Gift shop. Restaurant.*

The first visitors to this subterranean wonderland descended deep into the earth by rope in 1878, discovering one enormous cavern after another. Today's guests are taken through on comfortable, hour-long conducted tours, but the sights encountered are the same. Every color of the rainbow is reflected from the cavern walls, the stalactites, and stalagmites. Among the highlights is the unique ***Great Stalacpipe Organ**, in which the natural acoustic qualities of the rocks are electronically activated to produce concert-quality music.

Admission to the caverns includes a visit to the adjacent **Historic Car and Carriage Caravan**, an exhibition of some 140 wheeled vehicles dating from as long ago as 1625. Its treasures include an 1892 Benz, a 1906 Ford, a 1908 Baker Electric, a 1911 Hupmobile, a 1913 Stanley Steamer, and Rudolph Valentino's 1925 Rolls Royce.

The town of **New Market** (6), about 12 miles west on US-211, remembers its Civil War past at the poignant **New Market Battlefield Historical Park**. Spread over 280 acres of land where the costly Battle of New Market raged on May 15, 1864, the site includes the **Hall of Valor** with its artifacts, dioramas, and films dealing with the tragic conflict. There is also a restored farmhouse where the wounded were treated, and walking tours of the battlefield. The complex is operated by the Virginia Military Institute to honor their cadets who fought and died in this desperate battle. ☎ *(540) 740-3101. Open daily 9–5. Closed Thanksgiving, Christmas, and New Year's. Adults $5, children $2.* &.

Nearby is the separate **New Market Battlefield Military Museum**, a private collection of over 2,000 artifacts from all American wars, from the

Revolution to the present. ☎ *(540) 740-8065. Open mid-March to Dec. 1. Adults $6, seniors $5, children (7–15) $3.* ♿.

Another notable cave in the area, this one accessible to the handicapped, is **Shenandoah Caverns** (7). Visitors descend 220 feet by elevator, emerging in a wondrous subterranean world of glistening formations. Take Route I-81 four miles north to Exit 269. ☎ *(540) 477-3115. Open daily, 9–4:15, 5:15, or 6:15 depending on season. Adults $12, seniors $10.50, children (5–14) $5.50, under 5 free. Cave temperature is 56° F. Free picnic area.* ♿.

At this point you could return to Washington via routes I-81 or US-340, followed by I-66—or continue down **Skyline Drive**. Following the latter, you can choose from over seven picnic areas. **Panorama** (8) near Mile 31, boasts a restaurant and a host of other facilities including a trail to nearby Marys Rock. The road tunnels under this as it continues south to **Skyland Lodge** (9) near Mile 42. Founded in 1894 as a summer retreat, the lodge has grown into a 186-room complex complete with restaurant, shops, horseback riding, pony rides, and the Stony Man Nature Trail. ☎ *(800) 999-4714 for lodging information. Open early April through Nov.* ♿.

Just down the road is the **Byrd Visitor Center** (10), complete with exhibits on local natural history, ranger programs, information, and other National Park services. ☎ *(540) 999-3283. Open Apr.–Dec., daily 9–5, and possibly weekends the rest of the year.* ♿. The **Big Meadows Wayside** and **Big Meadow Lodge** (11), practically next door, offer various accommodations, restaurants, service station, picnic grounds, and nature trails. *Open mid-May through Oct.*

You have so far driven only about half of the Skyline Drive. Beyond this, there are three additional picnic areas and the beauty continues. The next exit is at **Swift Run Gap**, Mile 65.7, where US-33 can take you east to US-29, leading north back to Washington. If you want to go all the way, the final exit is at Rockfish Gap, 18 miles west of Charlottesville.

Section IV

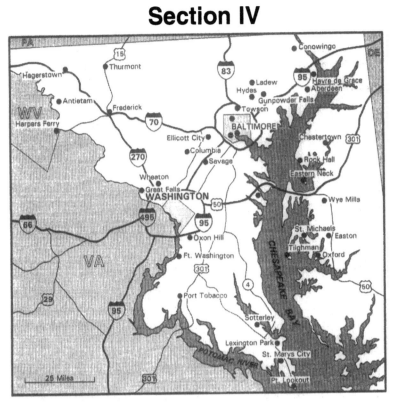

DAYTRIPS TO
MARYLAND

Practically surrounding Washington, Maryland offers the greatest choice of daytrip destinations within the shortest distance from the nation's capital. As in Virginia, there are plenty of preserved Colonial towns and Civil War sites, grand mansions and natural beauty spots. The Chesapeake Bay region, especially on the Eastern Shore, has a quiet charm you won't find elsewhere. Maryland is also blessed with Baltimore, easily one of the most interesting, urbane cities in America, and surely among the most enjoyable.

This section ventures briefly into West Virginia for a look at Harpers Ferry, an historically important town that's famous for its spectacular views.

Those with more leisure time can link several of the excursions together into a mini-vacation, staying overnight at inns along the way.

Montgomery County

Suburban Maryland begins in Montgomery County, an area rich in widely-spaced attractions appealing to a broad range of interests. You won't want to see them all, so it makes little sense to attempt an itinerary. Instead, pick out those that catch your fancy and head directly to them.

Among the highlights are a chance to jump back in time aboard a C&O canal boat, ride a 1920's carousel, and go for a trip on an historic trolley car. There are also such beauty spots as the Great Falls of the Potomac, and the lovely Brookside Gardens. Those in need of exercise can stroll down several nature trails, or take a walking tour of historic old Rockville.

GETTING THERE:

By car, Great Falls is about 16 miles northwest of downtown Washington, passing Glen Echo and the Clara Barton site along the way. Rockville lies about 17 miles north of central D.C., while the Trolley Museum and Wheaton Park are a few miles east of it. Use the map to locate the sites, then a more detailed road map to plot your route.

PRACTICALITIES:

Most of the sites are open daily, except on Thanksgiving, Christmas, or New Year's Day. **Canal boat rides** operate from mid-April through October, on Wednesdays through Sundays. The Glen Echo **Carousel** runs on weekends and Wednesdays from May to September. The **Trolley Museum** has a complex schedule, basically operating on weekends all year round, and on Memorial Day, July 4th, and Labor Day. During July and August it also runs on Wednesdays.

For further information, phone the sites directly or contact the **Conference & Visitors Bureau of Montgomery County,** 12900 Middlebrook Road, Suite 1400, Germantown, MD 20874, ☎ 301-428-9702 or 800-925-0880, Internet: www.cvcmontco.com.

FOOD AND DRINK:

You'll find a vast assortment of restaurants all over these affluent suburbs, including:

Old Angler's Inn (10801 MacArthur Blvd., near the southeast corner of Great Falls Park) Long a favorite rendezvous, this 1860 inn now features contemporary American cuisine. Reservations advised, ☎ 301-365-2425. X: Mon. $$ and $$$

Normandie Farm (10710 Falls Rd., MD-189, Potomac, near Great Falls) French provincial cuisine served in a romantic, rustic atmosphere. Reservations suggested, ☎ 301-983-8838. X: Mon. $$

Cottonwood Café (4844 Cordell Ave., near Woodmont Ave., Bethesda) Southwest American cuisine with an accent on healthy dishes. ☎ 301-656-4844. X: Sun. lunch. $$

Würzburg Haus (7236 Muncaster Mill Rd., MD-115, in Red Mill Shopping Center, just north of Rockville) It's a little bit out of your way, but if you crave German food, this is the place. ☎ 301-330-0402. $$

Tako Grill (7756 Wisconsin Ave. at Cheltenham Rd. in Bethesda) A popular, modern place serving a broad range of Japanese dishes at affordable prices. ☎ 301-652-7030. $ and $$

Foong Lin (7710 Norfolk Ave., at Fairmont Ave. in Bethesda) All sorts of Chinese specialties in a friendly setting. ☎ 301-656-3427. $

Original Pancake House (7700 Wisconsin Ave. in Bethesda) Pancake, crêpes, sandwiches, salads, and the like. X: evenings. ☎ 301-986-0285. $

Fritzbe's (1592 Rockville Pike, MD-355, in Rockville) American favorites, from salads and sandwiches to full meals. ☎ 301-984-8890. $

There are both seasonal concessionaires and picnic facilities at the C&O Great Falls Park, and at Glen Echo Park.

LOCAL ATTRACTIONS:

Numbers in parentheses correspond to numbers on the map.

*C&O CANAL NATIONAL HISTORICAL PARK at GREAT FALLS (1), 11710 MacArthur Blvd., Potomac, MD 20854, ☎ 301-299-3613, Internet: www.nps.gov/choh. *Park and museum open daily 9–5. Closed Thanksgiving, Christmas, and New Year's Day. Boat rides Wed.–Sun.; mid-April through Oct. Park entrance $4 per vehicle. Boats rides: Adults $7.50, seniors $6 and children $4. Exhibits. Picnic facilities. Snack bar.* ♿, *partial access.*

The **Chesapeake and Ohio Canal** (see page 00), incorporating sections of George Washington's Potomack Canal of 1785, was begun in 1828 as a shipping route from Georgetown to Pittsburgh, running a projected distance of 364 miles. By 1850 it had reached 184.5 miles west to Cumberland, MD, when construction ceased due to competition from

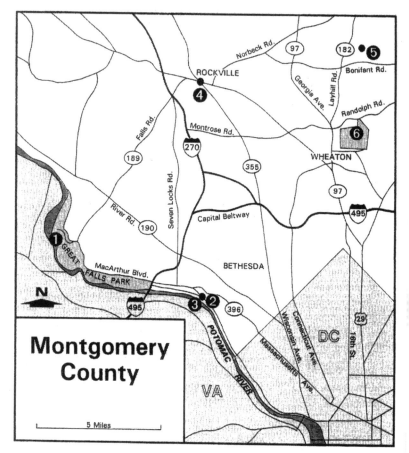

Montgomery County

N

5 Miles

the vastly more efficient B&O Railroad. The canal remained in service until 1924, became derelict, and was later partially restored as a National Historical Park. The section around **Great Falls Tavern**, like that at Georgetown (see page 00), today looks much as it did in the 19th century. The 60-minute mule-drawn ***boat rides** are a lot of fun as they work their way through a lock, with costumed crew members telling canal stories and history. The old tavern of 1830 is now a **museum** of canal-era artifacts, and you can take a wonderful walk along the towpath to the glorious ***Great Falls** of the Potomac River.

GLEN ECHO PARK (2), 7300 MacArthur Blvd., Glen Echo, MD 20812, ☎ 301-492-6282. *Park open daily except Thanksgiving, Christmas, and New*

Year's. Carousel rides May–Oct., weekends noon–6 and Wed. 10–2. Museum daily 10–5. Many programs and performances on varying schedules. Park is free, rides 50¢, performance prices vary. Picnic facilities. Snack bar in season.

Begun in 1891 as a Chautauqua cultural society, Glen Echo became a popular amusement park in 1911, remaining in business until 1968. Many of its rides survive as artifacts of that era, but only the **Dentzel Carousel** of 1921 still operates. Taken over in 1976 by the National Park Service, Glen Echo lives again as a cultural arts center with painters, potters, puppeteers, and all kinds of performers busy creating. There's a museum, and various theatrical shows.

Practically next door, and using the same parking lot, is the:

CLARA BARTON NATIONAL HISTORIC SITE (3), 5801 Oxford Rd., Glen Echo, MD 20812, ☎ 301-492-6245, Internet: www.nps.gov/clba. *Open daily 10–5. House shown by guided tour on the hour 10–4. Closed Thanksgiving, Christmas, New Year's Day. Tours. Free. &, partial access.*

Clara Barton (1821–1912), the founder of the American Red Cross, used this house as her home and headquarters from 1897 until her death in 1912. Erected on land donated by the developers of the adjacent Chautauqua, it also served as a home for as many as 25 volunteers as well as housing offices of the Red Cross. The building was saved from possible destruction in 1963 by a local group of concerned citizens, and deeded to the National Park Service in 1975. Of particular interest are the deep closets used to store disaster relief supplies, and the restored Red Cross offices.

Rockville (4) has been the county seat since 1776, and has a lovely old downtown area with historic houses. A visit to the town should begin at the **Beall-Dawson House** of 1815, now used by the local historical society. Its interior is filled with furnishings from the Federal and Victorian periods, and has an adjacent **medical museum** in a Civil-War era doctor's office. The gift shop here offers a *Walking Guide to Peerless Rockville* booklet for your self-guided tour. *103 W. Montgomery Ave. (MD-28),* ☎ *301-762-1492. Open Tues.–Sat. noon–4, and first Sun. of each month 2–5. Closed New Year's Day, July 4 and Dec. 25. Adults $3, seniors and students over 13 $2.* Among the sights in town are the old **B&O Railroad Station** and Wire Hardware Company at Baltimore Road and Church Street and, strangely, the **graves of F. Scott and Zelda Fitzgerald** by St. Mary's Church at 520 Viers Mill Road, corner of Rockville Pike (MD-355).

A few miles to the east is the:

NATIONAL CAPITAL TROLLEY MUSEUM (5), 1313 Bonifant Rd., Silver Spring, MD 20905, ☎ 301-384-6088, Internet: www.dctrolley.org. *Open Jan.–Nov., weekends, Memorial Day, July 4, and Labor Day, noon–5; plus Wed. during July and Aug. 11–3, and weekends in Dec. 5–9 p.m. Admission free. Trolley rides: Adults $2.50, children ages 2–17 $2, under 2 free. Last trolley departs 30 minutes before closing. Gift shop.*

A magnificent collection of trolleys from Washington, Alexandria, New York, and as far away as Graz, Austria take turns clanging their way through scenic Northwest Branch Park, much to the delight of passengers. Volunteers maintain the cars and tracks, and host a variety of special events. The Visitor Center has exhibits on the history of Washington's streetcars, an operating model trolley line as it looked in the 1920s, and an interactive computer exhibit.

WHEATON REGIONAL PARK and BROOKSIDE GARDENS (6), 1500 Glenallan Ave. near Randolph and Kemp Mill roads, Wheaton, MD 20902, ☎ 301-949-8230. *Open daily 9–5. Closed Christmas. Nominal charge for some park activities.* &.

Wheaton's famous **Brookside Gardens** are lovely throughout the year, and especially so in fall. Whatever the season, there's always something blooming in the conservatories. The Japanese Garden with its teahouse and tranquil ponds attracts many visitors.

Elsewhere in the park is a **Nature Center** and a host of outdoor recreational facilities, including horseback riding, skating, bike trails, an antique carousel, a miniature train ride, and a small children's farm.

*Annapolis

Maryland's capital since 1695, and home to the United States Naval Academy since 1845, the seafaring town of Annapolis remains one of the most attractive daytrip destinations in the Washington area. Although it boasts many fine Colonial buildings along its shady streets, this is really a thriving town of today, complete with a youthful population of students, "middies," and government workers.

Annapolis was founded in 1649 and later named for Princess Anne, who became Queen of England in 1702. From November 1783 until August 1784 it was the capital of the United States.

A leisurely stroll through the compact Historic District will take you past the colorful docks, where you can enjoy a boat ride, then to the U.S. Naval Academy for a guided tour. Following that are several historic houses than can be visited, an amble across the campus of St. John's College, a tour of the oldest State House to remain in use in America, and a few intriguing museums before returning to the docks for a bit of people watching at one of the outdoor cafés.

GETTING THERE:

By car, Annapolis is about 30 miles east of Washington via Route US-50. Take Exit 24 onto Rowe Boulevard (MD-70), heading southeast into town. The best place to park is at the Navy-Marine Corps Stadium on your right, from which a shuttle bus runs into the Historic District every 20 minutes on weekdays only, from 6:30 a.m. to 8 p.m. Otherwise, use one of the commercial lots or garages downtown. Street parking is usually metered, always limited to two hours per day, and subject to merciless ticketing.

Buses operated by Greyhound/Trailways provide limited service between Washington and Annapolis, ☎ 800-231-2222 for information.

PRACTICALITIES:

Most of the sites are open daily, except on Thanksgiving, Christmas, or New Year's Day. A few minor attractions close on Mondays, and on some weekdays during January and February.

Taken all the way, the suggested walking tour is almost four miles in length.

For further information, contact the **Annapolis & Anne Arundel County Conference & Visitors Bureau**, 26 West Street, Annapolis, MD 21401, ☎ 410-280-0445, Internet: www.visit-annapolis.org. They have a convenient branch kiosk on the City Dock, open April through October, daily 10–5.

FOOD AND DRINK:

Annapolis abounds in lively tourist-oriented restaurants, mostly in the moderate price range. Some choices are:

Treaty of Paris (Maryland Inn, 16 Church Circle, a block northwest of the State House) Reservations are strongly recommended for dining at this classic 18th-century inn, where Continental and New American cuisine is prepared to perfection. ☎ 410-216-6340. $$$

Middleton Tavern (2 Market Space) Established in 1750, this rustic waterfront tavern offers seafood and American cuisine, both indoors and out. ☎ 410-263-3323. $$

McGarvey's Saloon (8 Market Space) Fans of micro-brewed beer will love the suds here. Seafood, steaks, burgers and the like are popular with a young crowd. ☎ 410-263-5700. $$

Riordans Saloon (26 Market Space) Crabcakes, prime ribs, and similar dishes are featured in the noisy upstairs dining room of this old pub. ☎ 410-263-5449. $$

Buddy's Crabs & Ribs (100 Main St., at Market Place) This huge warehouse of a place is upstairs, overlooking the waterfront. Its name is its menu. ☎ 410-219-1800. $ and $$

Chick & Ruth's Delly (165 Main St., south of the State House) Maryland's politicos eat here, and many of the sandwiches are named for the more infamous of them. Deli atmosphere, always open. ☎ 410-269-6737. $

SUGGESTED TOUR:

Numbers in parentheses correspond to numbers on the map.

Begin your walk at the **City Dock** (1), where you'll find a seasonal branch office of the helpful **Visitors Bureau**. Here you can get maps, brochures, and information on special events. Ask them about the delightful ***boat trips** offered by several different operators, some as short as 40 minutes.

At the end of the harbor is the restored **Market House** of 1858, again offering all sorts of foods, ready-to-eat and otherwise. The old brick **Victualling Warehouse** (2), just across the street, was built in the 18th century and used during the Revolution to store supplies for the

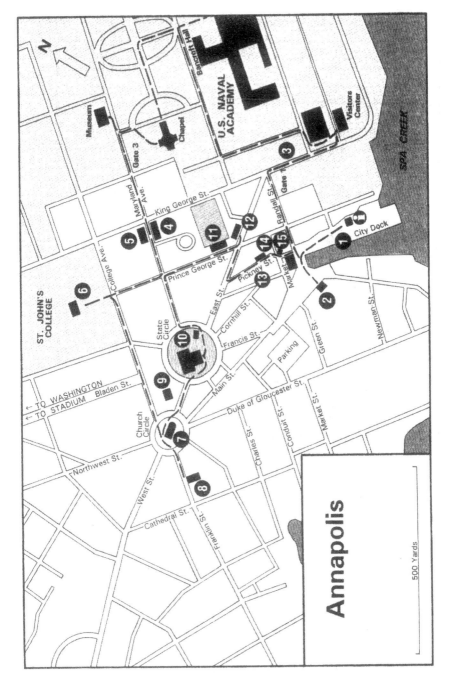

Annapolis

500 Yards

Continental Army and Navy. Today it houses the **Maritime Museum**, a small exhibition of Annapolis' history. If you wish, you can rent an audio-tour cassette guide here for a walking tour of the town. ☎ *410-268-5576. Open daily, 11–4:30.*

Follow the map around to the:

*UNITED STATES NAVAL ACADEMY (3), Annapolis, MD 21402, ☎ 410-263-6933, Internet: www.nadn.navy.mil. *Visitor Center open March–Dec. 9–5, Jan.–Feb. 9–4. Tours daily except Thanksgiving, Christmas, and New Year's; June through Labor Day, Mon.–Sat. 9:30–3:30, Sun. 12:15–3:30; Sept.–Nov. and Apr. through Memorial Day, Mon.–Fri. 10–3, Sat. 9:30–3:30, Sun. 12:15–3:30; Dec.–March, Mon.–Fri. 10–2:30, Sat. 9:30–3:30, and Sun. 12:30–2:30. Tours: Adults $5.50, seniors over 62 $4.50, students 1st–12th grades $3.50, under 6 free. Grounds free. Gift shop. Snack bar. &.*

Enter the grounds through Gate 1, at the foot of King George Street, and head directly for the **Armel-Leftwich Visitor Center** in Ricketts Hall, where you can join one of the frequent **guided tours** or get information for exploring on your own. Founded in 1845, the academy has some 4,000 students in training to be naval officers. They live in one of the world's largest dormitories, **Bancroft Hall**. The **Chapel**, where naval hero John Paul Jones is buried, has wonderful stained-glass windows. Seafaring artifacts, naval prints, and priceless ship models in wood, bone and gold many of which are by Tiffany Studios fill the **Academy Museum** in Preble Hall, as well as the U.S. Naval Institute bookstore.

Exit onto Maryland Avenue and head west to the:

HAMMOND-HARWOOD HOUSE (4), 19 Maryland Ave., ☎ 410-269-1714. *Open Mon.–Sat. 10–4, Sun. noon–4. Closed Thanksgiving, Christmas, New Year's. Adults $5, students (6–18) $3, under 6 free. Gift shop. &, by prior arrangement.*

William Buckland, a famous Colonial architect, designed this splendid mansion in 1774 for planter and legislator Mathias Hammond. It is considered to be the most important historic house in Maryland because it is the pinnacle of the Georgian style in America. This building, his last and arguably his greatest, is now filled with exquisite period furniture and fine arts, and is shown daily by guided tour. Especially renowned for his carved woodwork, Buckland has also created the interiors at Gunston Hall in Virginia (see page 000) and across the street from the Hammond-Harwood House at the Chase-Lloyd House.

Directly across the street is the:

CHASE-LLOYD HOUSE (5), 22 Maryland Ave., ☎ 410-263-2723. *Open Mar.–Dec., Tues.–Sat., 2–4; closed Jan. and Feb. Admission $2.*

Samuel Chase (1741–1811), a signer of the Declaration of Independence, was also one of America's first Supreme Court justices. Long before that, in 1769, he began construction on this house, which he sold unfinished to a rich planter named Edward Lloyd IV in 1771. Lloyd hired architect William Buckland (see above) to make it beautiful. You can see the lovely results, but only in a few rooms of the first floor as the rest of the house has long been used as a retirement home for elderly women. The mansion's most noted features are its spectacular "flying" *stairway and the carved marble mantlepiece in the parlor.

Turn north on Prince George Street to **St. John's College** (6), a small liberal arts school renowned for its Great Books curriculum and intellectual prowess. Founded in 1696 as King William's School, it claims to be the third-oldest college in the nation. A long brick path leads up to **McDowell Hall**, a grandiose structure built in 1742 as the Colonial governor's residence. Also on campus is the **Elizabeth Myers Mitchell Art Gallery** with its changing exhibitions (☎ *410-626-2556, open daily except Mon.*), and the ancient **Liberty Tree**, a tulip poplar believed to be over 400 years old. *Tours by appointment,* ☎ *410-263-2371.*

Continue west on College Avenue to Church Circle and **St. Anne's Church** (7). Built in 1859 on the site of a late 1600's church, it still uses a silver communion service presented to it by King William III in 1695. Inside, there's an interesting altar screen, and a stained-glass window depicting St. Anne and the Virgin. The graveyard holds the remains of Maryland's last Colonial governor, Sir Robert Eden. ☎ *410-267-9333. Open daily.*

Franklin Street leads west to the **Banneker-Douglass Museum of Afro-American Life and Culture** (8), which chronicles the African-American experience in Maryland and elsewhere through changing exhibitions, lectures, films and cultural activities. The museum is housed in the former Mount Moriah African Methodist Episcopal Church, an historic Victorian Gothic structure of 1874. ☎ *410-974-2893. Open Tues.–Fri. 10–3, Sat. noon–4. Free.*

Head down School Street, passing the **Governor's Mansion** (9) on your left. Built in 1868 in the Victorian style, it was remodeled in 1935 in the Colonial Revival manner, and houses a fine collection of Maryland antiques. *Tours by appointment, Tues.–Thurs. 10–2,* ☎ *410-974-3531.* &.

In the center of State Circle stands the:

*MARYLAND STATE HOUSE (10), ☎ 410-974-3400, Internet: www.mdis fun.org. *Open every day except Christmas, Mon.–Fri. 9–5, Sat. and Sun. 10–4. Free. Tours daily at 11 and 3, except Thanksgiving, Christmas, and New Year's. Visitors Center. ᕂ.*

Maryland's capitol, begun in 1772, is the oldest State House in the nation to remain in continuous legislative use, and the only one to have ever served as the nation's capitol. The Continental Congress met here from November 26, 1783, to August 13, 1784; this is where George Washington resigned as commander-in-chief in 1783; and where the Treaty of Paris ending the Revolutionary War was ratified in 1784.

In addition to the twice-daily guided tours through the major chambers, there are also various exhibits of historic artifacts, and a visitors center where you can get all kinds of information about Maryland.

A few steps east of the State House, on the same grounds, stands the tiny **Old Treasury Building** of 1735, the oldest public building in the state. *Open by appointment, ☎ 410-267-7619.* Now follow the map to the:

*WILLIAM PACA HOUSE & GARDEN (11), 186 Prince George St., ☎ 410-263-5553 or 800-603-4020, Internet: www.annapolis.org. *Open March–Dec., Mon.–Sat. 10–4, Sun. noon–4; Jan.–Feb., Fri.–Mon. only. Closed Thanksgiving, Christmas, and New Year's. Adults $7, seniors $6.50, children (6–18) $3.50, under 6 free. Gift shop.*

Yet another Annapolis resident who affixed his signature to the Declaration of Independence, William Paca (1740–99) was also governor of Maryland from 1782 until 1785. He built this magnificent Georgian mansion between 1763 and 1765 and, behind it, developed a fabulous ***garden** with formal parterres, waterways, a Chinese bridge, and a miniature wilderness. Nearly all was lost when the house became part of a hotel and the garden was paved over. In 1965 the hotel was pulled down to make way for a high-rise apartment house, but preservationists bought the property, saved the remains, dug up the garden, ran the most elaborate archaeological tests on everything, and were able to accurately reconstruct the whole site. Now fully restored, the house is furnished with period antiques dating from the time that the Pacas were in residence.

Near the corner of East Street stands the **Brice House** (12) of 1766, a fine example of Colonial craftsmanship whose splendid interior may be seen by appointment. ☎ *410-267-8149.* Head west on East Street, turning down Pickney Street to the **Barracks** (13) at number 43. As the name implies, this former dwelling was used during the Revolution to house soldiers awaiting battle, and is furnished to depict their lifestyle. It's open by appointment only, ☎ *410-267-7619*. Almost across the street is a rather stark tavern of around 1715, the **Shiplap House** (14), which just might be the oldest surviving building in town, and is said to be haunted. Again, you can visit its restored interior by prior arrangement, ☎ *410-267-7619*. Another sight you'll have to call ahead for is the **Tobacco Prise House** (15) at number 4. Maryland's significant tobacco industry is recalled in this restored 19th-century warehouse with exhibits and antique equipment, ☎ *410-267-7619*.

You are now back at the City Dock (1), where you can relax at a café or tavern, or just watch the boats.

Howard County

C onvenient to both Washington and Baltimore, Howard County
combines the best of suburbia with the genuinely rural. One of
its main towns is older than the nation itself, while another was
just farmland barely 30 years ago. A daytrip here offers the chance to
explore the historic old mill town of Ellicott City, the terminus of
America's first railroad line in 1830. Its old station is a museum now,
attracting both rail fans and normal people alike with its evocation of
railroading's earliest days. There's also a firehouse museum, restored
stone workers' houses, unusual shops, galleries, and a thriving arts-and-
crafts scene.

At the opposite end of the spectrum, but only a few miles away, is
Columbia, a completely planned city begun from scratch in 1966. And in
nearby Savage a 19th-century factory complex has been lovingly
restored as a handsome center for crafts, studios, antiques, and interesting stores.

GETTING THERE:

By car, Ellicott City is about 30 miles northeast of downtown
Washington via Route **US-29**.

Return south on US-29 to Columbia.

For Savage, head south on US-29, then east on **MD-32** to **US-1**, turning south there and following signs.

PRACTICALITIES:

Most of the sites along this trip are open daily; note however that
the B&O Railroad Station Museum is closed on Tuesdays in summer,
and on Tuesdays through Thursdays from Labor Day to Memorial Day.
The Firehouse Museum is open on Sundays only, closed on Easter and
Thanksgiving weekends, and closed from Christmas through New Year's
Day.

For further information contact the **Howard County Tourism Council**,
8267 Main St., Ellicott City, MD 21043, ☎ 410-313-1900 or 800-288-TRIP,
Internet: www.howardcountymdtour.com.

FOOD AND DRINK:

Some choice restaurants are:

King's Contrivance (10150 Shaker Drive, east of US-29, just north of MD-32, Columbia) Fine dining in a romantic old country mansion; French and Continental cuisine. Reservations advised, ☎ 410-995-0500. X: weekend lunch, some holidays. $$ and $$$

Crab Shanty (3410 Plumtree Drive, US-40W west of junction with US-29, Ellicott City) Some of suburbia's best seafood is served here, and for landlubbers there's also beef and chicken. ☎ 410-465-9660. X: Sat. lunch. $$

Bombay Peacock Grill (10005 Old Columbia Rd., at Eden Brook Dr., Columbia) Excellent Indian cuisine, with a great lunch buffet. ☎ 410-381-7111. $$

Clydes of Columbia (10221 Wincopin Circle, in the center of Columbia) This tavern features a wide range of American dishes, from sandwiches to full meals. ☎ 410-730-2829. $ and $$

China Chefs (10801 Hickory Ridge Rd. and Cedar Lane, south of Little Patuxent Pkwy., near the hospital) Good-value Chinese cuisine, especially the Szechwan dishes. ☎ 410-730-1200. $

The Canopy (9319 Baltimore Nat'l Pike, US-40, in Ellicott City) A pit stop for Baltimore-style sandwiches. ☎ 410-465-5718. $

LOCAL ATTRACTIONS:

Numbers in parentheses correspond to numbers on the map.

Ellicott City (1) was settled in 1774 by three Quaker brothers from Pennsylvania named Ellicott. Here, on the banks of the Patapsco River, they built a gristmill and a wharf for shipping their grain. Ironworks and rolling mills followed, and in 1830 the booming industrial town became the first railroad terminus in America when a locomotive named "Tom Thumb" puffed its way down 13 miles of track from Baltimore. The first U.S. President to ride the rails, Andrew Jackson, boarded his train here in 1833.

Much of Ellicott City's early 19th-century industrial past remains intact, preserved as specialty shops, antique dealers, restaurants, and the like. Its narrow streets and winding alleyways, lined with tiny stone houses and even log cabins, reveal some surprising sights, especially along **Tongue Row.**

That first train station, built in 1830, is now the:

*B&O RAILROAD STATION MUSEUM, 2711 Maryland Ave. at Main St., ☎ 410-460-1944. *Open Memorial Day to Labor Day, Wed.–Mon. 11–4; rest of year Fri.–Mon. 11–4. Closed major holidays. Adults $3, seniors over 64 $2,*

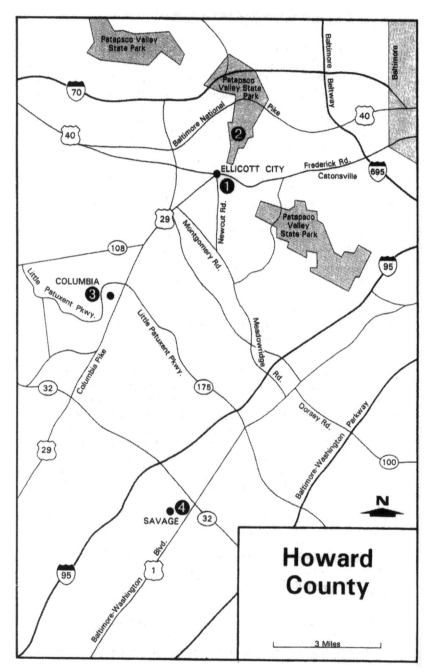

under 13 $1. Gift shop.

The first 13 miles of railway in America are brought back to life with an **operating HO-gauge model**, one of several fascinating attractions in an 1885 freight house adjacent to the original granite stone station of 1830. There are also displays of railroading artifacts, a video on the history of the B&O, and restored rooms including the freight agent's living quarters. Outside, you can examine a partially-excavated turntable from the mid-1800s, and explore the insides of a 1927 caboose.

Elsewhere in town is the **Firehouse Museum** with its small collection of historic firefighting artifacts, housed in an 1889 building that served as the firehouse until 1923. *3829 Church Rd., just off Main St.* ☎ *410-313-2762 or 410-313-2602. Open Sundays only, noon–4. Closed Easter and Thanksgiving weekends, and from Christmas through New Year's. Free.* While strolling around, take a look at the **Howard County Courthouse** of 1843 at 8370 Court Avenue, and the nearby **Historical Society Building** with its adjacent pre-1790 library.

Just north of Ellicott City is the **Patapsco Valley State Park** (2), a fine place for a nature break or a picnic. Woodland trails, a scenic overlook, fishing, and various other activities are among its offerings. *8020 Baltimore National Pike (US-40),* ☎ *410-461-5005. Nominal fee per vehicle.*

Columbia (3), population 76,000 and growing fast, didn't even exist a few decades ago. Nine planned communities begun in 1966 surround a central urban area reached via the Little Patuxent Parkway. Naturally, there's an enormous mall, but there's also **Lake Kittamaqundi** (☎ *410-730-1112*) with its picnic facilities, boat rentals, and fishing conveniently near the town center. The **Maryland Museum of African Art**, also close by, exhibits traditional arts and crafts from African societies. *5430 Vantage Point Rd.,* ☎ *410-730-7105. Open Tues.–Fri. 10–4, Sun. noon–4, closed holidays. Adults $2, seniors and children 2–12 $1.*

Savage (4), south of I-95 at Route 32, isn't quite as new as Columbia. In fact, its historic **Savage Mill** complex dates from as far back as 1822 and continued to produce cotton duck for sail canvas until after World War II. Today, it's been carefully restored and its interiors converted into a combination museum, arts-and-crafts center, antiques emporium, and upscale shopping experience. *8600 Foundry St., Mill Box 2022, Savage, MD 20763,* ☎ *410-792-2820. Open daily 10–6, until 9 on Thurs., Fri. and Sat. Free entry. Restaurants.* &.

Next to the mill is the unique **Bollman Truss Railroad Bridge** of 1869, the only one of its type left in the world, and now an historic landmark. **Savage Park**, also adjacent to the mill, offers nature trails and a picnic area.

*Baltimore's Inner Harbor

Not so very long ago, "Bawlamer" just wasn't much of a tourist destination. How times have changed! Ever since the stunning renaissance of its Inner Harbor breathed new life into a decaying waterfront, Baltimore has become a symbol of urban renewal at its best. Exciting changes, underway since the 1960s in the downtown business district, began to totally transform the harbor with the 1980 opening of Harborplace, followed by the National Aquarium in 1981. Each successful attraction encouraged others, until the entire mile-and-a-half-long stretch from Oriole Park to Little Italy became chockablock with worthwhile sights, some among the best of their kind in the nation.

One of America's great cities, Baltimore is also among its oldest. Established in 1729, it was named in honor of George Calvert (1580–1632), the first Lord Baltimore and the founder of Maryland. Its fine natural harbor at the end of the Patapsco River on Chesapeake Bay made it a major shipbuilding center and commercial port from the very start. During the Revolutionary War it briefly served as the capital of the infant nation, and successfully defended itself against British attack throughout the War of 1812. As an industrial center, it prospered well into the 20th century until after World War II. Then, as America's competitiveness in manufacturing declined, Baltimore experienced the same problems facing other older cities. Prompt, bold action on the part of leading citizens and an activist mayor have brought the city back to life with new business ventures, making it more attractive than ever.

Along this walking tour you can visit what many regard as the world's most exciting aquarium, board an historic warship, climb through a submarine, take boat rides around the harbor, enjoy the local seafood specialties, learn something at a hands-on science center, shop till you drop, sit at outdoor cafés overlooking the whole scene, and explore a preserved seafaring neighborhood. As you stroll along, you'll discover that Baltimore is not only interesting, it's just plain fun as well! And, for those with kids in tow, it may be the best of all possible trips.

While you're here, why not see more of this amazing city? The next two chapters explore other fascinating parts of town, either on foot or by car. After that, the book takes a look at nearby areas to the north, as previous chapters visited those to the south. If you stay over for a few days, you'll find that Baltimore makes an excellent base for all but the southernmost of the one-day excursions described in this book.

GETTING THERE:

By car, downtown Baltimore is about 40 miles northeast of downtown Washington via Route I-95. Get off at Exit 53 and follow I-395 north to Oriole Park at Camden Yard. Turn right on Pratt Street, keeping an eye out for the first available parking lot.

Trains operated by **Amtrak** provide frequent service between Washington's Union Station and Baltimore's Penn Station. The run takes about 35 minutes. For current schedules and fare information, ☎ 800-USA-RAIL, Internet: www.northeast.amtrak.com. From Penn Station in Baltimore, board a MTA bus on St. Paul Street to Inner Harbor, or walk 1.5 miles south along Charles Street.

Alternatively, on weekdays you can save quite a few dollars by taking a slower **MARC** commuter train from Washington's Union Station to either Penn Station in Baltimore (50 minutes), or Camden Station near Baltimore's Inner Harbor (1 hour). These are two completely different routes. Your savings will be even greater if you buy a round-trip ticket. There is no MARC service on weekends. ☎ 800-543-9809 or, in MD, 800-325-7245 for current information.

PRACTICALITIES:

Good weather will enhance your visit to the Inner Harbor, which is especially enjoyable between mid-spring and mid-fall. If you do come in the dead of winter, however, there are enough museums and other indoor attractions to keep you happily occupied all day long.

Nearly all of the sights are open daily, except possibly on Thanksgiving, Christmas, and New Year's. A few other exceptions are: the Public Works Museum closes on Mondays, as does the Museum of Industry, which also closes on Tuesdays in the off-season.

Advance reservations (see below) are advisable for the National Aquarium during the peak tourist season. Otherwise, try to stop by their ticket booth as early as possible to avoid long waiting lines.

Not including any side trips, the suggested walk is only two miles long, level all the way.

For further information, contact or visit the **Baltimore Area Visitors Center** at 451 Light Street, Baltimore, MD 21202, near Harborplace. ☎ 410-837-4636 or 800-282-6632, Internet: www.baltimore.org. They have a convenient branch booth on the west side of the harbor.

FOOD AND DRINK:

You'll find countless places to eat around the Inner Harbor, especially in the two pavilions of the Harborplace. The food court upstairs in the Light Street Pavilion has an eclectic selection of the world's cuisines at modest prices, with both indoor and outdoor waterside seating.

Among the better full-service restaurants, both here and at Fell's Point, are:

Phillips (Light St. Pavilion, Harborplace) Abundant seafood platters, live entertainment, and a waterside patio make this one of the harbor's most successful restaurants. ☎ 410-685-6600. $$

Paolo's (Light St. Pavilion, Harborplace) A slick, very popular spot for modern Italian/American dishes. Right on the harbor, indoor/outdoor dining. ☎ 410-539-7060. $$

Planet Hollywood (Pratt St. Pavilion, Harborplace) Burgers, salads and such in a setting of Hollywood glitz. ☎ 410-685-7827. $ and $$

Capitol City Brewing (Light St. Pavilion, Harborplace) Micro brews, burgers, and fancier dishes. ☎ 410-539-7468. $ and $$

Bertha's (734 S. Broadway, at Lancaster St., Fell's Pt.) Everyone comes to Bertha's for mussels, or for other good seafood. There's also an afternoon tea, for which reservations are needed. ☎ 410-327-5795. $ and $$

Donna's (Pratt St. Pavilion, Harborplace) A clean, contemporary place for marvelous sandwiches, salads, foccacia, and the like. ☎ 410-752-9040. $

Hard Rock Café (Power Plant, 601 E. Pratt St. at Market Place) Good burgers and salads with loud rock music and memorabilia. ☎ 410-347-7625. $

SUGGESTED TOUR:

Numbers in parentheses correspond to numbers on the map.

You might as well begin your walk with an overview. The **World Trade Center** (1), right on the Inner Harbor, is the world's tallest pentagonal building, and offers a splendid *view from its 27th-floor **Top of the World** observation deck. Along with the panorama, you get multi-media presentations and hands-on exhibits on the history of Baltimore. ☎ *410-837-8439. Open Mon.–Sat. 10–5, Sun. noon–5. Adults $3, seniors and children 5–15 $2. Gift shop.* ♿.

Close by is the city's number-one attraction, the:

***NATIONAL AQUARIUM IN BALTIMORE** (2), Pier 3, 501 East Pratt St., ☎ 410-576-3800, TDD 410-625-0720, Internet: www.aqua.org. *Open: Jul. and Aug. 9–8 daily; Nov.–Feb. Sat.–Thurs 10–5, Fri. 10–8; March–June, Sept.

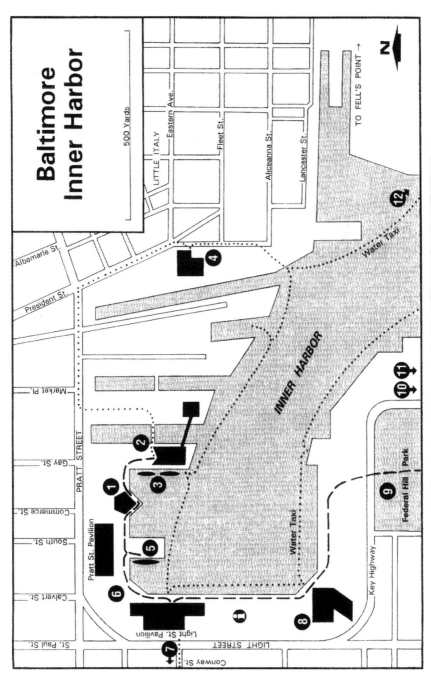

and Oct., Sat.–Thurs. 9–5, Fri. 9–8. Adults $14, seniors $10.50, children 3–11 $7.50, under 3 free. Reserved advance tickets through TicketMaster, ☎ *410-481-SEAT, out of state 800-551-SEAT. Gift shop. Café with light lunches.* ⅗.

Plan to spend at least two hours immersed, as it were, in this aquatic world of wondrous sights. Seven levels of exhibits feature over 10,000 creatures from all over the world, including such exotic species as poison-dart frogs, piranha, sharks, and stingrays. Moving sidewalks on elevated bridges transport visitors from habitats as diverse as the frozen Icelandic coast to tropical rain forests. In the **Marine Mammal Pavilion** you'll see bottlenose dolphins performing in an educational show enhanced with hands-on experiences, and in the **Aquarium Rain Forest** you'll walk through a jungle filled with the strangest creatures. The **Children's Cove** allows young explorers to handle live marine animals as they stroll along a rocky seashore and even more hands-on opportunities are offered at the **Exploration Station.**

Adjacent to the aquarium are the floating vessels of the:

BALTIMORE MARITIME MUSEUM (3), Pier 3, E. Pratt St., ☎ 410-396-3854. *Open Mon.–Fri. 11–5, Sat.–Sun. 10–5. Adults $5.50, seniors over 59 $4.50, children 5–12 $3, active duty military with ID $2.*

The star attraction here is a self-guided tour of the last American submarine to sink an enemy ship during World War II, the **U.S.S.** *Torsk.* This fierce-looking warrior first put to sea on the final day of 1944, fought in the Pacific, and later saw duty in Lebanon and in the naval blockade of Cuba. You can also climb aboard the lightship *Chesapeake,* a fully operational floating lighthouse built in 1930; as well as the retired Coast Guard Cutter *Taney,* a survivor of Pearl Harbor.

From here, you might want to make a little **side trip** by Water Taxi (see below) or on foot to the:

BALTIMORE PUBLIC WORKS MUSEUM (4), 751 Eastern Ave., ☎ 410-396-5565. *Open year-round Tue.–Sun. 10–4. Adults $2.50, seniors and students $2, children (6–17) $1.50.* ⅗, *limited access, call ahead.*

Children, especially, might enjoy learning about the unusual side of things most people take for granted, like municipal water supply, sewage, roads, and bridges. Located in a functioning, historic pumping station, America's first museum of its kind features exhibitions, multimedia shows, a "Streetscape" outdoor re-creation of underground utilities, and various children's activities including a hands-on construction site, water meter tracings and interactive computer programs.

Return to the foot of Pier 3 and stroll over to the:

U.S.S. *CONSTELLATION* (5), Pier 1, 301 E. Pratt St., ☎ 410-539-1797, Internet: www.constellation.org. *Open daily 10-8. Adults $6, seniors $4.75, children $3.50, under 4 free.*

The U.S.S. *Constellation* was first built in 1797 as one of the original six frigates commissioned by the U.S. Congress. It was also the first American-built ship to defeat an enemy man-of-war on the high seas, during a long-forgotten conflict with France that took place in the Caribbean from 1798 until 1801. Later fighting in the Barbary Wars against Tripoli, the *Constellation* also saw action against the British in the War of 1812.

Totally rebuilt in Norfolk in 1853 as a sloop of war, its career extended through the Civil War, then as a training vessel at the U.S. Naval Academy, and finally as a relief flagship during World War II! Decommissioned in 1955, it was returned to the port where the original *Constellation* was first built, Baltimore.

By 1994 the ship had, unfortunately, deteriorated so badly that a complete restoration became necessary, and it was put into dry dock. Five years of work there have returned it to its Civil War appearance as a sloop. In 1999 it was returned to its Inner Harbor dock and once again opened to the public.

Although this tour is designed to be taken on foot, you can also get around by **Water Taxi**, a highly useful, enjoyable, and surprisingly inexpensive water bus service that makes about a dozen stops on routes stretching from here to Fell's point. ☎ *410-563-3901 or 800-658-8947. Service daily year-round. Runs at 12–15 minute intervals in season, less at other times. Tickets for unlimited use on day of purchase: Adults $3.50, children 10 and under, $2.25.*

If you'd like to take to the water on your own, you can rent **Paddle Boats** by the hour at the dock here. ☎ *410-563-3901. Daily, weather permitting, March–Oct.*

The opening of **Harborplace** (6) in 1980 was really the key to the economic rebirth of Baltimore's Inner Harbor. Often imitated by other cities, this glass-enclosed shopping and dining complex overlooking the water has been a phenomenal success largely because it is such an enjoyable place to visit. It consists of two main structures, the **Pratt Street Pavilion** and the **Light Street Pavilion**, separated by an amphitheater with free outdoor entertainment. The complex is connected to another shopping mall, **The Gallery**, as well as much of downtown Baltimore, by the overhead **Skywalk**. *Open Mon.–Sat. 10–10, Sun. noon–8.* ☎ *410-332-4191, Internet: www.harborplace.com.*

From here, you can make a little **side trip** to the **Old Otterbein Church** (7) of 1785. Built by German immigrants, it is the oldest surviving church in town. Some of the surrounding neighborhood also dates from the late 18th century, and has been restored through a 1970's program of "Urban Homesteading" in which abandoned houses were sold for a dollar apiece to people who would agree to renovate them with "sweat equity," and then live in them. To get there, cross Light Street and head west on Conway Street for two blocks.

Back at the Inner Harbor, continue south along the waterfront, passing the Visitors Center's handy branch kiosk where you can get current tourist information. While you're there, you might want to ask about the **harbor cruises** offered by several different firms, which depart from this area.

Continue south to the:

MARYLAND SCIENCE CENTER (8), 601 Light St., ☎ 410-685-5225, TDD 410-962-0223, Internet: www.mdsci.org. *Open mid-June to Labor Day, Mon.–Thurs. 10–6, Fri.–Sun. 10–8; remainder of the year Mon.–Fri. 10–5, weekends 10–6. Closed Thanksgiving and Christmas. Adults $10; seniors and students 13–17 $8. Children 4–12 $7. Science store. Additional showings of IMAX on Fri.–Sat. evenings at 8:30, 7:30 off-season, $7.* ♿.

Children, and adults too, can easily spend hours exploring the mysteries of the world around them in this modern, hands-on, user-friendly, fun-filled playpen for budding scientists. Admission also includes a stunning show at the **IMAX Theater**, whose five-story screen envelopes its audience with sensational images, and the **Davis Planetarium** for a stellar voyage. The **Crosby Ramsey Observatory** on the roof holds regular public sessions to observe the night sky through an 8" diameter telescope. Special events are held for eclipses and comets, and the telescope can be used to transmit images to the Davis Planetarium theater for special audience viewing. Besides the regular exhibits, there's always something new on at the Science Center.

Turn east past the marina, and uphill across Key Highway into **Federal Hill Park** (9) for the best ***view** of Baltimore. During the Civil War this was the site of Union fortifications, although Baltimore remained rather ambivalent in its loyalties.

About a half-mile to the southeast, reached either on foot, by bus, or by water taxi (see above), is the:

BALTIMORE MUSEUM OF INDUSTRY (10), 1415 Key Highway, ☎ 410-727-4808. *Open Memorial Day to Labor Day, Tues.–Fri. and Sun. noon–5, Sat. 10–5; remainder of the year, Thurs., Fri., and Sun. noon–5, Sat. 10–5, Wed. 6 p.m.–9 p.m. Closed Thanksgiving, Christmas Eve, Christmas. Adults $3.50, seniors over 60 and students with ID $2.50, families $12. Tug tour Mon.–Fri. 9–5, adults $2.50, children ages 6–18 $1.75.* ♿.

Another great place to bring the kids, the Museum of Industry takes visitors back to the wonderful age of sweatshop labor. Its waterfront location, in an 1870 oyster cannery set amid reminders of an industrial past, is the perfect place to experience the factory jobs of yesterday. Children can become "workers" in the Kid's Cannery, or punch in on a truck assembly line. You can also print your own handbills on an 1880 job press, visit a machine shop, and feel the power of the only operating steam tug in America, the S.S. *Baltimore* of 1906. There's a serious side to this, too, in the historical displays of the city's early industrial history.

Game for more? Bus number 1 or a mile-and-a-half-long hike southeast along Key Highway and Fort Avenue takes you to that most Star-Spangled of places, the:

FORT McHENRY NATIONAL MONUMENT (11), end of East Fort Ave., ☎ 410-962-4290, Internet: www.nps.gov/fomc. *Open June–Labor Day, daily 8–8; remainder of year, daily 8–5. Closed Christmas and New Year's. Admission $5, seniors and under 17 free. Commercial boat service to/from Inner Harbor. Picnicking. Walking trails. Ranger programs.* ♿.

A replica of the famous flag that inspired the national anthem flies over the fort where the British were defeated in the War of 1812. Francis Scott Key, a Washington lawyer sent to negotiate for the release of a Maryland doctor held by the British, was detained during the battle and witnessed first-hand the American triumph. Overjoyed, he immediately began composing the poem that was later set to the tune of an old English drinking song, and became known as *The Star-Spangled Banner*. The actual flag is in the Smithsonian's National Museum of American History in Washington (see page 34). It was sewn by a Baltimore lady, whose house is described on page 211.

Tours begin in the Visitor Center with an exhibition of historical artifacts, followed by an introductory film, after which you can explore the fort.

Another nice place to visit, especially late in the day, is the preserved old seafaring neighborhood of **Fell's Point** (12). Some 350 historic houses dating from the 18th and 19th centuries line the cobblestone streets; many of these now house shops, galleries, cafés, restaurants, and inns. Once the center of Baltimore's shipbuilding industry, this is now a delightful area in which to stroll around while soaking up the atmosphere. It can be reached by boat from Fort McHenry (summer only), by water taxi from the Museum of Industry or the Inner Harbor, or by land from the Inner Harbor.

Trip 27

Downtown Baltimore

Thousands of visitors descend on Baltimore to savor its Inner Harbor, but usually miss out on the more sophisticated treats that lie just north of the docks. If the waterfront is a playground for kids (and the child that lives in most everyone), downtown Baltimore is for grown-ups with developed tastes. Its historical and cultural highlights include restored houses and mansions from the 18th and 19th centuries, one of the nation's foremost art galleries, its first cathedral, an elegant neighborhood filled with unusual shops and restaurants, a market that has thrived since 1782, and a skywalk above the traffic in the booming business district.

GETTING THERE:

See the travel information for Baltimore's Inner Harbor on page 000.

PRACTICALITIES:

Avoid making this trip on a Monday, when most of the attractions are closed. A few close on Sundays instead, and several also close on some major holidays. Since the route takes you through the heart of the business district, you'll find more activity on weekdays.

The suggested walking tour is about three miles long, and somewhat hilly in spots. There's plenty of public transportation in this area if you get tired.

For further information, contact the **Baltimore Area Visitors Center** at 451 Light Street, near the Inner Harbor, ☎ 410-837-4636 or 800-282-6632, Internet: www.baltimore.org.

FOOD AND DRINK:

There's a wealth of good restaurants in this area, especially around North Charles Street. Among the best lunch choices for casual tourists are:

Sotto Sopra (405 N. Charles St. at Mulberry St.) Creative Italian cuisine served with grace and style. Reservations suggested, ☎ 410-625-0534. X: weekend lunches, major holidays. $$ and $$$

Kawasaki (413 N. Charles St., 3 blocks south of the Walters Art

Gallery) Superb Japanese cuisine at reasonable prices. Kawasaki is famous for its sushi and sashimi, but there's also teriyaki and tempura. ☎ 410-659-7600. X: Sat. lunch, Sun. $$

Purple Orchid (419 N. Charles St. at Franklin St.) Sophisticated cuisine combining French and Asian influences. ☎ 410-837-0080. X: weekend lunches. $$

Louies's Bookstore Café (518 N. Charles St., a block south of the Walters Art Gallery) Walk through the bookstore to reach the café, where an eclectic menu offers light lunches and dinner, both indoors and out. ☎ 410-962-1224. X: Sun. $

Akbar (823 N. Charles St., 2 blocks north of the Washington Monument) Tandoori as well as vegetarian dishes are featured in this small Indian restaurant, long a neighborhood fixture. ☎ 410-539-0944. $

Woman's Industrial Exchange (333 N. Charles St., 3 blocks south of the Walters Art Gallery) A wonderfully old-fashioned dining institution with simple food like Grandma used to make. ☎ 410-685-4388. X: weekends. $

Donna's Coffee Bar (2 W. Madison, at N. Charles St., a block north of the Walters Art Gallery) Salads, sandwiches, and fancier fare in a California-style eatery. ☎ 410-385-0180. $

SUGGESTED TOUR:
Numbers in parentheses correspond to numbers on the map.

Begin your walk on the north side of the Inner Harbor, following Pratt Street east across the expressway to Albemarle Street.

THE STAR-SPANGLED BANNER FLAG HOUSE and 1812 MUSEUM (1), 844
E. Pratt St., ☎ 410-837-1793. *Open Tues.–Sat. 10–4, last tour at 3:30. Adults $4, seniors $3, children $2. Gift shop. &, partial access.*

Little did Mary Pickersgill realize, as she stitched together a gigantic 30x42-foot American flag for nearby Fort McHenry, that her creation would inspire the national anthem. Mary's house and seamstress shop was built in 1793, and has been authentically restored with period furnishings, some of which belonged to her. The adjacent structure houses a museum of the War of 1812, with documents, artifacts, weapons, and an audiovisual show about the conflict. After viewing this, visitors are taken on a tour of the Pickergill house, ending in the garden. Here, an unusual outdoor map depicts the continental United States in stones native to each state. The museum also offers monthly programs, open hearth cooking and hands-on activities for children.

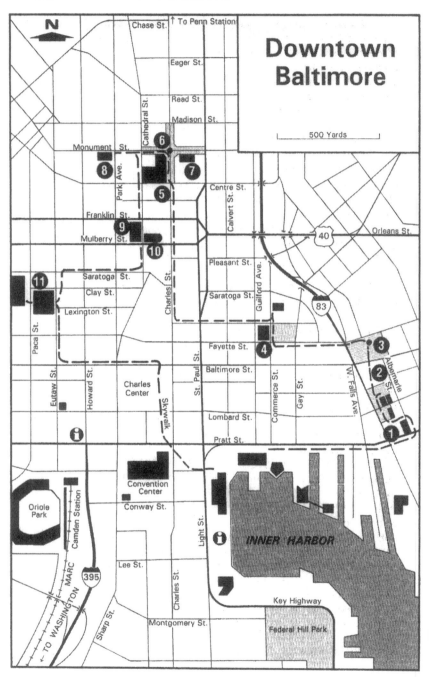

Downtown Baltimore

Follow the map north to the restored **Home of Thorowgood Smith** (2), a circa-1790 town house that is the sole survivor of a neighborhood of merchants, artisans, and "gentlemen." Thorowgood Smith (1743–1810) lived here until 1804, when he became Baltimore's second mayor. Later used as a hotel, and finally as a secondhand-auto-parts shop, it was fully restored as the headquarters of the Women's Civic League in 1972, and also serves as a sort of tourist-information center. You're welcome to visit and find out all about this eminent citizen. *9 N. Front St.,* ☎ *410-837-5424. Open Tues.–Fri. 9–2. Free.*

You can't miss seeing the 215-foot-high **Shot Tower** (3), where molten lead was dropped through sieves at the top, falling into water at the bottom as it formed into gunshot. One of the few survivors of its type, it was used from 1829 until 1892, producing half a million 25-pound bags of shot a year.

Turn west on Fayette Street to Baltimore's impressive **City Hall** (4) of 1875, a marvelously Victorian structure with mansard roofs and a gilt dome. *100 N. Holliday St. Tours by appointment,* ☎ *410-837-5424. Free.*

Head west on Lexington Street, climbing uphill to North Charles Street, and turning right on what perhaps is Baltimore's most interesting thoroughfare. As you continue north on Charles Street, you'll pass numerous specialty shops, art galleries, and restaurants. At the corner of Centre Street stands the fabulous:

*WALTERS ART GALLERY (5), 600 N. Charles St., ☎ 410-547-9000. *Open Tues.–Fri. 10–4, Sat. and Sun. 11–5, remaining open on Thurs. until 8. Closed Mon., New Year's, July 4, Thanksgiving, Christmas. Adults $6, seniors over 64 $4, students with ID $3, children 6–17 $2. Free to all Sat. 11–1 and first Thurs. of month 5–8. Museum shop. Special exhibitions. ♿, use Centre St. entrance.*

What a joy! The Walters is the perfect art museum for daytrippers, being neither too large nor too small. Its exquisite collections are easily explored, and displayed under the most ideal of conditions. William Walters (1819–94) was a wealthy patron of the arts whose splendid collections of 19th-century works and Asian porcelains were greatly enhanced by his son Henry Walters (1848–1931). The latter's collecting genius transformed this into one of the finest private collections in America. His original gallery, an Italianate *palazzo* of 1904, remains the central part of the museum, which has since been expanded by a modern 1974 wing and a 1991 renovation of an adjoining mansion of 1850. Both the museum structure and its priceless contents were bequeathed to the City of Baltimore by Mr. Walters in 1931.

Among the treasures, ranging from the art of ancient Egypt to Art Nouveau and spanning 5,000 years of history, are works representing

Greek, Roman, Etruscan, Near Eastern, Islamic, Byzantine, Early Christian, and medieval cultures. The *Asian collections are in a class by themselves, shown in the setting of a private mansion. *European and American art, from the Renaissance through the 19th century, include such gems as Ingres' *Odalisque with Slave*, Delacroix's *Christ on the Sea of Galilee*, Millet's *Breaking Flax*, Manet's *At the Café*, and Monet's *Springtime*. Additionally, as you stroll around you'll find Egyptian mummies, illuminated manuscripts, armaments, and much, much more.

Just outside the Walters is Baltimore's most urbane spot, **Mount Vernon Square** (6), in the center of which stands the 178-foot-tall **Washington Monument**. Begun in 1815, it was the nation's first major monument to George Washington. Visitors can enter the base to see exhibits on his life, and climb the 228 steps for a magnificent *panoramic view. ☎ *410-396-0929. Open Wed.–Sun., 10–4, closed holidays. Donation $1.*

Walk around the park, which extends for a block down each of the four streets. On the south side of East Mount Vernon Place is the famed **Peabody Conservatory of Music** (7), founded in 1857 and now a part of Johns Hopkins University. It is the oldest music school in the United States. The adjacent **Peabody Library** has a gorgeous interior with six stories of wrought-iron stacks surrounding a skylit atrium, which may be visited. *17 E. Mt. Vernon Pl., ☎ 410-659-8165. Open Mon.–Fri. Free.* Dominating the northeast corner of the square is the Victorian Gothic **United Methodist Church** of 1872, and all around you are elegant stone townhouses from that period. Continue west on Mount Vernon Place to Cathedral Street.

From here you might want to make a small side trip to the:

MARYLAND HISTORICAL SOCIETY (8), 201 West Monument St. at Park Ave., ☎ 410-685-3750. *Open Tues.–Sat. 10–5, Sun. 11–5. Closed Mon. and major holidays. Adults $4, seniors over 64 and children 12–17 $3. Museum shop.* ♿.

This often-overlooked museum celebrates Maryland's history with a wealth of fascinating displays. Here you'll see the original manuscript of Francis Scott Key's immortal poem *The Star-Spangled Banner*, along with a bomb that failed to burst in air during the battle at Fort McHenry in 1814. There's also the reconstructed pilothouse of a century-old Chesapeake Bay steamboat, an exhibition on the Civil War, a dollhouse that belonged to the family of H.L. Mencken, room settings with period furniture, paintings by the renowned Peale family, and an enormous collection of 19th-century American silver. Thousands of items from the now-defunct Baltimore City Life Museums are being put on display as space becomes available.

Return to Cathedral Street and head south to the **Enoch Pratt Free Library (9)**, one of the largest in the nation. Inside are special collections and exhibits devoted to the lives of Baltimore writers Edgar Allan Poe and H.L. Mencken. *400 Cathedral St.,* ☎ *410-396-5500. Open Mon.–Wed. 10–8, Thurs. and Sat. 10–5.* Directly across the street stands America's oldest Roman Catholic cathedral, the neoclassical **Basilica of the Assumption** (10). Begun in 1806 and completed in 1821, it was designed by Benjamin Latrobe of U.S. Capitol fame. The nation's first Catholic archbishop, John Carroll (1735–1815), founder of Georgetown University, was the first bishop of this church and is buried beneath its sanctuary. Step inside to admire the oldest known *cathedra* in America, the High Altar of 1822, and stained-glass windows installed in the 1940s. ☎ *410-727-3564. Open Mon.–Fri. 7:30–5.*

Continue down Cathedral Street and turn right onto Saratoga Street. A left on Eutaw Street brings you to the **Lexington Market** (11), founded in 1782 and now housed in several modern buildings. With over 140 shops, it is the oldest continuously operating market in the United States, and offers an incredible variety of foods and related items. ☎ *410-685-6169. Open Mon.–Sat. 8:30–6.*

Return to Eutaw Street and head south to Baltimore Street. From here you can see one of the city's more unusual landmarks, the **Bromo-Seltzer Clock Tower** of 1911. Soaring 290 feet above the corner of Lombard Street, it was inspired by the Palazzo Vecchio in Florence and was once topped by a huge, illuminated bottle of the antacid. The clock of this former corporate headquarters still tells time by the 12 letters of its name.

Stroll east along Baltimore Street past the Baltimore Arena and the Omni Hotel, then ascend to the upper pedestrian level of **Charles Center**. From here follow the **Skywalk**, an elevated walkway connecting various buildings in the rejuvenated downtown business district, south to the Pratt Street and the Inner Harbor.

West Baltimore

J ust because you've been to both the Inner Harbor and downtown doesn't mean that you've seen Baltimore. There are still plenty of attractions left in this All-American city, several of which are along the suggested tour route and can be reached on foot or by car. Beyond that lies an eclectic selection of scattered sights that will appeal to more specialized tastes; these are described in the next chapter.

Baseball fans surely won't want to miss the fabulous Oriole Park or the Babe Ruth Birthplace; nor will any real railfan leave Baltimore without visiting that pantheon of locomotion, the B&O Railroad Museum. A beautifully-maintained pre-Revolutionary mansion, surrounded by its own park, may be seen on tours. Heading back into town, there is a unique museum of dentistry and, nearby, the spooky grave of Edgar Allan Poe.

GETTING THERE:

See the travel information for Baltimore's Inner Harbor on page 000.

PRACTICALITIES:

The two major sights along the walking route are open daily, except for a few holidays. You can get a good view inside Oriole Park at any time, but tours are only held on days when there are no afternoon games. The Mount Clare Mansion, a bit out of the way, is closed on Mondays, holidays, and the month of January. Its tour hours are at very specific times.

A car is recommended if you plan on following the entire route, or you might want to do just the first half of it on foot, returning along Pratt Street by bus number 31 from the B&O Museum, or from near the Mount Clare Mansion. Should you hoof it all the way, the total distance is about three miles excluding a possible two-mile side trip to the Mount Clare Mansion.

For further information, stop by the **Baltimore Area Visitors Center** at 451 Light Street, near the Inner Harbor, ☎ 410-837-4636 or 800-282-6632, Internet: www.baltimore.org. They can show you how to use the MTA public transit system.

FOOD AND DRINK:
There are precious few decent places to eat along this route, so you might consider having lunch at the nearby Inner Harbor, some of whose restaurants are listed on page 000. Otherwise, you might try:

Donna's at University Hospital (22 S. Green St. at Baltimore St., 2 blocks northeast of the Babe Ruth Museum) A coffee shop with great sandwiches, salads, and trendy tidbits. ☎ 410-328-1962. X: weekends. **$**

Faidley's (in the Lexington Market, Lexington St. at Paca St., 2 blocks northeast of Poe's Grave) A standup raw bar for shuckers, crab cakes, and the like. A genuine Baltimore experience. ☎ 410-727-4898. **$**

SUGGESTED TOUR:
Numbers in parentheses correspond to numbers on the map.

From the Inner Harbor, head west along Pratt Street (Lombard Street if you're driving) past the **Baltimore Convention Center**, on your left. Two blocks farther, and a block to the south, is the nicely-renovated **Camden Station**, an old train terminal dating from 1856. A modern station of the same name stands right behind.it, serving MARC commuter trains to Washington along with Baltimore's Light Rail transit system. Immediately west of this is the imposing 19th-century **Baltimore & Ohio Railroad Warehouse** that now houses the box office, shops, concessions, and management of the Baltimore Orioles baseball team. Standing next to it, you're just a fly ball away from one of Baltimore's newest attractions.

Unquestionably, the best way to see ***Oriole Park at Camden Yards** (1) is to attend a game, or take a guided tour of the facility. Failing that, you can just look in through the right-field fence and marvel at its appealing architecture that harks back to the intimate ballparks of yesteryear. Even though this thoroughly up-to-date stadium first opened in 1992, it looks old-fashioned with its real grass, traditional design, and friendly atmosphere. ☎ *410-547-6234. Guided tours hourly on days when there are no afternoon games. Mon.–Fri. 11–2, Sat. 10:30–2, Sun. 12:30–2. Adults $5, seniors and children under 12 $4.*

Another recent sports entry is just south of here. Opened in 1998, **Ravens Stadium** is home to the NFL Baltimore Ravens, formerly known as the Cleveland Browns. ☎ *410-261-7283.*

Continue west on Pratt Street, then a few steps south on Emory Street to the:

BABE RUTH BIRTHPLACE / BALTIMORE ORIOLES MUSEUM (2), 216 Emory St., ☎ 410-727-1539, Internet: www.baberuthmuseum.com. *Open* *daily; Apr.–Oct. 10–5; Nov.–March 10–4; remains open until 7 when Orioles are playing at home. Adults $6, seniors $4, children 5–16 $3. Members and children under five free. Gift shop.* &.

Even though he played for the hated New York Yankees, Babe Ruth (1895–1948) remains a hero in Baltimore. The "Sultan of Swat" was born in this humble row house, which has been renovated as both a museum devoted to Ruth's life and the Official Baltimore Orioles Museum. Exhibits feature rare photos, game action highlights, vintage radio broadcasts and a treasure chest of Ruthian and Orioles memorabilia. All just a long fly ball from Oriole Park at Camden Yards.

Return to Pratt Street and follow it west to the:

*B&O RAILROAD MUSEUM (3), 901 W. Pratt St., ☎ 410-752-2490, Internet: www.borail.org. *Open daily 10–5. Closed on Thanksgiving, Dec. 25 and Easter. Adults $6.50, seniors $5.50, children 3–12 $4, under 3 free. Half-hour train rides on Sat. and Sun. $2. Gift shop.* &.

If you like trains, you'll love this museum. American railroading began here at Mount Clare in 1828 when the first stone of the Baltimore & Ohio Railroad was laid by Charles Carroll, the last surviving signer of the Declaration of Independence. The **Mount Clare Station** of 1851 still stands, and is used today as the museum's entrance. Adjoining it is the magnificent, almost Gothic, ***Roundhouse** of 1884, beautifully preserved and filled with historic locomotives and rolling stock. Replicas of the earliest equipment, including the first American-made locomotive, "Tom Thumb" of 1829, and a passenger car that strongly resembles a stage coach, are also on display. Another attraction is the working HO-gauge model railroad of 1956. There are also films to watch and artifacts to examine.

Outside, visitors can stroll through an extensive collection of loco-motives, passenger and freight cars, and unusual special-purpose equipment. These include some of the largest steam engines ever built, and more modern classics such as the Pennsylvania Railroad's GG-1 electric locomotive. **Rail excursions** to destinations as far away as Harpers Ferry, WV, are offered on some weekends throughout the year, ☎ *410-752-2393 for information and reservations.*

From here, you can return to the Inner Harbor by taking bus num-ber 31 from the stop on Pratt Street in front of the museum entrance. If you have a car, or if your feet are very ambitious, you might want to make a **side trip** west on Pratt (or Lombard) Street and south on Monroe Street to the:

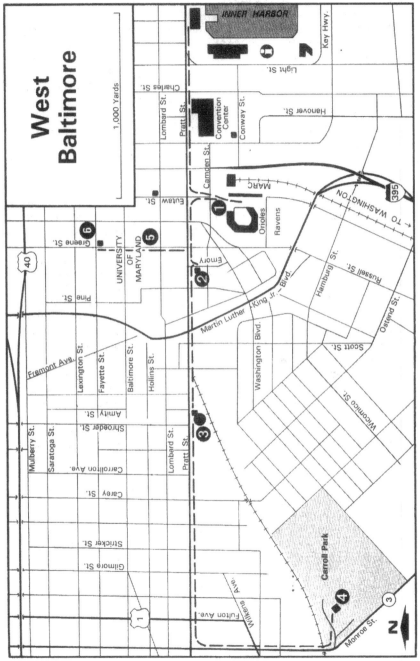

MOUNT CLARE MANSION (4), Carroll Park, 1500 Washington Blvd., ☎ 410-837-3262. *Open Tues.–Fri. with tours at 11, noon, 1, 2, and 3; weekends with tours at 1, 2, and 3. Closed Jan. and major holidays. Adults $6, seniors $5, students with ID $3, children 5–12 $1.* &.

George and Martha Washington, the Marquis de Lafayette, and John Adams were all guests of Charles Carroll, Barrister, and his wife Margaret Tilghman Carroll, here at Baltimore's oldest surviving residence. Charles Carroll Barrister, a distant cousin of Charles Carroll the signer of the Declaration of Independence, is credited with writing the Maryland Declaration of Independence and the Maryland Constitution. Begun in 1756, the mansion was the center of an 800-acre plantation, much of which is now Carroll Park. The house is unusual in that so many of its interior furnishings, and even everyday artifacts, belonged to the original owner and have been handed down through the generations under the same roof. One of Maryland's finest examples of Georgian architecture and Baltimore's only pre-Revolutionary mansion, Mount Clare has been open to the public as a museum since 1917.

From here, you can return to the Inner Harbor by bus number 31, which runs along Wilkens Avenue, then north on Gilmore and east on Pratt Street. Or walk. Either way, you might turn north on Green Street onto the University of Maryland campus to visit an unusual attraction that you can really sink your teeth into, namely the **Dr. Samuel D. Harris National Museum of Dentistry** (5). George Washington's lower denture resides here, as do the instruments used to treat Queen Victoria. Visitors can also learn all about oral health, flossing, root canals, and other fascinating subjects. *Open Wed.–Sat. 10–4, Sun. 1–4, closed major holidays. Adults $4.50, seniors and students with ID $2.50, under 7 free.* ☎ *410-706-0600.*

Continue north on Greene Street to the corner of Fayette Street, where you'll find the eerie **Westminster Churchyard** (7). Among the tombstones, some in open catacombs, is that of Edgar Allan Poe, whose short life ended in poverty and alcoholism. ☎ *410-706-2072. Open daily, dawn to dusk. Free. Tours on first and third Fri. evening and Sat. morning of each month, Apr.–Nov., call for reservations.*

Keep heading east into Charles Center, from which the elevated Skywalk leads back to the Inner Harbor.

Northern Baltimore

A rich selection of specialized attractions is spread all over the north central neighborhoods of Baltimore, especially around the campus of Johns Hopkins University. Art lovers have another great museum to relish, while those fascinated by handsome old mansions can savor two more. Then there's the Baltimore Zoo, the Great Blacks in Wax Museum, the Lacrosse Hall of Fame Museum and, finally, a ride into the past at the delightful Baltimore Streetcar Museum.

GETTING THERE:
See the travel information for Baltimore's Inner Harbor on page 000.

PRACTICALITIES:
The Baltimore Museum of Art is closed on Mondays, Tuesdays, and a few holidays, and offers free admission on Thursdays. Homewood and the Great Blacks Museum are closed on Mondays. The Lacrosse Hall of Fame Museum closes on Sundays and holidays, and the Baltimore Streetcar Museum operates on Sundays all year round, and also on Saturdays from June through October, but never on weekdays. Happily, the Baltimore Zoo is open every day except Christmas.

You'll need a car for this trip, unless you're an absolute master of the public transportation system or don't mind pedaling a bicycle. The distances involved are much too great for walking. A good map will come in handy.

For further information, contact the **Baltimore Area Visitors Center** at 451 Light Street, near the Inner Harbor, ☎ 410-837-4636 or 800-282-6632, Internet: www.baltimore.org.

FOOD AND DRINK:
Some good places for lunch are:

Polo Grill and Lounge (Doubletree Inn, 4 W. University Parkway, near the Lacrosse Museum) Classic American and Continental cuisine in a lovely dining room. Reservations advised, ☎ 410-235-8200. $$ and $$$

Jeannier's (105 W. 39th St., north of University Pkwy., near the Lacrosse Museum) French bourgeois cuisine in an atmosphere of faded gentility. ☎ 410-889-3303. X: Sat. lunch, Sun., holidays. $$

Ambassador Dining Room (3811 Canterbury Rd. at University Pkwy., near the Lacrosse Museum) Excellent British and Indian cuisine in a gracious setting. Lunch buffet. ☎ 410-366-1484. $$

Thai (3316 Greenmount Ave. at 33rd St., 2 miles east of the Art Museum) An old favorite for Thai cuisine, vegetarian or otherwise. ☎ 410-889-7303. X: Sun. lunch, holidays. $

Blue Nile (2101 N. Charles St. at 21st St.) Spicy Ethiopian dishes at low prices. BYOB. ☎ 410-783-0982. $

Donna's Charles Village (3101 St. Paul St. at 31st St., near the Art Museum) Donna's strikes again. A contemporary coffee shop in the California mode. ☎ 410-889-3410. $

LOCAL ATTRACTIONS:

Numbers in parentheses correspond to numbers on the map.

Since the sights cover such a wide range of interests, you'll have to pick and choose those that appeal to you.

*THE BALTIMORE MUSEUM OF ART (1), Art Museum Drive, N. Charles St. at 31st St., ☎ 410-396-7100, Internet: www.artbma.org. *Open Wed–Fri. 11–5; Sat., Sun. 11–6. Closed Mon., Tues., New Year's Day, July 4, Thanksgiving, and Christmas. Adults $6, seniors and full-time students $4, children 18 and under free. Free for all on Thursdays. Served by bus 3 or 11. Museum shop. &, wheelchairs on request at entrance.*

You'll find all manner of art from all over the globe on display in this immense neoclassical museum, ranging from antiquity to the contemporary. It is especially noted for its ***Cone Collection**, one of the world's finest accumulations of modern paintings and sculptures. Among its more than 85,000 treasures are many creations by Matisse, Picasso, Renoir, Cézanne, van Gogh, Gauguin, and other Post-Impressionists. The recently renovated **John Russell Pope Building** features period rooms, furnishings, decorative arts, and paintings from the 18th and 19th centuries. European **Old Masters** fill eight galleries, while other sections are devoted to Chinese ceramics and art from Africa, Oceania, and the Americas. Two **sculpture gardens** have 20th-century works from Rodin to Nevelson. **Special exhibitions** on a wide variety of visual media are held throughout the year.

A short distance to the north, on the campus of the university, is the:

HOMEWOOD HOUSE MUSEUM (2), 3400 N. Charles St., ☎ 410-516-5589. *Open Tues.–Sat. 11–4, Sun. noon–4. Closed Mon. and major holidays. Adults $6, seniors over 60 $5, under 18 $3. Tours. Gift shop.*

Charles Carroll of Carrolton, the last surviving signer of the Declaration of Independence, built this elegant country mansion in 1801 as a wedding present for his son, Charles Jr. The 140-acre estate is now the main campus of Johns Hopkins University, and the historic Federal mansion has been restored to its early-19th-century magnificence. The furnishings and decorations include items that were originally owned by the Carroll family.

A bit over a mile to the north is another grand mansion that you can visit:

EVERGREEN HOUSE (3), 4545 N. Charles St., ☎ 410-516-0341. *Open Mon.–Fri. 10–4, Sat. and Sun. 1–4. Closed New Year's Day, July 4, Memorial Day, Labor Day, Thanksgiving, and Dec. 25. Adults $6, seniors over 59 $5,* *students with ID $3. Museum shop. Tours.* &.

Surrounded by 26 acres of wooded estate, this 48-room Italianate mansion was built in the 1850s and was the home of Ambassador John W. Garrett and his descendants from 1878 until 1942. The family's fine collections of rare books, incunabula, prints, paintings, and porcelains are shown in the context of an elegant turn-of-the-century lifestyle. A full-scale restoration was completed in 1990 by the present owner, Johns Hopkins University.

Back at the north end of the main campus is:

THE LACROSSE MUSEUM AND NATIONAL HALL OF FAME (4), 113 W. University Parkway, ☎ 410-235-6882, Internet: www.lacrosse.org. *Open Mon.–Sat. 10–3, year round excluding holidays during which hours may vary. Adults $3, students $2, US Lacrosse members and children under 6 free. Gift shop.* &.

The 350-year history of America's oldest sport is thoroughly documented in this new museum, with videos and computers, photographs and art, vintage equipment and uniforms, plus a variety of lacrosse memorabilia and the brand new Hall of Fame gallery.

About 1.5 miles to the south is the:

BALTIMORE STREETCAR MUSEUM (5), 1901 Falls Rd., ☎ 410-547-0264. *Open Sun. 9–5 year-round, also Sat. noon–5 from June through Oct. Adults $5, children (4–11) and senior citizens $3, children under 4 free. Admission includes unlimited streetcar rides, audio visual show and all exhibits.*

Clang!, clang!, clang! go the trolleys at Baltimore's nostalgic remnant of an era that lasted from 1859 until 1963. That's the year that the last streetcar ceased operating in Baltimore, a victim of modern "progress." Visits to the museum begin at the **Visitors Center**, where you'll see exhibits on streetcar history and watch an audio-visual program. After that, you can enjoy a ride on a restored vehicle as it clickety-clacks its way up Jones Fall Valley past historic rail buildings before returning. At the end, stop by the carbarn to examine trolleys in various states of restoration.

About 1.5 miles to the east is the:

GREAT BLACKS IN WAX MUSEUM (6), 1601-03 E. North Ave., ☎ 410-563-3404. *Open Oct.–Jan. Tues.–Sat. 9–5, Sun. noon–5; Feb., July and Aug. Mon.–Sat. 9–6; Tues.–Sat. 9–6 rest of year. Closed on Dr. Martin Luther King's Holiday, New Year's Day, Labor Day-Sept. 30, Thanksgiving and Dec. 25. Adults $5.75, seniors over 55 and college students with ID $5.25, students 12–17 $3.75, children ages 2–11 $3.25.* &.

America's first and only wax museum of African-American history features over 100 life-size, realistic figures in dramatic historical scenes. The displays are arranged chronologically, covering such eras as ancient Africa, slavery, the Civil War, the Harlem Renaissance, and the Civil Rights movement.

Finally, about three miles to the west is the:

BALTIMORE ZOO (7), Druid Hill Park, ☎ 410-366-5466. *Open daily except Christmas, 10–4, with extended summer hours. Adults $8.50, seniors age 62 and up and children $5, under 2 free. On the first Sat. of every month all children are free before noon. Children's Zoo. Tram. Picnic tables. Various concessions. ♿.*

Over 2,250 mammals, birds, and reptiles inhabit the 180-acre spread of grassy slopes, caves, and forested hills that comprises the Baltimore Zoo. Visitors can stroll around or hitch a ride on the Zoo Tram, and kids can visit the eight-acre Children's Zoo or ride the carousel. Don't miss the latest attraction, the six-acre *African Watering Hole, where you can witness rhinos, zebras, and gazelles doing their thing.

Towson

J ust north of Baltimore lie several unusual attractions that are all too often overlooked. Conveniently located near the historic town of Towson, and easy to reach via Interstate highway, they make an interesting destination for a leisurely daytrip. This is also a good, short excursion for anyone staying in or around Baltimore. If your time is limited, be sure to at least see the Hampton National Historic Site—which could also be combined with nearby sights described in the next chapter.

GETTING THERE:

By car, take Route I-95 northeast to Exit 49, then I-695 (Baltimore Beltway) northwest to Exit 27, a bit over 50 miles from downtown Washington. Get off here and turn north on MD-146 for a very short distance. Immediately beyond the Interstate, turn right into Hampton Lane, being extremely careful not to enter the Beltway ramps adjacent to the lane. The Hampton Historic Site is less than a mile down the road, on the right.

Return to MD-146 and head south into Towson. Continue south on MD-45 (York Road) to Towson State University, on the right. The Asian Arts Center is in Room 236 of the Fine Arts Building.

Go back to the center of Towson and follow MD-45 (York Road) north as it bears to the left. The Fire Museum lies just beyond Exit 26 of the Interstate, on the right behind the Heaver Plaza office building.

PRACTICALITIES:

The Hampton Historic Site is open daily, except Thanksgiving, Christmas, or New Year's; while the Asian Arts Center is closed on weekends. Visits to the Fire Museum can be made on weekends from May through October, and also on Wednesdays through Fridays from June through August.

For further information, contact the **Baltimore County Conference and Visitors Bureau** at 435 York Rd./Towson Commons, Towson MD 21204, ☎ 410-583-7313 and 800-570-2836, Internet: www.visitbacomd.com.

FOOD AND DRINK:

The Towson area is full of good dining spots, including:

M. Gettier's Orchard Inn (1528 E. Joppa Rd., east of Towson) Creative French and Continental cuisine, with wide menu choices and a renowned chef. Reserve. ☎ 410-823-0384. $$ and $$$

Café Troia's (28 W. Allegheny Ave. in Towson, a few blocks north of the Asian Arts Center) Great Italian home cooking in a simple neighborhood restaurant. X: weekend lunch. ☎ 410-337-0133. $$

Paolos (Towson Commons, corner of York Rd. and Pennsylvania Ave., north of the Asian Arts Museum) Light Italian fare with an American touch, popular with a young crowd. ☎ 410-321-7000. $$

Ocean Pride (1534 York Rd. at Seminary Rd., north of the Fire Museum) An old favorite for crabs and beer. ☎ 410-321-7744. $ and $$

Hampton Tearoom (in the Hampton Historic Site) Both light and full luncheons, indoors or out. ☎ 410-583-7401. X: Sun. and Mon. $

Casa Mia (40 York Rd. at Burke Ave., Towson) Pizza, subs, and other Italian-Greek dishes. ☎ 410-321-8707. $

LOCAL ATTRACTIONS:

Numbers in parentheses correspond to numbers on the map.

*HAMPTON NATIONAL HISTORIC SITE (1), 535 Hampton Lane, Towson MD 21206, ☎ 410-823-1309. *Grounds open daily 9–5. Mansion open daily 9–5 except for Thanksgiving, Christmas and New Year's Day. Last tour at 4. Adults (17 years and up) to tour mansion, $5. Gift shop. Tearoom closed Sun. and Mon.*

One of the grandest American estates of the post-Revolutionary period, Hampton was built between 1783 and 1790 by Charles Ridgely from profits made during the war. In 1760, Ridgely was given the original 2,000 acres from his father, a plantation owner and merchant who settled here as early as 1745. Charles Ridgely's forceful personality and unerring business sense parlayed this modest inheritance into a mighty 24,000-acre agricultural/industrial/commercial empire that sustained six generations of the family dynasty for nearly two centuries. You'll hear all about them as you tour the 33-room Georgian mansion and marvel at its luxurious interiors.

Now reduced to a mere 62 acres, the Hampton estate has been maintained and operated by the National Park Service since 1948. Its beautiful landscaping and formal gardens may be enjoyed on a self-guided walking tour. Your visit can be made even more enjoyable by having lunch at the adjacent tearoom, which also has outdoor tables in season.

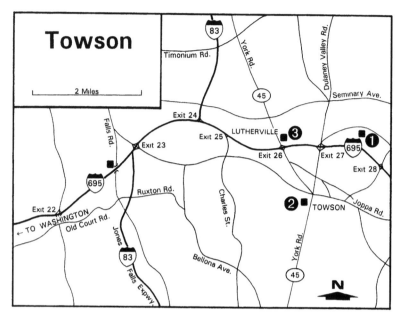

ASIAN ARTS CENTER/ROBERTS GALLERY (2), Room 236, Fine Arts Bldg., Towson State University, Towson, MD 21204, ☎ 410-830-2807. *Normally open Mon.–Fri. 11–4. Free.* ♿.

The superb permanent collections of Asian, African, and pre-Columbian art here are frequently augmented with changing contemporary exhibits.

FIRE MUSEUM OF MARYLAND (3), 1301 York Road, Lutherville, MD 21093, ☎ 410-321-7500, Internet: www.firemuseummd.org. *Open May–Oct. on weekends Sat. 11–4, Sundays 1–5; Jun.-Aug. Wed.–Sat. 11–4, Sun. 1–5. Adults $5, seniors and fire-fighters $4, children 4–15 $3, under 4 free, $12 family (two adults and children 4–15).* ♿.

Ring the bell, sound the siren, and operate a pump as you learn all about fighting fires in one of America's finest museums of its type. Over 60 major pieces of equipment are displayed here, with engines dating from 1822 to 1957. There's a re-created Central Office from which fire-fighters were dispatched, plenty of colorful memorabilia from all over, and a film on fire-fighting history. Lovingly restored by dedicated volunteers, the historic rigs and other artifacts make this a highly worthwhile destination for all.

Baltimore & Harford Counties

S everal of Central Maryland's most interesting sights straddle the line between Baltimore and Harford counties, and make enjoyable daytrip destinations from the Washington or Baltimore areas. On this excursion you can visit one of the most renowned vineyards on the East Coast to sample their wine, enjoy a fabulous, whimsical topiary garden surrounding an eccentric manor house, and explore a rambling state park with an old covered bridge and 18th-century mill. Elements of this tour could easily be combined with one or more of those described in the previous chapter to make a custom itinerary.

GETTING THERE:

By car, take Route **I-95** northeast through Baltimore to Exit 64, then **I-695** (Baltimore Beltway) west to Exit 31 North. From there head 4 miles north on **MD-147**, turning left on Long Green Pike for 32 miles to the Boordy Vineyards, on the left. The total distance from Washington is about 60 miles.

Continue north on Long Green Pike a short way and turn left on Hydes Road to Knoebel, then continue northwest on Manor Road to **MD-146**, Jarrettsville Pike. Turn right here and follow it north to the Ladew Topiary Gardens.

Go north a short distance, then southeast on **MD-152**, Fallston Mountain Road, crossing **US-1**. Continue to Jerusalem Road, turning right to the Jerusalem Mill. The Jericho Covered Bridge is just south of this, on Joppa Road.

Continuing southeast on MD-152 will return you to I-95 at Exit 74, from which you can head back to Baltimore and Washington.

PRACTICALITIES:

Boordy Vineyards is open daily all year round, and you can explore Gunpowder State Park at any reasonable time, but the Ladew Topiary Gardens are open only from mid-April through the end of October.

For further information, contact the sites directly; or contact **Baltimore County Conference and Visitors Bureau,** ☎ 410-583-7313 and 800-570-2836, Internet: www.visitbacomd.com; or **Discover Harford County Visitor Center,** ☎ 410-939-3336, 800-597-2649, Internet: www.harfordmd.com.

FOOD AND DRINK:

Some choice restaurants in the area are:

Peerce's Plantation (Dulaney Valley Rd. at Loch Raven Rd., Phoenix, about 4 miles west of Boordy) Reservations are suggested for this lovely country restaurant, serving Continental and seafood dishes, both indoors and out. ☎ 410-252-3100. $$$

Josef's Country Inn (2410 Pleasantville Rd., MD-152, Fallston, 2 miles north of Jerusalem Mill) German cuisine in a cozy Bavarian setting; often crowded, so try to make reservations. ☎ 410-877-7800. $$

Scotto's (5 Bel Air S. Pkwy., Rt. 24, Bel Air) Excellent Italian dishes between the strip malls. ☎ 410-515-2233. $$

Du Claw Brewing Company (16-A Bel Air S. Pkwy., Rt. 24, Bel Air) A brew pub with steaks and other American favorites. ☎ 410-515-3222. $$

Ladew Café (Ladew Topiary Gardens) Light lunches and Sunday brunch. ☎ 410-557-9570. $

LOCAL ATTRACTIONS:

Numbers in parentheses correspond to numbers on the map.

BOORDY VINEYARDS (1), 12820 Long Green Pike, Hydes, MD 21082, ☎ 410-592-5015, Internet: www.boordy.com. *Open all year, Mon.–Sat. 10–5, Sun. 1–5. Closed New Year's Day, Easter, July 4th, Thanksgiving and Dec. 25. Tours on the hour, 1–4. Free. Special events. Wine shop.*

Maryland's oldest and largest winery was established in 1945, long before small vineyards came into fashion. Its wines are highly regarded by knowledgeable lovers of the juice, and are mostly made from the traditional European varieties. Your tour begins with a stroll through the vineyards themselves, then goes inside a renovated 19th-century barn to the winemaking and barrel-aging rooms, where the powerful aroma of maturing vintages prepares you for the final treat. Here you can sample a generous variety of the different types and, if you wish, purchase a few bottles to take home. The whole experience is refreshingly unpretentious.

*LADEW TOPIARY GARDENS (2), 3535 Jarrettsville Pike, Monkton, MD 21111, ☎ 410-557-9570. *Open mid-April through Oct.; Mon.–Fri. 10–4, weekends 10:30–5, last house tour one hour before closing. Combined house & gardens: Adults $8, seniors over 62 and students with ID $7,*

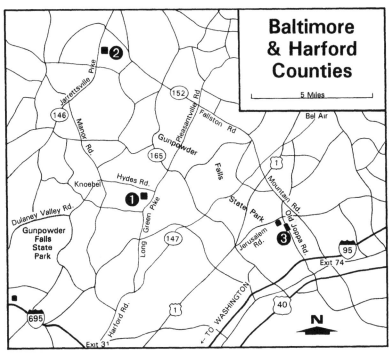

Baltimore & Harford Counties

5 Miles

children under 12 $2. Gardens only: Adults $6, seniors over 62 and students with ID $5, children under 12 $1. Gift shop. Special events. Café, serves light lunch. &.

Harvey Ladew was a wealthy Renaissance man with eccentric tastes and a marvelous sense of humor, all of which comes across in this most enjoyable of estates. After purchasing the 22-acre retreat in 1929, he set about transforming it into what the Garden Club of America calls "the most outstanding topiary garden in America." Shrubs and plants are sculpted into whimsical figures such as horses, their riders, foxes, and hounds; a reference to Ladew's hunting exploits with such notables as King Edward VII of England. His friend T.E. Lawrence, of Arabian fame, is represented by a topiary camel!

Ladew's house is every bit as odd as the shrubbery. The Oval Library, considered to be one of the most beautiful rooms in America, was added solely because he had purchased a massive desk that wouldn't fit in any of the rooms. It also has a secret panel that he used to escape from boring guests. More reminders of his fun-loving personality are evident throughout the house, making this a really delightful place to visit.

GUNPOWDER FALLS STATE PARK (3), 10815 Harford Rd., Glen Arm, MD 21057, ☎ 410-592-2897. *Open daily 10–sunset. Historic sites, nature walks, hiking/biking/equestrian/cross-country ski trails, boating, fishing, hunting, picnicking.*

Spread over nearly 12,000 acres, this rambling state park follows the meanderings of its namesake creek and its branches, offering miles of recreational opportunities along the way. Among its historic site is the **Jerusalem Mill** of 1772, located right on Jerusalem Road just west of Route 152, halfway between US-1 and I-95. Almost around the corner from this, on Joppa Road, is the picturesque **Jericho Covered Bridge.** Erected about 1865, it still carries some traffic. Park your car nearby and take a stroll through it, noticing the "lattice truss" construction of timbers organized in a series of triangles that distribute stress to achieve great strength from simple materials.

Eastern Harford County

The northern head of Chesapeake Bay, where the broad Susquehanna River empties into the largest estuary in the United States, offers an unusually rich variety of attractions. Here the fresh waters of inland mountain streams mix with the salty brine of the ocean. And here, too, reminders of America's maritime past combine with the realities of today's world.

Havre de Grace, with its subdued nautical flavor, is the perfect little escape from the pressures of Washington and Baltimore. Its downtown Historic District features dozens of interesting structures built between the 1780s and the late Victorian period. There is also a lighthouse of 1827 that remains in use today, a modern museum of decoy carving, a maritime museum, a restored segment of the old Susquehanna & Tidewater Canal, and other attractions open to visitors. According to tradition, the town was given its name by the Marquis de Lafayette, who was reminded of his native France. In 1791 it narrowly escaped becoming the nation's capital, as did several other towns. During the War of 1812 Havre de Grace was torched and largely destroyed by the British, but soon prospered again with the coming of the canal and railroad eras.

Just a few minutes south, in Aberdeen, is the U.S. Army Ordnance Museum, possibly the most extensive collection of military weapons to be found anywhere. Its 25-acre site contains some 225 tanks, artillery pieces, and rockets from all over the world; while its indoor museum houses armaments and military oddities from many nations.

Besides the expected amenities, the nearby Susquehanna State Park rewards its visitors with an operational 18th-century grist mill, a 19th-century mansion that you can visit, and a ten-acre living history museum of rural life around 1900.

GETTING THERE:

By car, Aberdeen is about 70 miles northeast of Washington via Route I-95. From Exit 85, take **MD-22** southeast to the Aberdeen Proving Grounds, a distance of about 3 miles, and continue straight past the Military Police gate to the museum on your right.

Return to Aberdeen town and turn right (northeast) onto **US-40**, which brings you to Havre de Grace in about 5 miles. *To get there directly from Washington, take I-95 to Exit 89, then MD-155 into town.*

Leave Havre de Grace on **MD-155**, heading northwest to I-95. To visit the State Park and Conowingo, continue straight ahead and in about a quarter-mile turn right (north) on Earlton Road, following it for a half-mile. Turn left on Quaker Bottom Road and enter the park. Continue north on local roads for Conowingo.

PRACTICALITIES:

The Ordnance Museum in Aberdeen is open daily. In Havre de Grace, the Decoy Museum is open daily except on major holidays, while the Lighthouse, Maritime Museum, and Susquehanna Museum are usually open on Saturdays, Sundays or weekends only, from late spring until early fall. Within the Susquehanna State Park, the Steppingstone Museum, Carter Mansion, and Rock Run Mill are open on weekends only, from late spring until Labor Day or early fall. As you can see, this makes a good weekend trip in summer.

The **Discover Harford County Visitor Center** is located in the Old City Hall Building, Havre de Grace, MD, ☎ 410-939-3336, 800-597-2649, Internet: www.harfordmd.com. Another good source of current information is the **Havre de Grace Chamber of Commerce**, 224 North Washington St., P.O. Box 339, Havre de Grace MD 21078, ☎ 410-939-3303, or 800-851-7756, Internet: www.graf.com/hdg/chamber.

FOOD AND DRINK:

Havre de Grace is graced with a good selection of fine restaurants, including:

The Crazy Swede (400 N. Union Ave., in the Historic District) Surf 'n Turf specialties in a maritime setting. ☎ 410-939-5440. Lunch $$, dinner $$$

Bayou (927 Pulaski Hwy., US-40, north of Revolution St.) An unusually good value for seafood and meat dishes, especially at lunch. Reservations advised for peak periods. ☎ 410-939-3565. $ and $$

MacGregors (331 St. John St., left off MD-7 in Havre de Grace) A smart dining room overlooking the Susquehanna River; American cuisine. ☎ 410-939-3003. $ and $$

Fortunato Brothers (103 N. Washington St., north of Congress St. in the Historic District) Pizza, salads, and traditional Italian dishes in a popular midtown restaurant. ☎ 410-939-1401. $

LOCAL ATTRACTIONS:

Numbers in parentheses correspond to numbers on the map.
U.S. ARMY ORDNANCE MUSEUM (1), Aberdeen Proving Ground, MD 21005-5201, ☎ 410-278-3602. *Open daily 10—4:45; closed all national holi-*

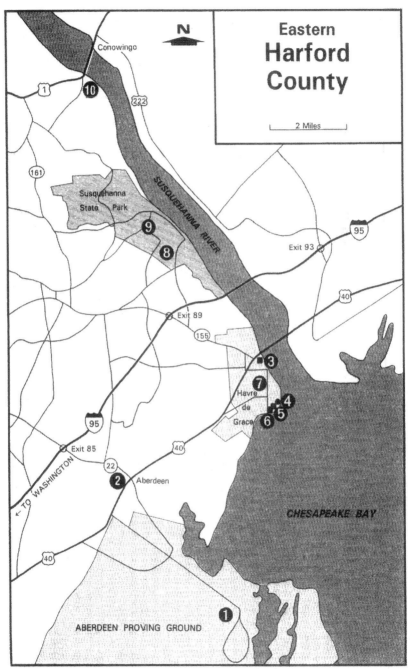

Eastern **Harford County**

2 Miles

days except Armed Forces Day, Memorial Day, Independence Day, and Veterans' Day. Free. Gift shop. &, most areas.

It seems somehow fitting that weapons of the past are preserved and exhibited on the very same army post where tomorrow's weapons are being tested today. Indeed, the museum is more than a collection of historic relics; it serves primarily as a repository of solutions to weapons design problems, and as such is an invaluable source of information for contemporary engineers. Much of this knowledge comes from the vast assortment of foreign equipment, especially from captured enemy ordnance sent here for evaluation and intelligence purposes.

Lined up like soldiers on a parade ground are some 250 tanks, rockets, and artillery pieces from all over the world, some dating from well before World War I. Among the star attractions is **"Anzio Annie,"** an enormous railway gun employed by the German army in 1943 to hurl 550-pound shells at Allied troops attempting to storm the Italian shores. A sinister **V-2 rocket**—the world's first ballistic missile, used by the Nazis to terrify London—lurks beneath a metal canopy not far from the American **Atomic Cannon** of the 1950s.

Inside the museum building you'll see the fantastic **Locomobile** that served as General Pershing's staff car in World War I, some rather strange early tanks, and two floors of displays on the evolution of small arms, ammunition, machine guns, and other instruments of war.

While in Aberdeen you might want to stop at the **Ripken Museum** (2), which displays personal possessions and memorabilia of baseball star Cal Ripken Jr. *3 West Bel Air Ave., off US-40. Open Memorial Day to Labor Day, Sun.–Fri. noon–3, Sat. 11–4; rest of year Fri. and Sun.–Mon. noon–3, Sat. 11–4. Adults $3, seniors $2, children $1.* ☎ *410-273-2525.*

Now head northeast on US-40 to Havre de Grace and its attractions:

SUSQUEHANNA LOCKHOUSE MUSEUM (3), Erie & Conesto streets, Havre de Grace, MD 21078, ☎ 410-939-5780. *Open on Saturdays from May through October, 1–5; also on Fridays from Memorial Day through Labor Day. Free.*

Even if the museum itself isn't open, you may still want to stop by to examine the short reconstructed canal lock section at the northern end of Havre de Grace. The long-defunct **Susquehanna & Tidewater Canal** opened in 1839, running northwest from here for about 45 miles to Wrightsville, PA, where it connected with the Central Division of the Pennsylvania Canal. This combination of waterways, along with a branch to Lancaster, opened all of central Pennsylvania to trade with the seaport of Baltimore. Leisurely moving at about three miles an hour, the mule-drawn canal boats encountered 28 locks along the way, lifting them a total of 233 feet. After peaking around 1870, however, the hopelessly inefficient canals lost out to competition from the railroads, and by the turn of the century were mostly a part of history.

The museum occupies the former lock tender's modest house of 1840, and is filled with artifacts from that era along with many items recalling the entire town's history. You'll get a friendly tour of both floors, and get to watch a short video about the canal in its heyday.

CONCORD POINT LIGHTHOUSE (4), Concord & Lafayette streets, Havre de Grace, MD 21078, ☎ 410-939-9040. *Open for climbing on Sundays from April through Oct., 1–5. Free.*

Built in 1827 and still in use today, this is the oldest continuously-operated lighthouse in Maryland. It marks the hazardous point where the Susquehanna River meets the tidal flow of Chesapeake Bay. Whale-oil lamps provided the original illumination, but this was modernized in 1854 and electrified in 1920. Climbing to the lantern room, less than 30 feet up a spiral staircase, will give you an excellent ***view** of the area while allowing a close examination of the antique Fresnel lens.

Back on the ground, walk around to see the cannon used in defense of the town against the British during the War of 1812. The adjacent lighthouse keeper's house is currently under restoration and will eventually house displays on the life and activities of 19th-century keepers.

HAVRE DE GRACE MARITIME MUSEUM (5), 100 Lafayette St., Havre de Grace, MD 21078, ☎ 410-939-4800. *Open on weekends from May through Sept., 1–5. Donations accepted.*

Only part of this ambitious new museum project is open yet, but even that has interesting displays on the maritime heritage of the Upper Chesapeake Bay, including a 55-foot oystering sloop from 1904, various artifacts, memorabilia, and photographs.

HAVRE DE GRACE DECOY MUSEUM (6), Giles & Market streets, Havre de Grace, MD 21078, ☎ 410-939-3739, Internet: www.decoymuseum.com. *Open daily except major holidays, 11–4. Adults $4, seniors & children over 8 $2. Gift shop. &.*

Havre de Grace has long been a center for the art of making duck (and goose) decoys used in waterfowl hunting, a local tradition of the bay area. Hundreds of examples of this genre are beautifully displayed in a modern museum, ranging from simple working decoys to fancy "decoratives." On weekends, guest carvers demonstrate their craft in a functioning workshop, while some of the local lore is colorfully discussed by mannequins in an unusual tableau.

HAVRE DE GRACE HISTORIC DISTRICT (7), extending approximately from Union Avenue east to Market St. and from Fountain St. north to Warren St. *Free brochure/map available from the Chamber of Commerce tourist office at 224 North Washington St., or at most attractions in town.*

Park your car and take a stroll through this compact area whose oldest structure, the **Rodgers House** at 226 North Washington St., dates from 1787. It was once the home of Admiral John Rodgers, the ranking naval officer in the War of 1812 who later served as Secretary of the Navy, and remained in his family for nearly a century. Other outstanding buildings date from the prosperous Canal Era (1830–50) and the boom times of the Victorian Age (1880–1910).

SUSQUEHANNA STATE PARK (8), Route 155, Havre de Grace, MD 21078. ☎ 410-557-7994. *Open daily 10–sunset. Fee parking available. Historic sites, nature walks, picnicking, playground, camping, boating, fishing, skiing.*

Occupying some 2,500 acres along the west bank of the Susquehanna River, this is easily one of Maryland's most attractive parks. It is particularly noted for its historic sites, including the **Rock Run Mill** of 1794, where volunteers use waterpower to grind cornmeal on summer weekends from 2–4. *Mill open from Memorial Day through Labor Day, weekends 10–6. Free.* ☎ *410-939-0643.* Two other attractions are the **Carter Mansion**, an early-19th-century 13-room house filled with period antiques; and the **Jersey Toll House**, now used for exhibits on local natural history. *Both open at the same times as the mill, free.* Also within the park is the Steppingstone Museum, described below.

STEPPINGSTONE MUSEUM (9), 461 Quaker Bottom Road in Susquehanna State Park, Havre de Grace, MD 21078. ☎ 410-939-2299. *Open May through early Oct., weekends only, 1–5. Adults $2, children free. Special events throughout the year. Gift shop.*

Rural life from 1880 through 1920 is re-created on this 10-acre farm site, where you can watch volunteers demonstrate the old crafts such as blacksmithing, barrel-making, woodworking, and tinsmithing.

Before heading home, you might want to head north a few miles through **Darlington** to see the mighty **Conowingo Hydroelectric Dam** (10), which carries U.S. Route 1 across the broad Susquehanna River. Behind it is a 14-mile-long recreational lake with numerous aquatic activities. *For information about tours of the facility and use of the lake* ☎ *410-457-5011.*

Frederick

F rederick has been through a lot in the last 250 years, playing important roles in both the Revolution and the Civil War. By the 1960s,
however, the town had clearly seen better days as businesses
moved out and the downtown deteriorated. Its rebirth, so to speak,
came in the mid-70s when a group of determined citizens got to work
restoring the Historic District as a tourist attraction. Today's visitors can
enjoy a variety of historic sites, museums, shops, and galleries in 18th-
and 19th-century settings.

A few miles to the north are the lovely Catoctin Mountains with
both state and national parks, as well as other attractions. South of the
town, the Civil War is remembered at Monocacy National Battlefield
Park.

By staying overnight or longer, this trip could easily be combined
with the ones to nearby Hagerstown, Harpers Ferry, or Gettysburg.

GETTING THERE:

By car, Frederick is about 50 miles northwest of Washington. From
the Beltway, take Route **I-270**, which becomes **US-40** as it enters the
town. Get off at Exit 6 and head east on West Patrick Street into the
Historic District.

Return to the same junction and take **US-15** north about 15 miles to
Thurmont for the Catoctin Mountain parks.

For Monocacy Battlefield, return to Frederick and take **MD-355**
south about three miles.

PRACTICALITIES:

Frederick pretty much closes down in winter, its attractions hiber-
nating from November or December through March. Some sites are
closed on weekdays, even in the warmer months. The Barbara Fritchie
House is always closed on Tuesdays and Wednesdays, on weekdays in
October and November, and all the time from December through
March. The best time to make this trip is on a weekend, Thursday, or
Friday, from April through September.

For further information contact the **Tourism Council of Frederick**

County, 19 East Church Street, Frederick, MD 21701, ☎ 301-663-8687 or 800-999-3613, Internet: www.visitfrederick.org. They have a Visitor Center at that address.

FOOD AND DRINK:

Some choice restaurants are:

Brown Pelican (5 E. Church St., near the Visitor Center) Specializing in veal and seafood, this is regarded as the best dining spot in town. Reservations suggested, ☎ 301-695-5833. $$ and $$$

Red Horse Steak House (996 West Patrick St., US-40 west of US-15) Steak and seafood for over 30 years; with a cigar lounge. ☎ 301-663-3030. X: weekend lunches, major holidays. $$

Tauraso's (Everedy Sq., 6 East St., in the Historic District) Choose the pub, patio, or formal dining room for Italian cuisine, seafood, meat, or vegetarian dishes. ☎ 301-663-6600. $ and $$

Di Francesco's (26 N. Market St., between W. Patrick and Church streets) A casual place for homestyle Italian dishes. ☎ 301-695-5499. $ and $$

Cozy Restaurant (105 Frederick Rd., MD-806, just off US-15, in Thurmont) A local institution for home cooking since 1929. Huge menu, buffet, and indoor/outdoor seating. ☎ 301-271-7373. $

LOCAL ATTRACTIONS:

Numbers in parentheses correspond to numbers on the map.

Begin exploring **Frederick** (1–6) at the town's **Visitor Center** (1), where you can get the latest information on these and other sites.

BARBARA FRITCHIE HOUSE AND MUSEUM (2), 154 West Patrick St., ☎ 301-698-0630. *Open Apr.–Sept., Mon., Thurs., Fri., and Sat. 10–4, Sun. 1–4; Oct.–Nov. Sat. and Sun. 1–4. Adults $2, seniors over 65 and under 12 $1.50.*

Barbara Fritchie (1766–1862) was the Civil War heroine immortalized in John Greenleaf Whittier's famous poem of 1863. Her reputed confrontation with Stonewall Jackson—" 'Shoot if you must, this old gray head, But spare your country's flag,' she said." —and his gallant response are the stuff that legends are made of. Fritchie's small house, from which the tattered Union flag flew as Confederate forces marched under it, has been reconstructed as a museum to her memory, and to commemorate a brief moment of decency in an otherwise brutal conflict. Inside, you'll see a short video, her possessions, and the bed in which she died.

Nearby is the **Roger Brooke Taney House/Francis Scott Key Museum**

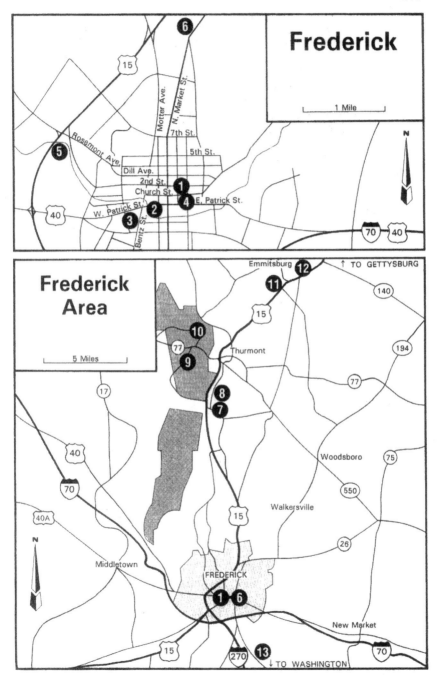

(3), located in the summer residence of former Chief Justice of the Supreme Court Roger Brooke Taney (1777–1864). The noted jurist will always be remembered for his decision in the infamous Dred Scott case of 1857. Key, a sometime resident of Frederick, wrote the *Star Spangled Banner* (see page 209) and once shared a law practice with Taney. Memorabilia of both men are displayed along with restored slave quarters. *123 S. Bentz St., ☎ 301-663-8687. Open Apr.–Oct., weekends and by appointment, call first. Nominal admission.*

The **Historical Society of Frederick County** (4), also in town, occupies a Federal-style mansion of about 1820, filled with architectural details, period furnishings, and items related to the Revolution and the Civil War. Guided tours are given, and there's a lovely boxwood garden. *24 E. Church St., ☎ 301-663-1188, Internet: www.fwp.net/hsfc. Open Mon.–Sat. 10–4, Sun. 1–4. Adults $2 donation, under 17 free.*

Located a few blocks northwest of the Historic District, the **Schifferstadt Architectural Museum** (5) centers around an early German-American farmhouse of 1756 and its 18th-century garden. *1110 Rosemont Ave., off US-15, ☎ 301-663-3885. Open Apr.–mid-Dec., Tues.–Sun., call for hours. Donation.*

THE CHILDREN'S MUSEUM OF ROSE HILL MANOR PARK (6), 1611 N. Market St., ☎ 301-694-1648. *Open Apr.–Oct., Mon.–Sat. 10-4, Sun. 1–4; Nov. Sat. 10–4, Sun. 1–4. Group reservations welcome Mar.–Dec. Admission. Gift shop. Picnic facilities. ᵬ.*

Situated in a park near the north end of town, Rose Hill, once the retirement home of Maryland's first elected Governor some 200 years ago, is now a special treat for elementary-school- aged children. This 1790's mansion and estate is now a museum of 19th-century family life, where costumed guides help visitors to understand their heritage. Hands-on activities abound in the manor house, gardens, orchard, blacksmith shop, and log cabin. There's also a **Carriage Museum** with restored vehicles. Its **Farm Museum** exhibits may be toured by prior request.

The **Catoctin Mountains**, north of Frederick along US-15, are especially nice to visit in the fall foliage season. Exiting onto MD-806 and continuing north brings you to the ruined **Catoctin Furnace** (7) of 1774, where iron was produced for Revolutionary and Civil War armaments by workers living in a village of stone cottages. Interpretive signs explain all. A bit farther up the road is the **Catoctin Mountain Zoological Park** (8). Over 300 specimens of rare and endangered mammals, birds, and reptiles may be seen in this wooded environment, complete with a

Discovery Room, Monkey Islands, and a petting area. *13019 Catoctin Furnace Rd., Thurmont,* ☎ *301-271-3180 or 301-271-4922, Internet: www.fwp.net/cwpzoo. Call for fees. Open daily 9–6 Apr.–Oct.*

Two wilderness areas lie a short distance west of Thurmont on MD-77. **Cunningham Falls State Park** (9), on the south side of the road, offers an easy walk to its 78-foot waterfalls and scenic overlook. There are also picnic facilities, swimming, fishing, canoe rentals, and nature trails around the William Houck Area just south of MD-77. ☎ *301-271-7574,* ♿. North of the road is the National Park Service's **Catoctin Mountain Park** (10), site of the President's famous Camp David retreat. You can't visit this, but the park holds other attractions that are open to the public. Stop at the Visitor Center for a brochure/map before exploring the miles of nature trails—one of which leads to a restored whiskey still from Prohibition days! ☎ *301-663-9388, Internet: www.nps.gov/cato. Open daily except Thanksgiving, Christmas, and New Year's. Free. Picnic facilities. Exhibits. Rock climbing. Cross-country skiing. Fishing. Camping (fee).* ♿, *partial access.*

A few miles farther north on US-15 is the **National Shrine Grotto of Lourdes** (11), the oldest replica of the French shrine in the Western Hemisphere. Located above the campus of Mount St. Mary's College, it is one-third the size of the original. ☎ *301-447-5318. Open year-round; services Easter–Oct.* While there you might want to continue north a bit to the **National Shrine of St. Elizabeth Ann Seton** (12), dedicated to the first American-born saint, who lived from 1774 until 1821 and founded early charities. *333 S. Seton Ave., Emmitsburg.* ☎ *301-447-6606, Internet: www.setonshrine.org. Open daily 10–4:30. Closed Christmas, last two weeks of Jan., and Mondays from Nov.–Mar. Free.* ♿.

On the way back to Washington, just south of Frederick, you'll pass **Monocacy National Battlefield Park** (13). Although won by the Confederacy, the Civil War battle fought here on July 9, 1864 is credited with having saved Washington from attack. Union forces, decimated though they were, managed to delay Confederate General Jubal Early's advance just long enough for Northern reinforcements to enter the capital. To reach the battlefield, get off I-270 at Exit 31, go east less than a mile to MD-355, and turn south, crossing the Monocacy River. ☎ *301-662-3515. Visitor Center open Wed.–Sun. 8–4:30. Closed major holidays. Free.* ♿.

Hagerstown and Antietam

History buffs will find much to scrutinize in the Hagerstown area. Whether your interests lie in Colonial America, the Civil War, the canal era, or early railroading, there's enough here to keep you happily probing all day long.

First settled in 1739, the town still preserves its founder's house in perfect Colonial condition. Near it are two small art galleries, and a roundhouse museum celebrating the seven railroads that once made Hagerstown their hub. The only surviving original fort from the French and Indian War is nearby, adjacent to the historic C&O Canal of the early 19th century. Antietam Battlefield, south of Hagerstown, commemorates the bloodiest single day of the Civil War. And, if you'd rather go back millions of years into geologic time, there's always the subterranean splendors of Crystal Grottoes.

By staying overnight, this trip could be combined with the previous one to Frederick, or with Harpers Ferry.

GETTING THERE:

By car, Hagerstown is about 75 miles northwest of Washington via routes **I-270** and **I-70**. Get off at Exit 32 and follow **US-40** north into town.

Fort Frederick lies about 18 miles west of Hagerstown via **I-70** to Exit 12, then south a mile on **MD-56**.

Antietam Battlefield is about 15 miles south of Hagerstown via **MD-65**. From there you can take MD-34 east, passing Crystal Grottoes, and US-40 south to its junction with I-70 for the return to Washington.

PRACTICALITIES:

Several of the sites in Hagerstown are closed in winter, and on Mondays all year round. A few also close on Tuesdays. The Roundhouse Museum closes on Mondays through Thursdays. Check the individual listings before making this trip.

For further information contact the **Washington County Convention & Visitors Bureau**, 16 Public Square, Hagerstown, MD 21740, ☎ 301-791-3246 or 800-228-7829.

FOOD AND DRINK:

Schmankerl Stube (Potomac and Antietam streets, downtown Hagerstown) Authentic Bavarian cuisine in an Old World setting, with an outdoor beer garden. ☎ 301-797-3354. X: Mon. $$$

Antrim House (Fountainhead Plaza, Pennsylvania Ave., US-11N, Hagerstown) A family-style restaurant offering sandwiches to full meals, especially seafood. ☎ 301-797-8111. $ and $$

Richardson's (710 Dual Hwy. (US-40), east of town) A good-value place for seafood, chicken, and other dishes. Salad bar. ☎ 301-733-3660. $

Family Time Restaurant (18213 Maugans Ave., just west of Exit 9 on I-81) A wide variety of favorite dishes, with a salad bar and lunch buffet. ☎ 301-733-0767. $

In addition, you'll find **picnic facilities** at Fort Frederick State Park.

LOCAL ATTRACTIONS:

Numbers in parentheses correspond to numbers on the map.

Most of the sites in Hagerstown are concentrated around City Park, but the compact old downtown area also has its attractions. Near the center of this is the **Miller House** (1), home to the Washington County Historical Society and open to the public as a small museum. Inside this Federal-style 1820's building you can see a turn-of-the-century general store, a three-story spiral staircase, local clocks, dolls, and pottery, and a fine collection of C&O Canal and Civil War artifacts. While here, you might ask about other worthwhile sights in the same neighborhood. *135 W. Washington St., ☎ 301-797-8782. Open Apr.–Nov., Wed.–Sat. 1–4. Variable Dec. schedule. Closed major holidays. Adults $3, seniors $2, students with ID free.*

City Park (2–4) is graced with a 50-acre lake, lots of waterfowl, and three attractions. The first of these is the:

HAGER HOUSE (2), 110 Key St., City Park, ☎ 301-739-8393. *Open Apr.–Dec., Tues.–Sat. 10–4, Sun. 2–5. Closed last week of Nov.–first Tues. in Dec. Adults $3, children 6–12 $2. Special events.*

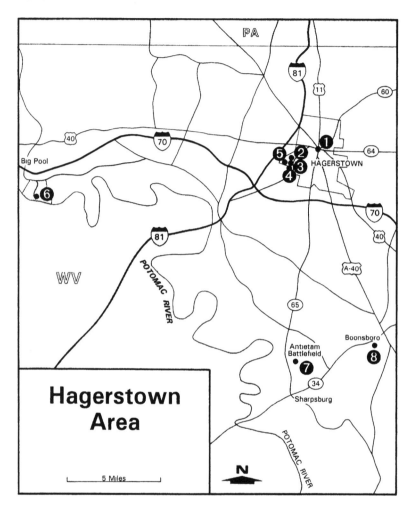

Hagerstown
Area

5 Miles

N

Jonathan Hager, a young German immigrant in search of adventure, purchased 200 acres of wilderness here in western Maryland in 1739 for the sum of £44. Choosing a location above a spring, he built a virtually indestructible frontier house with stone walls some 22 inches thick. With its own water supply, the structure could also serve as a fort in case of Indian attack. As Hager prospered with his trading post that became Hagerstown, he and his family outgrew the house and sold it in 1745 to one Jacob Rohrer, whose descendants kept it until 1944. After that it was presented to the town, restored to its Colonial condition, and opened to the public as a museum.

Completely outfitted with period furnishings and set in a lovely park, the Hager House offers a delightful journey into the past. Adjacent to it is the **Hager Museum**, where you can see "Little Heiskell," a weather vane in the shape of a Hessian soldier that was commissioned by Jonathan Hager and now serves as the town's symbol.

Elsewhere in the park is the **Washington County Museum of Fine Arts** (3), with exhibitions ranging from Old Masters to contemporary art and excellent collections of 19th-century American pieces. *City Park, Virginia Ave.,* ☎ *301-739-5727. Open Tues.–Sat. 10–5, Sun. 1–5. Closed New Year's Day, Good Friday, July 4th, Thanksgiving, Dec. 24, 25, and 31. Free.* ♿. Local art is displayed in the nearby **Mansion House Art Center** (4), a Georgian-style structure of 1846. ☎ *301-797-6813. Open Thurs.–Sat. 10–4, Sun. 1–5.*

Just across the tracks is the **Hagerstown Roundhouse Museum** (5), where the seven railroads that made Hagerstown their hub are celebrated with displays of historic equipment, memorabilia, photos, and archives. *300 S. Burhans Blvd.,* ☎ *301-739-4665. Open year-round Fri.–Sun. 1–5. Adults $2.50, children 12 and under 50¢, under 3 free. Gift shop.*

Fort Frederick State Park (6), 18 miles west of Hagerstown, preserves the sole surviving original fort from the French and Indian War. Hastily built of stone in 1756 after General Braddock's defeat near Fort Duquesne, the fortress also housed Hessian prisoners during the Revolution and was used as a garrison early in the Civil War. Re-enactments of historical battles are held at various times throughout the year. An orientation film is shown at the Visitor Center, and there's a museum of artifacts as well as the usual park amenities including picnic facilities, nature walks, hiking trails, fishing, boating, camping, bike rentals, and cross-country skiing. The park overlooks the adjacent **C&O Canal National Historical Park** (see page 88 and 187), which stretches nearly 185 miles from Georgetown DC to Cumberland MD but is only a few yards wide. You can walk along the towpath here to several historic locks and aqueducts. *Ft. Frederick State Park, 11100 Ft. Frederick Rd., Big Pool, MD 21711,* ☎ *301-842-2155. Free. Snack bar.* ♿.

About 15 miles south of Hagerstown is the:

*ANTIETAM NATIONAL BATTLEFIELD (7), Box 158, Sharpsburg, MD 21782, ☎ 301-432-5124, Internet: www.nps.gov/anti/. *Open daily 8:30–5 (6 in summer). Closed Thanksgiving, Christmas, and New Year's Day. Adults*

$2, $4 per family and children under 16 free. Cassette audiotape tour rentals $5. Visitor Center. Special events. Mostly &.

The bloodiest single day in American military history occurred here on September 17, 1862 when over 23,000 men were killed or wounded in a savage battle that decided little. Numerically superior Union forces under General George B. McClellan narrowly forced a retreat of the Confederate Army of Northern Virginia under General Robert E. Lee, but at such expense that McClellan was soon relieved of command for his failure to pursue Lee into Virginia. One major outcome of the battle, however, was the Emancipation Proclamation issued by President Lincoln that altered the purpose of the war from just reuniting the country to ending slavery.

Begin your tour at the **Visitor Center**, where a 26-minute award-winning film re-creating the battle is shown on the hour, and where there's a museum of battle artifacts to examine. A free brochure/map will guide you through the battlefield, or you can rent a cassette tape guide.

On the way back to Washington, you might want to have a little underground adventure at Maryland's only commercial cave. **Crystal Grottoes Caverns** (8) offers a journey back in geologic time to a subterranean world of colorful stalactites and stalagmites, columns, ribbons, and other kinds of unusual formations. The guided tour takes about 40 minutes and is easy to follow. *19821 Shepherdstown Pike (MD-34), Boonsboro, MD 21713. ☎ 301-432-6336. Open Apr.–Oct., daily 10–5; Nov.–Mar., weekends only 11–4. Adults $8.50, children under 12 $4.50.*

Harpers Ferry, West Virginia

Radical abolitionist John Brown (1800–59) put Harpers Ferry on the map on October 16, 1859, when he led a small group of followers on a raid of the U.S. arsenal there. Although soon captured by Federal troops commanded by then-Colonel Robert E. Lee and Lieutenant J.E.B. Stuart, and quickly hanged, Brown through his actions ignited passions that led inevitably to the Civil War. During that conflict Union soldiers marched to the song "John Brown's Body" in honor of their martyr.

Harpers Ferry was a strategically vital place long before John Brown was born. Located in rugged mountain terrain at the confluence of the Shenandoah and Potomac rivers, and at the junction of three states, it was first settled in 1733 by one Peter Stephens, who ran a ferry service. This was taken over in 1747 by a miller named Robert Harper. A Federal arsenal and rifle factory, established in 1796 at the urging of President George Washington, made the little town important. The coming of the C&O Canal and the B&O Railroad in the 1830s brought additional prosperity, but destruction during the Civil War later caused a serious decline. Today, much of Harpers Ferry is preserved as a National Historical Park, and the town thrives on a booming tourist trade.

Beyond its historic value, a trip to Harpers Ferry is more than worthwhile for the scenic splendor alone. For those who can stay overnight, this excursion combines well with the previous ones to Frederick and Hagerstown.

GETTING THERE:

By car, Harpers Ferry is about 70 miles northwest of Washington. Take Route **I-270** to Frederick, then **US-340** west across the Potomac and Shenandoah rivers to the Visitor Center. Park there and take the shuttle bus; do not drive in town.

Trains operated by both Amtrak ☎ (800-USA-RAIL) and MARC ☎ (800-325-RAIL) provide service between Washington and Harpers Ferry, but only at times inconvenient for daytrippers. This is a viable option if you can stay overnight.

PRACTICALITIES:

The sites are open daily all year round (except Christmas), but some commercial establishments close in winter—at least on weekdays. Park activities are mostly held in summer, with a few on weekends only in fall and spring. The views here are especially lovely during the fall foliage season.

For further information contact the **Jefferson County Visitor & Convention Bureau**, P.O. Box A, Harpers Ferry, WV 25425, ☎ 304-535-2627 or 800-848-TOUR, Internet: www.jeffersoncountycvb.com. Another source is the **West Virginia Welcome Center**, Hwy. US-340, across from the Visitor Center, Harpers Ferry, WV 25425, ☎ 304-535-2482, Internet: www.state.wv.us.

FOOD AND DRINK:

Among the tourist-oriented eateries in town are the:

Anvil Restaurant (1270 Washington St. at Old Furnace Rd.) Popular American dishes, with a focus on seafood—all served in a rustic atmosphere. ☎ 304-535-2582. X: Mon., also Tues. from Jan.–Mar. $ and $$

Garden of Food (High St.) Burgers and other light lunches. (304-535-2202. $

Back Street Café (Potomac St.) Salads and sandwiches, indoors or out. ☎ 304-725-8019. $

This is a great place for a **picnic**; supplies are available in town, and the National Historical Park has free facilities.

LOCAL ATTRACTIONS:

Numbers in parentheses correspond to numbers on the map.

Begin at the **Visitor Center** (1) of the **Harpers Ferry National Historical Park**, located just off US-340, west of the Lower Town. Here you can park your car, see various exhibits, get information, possibly join a tour, and board a shuttle bus to the Lower Town. *☎ 304-535-6298, Internet: www.nps.gov/hafe. Open daily 8–5, remaining open until 6 in summer. Closed Christmas. Park use fee $5 per car or $3 per person without car. Seniors 62+ free (with Golden Age card). Tours. Picnic facilities.* &.

The **Lower Town** is almost two miles east of the Visitor Center, and is reached by shuttle bus or on foot. Make your first stop there at the **Stagecoach Inn** (2) of 1826, which now serves as the Park Information Center and bookstore. Adjacent to this are exhibitions on the industrial history of Harpers Ferry. Cross Shenandoah Street to the **Master**

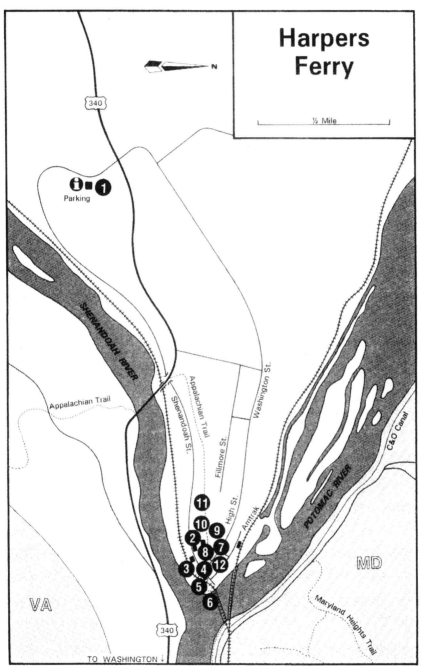

Armorer's House (3), built in 1858 as a residence for the armory's chief gunsmith. It is now a museum of gunmaking. Next door is a **Dry Goods Store** of the mid-19th century, restored as it would have been just before the Civil War.

The **John Brown Museum** (4), on Shenandoah Street between High and Potomac streets, offers a film on John Brown's life along with related memorabilia. Across the street is **John Brown's Fort** (5), actually the armory's enginehouse, in which he and his raiders took refuge as the town was stormed by militia units on October 17, 1859. Marines under the command of then-Colonel Robert E. Lee, arriving by train from Washington, captured the "fort" after a short battle the following morning. Brown, along with his surviving followers, was taken into custody, swiftly tried, and quickly hanged. On the day of his execution, he wrote a prophetic note predicting the bloodshed to come. His slave insurrection had failed, and there was now no option other than Civil War.

A walk under the railroad tracks leads to **The Point** (6) at the very confluence of the rivers, from which three states can be seen. Stroll up Potomac Street, passing the **Whitehall Tavern**, and bear left to High Street. There are two **Civil War Museums** (7) here that recall life in Harpers Ferry during the constant turmoil of war. Close by is the **Black History Exhibit** (8) and the base of the **Stone Steps** that lead steeply to the town's upper levels. Climb these to the **Harper House** (9) of 1775, built by the town's founder and now furnished as it was in his day. **St. Peter's Catholic Church** (10), not a part of the park, was built around 1830, survived the war, and remains in use today. It offers a magnificent view, but not quite as spectacular as the panorama that unfolds higher up the mountainside at *Jefferson Rock** (11). Thomas Jefferson visited this spot in 1783, and is supposed to have remarked that the view was "worth a voyage across the Atlantic."

Back in town, you might want to stop at the privately-owned **John Brown Wax Museum** (12), where the famous raid is brought to life through the media of sound and animation. *High St., ☎ 304-535-6342. Open daily mid-March–early Dec., weekends Jan.–March. Adults $2.50, seniors $2, students 12–18 $1.50, children 6–11 75¢.*

Located just six miles southwest of town is the recently-renovated **Charles Town Races**, where fans can experience live horse racing, simulcast racing from around the globe and over 1,000 video slot machines. *US Rte. 340, ☎ 800-795-7001, Internet: www.ctownraces.com. Open daily Mon.–Sat. 9 a.m.–2 a.m. and Sun. 1 p.m.–2 a.m.*

Serious hikers can enjoy a visit across the river on the **Maryland Heights Trail**, a rugged section of the park in Maryland that offers fabulous views and Civil War ruins along with steep climbs. Ask at the Visitor Center for a free trail map. Rock climbers must register before attempting the dangerous cliffs.

Prince George's and Charles Counties

You don't have to go far from Washington to enjoy a genuine old-time rural experience. The Oxon Hill Farm is in fact immediately south of the capital, barely seven miles from the Washington Monument, yet it preserves a traditional 19th-century way of life.

Plantation farming of the 18th century is kept alive for visitors at the nearby National Colonial Farm on the shores of the Potomac. Fort Washington, the capital's first line of defense in the War of 1812, is just across the Piscataway Creek and offers a look at 19th-century military life along with a great view of Mount Vernon.

One of the great dramas of the Civil War occurred in this area as a wounded John Wilkes Booth fled Washington after assassinating President Lincoln. Two houses associated with the plot are open as living-history museums, where tales of murky loyalties and all-too-quick justice are recalled by costumed docents.

Port Tobacco, one of the oldest English settlements in the New World, began life around 1640 but later practically disappeared. Rediscovered and restored, it is now an unusual remembrance of a time when tobacco was king.

Several of the attractions on this short excursion are especially suitable for children, and are fortunately quite inexpensive (or even free!), courtesy of the National Park Service.

GETTING THERE:

By car, Oxon Hill Farm lies immediately south of Washington at the intersection of MD-210 and the Capital Beltway I-95, Exit 3.

Continue south on MD-210 about four miles, then turn right onto Fort Washington Road for some three miles to the National Park. For the National Colonial Farm, return to MD-210 via Old Fort Road, go south about three miles, and west on Bryan Point Road to the farm.

The Surratt House is a few miles to the east on MD-223, just south of the town of Clinton on Brandywine Road. For Dr. Mudd's House continue south on MD-5, turning left on MD-382, then right on MD-232,

Bryantown Road.

Return on MD-5 and turn south on **US-301** to La Plata, where you turn right on **MD-6** for three miles. Go south on Chapel Point Road a half-mile to the Port Tobacco Restored Area.

PRACTICALITIES:

The rural attractions are open every day except Thanksgiving, Christmas, and New Year's Day (the Colonial Farm is also closed on Mondays). Those wishing to see the Surratt and Mudd houses should come on a weekend between mid-spring and mid-fall, or check the few other times that they're open. Port Tobacco sites are basically open on weekends from April through November, plus a few other days in summer.

For further information contact the **Prince George's County Visitors Bureau**, 9200 Basil Ct., #101, Largo, MD 20774, ☎ 301-925-8300 or 888-925-8300, or **Charles County Tourism**, P.O. Box B, La Plata, MD 20646 ☎ 301-645-0558, 800-766-3386, Internet: www.govt.co.charles.md.us.

FOOD AND DRINK:

Wayfarer Restaurant (in Clinton, on MD-5 a mile south of MD-223, at the Colony South Hotel) An attractive place for beef, poultry, seafood, and pasta dishes. ☎ 301-856-3343. $$

Red River Barbeque & Grille (in Waldorf, on US-301, a half-mile south of MD-228) Southwestern cooking and ambiance. ☎ 301-374-6700. $$

Why not have an enjoyable **picnic lunch**? Free tables and facilities are available at Oxon Hill Farm, Fort Washington, and the National Colonial Farm.

LOCAL ATTRACTIONS:

Numbers in parentheses correspond to numbers on the map.

The first three attractions are mostly outdoors, bringing history to life in a rural setting:

OXON HILL FARM (1), Oxon Hill Rd. off MD-210, Oxon Hill, MD 20745, ☎ 301-839-1177. *Open daily 8–4:30. Activities curtailed from Dec. through March. Closed Thanksgiving, Christmas, and New Year's. Free. Picnic facilities. Nature trail.* ♿.

Run by the National Park Service, Oxon Hill is a living-history farm that preserves rural life as it was in Maryland and Virginia around the turn of the century. Visitors may join in the fun as cows are milked and

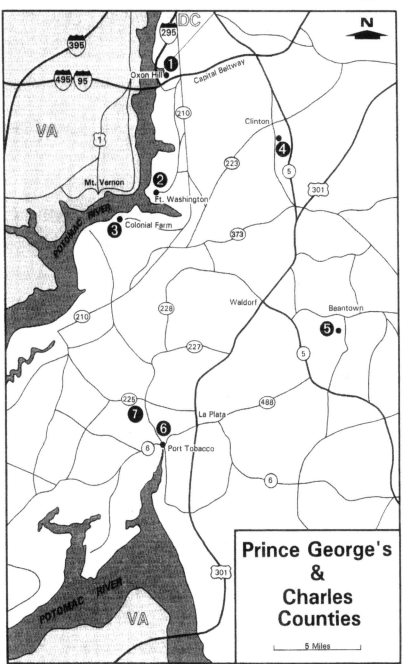

Prince George's
&
Charles
Counties

5 Miles

eggs collected. The usual barnyard animals are here, most of them tame enough to be petted by children. You can also watch the crops grow (helpful signs tell you what they are), see chores tended to, and perhaps even take a hayride.

FORT WASHINGTON PARK (2), Indian Head Hwy., MD-210, Fort Washington, MD 20744, ☎ 301-763-4600. *Park open daily 8–dusk, Visitor Center daily 9–5. Closed Christmas and New Year's. Use fee: $4 per vehicle or $2 per pedestrian or cyclist. Seniors free. Hiking trail. Picnic facilities. Tours.* ♿.

Another offering of the National Park Service, Fort Washington was built between 1814 and 1824 on the site of Fort Warburton, which was destroyed by its own commander during the War of 1812 to prevent its falling into the hands of the British. This was Washington's first line of defense against naval attack, and served well through the Civil War. Today's visitors can cross the drawbridge to tour the massive fortifications, visit the small museum, and get a wonderful view across the Potomac to Mount Vernon.

NATIONAL COLONIAL FARM (3), 3400 Bryan Point Rd., Accokeek, MD 20607, ☎ 301-283-2113, Internet: web.gmu.edu/bios/potamac/af. *Open Tues.–Sun. 10–4. Closed Mon., Thanksgiving, Christmas, and New Year's. Adults $2, children 50¢ (maximum $5 per family). Tours. Picnic facilities.*

Step back even further in time at this re-created 18th-century Tidewater tobacco plantation, where agricultural methods of the 1750s are carried on by workers in period costume. Along with the favorite Colonial cash crop is a kitchen garden, a herb garden, an orchard, and grape arbors for wine production. Typical livestock of the era meander about the barnyard, while the authentically re-created buildings include a small frame farmhouse, a kitchen dependency, a smokehouse, and an outhouse.

The next two attractions recount the bizarre story of John Wilkes Booth's flight to Virginia after assassinating President Lincoln at Ford's Theater in Washington on April 14, 1865 (see page 69):

MARY SURRATT HOUSE AND TAVERN (4), 9118 Brandywine Rd., Clinton, MD 20735, ☎ 301-868-1121. Internet: www.clark.net/pub/surratt/surratt.htm/. *Open March–mid-Dec., Thurs.–Fri. 11–3 and Sat.–Sun. noon–4. Adults $3, less for seniors and children. Research library. Book store. Gift* shop. &.

Mary Elizabeth Surratt (1823–65) had the dubious distinction of being the first woman to be hanged by the U.S. government. Ironically, she was very likely innocent of any role in the Lincoln assassination plot—although her young son was probably guilty, and he went free. Her house was also the local post office, tavern, and gathering place for a community whose sympathies, like those of other southern Maryland towns, favored the Confederacy—and it was almost surely used as a safe house for Rebel agents. Now restored, the house is shown on tours by costumed docents who will relate the whole story to you, and leave you wondering about the kind of justice that often accompanies national hysteria. Another popular tour offered by the museum is by bus, tracing the entire escape route of John Wilkes Booth from Ford's Theatre to the site of Garrett's Farm.

DR. SAMUEL A. MUDD HOUSE MUSEUM (5), Rt. 232, Waldorf, MD 20646, ☎ 301-934-8464. *Open early April–late Nov., Sat.–Sun. noon–4 and Wed. 11–3. Adults $3, less for children. Tours. Gift shop.*

Although presumably innocent of having knowingly committed a crime, Dr. Samuel A. Mudd (1833–83) was sentenced to life imprisonment for treating the wounds of a fugitive-in-disguise whose real name was John Wilkes Booth, and who was headed for supposed safety in Virginia. Whether Dr. Mudd even knew of Lincoln's assassination is doubtful, but so high were public feelings about the deed that anyone even remotely connected to it was persecuted. Fortunately, Dr. Mudd was pardoned four years later by President Andrew Jackson. Costumed docents, some actually descendants of the good doctor, will take you through the restored house as they relate the story.

About 15 miles farther south is the historic village of **Port Tobacco** (6), the ancestral home of a vanished Native American culture and one of the earliest English settlements in the New World. Officially colonized in the 1640s as Charlestown, it was a major seaport for shipping the filthy weed, thus its popular name. During the 19th century, however, the creek silted up and became a tidal marsh, plunging the town into economic decline. Abandoned as the county seat after the courthouse burned down in the 1890s, Port Tobacco all but disappeared. Today, only a few original buildings remain, along with some reconstructions. These are operated as a **museum** of local life from early Colonial days through the Civil War.

Begin your visit at the reconstructed **Charles County Courthouse** of 1819, where you can see historical exhibits and watch a 30-minute video on the town's story. ☎ *301-934-4313. Open Apr.–May and Sept.–Dec., weekends only, noon–4; and June–Aug., Wed.–Sun., noon–4. Schedules vary; call ahead to confirm. Nominal admission. Gift shop.* ♿. Other buildings that can be visited include the authentically-furnished 18th-century **Catslide House** with its hands-on Children's Museum, and the original 19th- century **One-Room Schoolhouse** with period furnishings.

Another nearby site is the **Thomas Stone Haberdeventure Plantation** (7), located on Rose Hill Road between Maryland routes 6 and 225, four miles west of La Plata. One of the four Maryland signers of the Declaration of Independence, Thomas Stone (1743–87) was a successful lawyer, politician, and businessman who eventually expanded his plantation to encompass some 1,077 acres. Haberdeventure, its name, remained in the Stone family until 1936. It was purchased by the National Park Service in 1981, and recently restored to its original appearance. ☎ *301-934-6027 Internet: www.nps.gov/thst/, 6655 Rose Hill Rd., Port Tobacco, MD, 20677. Open Memorial Day through Labor Day, daily 9–5; and on Thursdays through Mondays the rest of the year, 9–5. Closed Christmas and New Year's Day. Tours, orientation video, exhibits, and picnic facilities.*

St. Mary's County

Maryland's history began in 1634 at St. Mary's City, the fourth-oldest English settlement in the New World and the colony's first capital. Once a thriving place, St. Mary's faded away after the capital moved to Annapolis in 1695, and was largely forgotten about. In recent years the town has come back to life as a sort of mini-Williamsburg-in-the-making, offering visitors a chance to experience 17th-century Colonial life as it was, without the tourist throngs. Here you can probe an early tobacco plantation, a replica of the sailing ship that brought Maryland's first colonists from England, the reconstructed State House of 1676, various other living-history sites, and even try a lunch in a Colonial garden setting.

A different kind of history is revisited at Point Lookout State Park, the site of a Civil War fortress and prison overlooking Chesapeake Bay. Those interested in more recent military matters will enjoy a stop at the Naval Air Test and Evaluation Museum, where several of the actual craft that made naval aviation history may be inspected.

Sotterley Plantation, the last stop on this excursion, traces its traditions back to the 15th-century Wars of the Roses, fought in England long before the first colonists ever set foot on these shores. Its story is a fascinating one, as is its beautifully-preserved early-18th-century architecture and lovely setting.

GETTING THERE:

By car, St. Mary's City is about 75 miles southeast of Washington. Take Route **MD-4** (Pennsylvania Avenue extension), crossing the Patuxent River at Solomons, and turn left onto **MD- 235**. Continue south through Lexington Park and turn right onto Mattapany Road for two miles, then left on **MD-5**, and follow signs.

St. Inigoes is four miles south of St. Mary's City on MD-5. Continue another nine miles to Point Lookout.

Return on MD-5, turning right on MD-235 back to Lexington Park, where you'll find the Naval Air Museum.

If you're visiting Sotterley, continue north on MD-235 to Hollywood, then go right on MD-245. You can return to Washington via MD-235,

MD-5, and US-301.

PRACTICALITIES:

Historic St. Mary's City is open daily from the beginning of April through the last weekend in November. The Naval Air Museum is open Tuesday through Sunday, 10-5 year-round. Sotterley Plantation is closed on Mondays and from November through April.

For further information contact **St. Mary's County Tourism**, P.O. Box 653, Leonardtown, MD 20650, ☎ 301-475-4411 or 800-327-9023.

FOOD AND DRINK:

Among the best choices for lunch are:

Spinnakers at Point Lookout Marina (Wynne Rd., Ridge, 8 miles south of St. Mary's City) Famous for its soft-shell crabs and other seafood delights, served in a friendly atmosphere. ☎ 301-872-4340. X: Tues. $$

Farthing's Kitchen (Historic St. Mary's City site) Colonial and modern lunches in a period garden setting. ☎ 301-862-0988. $ and $$

Aloha (2025 Wildewood Ctr., MD-235 in California, between St. Mary's City and Sotterley) Szechuan, Hunan, and Mandarin dishes—all in a Polynesian setting. ☎ 301-862-4838. $

Free **picnic facilities** are available year-round at Historic St. Mary's City and at Point Lookout State Park (with the exception of a $3 summer weekend and holiday charge).

LOCAL ATTRACTIONS:

Numbers in parentheses correspond to numbers on the map.

*HISTORIC ST. MARY'S CITY (1), MD-5 south of Lexington Park, St. Mary's City, MD 20686, ☎ 301-862-0990 or 800-SMC-1634, Internet: www.webgraphic.com/home. *Sites open April–Nov., Wed.–Sun. 10–5. Closed Thanksgiving. Adults $7.50, students with ID $5.50, children (6–12) $3.50. Living history activities. Hiking trails. Gift shop. Restaurant.* ⅃.

Practically lost for centuries, America's fourth oldest permanent English settlement was restored by the State of Maryland and opened to the public in 1984 as a living-history museum. Until 1695 it had been the capital of the colony, but after the politicians moved to Annapolis this tiny port all but vanished from memory.

The first settlers to step ashore here arrived from England in March, 1634. Led by Leonard Calvert (1606–47), brother of the Royal Proprietor, Lord Baltimore, the party consisted of 18 gentlemen, one Catholic priest, and some 140 indentured servants. From the very beginning, the colony of Maryland was intended as a haven for persecuted Catholics,

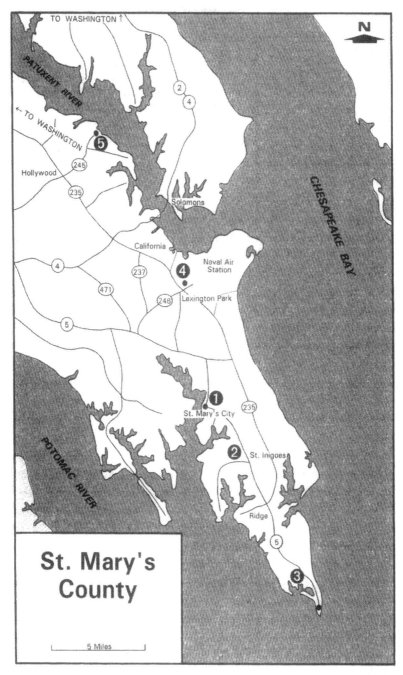

N

TO WASHINGTON ↑

PATUXENT RIVER

← TO WASHINGTON

Hollywood

(2)
(4)

(245)

(235)

Solomons

California

(4)

(237)

(471)

Naval Air Station

(246)

Lexington Park

(5)

CHESAPEAKE BAY

POTOMAC RIVER

(235)

St. Mary's City

St. Inigoes

Ridge

(5)

St. Mary's County

5 Miles

and as early as 1649 passed a statute providing freedom of worship.

Among the sites to visit is the reconstructed **State House** of 1676, a replica of the state's first public building. With luck, you'll be able to see the past brought to life with living reenactments of long-ago trials. Riding at anchor nearby is the 42-ton square-rigged *Maryland Dove*, a full-scale reproduction of one of the two ships that brought the first colonists. Visitors can board it to learn all about life at sea on such an improbably small vessel (the other ship, the *Ark*, was 300 tons and carried most of the passengers), and join in the fun as little dramas are acted out once again.

The **Godiah Spray Tobacco Plantation**, a complete working re-creation of a 17th-century farm, is staffed with costumed members of the fictional "Spray family" and their "indentured servants." They'll invite you to try your hand at the various chores, and tell you about the wondrous crop that brought prosperity to Colonial Maryland. If all this activity makes you hungry, you can stop at **Farthing's Kitchen** for a bite, or just to look around the reconstructed 17th-century inn. Other sights include the **Margaret Brent Memorial Garden & Gazebo**, honoring the first Colonial woman to demand the right to vote (she didn't get it), the **Woodland Indian Hamlet** and re-created buildings in the town center, and the **Brentland Farm Visitors Center** with its exhibit hall.

Continue down MD-5 to the hamlet of St. Inigoes, where you'll find the **St. Ignatius Church** (2), built in 1758 on the site of the first Roman Catholic mission in the English colonies. The churchyard here is among the oldest in the nation, dating from the 1640s. *Villa Rd. off MD-5.* ☎ *301-872-5590.* In a few more miles you'll come to the:

POINT LOOKOUT STATE PARK (3), P.O. Box 48, Scotland, MD 20687, ☎ *301-872-5688. Park open daily. Visitor center and museum open weekends April, May, Sept. and Oct. 10–6, and daily 10–6 from Memorial Day through Labor Day. Nominal use fee. Boating. Camping. Fishing. Nature walks. Picnic facilities.*

Today this 1,000-plus-acre park offers wonderful ***views** at the confluence of Chesapeake Bay and the Potomac River, but during the Civil War this was the site of a particularly horrible Union POW camp. Well over 3,000 Confederate soldiers died in captivity here as a result of inhumane conditions, just across the river from Rebel territory in Virginia. Their suffering is remembered in a **Civil War Museum** and in the remains of **Fort Lincoln**, built by their forced labor. No wonder the place is allegedly haunted.

Heading north again soon brings you to the:

NAVAL AIR TEST & EVALUATION CENTER MUSEUM (4), Three Notch Rd., MD-325, Lexington Park, MD 20653, ☎ 301-863-7418. *Open Tues.–Sun. 10–5, year-round. Closed New Year's Day, Easter, Thanksgiving, Christmas. Donations accepted. Model shop.*

Located just outside the North Gate of Patuxent Naval Air Station, this is the only museum in America dedicated to the test and evaluation of naval aircraft. A number of vintage aircraft are on display outside, including some rather odd items, while the indoor exhibits include models, historical artifacts, a trainer cockpit, and audio-visual displays.

On the way back to Washington, just east of Hollywood on MD-245, is the:

SOTTERLEY PLANTATION (5), Hollywood, MD 20636, ☎ 301-373-2280 or 800-681-0850, Internet: www.eaglenet.com/sotterley/. *Grounds open year-round Tues.–Sun. 10–4. Manor House tours available Tues.–Sun., May–Oct. Adults $7, children $3, under five free. Tours for adult groups of 15 or more $5 per person. Gift shop.*

Sotterley takes its name from Sotterley Hall in Suffolk, England, once owned by the Satterlee family. Unfortunately, they were supporters of the Lancastrians during the Wars of the Roses, and so lost their property upon the accession to the throne of Edward IV in 1461. That estate was given to the loyal Plater family. Later generations of the Platers moved to Maryland in the New World, where they owned the ancestral home's namesake, Sotterley Plantation. To complete the story, in 1910 the plantation was sold to Herbert Satterlee, a descendant of the original dispossessed family of the 15th century!

Not only is the story interesting, but so is the architecture. Built around 1717, the house is an elegant mixture of styles, full of strange little oddities. These are shown on guided tours, after which you can explore the grounds of this working plantation. Don't miss the restored slave cabin, farm museum, and "necessary."

Upper Eastern Shore

Much of Maryland's watery Eastern Shore lies too far from Washington for a comfortable daytrip, but fortunately some of its best sights are found not far north and south of the easily accessible Chesapeake Bay Bridge. This scenic drive heads north along the edge of the bay to several unspoiled wildlife refuges where you can momentarily escape into a world of nature, and to a wonderfully preserved Colonial town whose colorful past can be explored on an easy walking tour. As a bonus, you can savor some of the fresh seafood delights for which the area is so justly renowned.

Those with more time might stay overnight and combine this trip with the next one, or with Annapolis. Alternatively, the Eastern Shore can also be visited en route to Trips 40 and 41 in Delaware.

GETTING THERE:

By car, Chestertown is about 70 miles northeast of Washington via Route **US-50**, Annapolis, the Chesapeake Bay Bridge, Stevensville, and Grasonville. At Queenstown turn left onto **US-301**, then exit at **MD-213** North and continue through Centreville and Church Hill into Chestertown. Turn left at Cross Street (MD-289), parking near High Street and the Town Square.

To reach Rock Hall, continue on **MD-20** (High Street) for about 12 miles to the southwest. Another eight miles south on **MD-445** brings you to the Eastern Neck National Wildlife Refuge.

You'll have to come back pretty much the same way, or swim.

PRACTICALITIES:

This scenic drive can be taken at any time in good weather, but it's especially nice in spring and fall. The few indoor attractions are of minor interest, so don't plan your trip around their opening times. Bear in mind that traffic across the Chesapeake Bay Bridge can be fierce on summer weekends.

For further information contact the **Queen Anne's County Visitors Service**, 425 Piney Narrows Rd., Chester, MD 21619, ☎ 410-604-2100; or the **Kent County Tourism Office**, 400 South Cross Street, Chestertown, MD 21620, ☎ 410-778-0416. Internet: www.kentcounty.com.

FOOD AND DRINK:

Some choice restaurants are:

The Narrows (US-50 at the Kent Narrows Bridge, Grasonville) More upscale than its neighbors, The Narrows specializes in crabs but also provides other dishes. Outdoor seating in season. ☎ 410-827-8113. $$ and $$$

Harris' Crab House (433 Kent Narrows Way N., Grasonville) A large, casual, and popular place at the Kent Narrows Bridge for crabs and beer, with outdoor tables on the deck as well as a dining room. Landlubber food is offered, too. ☎ 410-827-9500. $$

The Old Wharf Inn (Cannon St. at the harbor in Chestertown) Seafood, steaks, and other American dishes, overlooking the historic harbor. ☎ 410-778-3566. $$

Angler (3015 Kent Narrows Way S., US-50, Exit 42, Grasonville) Fresh seafood served with an authentic local touch. ☎ 410-827-6717. $ and $$

Holly's Restaurant (US-50 at Jackson Creek Rd., Grasonville) Venerable and unpretentious, this establishment offers good cooking at modest prices. ☎ 410-827-8711. $

LOCAL ATTRACTIONS:

Numbers in parentheses correspond to numbers on the map.

The Eastern Shore begins just as soon as you cross the Chesapeake Bay Bridge, at the small town of **Stevensville** (1). If you stop, you might want to take a look at the **Cray House** on Cockey's Lane, a gambrel-roofed wooden house of 1839 that's furnished with period middle-class pieces and occasionally open to the public. The nearby **Stevensville Train Station** of 1902, also on Cockey's Lane, today has model trains instead of real ones. **Christ Church** houses the oldest Episcopal congregation in Maryland, and exhibits a 17th-century communion chalice in its odd Carpenter Gothic structure of 1880, built with bricks from the original church of 1652. *117 E. Main St.,* ☎ *410-643-5921.*

Continue down the road to **Grasonville** (2), which has numerous seafood restaurants. Just south of this, reached via Perry's Corner Road, is the **Horsehead Wetlands Center** (3). Managed by the Wildfowl Trust of North America, this 310-acre nature preserve is home to colorful flocks of waterfowl and many other bird species, along with resident deer, foxes, otters, and so on. Visitors can use the blinds and observation towers, see the various exhibits, go for nature walks, or even have a picnic. ☎ *410-827-6694. Open daily except Christmas, 9–5. Nominal admission charge. Pets prohibited. Gift shop.*

Queenstown (4) has a number of factory-outlet stores, but it also has the **Historic Queen Anne's County Courthouse** of 1708 that served until 1749. *MD-18 off US-301. Tours by appointment,* ☎ *410-827-7646.*

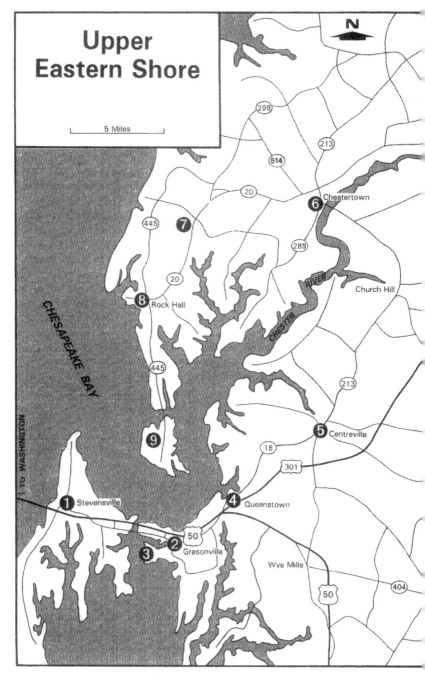

Upper Eastern Shore

5 Miles

Continue on to **Centreville** (5), home of the present **Queen Anne's County Courthouse**, built in 1791. Of course, there's a statue of England's Queen Anne (1665–1714) here, seated in a Queen Anne chair. It was dedicated in 1977 by England's Princess Anne, who is unlikely to become a queen. *122 N. Commerce St. (MD-213),* ☎ *410-827-7646. Open Mon.–Fri. 9–4. Free.*

Head north on MD-213 into Kent County and **Chestertown** (6), founded in 1706 around a courthouse of 1698. Like Boston, the town is famous for its tea party, in which rampaging locals boarded an English ship in 1774 and tossed a cargo of British tea into the harbor, apparently along with some of the crew. Several square blocks of the old town, mostly from the Chester River north to Mill street, and from Maple Avenue west to Cannon Street, are exceptionally well preserved, and marked with historical identification plaques. These correspond to a free printed walking-tour map available at the Chamber of Commerce *400 S. Cross St.,* ☎ *410-778-0416* and other places. The **Geddes-Piper House** of the 1780s now houses the Historical Society of Kent County and may be visited. *101 Church Alley, off Queen St. between Maple and High,* ☎ *410-778-3499. Open weekends, 1–4.* Among the period furnishings is a splendid collection of teapots, once owned by the same merchant from whose ship the infamous tea was dumped.

Head west on MD-20 towards Rock Hall. Along the way you'll pass the entrance of **Chesapeake Farms** (7), a 3,000-acre wildlife research and demonstration area. You may drive through its various habitats along a signposted six-mile car route, following a free brochure/map available at the nearby office. *7319 Remington Drive,* ☎ *410-778-8400. Open Feb.–mid-Oct. Free.*

Continue on to the bayside village of **Rock Hall** (8), a stop on the old travel route from Virginia to Philadelphia and the North. The town's colorful history is celebrated at the small **Rock Hall Museum**, a miscellaneous collection of all kinds of local artifacts. *Municipal Bldg., S. Main St. (MD-445),* ☎ *410-778-1399. Open Wed.–Fri. and Sun. 2–4:30, and Sat. 10–noon.* Also see the **Waterman's Museum** with exhibits on oystering, crabbing, fishing, historical photographs, local carving, boats and a replica of an old shanty. *Rock Hall,* ☎ *410-778-6697. Open Sat., Sun. and holidays from 10–5. Obtain key from marina next door for weekday entrance. Free.*

If you really want to leave civilization behind, just head south on MD-445 a few miles to the **Eastern Neck National Wildlife Refuge** (9). A paradise for migrating waterfowl operated by the U.S. Fish and Wildlife Service, this is a wonderful getaway for humans, too. You can hike through a variety of habitats on several short trails, and enjoy great views of Chesapeake Bay and the Chester River. *1730 Eastern Neck Rd. (MD-445),* ☎ *410-639-7056. Open daily, dawn to dusk. Free.* ♿

Trip 39

Central Eastern Shore

Several of the Eastern Shore's most rewarding sights are found in Talbot County, between the Chesapeake Bay Bridge and the Choptank River. Here you'll encounter much of the maritime flavor and culture unique to this region, explore its past, taste its food, and perhaps even go for a boat ride or two.

If you're staying over, this trip combines well with the previous one, and also with Annapolis.

GETTING THERE:

By car, Easton is about 70 miles east of Washington via Route **US-50**, Annapolis, and the Chesapeake Bay Bridge.

Head west about 10 miles on **MD-33** to St. Michaels, then another 15 miles to Tilghman Island.

Return by the same (and only) route through St. Michaels, turning south on **MD-329** and a local road to Bellevue. Take the ferry to Oxford (or drive a very roundabout route), then **MD-333** and local roads back to US-50.

PRACTICALITIES:

Other than scenery and the colorful Eastern Shore ambiance, the major attraction of this excursion is the mostly outdoor Chesapeake Bay Maritime Museum at St. Michaels. Fortunately, this is open every day except Thanksgiving and Christmas Some of the minor cultural sites are open on weekends in season only. Note that the Oxford-Bellevue Ferry does not operate from December through February, during which time drivers have to make a lengthy detour or not go to Oxford. Fine weather is essential for enjoying this trip.

For further information contact the **Talbot County Chamber of Commerce**, P.O. Box 1366, 210 Marlboro Ave., Easton, MD 21601, ☎ 410-822-4606, Internet: www.talbotchamber.org.

FOOD AND DRINK:

Among the many good restaurants in this area are:

The Inn at Perry Cabin (308 Watkins Lane, St. Michaels) Superb

Continental cuisine served in the most elegant of country inns. Dress accordingly and make reservations. ☎ 410-745-2200. $$$

Crab Claw (156 Mill St. at Talbot St., St. Michaels) Crabs and other seafood, with a few landlubber options. Great view. ☎ 410-745-2900. X: Dec.-Feb. $$

Town Dock (125 Mulberry St., at the harbor, St. Michaels) Enjoy a great view of the harbor from any table in this large seafood restaurant. ☎ 410-745-5577. $ and $$

Legal Spirits (42 E. Dover St. at Harrison St., Easton) Prohibition and the Roaring Twenties is the theme of this casual pub, serving steaks, burgers, seafood, and the like. ☎ 410-820-0033. $ and $$

Washington Street Pub (20 N. Washington St., Easton) Burgers, sandwiches, and like in a pub. (410-822-9011. $

Additionally, some of the restaurants described in the previous chapter are also convenient for this trip.

LOCAL ATTRACTIONS:
Numbers in parentheses correspond to numbers on the map.

The hamlet of **Wye Mills** (1) is right on the border between Queen Anne's and Talbot counties, just south and west of US-50 via MD-404. It is named after its 1671 gristmill that, after being rebuilt in 1720 and 1840, stills grinds out flour and yellow cornmeal as it has for over three centuries. George Washington's hungry troops at Valley Forge survived on provisions from here; you can buy a bag, too, as you tour the mill. *MD-662, Wye Mills,* ☎ *410-827-6909. Open daily Apr.–Oct., weekdays 10–1, weekends 10–4. Donations accepted. Gift shop.*

Close to the mill is **Wye Oak State Park**, a 29-acre spread surrounding Maryland's state tree, the 450-year-old Wye Oak. At 95 feet in height and 21 feet in circumference, this is thought to be the largest white oak in America, and surely the only one to rate its very own park.

Rejoin US-50 by heading south on MD-662, then continue down to **Easton** (2). Route MD-331 (Dover Road) will bring you west into the center of town. First settled in 1682, Easton is the beautifully-preserved and quite prosperous county seat. Among its attractions is the **Talbot County Courthouse** of 1794, where branch offices of the state government were located in the days when the Eastern Shore was a remote, isolated place. The **Historical Society Museum**, two blocks south of this, has changing exhibits of local history in its three galleries. They also offer a walking-tour pamphlet, and visits to other historical houses and gardens in town. *25 S. Washington St.,* ☎ *410-822-0773.*

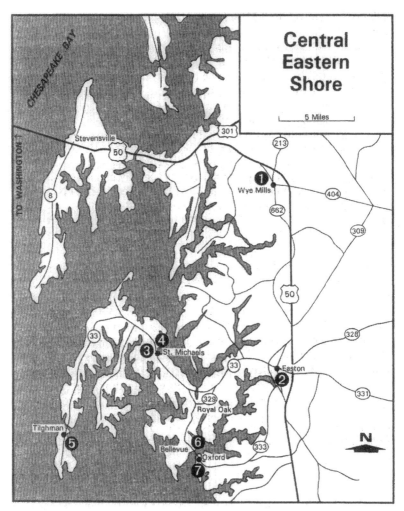

Open Tues.–Fri. 11–3, Sat. 10–4. Adults $3 for museum, $3 for house tours, $5 combined; children 10 and under free.

Also in Easton is the **Academy of the Arts** with its exhibitions of paintings, sculptures, photographs, and so on. *106 South Street,* ☎ *410-822-0455, Internet: www.art-academy.org. Open Mon.–Sat. 10–4, Wed. until 9.* ♿. Return to Washington Street and stroll south a few blocks to the **Third Haven Friends Meeting House.** Built by Quakers in 1682, this is thought to be the oldest wood-frame house of worship to remain in continuous use in America. William Penn himself spoke here, and Lord

Baltimore attended services. *405 S. Washington St.,* ☎ *410-822-0293. Open daily 9–5. Free.*

Follow the map west to **St. Michaels** (3), the little "town that fooled the British." During the War of 1812 this strategic shipbuilding center fell under naval attack, but was saved by the simple expedient of blacking itself out during the night and hoisting lanterns high into the treetops so that the British gunners would aim too high. It worked, and only one house was struck. This so-called "Cannonball House" is still there, on Mulberry Street on the northwest side of **St. Mary's Square**. This lovely little bit of public space is well worth perusing on foot. If it's open, pay a visit to the **St. Mary's Square Museum**, where local history is explored in two vintage buildings. ☎ *410-745-9561. Open May–Oct., weekends only, 10–4. Donation.* Spend some time just ambling around St. Michaels and absorbing its atmosphere, then visit the premier attraction of this daytrip, the:

*CHESAPEAKE BAY MARITIME MUSEUM (4), Mill St. at Navy Point, St. Michaels, MD 21663, ☎ 410-745-2916, Internet: www.cbmm.org. *Open daily year round: Summer 9–7, fall & spring 9–5, winter 9–4. Closed Thanksgiving, Christmas and New Year's Day. Adults $7.50, seniors $6.50, children (6–17) $3. Family rate $18. Gift shop. Cruises.* ఉ.

You're in for a treat as you probe the 18 watery acres of restored buildings and boats that make up this marvelous museum. Its trademark feature is the **Hooper Strait Lighthouse** of 1879, a typical "screw-pile" affair of which only a few survive. There's a boatbuilding shop, a Watermen's wharf, waterfowling and Bay history buildings, and plenty of floating exhibits including a skipjack, a log canoe, and a bugeye. **Cruises** aboard the *Patriot*, lasting about 60 minutes, are offered daily from April through October, 10–4. ☎ *410-745-3100 for cruise information. Fares: $8.50, under 12 $4.*

By continuing along MD-33 you can make a nice little **side trip** across a drawbridge to **Tilghman Island** (5). Relatively uncommercialized, this old watermen's community is still home to a vanishing fleet of sail-powered fishing boats that co-exists with low-key tourism. Explore its delightful setting, then return through St. Michaels and turn south to Bellevue.

The **Oxford-Bellevue Ferry** (6) has been a vital traffic link on the Tred Avon River since 1683, making it probably the oldest private ferry in America to remain in continuous operation. Its short trip across the river saves you many miles of driving, and is fun besides. ☎ *410-745-9023. Operates every 20 minutes, weekdays 7–sunset, weekends 9–sun-*

set. No service from Dec. through Feb. One-way fares: Car and driver $5, each passenger 50¢, pedestrians $1, bicycles $2, motorcycles $3. Capacity 9 cars. RVs and trailers can be accommodated.

Oxford (7), the last stop on the trip, was founded in the late 17th century and is one of Maryland's oldest towns. Tobacco was once shipped directly to England from the busy port here, which at the time was second only to Annapolis in the number of ships that docked. The replica **Customs House** near the ferry landing recaptures some of the past, and may be visited when it's open. *Mid-Apr.–mid-Oct., Fri.–Sun. 3–5. Free.* Two blocks south on Morris Street (MD-333) is the **Oxford Museum**, focusing its attention on local history. ☎ *410-226-5122. Open mid-Apr.–mid-Oct., Fri.–Sun., 2–5. Free.*

Section V

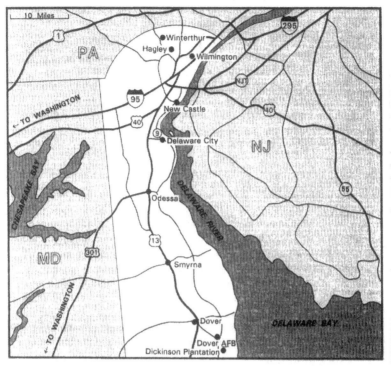

DAYTRIPS TO
DELAWARE

It may be tiny, but Delaware packs a lot of interest into less than 2,000 square miles. In the south, about 100 miles or so from Washington, you'll find historic towns dating as far back as the 17th and 18th centuries, including Dover and Odessa. New Castle, a bit to the north, was founded in 1651 and still preserves its unusual Dutch heritage. Visitors can travel by boat to a preserved Civil War fort in Delaware Bay, visit an 18th-century plantation, and enjoy nature preserves. But Delaware is primarily an industrial state, and one of the corporate capitals of America. With industry came wealth, lots of it, as is readily apparent when you visit the vast estates, châteaus, and marvelous gardens of the celebrated Brandywine Valley. Wilmington, too, has its cultural attractions, especially in its magnificent art museum.

Kent County

Dover became Delaware's capital in 1777, when invading British troops chased the Colonial Assembly out of New Castle (see page 280). The politicians apparently liked their new home, as they've stayed there ever since. Founded in 1683 by William Penn, this relaxed and rather quaint little town hardly looks like a state capital, but then again Delaware is a very small state.

There are enough attractions in and around Dover to keep you busy all day; however if you skip a few of these you might want to head north to the historic town of Smyrna, which has some off-the-beaten-track sites. In Dover you can visit the Old State House of 1792, browse through offbeat museums, and experience local agricultural life from Colonial days to the early 20th century. Just south of the capital is the immense Dover Air Force Base and its fine museum of vintage aircraft, and beyond that the John Dickinson Plantation of 1740, a reconstructed farm complex with its grand mansion and humble slave quarters. Smyrna offers several 18th- and 19th-century houses, including a Queen Anne country house of 1753 that you can visit on weekends.

GETTING THERE:

By car, Dover is about 100 miles east of Washington via Route US-50, Annapolis, the Chesapeake Bay Bridge, and routes US- 301, MD-302, MD-454, and DE-8.

PRACTICALITIES:

Most of the attractions are closed on Mondays, and some on Sundays as well. Check the individual listings in this chapter. The **Old Dover Days** celebration, when private historic houses and gardens are open to the public, is held on the first Saturday in May.

For further information, contact the **Delaware State Visitor Center**, Federal Street at Duke of York Street, Dover, DE 19903, ☎ (302) 739-4266. Another source is the **Kent County Convention & Visitors Bureau**, 9 East Loockerman St., Dover, DE 19901, ☎ (302) 734-1736 or (800) 233-KENT, Internet: www.visitdover.com.

FOOD AND DRINK:

Some dining choices are:

Blue Coat Inn (800 N. State St., near the north end of town) Early American specialties and seafood in a Colonial setting by a lake. ☎ (302) 674-1776. X: Mon. $$ and $$$

W.T. Smithers (140 S. State St., north of The Green) Creative American cuisine in an early-19th-century house. ☎ (302) 674-8875. $$ and $$$

Tango's Bistro (Sheraton Hotel, 1570 N. DuPont Hwy., US-13, Dover) Contemporary American cuisine in a bright, upscale setting. ☎ (302) 678-8500. $$

Captain John's (518 Bay Rd., near junction of US-13 and US-113, just east of town) This relaxed family eatery offers familiar American dishes and a salad bar, but no liquor. ☎ (302) 678-8166. $ and $$

In addition, you'll find a few decent luncheonettes in the vicinity of State and Loockerman streets in the historic district of Dover, and the usual fast-food emporiums along US-13.

LOCAL ATTRACTIONS:

Park at (or as close as possible to) the Visitor Center, from which you can easily walk to sites (1) through (6). You'll need a car to reach sites (7) through (11). *Numbers in parentheses correspond to numbers on the map.*

DELAWARE STATE VISITOR CENTER (1), Federal and Duke of York streets, ☎ (302) 739-4266. *Open Mon.–Sat. 8:30–4:30, Sun. 1:30–4:30. Free.* ♿.

Besides the wealth of free (and current!) information you can get here about Dover, Kent County, and all of Delaware, there are also changing exhibitions on related subjects, and a slide show on the historic sites. Upstairs is the new ***Sewell C. Biggs Museum of American Art**, a collection spanning some two centuries of fine art, furniture, and silver. Among the artists represented are Albert Bierstadt, Charles Wilson Peale, George Inness, and Gilbert Stuart. ☎ *(302) 674-2111. Museum open Wed.–Sat. 10–4, Sun. 1:30–4:30, closed major holidays. Free.*

OLD STATE HOUSE (2), South State Street at The Green, ☎ (302) 739-4266, Internet: www.destatemuseums.org/Statehs.htm. *Open Tues.–Sat. 10–4:30, Sun. 1:30–4:30, closed Mon. and State holidays. Free. Tours.* ♿.

Built in 1792, this is the nation's second-oldest State House in continuous use. Although the General Assembly moved to nearby Legislative Hall in 1934, the State House still remains Delaware's symbolic capitol. It contains an 18th-century courtroom, a ceremonial

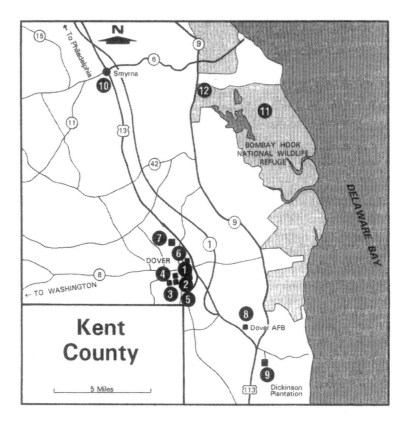

Governor's Office, legislative chambers, and county offices including a levy courtroom. Don't miss the larger-than-life portrait of George Washington in the Senate chamber, commissioned by the legislature in 1802.

Stretching out in front of the State House is **The Green**, a park-like meeting ground since the town's earliest days. A painting of King George III was burned here when the Declaration of Independence was read to the public in 1776, and it was on this site that Delaware's Continental Regiment was mustered for service in the Revolution. On the north side of the square is the former **Golden Fleece Tavern**, now private offices, where delegates met on December 7, 1787, to be the first to ratify the Constitution of the United States. This is why Delaware calls itself the "First State."

MEETING HOUSE GALLERIES (3), 316 South Governors Ave., ☎ (302) 739-4266, Internet: www.destatemuseums.org/Gallery *Open Tues.–Sat. 10–3:30, closed Sun., Mon., and state holidays. Free.* ㅎ.

Two old church buildings now house parts of the Delaware State Museum Complex on Dover's Meeting House Square, laid out by William Penn in 1717. The first of these is the **Old Presbyterian Church** of 1790, where the Delaware State Constitution was drafted in 1792, and the State Constitutional Convention convened in 1831. It is now home to a small but interesting museum of **local archaeology** that focuses in Native American life from prehistoric to Colonial times, and later developments.

The adjacent **1880 Gallery** houses reconstructed turn-of-the- century shops including a drugstore, a working printer's shop, a shoemaker's, a blacksmith's, and more.

JOHNSON VICTROLA MUSEUM (4), Bank Lane at New St., ☎ (302) 739-4266, Internet: www.destatemuseums.org/Victrola. *Open Tues.–Sat. 10–3:30, closed Sun., Mon., and State holidays. Free.* ㅎ.

The golden age of the American phonograph lives again when you visit this fabulous museum of Victrolas, where ghostly sounds from the past are played on wind-up machines. Eldridge Reeves Johnson, a local businessman, founded the Victor Talking Machine Company, which he sold to RCA in 1929. Ranging from early Edison cylinders to the beginnings of electronic radio-phonographs in the late 1920s, the amazingly complete displays here cover the pioneer days of recorded sound in a setting that re-creates a Victrola dealer's store of the period.

Another site in the neighborhood is the **Christ Episcopal Church** (5) of 1734, located at South State and Water streets. During the Revolutionary War it was repeatedly attacked by vandals, who unjustly considered all members of the Church of England to be Tories. Actually, one of the Revolution's great heroes (and a signer of the Declaration of Independence), Caesar Rodney (1728–84), is buried in the churchyard along with other famous Delawareans. ☎ *(302) 734-5731. Church open weekdays.*

A few blocks to the north stands the **Governor's House, "Woodburn,"** (6) at 151 Kings Highway. Erected in 1791, this Georgian residence has been the official Governor's mansion since 1966, and was once a station on the legendary Underground Railroad. ☎ *(302) 739-5656. Grounds open daily, house open Sat. 2:30–4:30.*

At the northern end of town, along Route US-13, is the:

Delaware Agricultural Museum and Village (7), 866 N. DuPont Hwy. (US-13), ☎ (302) 734-1618, Internet: www.agriculturalmuseum.org. *Open Jan.–Mar., Mon.–Fri. 10–4; Apr.–Dec., Tues.–Sat. 10–4 and Sun. 1–4. Adults $3, seniors (60+) and children (6–17) $2, under 6 free. Additional charge for special events. Gift shop.* ♿.

Farm life on the Delmarva Peninsula from Colonial times to the mid-20th century is brought back to life in this museum village, where you'll see exhibits ranging from milk bottles to a crop duster, an 18th-century log house to a Model T Ford. The re-created village on the banks of Silver Lake has a gristmill, a blacksmith's, a schoolhouse, a store, a train station, various farm buildings, and more.

Head south on US-13, soon bearing left onto US-113, which takes you to the:

AIR MOBILITY COMMAND MUSEUM (8), Dover Air Force Base, DE 19902-8001, ☎ (302) 677-5938, Internet: http://amcmuseum.org, also check www.dover.af.mil. *Open Mon.–Sun. 9–4, closed federal holidays. At the Main Gate of the Air Force Base get in the right-hand lane, and park at the Visitor Center. Go inside with your drivers' license, registration, and proof of insurance. Ask for a museum pass, then proceed by car through the gate and follow road signs to the museum. Free. Gift shop.* ♿.

The displays of historic military aircraft here include one of the few surviving B-17G bombers of World War II, a C-47 "Gooney Bird," a C-54 transport, an O-2A forward air control plane from the Vietnam conflict, and other former warplanes dating from the 1940s to the recent past. There is also a WWII Link Trainer, a F-106 flight simulator, and similar items.

Immediately south of the air base is the:

JOHN DICKINSON PLANTATION (9), Kitts Hummock Rd., near the junction of US-113 and DE-9, ☎ (302) 739-3277, Internet: www.destatemuseums.org/Dicknsn.htm. *Open Tues.–Sat. 10–3:30, Sun. 1:30–4:30 from Mar.–Dec., closed Mon. and State holidays. Closed Sun. in Jan. & Feb. Free. Tours. Partially* ♿.

John Dickinson (1737–1808), often called the "Penman of the American Revolution," was an influential writer, lawyer, and politician who served in the Continental Congress and helped draft the Articles of Confederation. His boyhood home, a plantation built by his father in

1740, has been restored to its late-18th-century condition and may be seen on guided tours. In contrast to the mansion are the re-created outbuildings, including the "log'd dwelling" that is typical of the mean living quarters used by slaves and poor tenant farmers.

Twelve miles north of Dover, on Route US-13, is the little town of **Smyrna** (10). This was once an important shipping center for local farm produce; today its past is recalled in several historic houses and public buildings. Find out more at the **Smyrna Visitors Center.** *5500 DuPont Highway (US-13),* ☎ *(302) 653-8910.*

Just east of Smyrna, on Route 9, is the **Bombay Hook National Wildlife Refuge** (11), a haven for migratory and resident waterfowl. A 12-mile auto tour route and various foot trails start at the visitor center. ☎ *(302) 653-6872. Open daily. Vehicle charge.* ♿. Near its entrance is the **Allee House** (12) of 1753, a brick farmhouse in the Queen Anne style that is furnished with local antiques. *Dutch Neck Road off DE-9,* ☎ *(302) 653-6872. Open weekends in spring and fall, 2–5 p.m. Free.*

New Castle and Odessa

M ost of America's Colonial heritage is British in nature, but here in northern Delaware you'll find much evidence of the Dutch and the Swedes, who arrived earlier. That's why their flags still fly from the Old Court House in New Castle, alongside the Union Jack and the Stars and Stripes. New Castle, once the state capital, has an exceptionally well-preserved historic district with houses and public buildings dating from as far back as the 1600s. Several of these can be visited as you stroll along the cobblestone lanes near the water's edge.

Civil War buffs—and anyone who likes boat rides—will enjoy a visit to Fort Delaware, a defensive bastion on Pea Patch Island in the middle of the Delaware River.

Finally, you can finish off the day at the Historic Houses of Odessa, a group of 18th- and 19th-century homes maintained and operated by the Winterthur Museum (see page 000) in the tiny village of Odessa.

GETTING THERE:

By car, New Castle is about 108 miles northeast of Washington via Route I-95. From Exit 5, just below Wilmington, take **DE-141** south to New Castle, then **DE-273** east to Delaware Street, following it to the Old Court House.

If you plan to visit Fort Delaware, take **DE-9** ten miles south to Delaware City and follow signs east to the state park. Continue south another ten miles on DE-9 to Odessa, turning north on **DE-299** to the historic houses.

For a faster route from New Castle directly to Odessa, take DE-273 west to **US-13, US-301** and follow it south to the historic houses. The distance is 18 miles.

Return to Washington from Odessa via **US-301** and **US-50**, going by way of Annapolis, a distance of 106 miles.

You might prefer to do this is reverse, especially if you'd like to have an evening dinner in New Castle or nearby Wilmington.

PRACTICALITIES:

Avoid taking this trip on a Monday, when everything is closed. Most of the sites also close completely during January and February, and on certain holidays. Fort Delaware is closed from October until the last weekend in April, and also on many weekdays, so call ahead. The famous **Yuletide in Odessa** festival is held in early December.

For further information, contact the sites directly.

FOOD AND DRINK:

You'll find the best selection of restaurants to be in and around New Castle, including:

Air Transport Command (143 N. DuPont Hwy., US-13, by the airport at New Castle) Continental American cuisine served in a replica World War II European farmhouse overlooking the runway. ☎ (302) 328-3527. $$

Lynnhaven Inn (154 N. DuPont Hwy., US-13, near the airport) A long-time favorite for steak and seafood in a Colonial setting. ☎ (302) 328-2041. X: weekend lunch. $$

Arsenal on the Green (30 Market St., near the Old Court House in New Castle) Classic American cuisine in an historic 1809 building. ☎ (302) 328-1290. X: Sun. lunch. $$

Cellar Gourmet (208 Delaware St., near the Old Court House in New Castle) Casual light dining in the cellar of an 1802 house, featuring sandwiches, quiche, soup, and the like. ☎ (302) 323-0999. $

Another good idea is to bring a **picnic lunch** with you to Fort Delaware State Park, where tables and grills are provided free. Fast-food places abound along Route 13 in the vicinity of New Castle.

SUGGESTED TOUR:

Numbers in parentheses correspond to numbers on the map.

Begin your tour in the historic town of **New Castle** (1–6), founded in 1651 by Peter Stuyvesant, the dictatorial Dutch administrator of the New Netherlands in America. Then known as Fort Casimir, the town held a strategic location commanding all traffic on the Delaware River. In 1654 it fell to the Swedes but was soon recaptured by the Dutch, who lost it to the British in 1664. William Penn first stepped foot in the New World here in 1682.

Park your car and start with the:

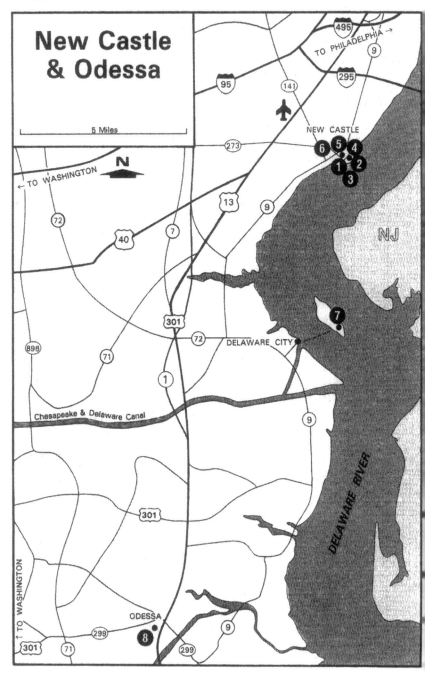

OLD COURT HOUSE (1), 2nd and Delaware streets, New Castle, DE 19720, ☎ (302) 323-4453. *Open Tues.–Sat. 10–3:30, Sun. 1:30–4:30, closed Mon. and holidays. Free. ♿, first floor only.*

Look at a map of Delaware and notice the peculiar circular line dividing it from Pennsylvania, a result of the Mason-Dixon survey of 1763-68. The exact center of this 12-mile radius is the handsome cupola atop the Old Court House. From the balcony beneath it fly the flags of the United States, Great Britain, Sweden, and Holland—the countries to which New Castle belonged to at one time or another.

Built in 1732, the Old Court House was used by the Colonial Assembly until Dover became Delaware's capital in 1777. The exterior has been restored to match an 1804 drawing, and the interior furnished as it was under British rule. Step inside and take the free guided tour, beginning in the **courtroom** with its prisoner's dock, witness stand, and judges' bench. Upstairs is the meeting room of Delaware's **Colonial Assembly**, and some other chambers lined with portraits of prominent figures in the state's history, including that of Thomas West (1577–1618), the 12th Baron de la Warre, after whom the river (and consequently the state) is named. He was the governor of Virginia and apparently never ventured this far north.

Leave the courthouse and continue down Delaware Street, turning left into The Strand to visit the:

GEORGE READ II HOUSE AND GARDEN (2), 42 The Strand, New Castle, DE 19720, ☎ (302) 322-8411, Internet: www.hsd.org. *Open Mar. through Dec., Tues.–Sat. 10–4, Sun. noon–4; closed Mon. and major holidays. Adults $4, students 13–21 $3.50, children 6–12 $2. Special events in May and Dec. ♿.*

Undoubtedly the most elegant residence in New Castle, the George Read II house was built between 1797 and 1804 by a prominent lawyer and son of a signer of the Declaration of Independence. Much of it is furnished in the style of the 1820s, while three contrasting rooms reflect the Colonial Revival tastes of a century later when the house was acquired by the Philip Lairds in 1920. Of particular note are the gilded fanlights, the silver hardware, and the elaborately carved woodwork. The house is surrounded on three sides by **landscaped gardens** laid out in the 1840's style of Andrew Jackson Downing.

Return along the other side of The Strand, taking a look down **Packet Alley**. A historical marker here informs you that this is where stage coaches bound for Maryland once met the packet boat from Philadelphia, making it a vital link in communications between North and South.

Continue on to a marker commemorating the spot where, on October 27, 1682, William Penn (1644–1718) first stepped foot on American soil. Originally a part of Pennsylvania, this area became unhappy with Penn's rule and in 1704 set up its own government as the colony, and later state, of Delaware.

Stroll through a riverside park called **The Battery** (3), with its sweeping views of the busy waterway and the Delaware Memorial Bridge to New Jersey. At the end of Delaware Street you'll see the curious little ticket office of the former **New Castle and Frenchtown Railroad**, the second-oldest rail line in the country. Built in 1832 and now restored, the office stands next to a rebuilt section of the original wooden tracks topped with iron strapping, attached to stone ties.

Return along Delaware Street and turn right onto Second Street, passing the Dutch-inspired **Town Hall**. Behind it is **The Green**, laid out by Peter Stuyvesant in 1655. Always a busy place, weekly markets and great fairs were held here from the earliest times. This was also the site of the town jail and gallows. To the right is the **Presbyterian Church** of 1707.

Turn left to visit **Immanuel Church** (4), founded as the first parish of the Church of England in Delaware in 1689 and completed in 1708. It was expanded and modified several times, and devastated by fire in 1980. A rebuilding in 1982 closely followed the design of 1820, complete with box pews. An unusual feature of the church is the rare set of change-ringing bells, used on special occasions. Several of Delaware's most illustrious early citizens are buried in the surrounding graveyard. *Open daily 10–5. Free. 100 Harmony St.* ☎ *(302) 328-2413.*

A left turn on Third Street brings you to the **Old Library Museum**, a strange hexagonal structure of 1892 that now houses the New Castle Historical Society and its exhibits on local history. *40 E. 3rd St.,* ☎ *(302) 322-2794. Open Sat. 11–4, Sun. 1–4, and Thurs.–Fri. when possible 11–4. Free.* Continue on to the **Old Dutch House** (5), virtually unchanged since it was first built around 1700 and today open to visitors. The furnishings are typical of New Castle's early Dutch settlers, down to the inevitable *klompen* (wooden shoes). *32 E. 3rd St.,* ☎ *(302) 322-2794. Open Mar.–Dec., Tues.–Sat. 11–4, Sun. 1–4; weekends only rest of year; adults $2, under 12 $1.* ♿.

A block west on Delaware Street stands the **Amstel House** (6) of 1738, once the home of Delaware's governor. Incorporating sections of an earlier house, it has a complete Colonial kitchen and many fine antiques. *Open at the same times as the Old Dutch House, above, same admission, combined ticket available.*

After enjoying New Castle, you might want to continue south on DE-9 to visit a Civil War fort, or head directly down US-13, US-301 to the Historic Houses of Odessa.

FORT DELAWARE STATE PARK (7), Pea Patch Island, opposite Delaware City, DE 19706, ☎ (302) 834-7941, Internet: www. destateparks.com/fdsp.htm. *Open from the last weekend of April through Sept.; Sat., Sun., holidays 10–6; also on some weekdays from mid-June through Labor Day. Call for current schedule. Admission including boat fare: Adults $6, ages 2–12 $4. Picnic facilities. Special events. Gift shop. ⅊.*

Park your car at the end of Clinton Street in Delaware City, opposite the old locks of the original **Chesapeake and Delaware Canal** of 1829. The canal has since moved south a mile or so, but there is still an active harbor here. At the adjacent State Park office you can buy your tickets and board the boat for a short cruise to the island. Upon landing, a jitney will take you to the fort.

Pea Patch Island, all 178 acres of it, supposedly acquired its name after a boat loaded with peas ran aground there, and the peas sprouted. Today it is mostly a **nature preserve** whose remote marshes provide habitat for herons, egrets, ibis, and other wading birds. An **observation tower** allows visitors to watch without disturbing the wildlife.

Fort Delaware, on the eastern end of the island, was built in 1859 on the site of earlier fortresses. It guarded the sea approaches to Wilmington, Philadelphia, and the Delaware Valley. Surrounded by a 30-foot moat and reached via a drawbridge, the massive bastion has 32-foot-high granite-and-brick walls that are up to 30 feet thick. During the Civil War it held as many as 12,500 Confederate prisoners of war at a time, of whom some 2,700 perished of diseases. The fort was modernized for the Spanish-American War, and again garrisoned during World War I. In World War II it was maintained by German POWs. Strangely, throughout its entire history, Fort Delaware never fired a shot in anger.

Visitors can explore nearly all of the fort, see period rooms and armaments, climb up to the ramparts, and even venture into the spooky dungeons. This is a great destination for kids!

Continuing ten miles farther south brings you to the:

HISTORIC HOUSES OF ODESSA (8), P.O. Box 507, Odessa, DE 19730, ☎ (302) 378-4069. *Open March through Dec., Tues.–Sat. 10–4, Sun. 1–4. Last combination tour at 3. Closed Mon., Easter, July 4, Thanksgiving, Dec 24–25, Jan., Feb. Adults $4 for one house, $6 for two, $7 for three. Seniors over 59 and students 12–17 $3 for one house, $5 for two, $6 for three. Children 5–11 $1 per house. Gift shop. Special events prior to Christmas.*

Then known as Cantwell's Bridge, tiny Odessa was once a prosperous little grain-shipping port on Appoquinimink Creek, an estuary of Delaware Bay. As business declined in the mid-19th century, however, it attempted to glorify its port facilities by renaming the town after the great Ukrainian seaport that was in the news then as a result of the Crimean War. It also made the fatal mistake of forcing the newfangled Delaware Railroad to bypass the town. The disastrous peach blight of the late 19th century didn't help matters, either. After that, Odessa just fell asleep until the 1950s, by which time its magnificent houses had become a tourist asset.

The Winterthur Museum of the Brandywine Valley (see page 293) now operates four historic properties in Odessa. These include the **Corbit-Sharp House** of 1774, a Georgian mansion built for the town's leading citizen. It is authentically furnished in the style of the late 18th century. Nearby is the **Wilson-Warner House**, a wealthy merchant's mansion of 1769 now furnished as it would have been in 1829, when an inventory was made during a bankruptcy sale. No longer an inn, the 19th-century Federal-style **Brick Hotel** has been renovated as an exhibition gallery of exceptionally ornate Victorian furniture in the manner of John Henry Belter (1804–63), the master of the Rococo Revival. Finally, there is the early-18th-century log-and-frame-built **Collins-Sharp House** presently used for educational programs such as hands-on hearth cooking for children.

Wilmington

You probably wouldn't think of Wilmington as a tourist destination; few people do. Yet, this bustling corporate headquarters city has several attractions that make the trip worthwhile. On top of that, it is only minutes from the world-class lures of the Brandywine Valley described in the next chapter (and also in the Pennsylvania section). Visitors can easily combine elements of this daytrip with some of those for a custom itinerary.

First settled by Swedish fur traders in 1638, the tiny colony of New Sweden was captured by the Dutch in 1655. A mere nine years later the English took over, and the town grew under William Penn's Quaker influence. Having an ideal port location, Wilmington was also blessed with abundant water power along its Brandywine River. This attracted early industrialists, especially the aristocratic du Ponts who fled revolutionary France and founded the mighty chemical empire that dominates the area today.

If you're considering an overnight stay, this trip combines very well with those to Delaware's Brandywine Valley, Pennsylvania's Brandywine Valley, or New Castle and Odessa.

GETTING THERE:

By car, Wilmington is about 106 miles northeast of Washington via Route I-95. Get off at Exit 6 for the downtown sites, Exit 7 for the art museum and zoo, or Exit 9 for Rockwood.

Trains operated by Amtrak provide frequent service between Wilmington, Washington, and the Northeast Corridor. The ride from Washington takes about 90 minutes. Downtown sites are within possible walking distance of the station, but you'll need to take a bus (or car) to the others.

PRACTICALITIES:

Avoid Wilmington on a Monday or major holiday, when many of the attractions are closed. The History Museum is also closed on Sundays, as is Rockwood. Tours of the Grand Opera House are held on Thursdays only. The Wilmington and Western Tourist Railroad operates on summer weekends and some other times, but call first.

Shoppers will be delighted to know that Delaware has no sales tax.

Public transportation throughout the Wilmington area is operated by DART, ☎ (302) 652-DART or (800) 652-DART, Internet: www.dtcc.edu/dart for routes and schedules.

For further information, contact the **Greater Wilmington Convention & Visitors Bureau**, 100 West 10th St., Wilmington, DE 19801, ☎ (302) 652-4088 or 800-422-1181, Internet: www.wilmcvb.org.

FOOD AND DRINK:

Some good choices for lunch are:

Tavola Toscana (1412 DuPont St., between Pennsylvania and Delaware avenues, a mile south of the art museum) A great place for inspired Northern Italian cuisine. ☎ (302) 654-8001. X: weekend lunches. $$$

Waterworks Café (16th and French streets, 6 blocks northeast of the Grand Opera) Continental cuisine in a former waterworks on the river; indoor and outdoor dining. ☎ (302) 652-6022. X: Sat. lunch, Sun., Mon., holidays. $$

DiNardo's (405 Lincoln St. at 4th St., 2 miles west of the opera house) This boisterous, popular crab house serves great seafood in the most casual setting. ☎ (302) 656-3685. $$

Shipley Grill (913 Shipley St., near Willington Sq. in the heart of downtown) Steak and seafood with an imaginative touch. ☎ (302) 652-7797. X: Sun. lunch. $$

LOCAL ATTRACTIONS:

Numbers in parentheses correspond to numbers on the map.

DELAWARE HISTORY MUSEUM (1), 504 Market St. Mall, ☎ (302) 656-0637, Internet: www.hsd.org. *Open Tues.–Fri., noon–4; and Sat. 10–4. Closed Sun., Mon., and major holidays. Admission charged.* &.

Delaware's history comes alive in this restored five-and-dime from the 1940s. Exhibitions change, but focus on such subjects as business, maritime history, agriculture, and the ethnic background of the state's population.

Close by is **Willington Square** (2), a lovely group of 18th-century houses moved to this site in the 1970s.

Three blocks to the north stands the **Grand Opera House** (3), a

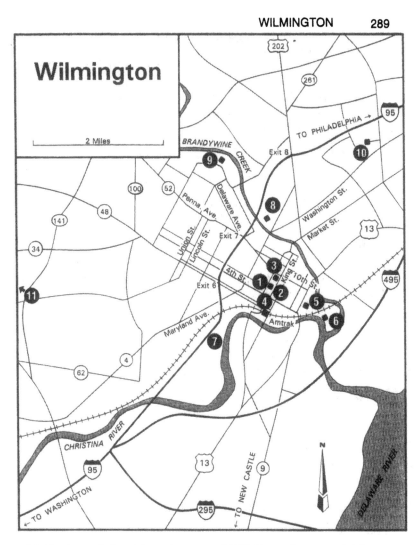

highly-decorated cast-iron structure of 1871. Recently restored, it is now Delaware's Center for the Performing Arts, where opera and symphonies are regularly performed. *818 Market St. Mall,* ☎ *(302) 658-7898, Internet: www.grandopera.org. Call for tour information.* ♿.

A few blocks to the south is one of America's oldest train depots, **Amtrak Station** (4). Fully restored to its Victorian splendor, it remains in constant use today.

About a mile east of Market Street are two reminders of Wilmington's earliest days. **Old Swedes Church** (5), now known as Holy

Trinity, was built in 1698 and is possibly the oldest house of worship in America to remain in use today. Originally Lutheran, it has been Episcopalian since 1791 but still contains some of the original furnishings, including the pulpit. Nearby, a small Swedish farmhouse of 1690 now contains a museum of 17th- and 18th-century artifacts. *606 Church St. ☎ (302) 652-5629. Open Mon.–Sat. 10–4. Admission $2.* The **Fort Christina Monument**, a short stroll to the east, marks the spot where the Swedes first stepped ashore in 1638. Nearby is an old log cabin of the type that the earliest settlers used.

The **Kalmar Nyckel Foundation** (6), on the shores of the Christina River just to the east, celebrates the first permanent European settlement in the Delaware Valley in 1638. Here you can see a replica of the ship, the *Kalmar Nyckel,* that brought those first Swedes here, along with a museum and a re-created 17th-century shipyard. Ten stories high and 139 feet long, the *Kalmar Nyckel* is Delaware's seagoing ambassador of good will and is sometimes out on a cruise. Check first to make sure it's in port. *1124 East 7th St., ☎ (302) 429-7447, Internet: www.kalnyc.org. Open Mon.–Sat. 10–4, Sun. noon–4, closed major holidays. Adults $8, seniors $6, children 7–12 $4.*

Another recent addition to Wilmington's cultural scene is the **First USA Riverfront Arts Center** (7), an enormous former ship assembly plant that was beautifully transformed into an exhibition venue featuring world-class temporary exhibitions. *800 S. Madison St., ☎ (302) 777-1600 or (888) 395-0005. Check ahead for current offerings.* Adjacent to it is the **Shipyard Shops** complex of upscale catalog outlets, **Frawley Stadium—** home of the Wilmington Blue Rocks Class A minor league baseball team ☎ *(302) 888-2015, Internet: www.bluerocks.com* —and the lovely **Tubman—Garrett Riverfront Park.**

Outside the central city are several other attractions, starting with the:

BRANDYWINE ZOO (8), 1001 N. Park Drive, ☎ (302) 571-7747. *Open daily 10–4. Admission charged Apr.–Oct.; Adults $3, seniors and children 3–11 $1.50. Free from Nov.–March.* ᕹ.

Although it's been a local landmark since 1905, the Brandywine Zoo takes a modern, enlightened approach to animal care. There are exotic species, of course, but the emphasis is on animals native to North and South America, and especially on presenting those native to Delaware in their natural habitat.

DELAWARE ART MUSEUM (9), 2301 Kentmere Parkway, ☎ (302) 571-9590, Internet: www.udel.edu/delart. *Open Tues.–Sat. 9–4., Sun. 10–4, remain-*

ing open until 9 on Wed. Closed Mon., Thanksgiving, Christmas, New Year's Day. Adults $5, seniors $3, students $2.50. Gift shop. &.

The greatest treasures in this modern museum are the works of Howard Pyle (1853–1911), a native of Wilmington who was virtually the father of American illustration and a founder of the Brandywine school. His students—N.C. Wyeth, Maxfield Parrish, Frank Schoonover and others—are also very well represented, as are other famous American artists such as Thomas Eakins, Winslow Homer, Andrew Wyeth, and a host of contemporary painters. The museum is also renowned for its vast collection of English Pre-Raphaelite paintings and decorative arts, displayed in Victorian settings.

ROCKWOOD MUSEUM (10), 610 Shipley Road, ☎ (302)761-4340, Internet: www.rockwood.org. *Open Tues.–Sat. 11–4. Adults $5, seniors $4, children 5–16 $2. Tours. Gift shop.* &.

Located in the eastern part of town, near Exit 9 of Route I-95, Rockwood is a gorgeous 19th-century country estate with a Rural Gothic manor house and lovely gardens. Its interior features English, European, and American decorative arts of the 17th, 18th, and 19th centuries. There is also a conservatory filled with period flora.

WILMINGTON & WESTERN TOURIST RAILROAD (11), Greenback Station on DE-41, 3 blocks north of the junction with DE-2, just west of Wilmington. ☎ (302) 998-1930, Internet: www.wwrr.com. *Operates every Sun., May–Dec.; every Sat. June–Aug., and at other times. Adults $7, seniors $6, children 2–12 $4. Gift shop.* &.

Ride behind an old steam or antique diesel locomotive as you chug your way through Red Clay Valley, stopping at a picnic grove before returning. What a nice way to end the day!

Delaware's Brandywine Valley

Extending north from Wilmington to the Pennsylvania border, Delaware's Brandywine Valley was one of the major birthplaces of America's industrial wealth. The Brandywine River provided ample waterpower for the mills while the lovely countryside made an ideal locale for the fabulous mansions that resulted from the profits.

This is the land of the du Ponts, an aristocratic French family who fled that country's revolution in the late 18th century and began the great DuPont chemical empire by opening a gunpowder mill on the banks of the Brandywine in 1802. Eventually they became extremely rich and established vast estates in the surrounding hills, filling them with exquisite treasures, magnificent homes, and beautiful gardens. Among those open to the public and included in the trip are Winterthur, noted for its period American antiques and natural landscaping; Hagley, the original du Pont home in America, adjacent to the company's first mills; and Nemours, a Louis XVI château that looks like a scene right out of France. For variety the trip also includes the picturesque little town of Centerville, an enchanting museum of toys and miniatures, and the Delaware Museum of Natural History.

The Brandywine Valley continues north into nearby Pennsylvania, where it offers some equally intriguing sights, described on pages 000-000. You might want to make a weekend of this by staying overnight and combining both trips.

GETTING THERE:

By car, Winterthur is about 115 miles northeast of Washington. Take Route I-95 to Wilmington, getting off at Exit 7 (Delaware Avenue) and heading a few miles northwest on **DE-52**. Centerville and the Museum of Natural History are also along this road, while Hagley, the Toy Museum, and Nemours lie slightly to the east on **DE-141** (see map).

Trains operated by Amtrak provide frequent, fast service between Washington's Union Station, points in Maryland, and Wilmington — where you'll need to rent a car for the remaining few miles of the trip.

PRACTICALITIES:

Most of the attractions on this daytrip are at their best during late spring and early fall, and can be crowded on summer weekends. Winterthur, the Museum of Natural History, and Hagley are open daily except for a few holidays. The Toy Museum closes on Mondays and some holidays. Nemours closes completely from December through April, and is always closed on Mondays. Reservations are suggested for the latter.

For additional information, phone the sites directly or contact the **Greater Wilmington Convention & Visitor Bureau**, 100 W. 10th St., Wilmington DE 19801, ☎ (302) 652-4088 or (800) 422- 1181, Internet: www.wilmcvb.org.

FOOD AND DRINK:

Some good places for lunch are:

Buckley's Tavern (5812 Kennett Pike, DE-52, in Centerville) Relaxed indoor-and-outdoor dining in a delightful little town; innovative American cuisine. ☎ (302) 656-9776. $$

Garden Restaurant (Winterthur Museum) Winterthur's full-service restaurant offers lunch on weekdays, teas on weekends, and champagne brunches on Sundays. Reservations required, ☎ (302) 888-4826. $$

Brandywine Brewing Company (3801 Kennett Pike, DE-52, at DE-141, Greenville) Steaks, chowders, burgers, sandwiches, pastas, and salads at a microbrewery. ☎ (302) 655-8000. $ and $$

Crossroads Café (Winterthur Museum) A cafeteria with a difference, Crossroads features themed "food stations" instead of the usual line. A wide variety of dishes is available. ☎ (302) 888-4600. $

Cappuccino Café (Winterthur Museum) Sandwiches, salads, desserts, and beverages right next to the museum. ☎ (302) 888-4600. $

LOCAL ATTRACTIONS:

Trying to see all of these attractions in the same day is practically impossible, so pick and choose carefully—allowing enough time to thoroughly enjoy those you do visit. You can always come back another time, or stay overnight! *Numbers in parentheses correspond to numbers on the map.*

*WINTERTHUR MUSEUM, GARDEN & LIBRARY (1), Route 52, Winterthur, DE 19735, ☎ (302) 888-4600 or (800) 448-3883; TDD (302) 888-4907, Internet: www.winterthur.org. *Open Mon.–Sat. 9–5, Sun. noon–5. Last ticket sale at 3:45. Closed New Year's, Thanksgiving, and Christmas. General admission: Adults $8, seniors and students (12–18) $6, children*

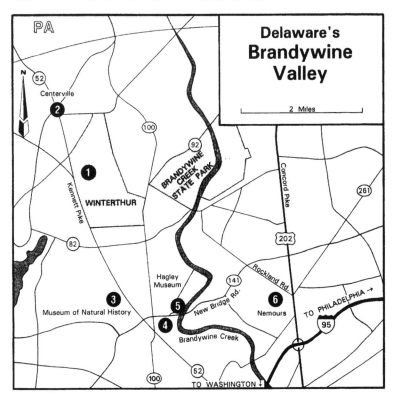

PA

N
52

Centerville

2

100

Delaware's
Brandywine Valley

2 Miles

92

BRANDYWINE
CREEK
STATE PARK

1

Concord Pike

261

WINTERTHUR

Kennett Pike

82

202

Hagley
Museum

141

Rockland Rd.

New Bridge Rd.

6

Nemours

TO PHILADELPHIA →

3

Museum of Natural History

5

4

Brandywine Creek

95

TO WASHINGTON ↓

100

52

(5–11) $4, children under 5 free. General admission includes Galleries, gardens, garden tram, and the Children's Touch-It Room. No reservations needed. Introduction Tour through selected period rooms, add $5, reservations advised. Decorative Arts tours of 1 or 2 hours for guests over 12, add $9 or $13 respectively, reservations needed. Special events. Gift shops. Café, cafeteria, full-service restaurant. ♿.

Admirers of the decorative arts come from all over the world to visit Winterthur, a vast estate whose nine-story ***mansion** contains some 175 period rooms furnished with 89,000 objects made or used in America between 1640 and 1860. Included are outstanding pieces of furniture, textiles, clocks, silver, needlework, porcelains, Oriental rugs, paintings, and anything else of quality that once decorated the finest American homes. This is indeed the foremost collection of its type on Earth, but you needn't take the full tour to appreciate it. Even a general admission visit of perhaps two hours or so will prove rewarding.

Adjoining the mansion (and beautifully spanning a creek) are the ***Galleries**, where many of the choicest items now reside in museum settings. There is also a theater with an introductory video show, and the **Touch-It Room** where children and their parents can pretend to be living in the past. A new addition is the renowned **Campbell Collection of Soup Tureens.**

Nearly a thousand acres of "naturalistic" ***gardens and woodlands** cover the gently rolling hills surrounding the mansion. These offer magnificent vistas and intimate little glens, and can be seen on foot or by riding the garden tram.

The estate was begun in 1837 by James Antoine Bidermann of Winterthur, Switzerland, who had married Evelina Gabrielle du Pont in 1816 and moved to America. Their heir preferred to remain in Europe, and so in 1867 the du Pont family bought the property. A descendant, Henry Francis du Pont (1880–1969), was born here and pretty much created what you see today—both the collections and the gardens. In 1951 he turned it all over to the nonprofit Winterthur Corporation, which opened it to the public.

A General Admission ticket allows you to explore the Galleries at leisure, stroll the gardens or ride the tram, and visit the Touch-It Room, all without reservations. For an additional fee you can take one of three different guided tours through selected period rooms in the mansion, ranging from one to two hours in length. Advance reservations are strongly advised for these special tours, although same-day arrangements are possible if space permits. Winterthur is exceptionally barrier-free, and makes exemplary efforts to accommodate handicapped visitors.

Just up the road is the delightful little village of **Centerville** (2), noted for its antique dealers, boutiques, and galleries. If you're shopping, remember that Delaware (Oh, happy state!) has no sales tax.

Turn around and return south on DE-52, again passing Winterthur, to the:

DELAWARE MUSEUM OF NATURAL HISTORY (3), Route 52, Greenville, DE, ☎ (302) 658-9111, Internet: www.delmnh.org. *Open Mon.–Sat. 9:30–4:30, Sun. noon–5, closed New Year's, Easter, July 4, Thanksgiving, Christmas. Adults $5, seniors $4, children (3–17) $3, children under 3 free. Gift shop. Nature films.* ♿.

Would you like to examine the world's largest bird egg? How about a 500-pound clam, an African watering hole, or a walk over the Great Barrier Reef? And how about wild dinosaurs? All of this and much, much more can be seen in this modern museum. Children of all ages have hands-on experiences in the Discovery Room, while stuffed animals await your visit in reproductions of their natural habitats.

Continue south and turn east on DE-141 to the:

DELAWARE TOY & MINIATURE MUSEUM (4), 3 Old Barley Mill Rd., DE-141, Wilmington, DE 19807, ☎ (302) 427-8697, Internet: http://thomes.net/toys. *Open Tues.–Sat. 10–4, Sun. noon–4. Closed major holidays. Adults $5, seniors $4, under 12 $3.*

Toys, games, trains, boats, planes, dolls and their houses, miniatures, and other reminders of childhood—from the 18th century to today, from America to Europe—it's all here, and it's fun to see.

Practically next door is the:

*HAGLEY MUSEUM (5), P.O. Box 3630, Wilmington, DE 19807, ☎ (302) 658-2400. *Open mid-March through Dec., daily 9:30–4:30; Jan. through mid-March, weekends 9:30–4:30, weekdays one tour only at 1:30. Closed Thanksgiving, Christmas, Dec. 31. Adults $9.75; seniors and students with ID $7.50, children (6–14) $3.50, under 6 free. Family rate $26.50. Bus to sites. Gift shop. Picnic facilities. ঙ most sites, some are difficult, inquire first.*

This is where it all began. E.I. du Pont de Nemours built his first black powder works on these 230 acres of riverside land along the Brandywine in 1802, harnessing abundant waterpower to drive the machinery that ground and mixed the ingredients of a superior gunpowder. Not only were the mills built here, but also the first du Pont mansion, situated dangerously close to the highly explosive works, where E.I. could keep his eye on things.

Many of the original mills and other early industrial buildings, some 19th-century workers' homes, the company's first office, and the original du Pont estate have been restored and are now operated as an historical museum, ready to be explored on foot or by bus. What is missing, understandably, is the gritty atmosphere of an early industrial site—you'll have to imagine for yourself the dirt, sweat, stench, and heat that must have made this a nasty place at the time. Well, you can't have everything.

Begin your visit at the **Henry Clay Mill** near the parking lot. Built in 1814 as a cotton-spinning mill, it was converted by the DuPont Company in 1884 for the manufacture of powder containers. Today it houses the visitor reception and a **museum** on the history of the site. Be sure to see the introductory video and the three-dimensional model of the valley with its interesting sound-and-light show.

From here you can either walk or take the little jitney bus to **Hagley Yard**, where skilled machinists demonstrate the use of old-time lathes, drill presses, and other devices in the ***Millwright Shop**. A walk-through exhibit explains the steps in manufacturing gunpowder, and you can take a guided tour to the waterside **Eagle Roll Mill** of 1839 to watch waterpower at work mixing the ingredients of black powder. Don't worry—the stuff isn't real, so it won't blow up.

Many of the workers lived on **Blacksmith Hill**, one of several communities built by the DuPont Company to provide decent housing. Most of the buildings are gone, but you can visit the well-preserved ***Gibbons-Stewart House** of 1846, where a foreman once lived. Workers' children learned their ABCs at the **Sunday School** of 1817, now restored to its original condition.

Farther along the river are the ***Birkenhead Mills**, where a reconstructed waterwheel still operates, and the **Engine House**, where you can watch a live demonstration of an 1870's stationary steam engine.

You'll have to take the bus to reach ***Eleutherian Mills**, located upstream beyond a public road. This is where the first mills were built in 1802, and where the founder, Éleuthère Irénée du Pont (1771–1834), lived. Although only foundations of the mills survive, the ***du Pont Family Home** of 1803 remained in the family until 1958, when it was restored as a museum. A guide will take you through lovely interiors that reflect the tastes of five generations of du Pont wealth. You'll also get to see the **First Office** of the DuPont Company, the **Workshop** where 19th- century experiments in chemistry were made, the **French Garden** of 1803, and the original **Barn**. The latter houses a Conestoga wagon and other 19th-century vehicles, along with early automobiles including a massive du Pont Auto from the 1920s, built in Wilmington.

For another glimpse of du Pont wealth, continue east on DE-141, turning right at Rockland Road and following signs to:

NEMOURS MANSION AND GARDENS (6), P.O. Box 109, Wilmington, DE 19899, ☎ (302) 651-6912. *Open May through November, tours Tues.–Sat. at 9, 11, 1, and 3; Sun. at 11, 1, and 3. Reservations strongly urged. Visitors must be over 16 years of age. Visit by tour only, $10. Many steps to climb. Allow at least 2 hours for the tour and arrive at least 15 minutes ahead of time.*

The du Pont's patriarch, Pierre Samuel du Pont de Nemours (1739–1817), was a French aristocrat closely associated with King Louis XVI, so it's no wonder that he fled to America in the aftermath of the French Revolution. It was against this background that his great-great-grandson, Alfred Irénée du Pont, built the fabulous ***château** of Nemours in 1909–10, and named it after the ancestral family home about 45 miles south of Paris. Some of the furnishings in its 102 rooms belonged to the king or his wife, Marie Antoinette. Others, equally valuable, date from as far back as 15th-century Europe.

The tour includes a bus ride through the formal ***gardens**, extending for a third of a mile from the mansion. Along the way you'll pass gates constructed in 1488 for Henry VII's Wimbeldon Manor in England, and others that once graced the palace of Catherine the Great in St. Petersburg, Russia. Finally, there's the garage with its **rare automobiles** built for the du Ponts from 1912 to 1951.

Section VI

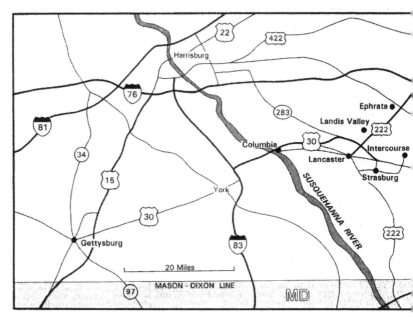

DAYTRIPS TO
PENNSYLVANIA

H eading north to Pennsylvania may seem like stretching the daytrip concept a bit far, but it's not. Gettysburg is only 78 miles from Washington, and none of the places described in this section are as distant as Williamsburg in Virginia. Excellent highways should get you to your destination in as little as 90 minutes. While driving to downtown Philadelphia may take slightly over two hours, it is also easily reached by frequent trains in considerably less time than that.

Southeastern Pennsylvania offers an amazing variety of sights. From the prosperous Pennsylvania Dutch countryside, where many farmers still live as their ancestors did over a century ago, to a major metropolis that is becoming more dynamic every day, this part of the Keystone State has something for everyone.

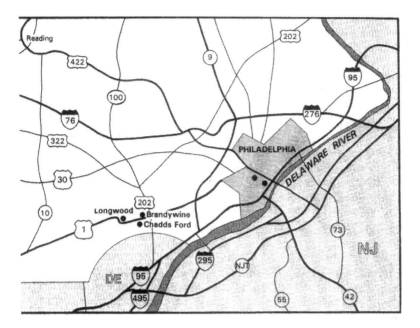

History buffs can retrace the beginnings of American independence, and explore important battlefields of both the Revolution and the Civil War. Art mavens will relish the world-class museums of Philadelphia and the Brandywine Valley. Food lovers will savor Lancaster County's hearty Pennsylvania Dutch cooking, Philly's tasty prole cuisine, the Brandywine Valley's sophisticated mushroom specialties, and delight in the regional farmers' markets. America's finest horticultural gardens are here, along with elegant mansions and estates that can be toured. For railfans and kids of all ages, a trip to Strasburg is like going to Heaven. And, if you haven't been to Philadelphia for a while, you're probably in for an unexpected urban surprise when you see how much it has changed for the better.

While this book is about daytrips, if you have more time, why not stay over and combine some of the excursions into a mini-vacation? In doing so, you could also include destinations in northern Maryland (Section IV) and Delaware (Section V).

Trip 44

*Gettysburg

A merican history took a profound turn during the first three days of July, 1863, when the tragic Battle of Gettysburg made the outcome of the Civil War inevitable. Until then, the Confederacy had high hopes for a negotiated peace and independence; afterwards, those hopes were dashed although the bitter struggle continued for another two years. More men fought, and more men died, at Gettysburg than in any other battle in North American history. Of the 163,000 soldiers involved, at least 50,000 became casualties, including an uncounted number who perished. It is to their memory that the 5,700-acre Gettysburg National Military Park was dedicated in 1895.

Those terrible events were perhaps best burned into the minds of Americans forever by the eloquent words of President Abraham Lincoln, who delivered his short *Gettysburg Address* here just four months after the carnage.

Almost 90 years later, another great American made his home near the sleepy college town of Gettysburg. General Dwight David Eisenhower (1890–1969), affectionately known as "Ike," bought a small dairy farm adjacent to the battlefield as a weekend retreat. Major improvements were made, and during his two terms as President the farm often served as a temporary White House, where leaders from around the world were entertained. Now a National Historic Site, the farm is open to the public.

Today, the battlefield remains much as it was in 1863 except, of course, for the monuments and graves. The natural lay of the land allows you to see the big picture from several vantage points, making the progress of the battle come alive. With just a bit of imagination, you can picture the Blue and Grey forces struggling to decide the fate of a nation.

Easily reached by highway, Gettysburg is a wonderful destination for a daytrip from Washington. You might even want to stay overnight. For those with more time, this is the perfect gateway for a trip east through Pennsylvania, perhaps stopping at Lancaster, the Pennsylvania Dutch country, Strasburg, Philadelphia, and the Brandywine Valley—all described on pages 307–359.

GETTING THERE:

By car, Gettysburg is about 78 miles northwest of Washington via Route **I-270** to Frederick, then **US-15** north past Emmitsburg, MD. Once in Pennsylvania, switch to **Business Route 15**, which brings you right to the Visitor Center.

PRACTICALITIES:

Visits may be made on any day except Thanksgiving, Christmas, or New Year's. The Eisenhower Farm, however, has a variable schedule that should be checked before making the journey.

Special events include the annual **Civil War Heritage Days** held in late June and early July, when the battle is re-enacted, and the **Anniversary of Lincoln's Gettysburg Address** on November 19th.

For further information, phone the sites directly or contact the **Gettysburg Convention and Visitors Bureau**, 35 Carlisle St., Gettysburg, PA 17325 (in the center of town), ☎ 717-334-6274, Internet: www. gettysburg.com.

FOOD AND DRINK:

Gettysburg has plenty of restaurants in all price ranges, including:

Herr Tavern & Publick House (900 Chambersburg Rd., US-30, a mile west of Gettysburg) An historic 1816 pub with overnight accommodations, near the battlefield. American and Continental cuisine. ☎ 717-334-4332. X: Sun. lunch. $$ and $$$

Dobbin House (89 Steinwehr Ave., a few blocks north of the Visitor Center) Built in 1776, this venerable tavern is the oldest building in Gettysburg, and offers both a casual pub and a gracious dining room, the latter for dinner only. ☎ 717-334-2100. $, $$ and $$$

JD's Grill (Quality Inn, 401 Buford Ave., US-30, west of town) Lunch or dinner in a Civil War setting. ☎ 717- 334-2200. $ and $$

Fast-food outlets abound along Steinwehr Avenue, just west of the Visitor Center. The park has several designated **picnic areas** where you can enjoy an alfresco lunch.

LOCAL ATTRACTIONS:

Park your car at the Visitor Center, from which you can walk to most of the sights. Unless you take the guided bus tour, however, you'll need the car to drive around the battlefield. Visits to the Eisenhower Farm can only be made by bus, leaving from the Visitor Center. *Numbers in parentheses correspond to numbers on the map.*

GETTYSBURG NATIONAL MILITARY PARK—VISITOR CENTER (1), Gettysburg, PA 17325, ☎ 717-334-1124. *Open daily 8–5. Closed*

Thanksgiving, Christmas, and New Year's. Park and museum free. Electric Map show: Adults $3, seniors (62+) $2.50, children (6–15) $1.50. Guide hire station. Bookshop. &, staff will assist for lower floor; free wheelchair loans.

NOTE: There are current plans to move the Visitor Center and Cyclorama to a nearby location, making them larger and more accessible; and to use a more appropriate style of architecture. Stay tuned.

Stop here first to pick up a free brochure/map for the self-guided Battlefield Tour, or possibly to hire a licensed guide who can ride along in your car. The fee for the latter is $30 (more for larger vehicles). You can also obtain other information about the official sites, and visit the bookstore.

Just behind the reception area is the superb **Gettysburg Museum of the Civil War**, featuring two floors of artifacts and exhibitions concerning all aspects of the conflict, from weapons to the daily lives of the participants. *Admission is free.*

Beyond this is the **Electric Map**, a 750-square-foot scale model of the battlefield as it was in 1863. The progress of the battle is explained with narration and hundreds of colored lights. This 30-minute show should be seen before touring the actual battlefield, as it helps you to understand the unfolding events. *Showings every 45 minutes from 8:15 until 4:15. Nominal admission, as above.*

A block south of the Visitor Center is the:

CYCLORAMA CENTER (2), ☎ 717-334-1124. *Open daily 9–5, closed Thanksgiving, Christmas, and New Year's. Exhibits, film show, overlook, and walking tour are free. Cyclorama show every 30 minutes 9–4:30, admission: Adults $3, seniors (62+) $2.50, and children (6–15) $2. &, steep ramp for Cyclorama show, free wheelchair loans.*

Way back in 1882, a French artist named Paul Phillippoteaux came to America to research and paint a massive 356-foot circular canvas depicting Pickett's Charge, the major offensive of the Battle of Gettysburg. Today, visitors stand in the center of this panoramic view as an exciting 20-minute sound-and-light program re-creates the fighting once again.

Elsewhere in this center, operated by the National Park Service, is an **exhibit** relating to **Lincoln's *Gettysburg Address***. During the summer months, the original draft of the two-minute speech is on display; the rest of the year it returns to the White House and a facsimile is substituted. Contrary to legend, it was not written on the back of an envelope.

While there, you can also see a free 10-minute film about the battle, visit the **overlook point** on the roof, and perhaps take the walking tour described below:

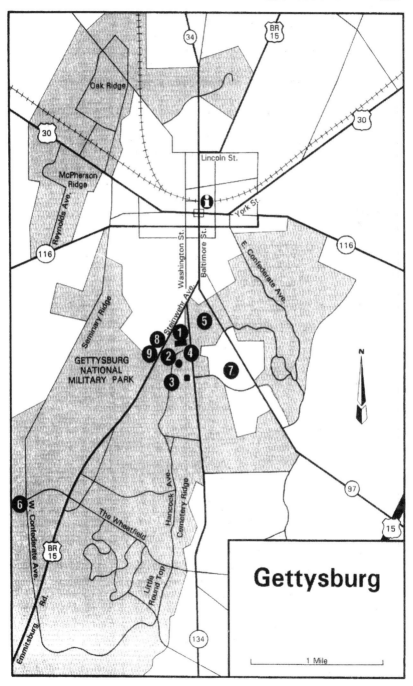

Gettysburg

1 Mile

HIGH WATER MARK WALKING TOUR (3), begins at the Cyclorama Center. Free. Ranger-led twice a day, or ask for a free descriptive brochure/map at the information desk and do it yourself. Most of the one-mile route is ૯.

This easy walk along Cemetery Ridge is a good orientation to the most critical moments of the battle, and shows you the turning point of the war from the eye-level perspective of the soldiers fighting it. Along the way you'll visit the farmhouse headquarters of the Union commander General George G. Meade, the site of **Pickett's Charge** where 12,000 Confederate soldiers attempted to pierce the Union lines, the stone wall where they lost momentum, and the **High Water Mark** where the tide of battle was reversed after an appalling slaughter.

You're now ready for the:

*BATTLEFIELD AUTO TOUR (4), begins at the Visitor Center. *18-mile circuit by car, bike, or bus. Free park entry. Free explanatory brochure/map for self-guided tours available at the Visitor Center. If desired, licensed guides may be hired at the Visitor Center for $30 (more for larger vehicles). Commercial cassette tape with narration and map available at the Wax Museum (8), for $12.95. Commercial guided bus tours offered by the Gettysburg Tour Center, 778 Baltimore St. ☎ 717-334-6296. ૯, partial access to sites.*

Allow at least two hours to make the suggested tour through the National Military Park, following the "Auto Tour" signs and stopping at the various points of interest. Along the way are several free observation towers where you can get good views, many explanatory signs, hundreds of cannon and monuments, historic structures, restrooms, and picnic sites. For hikers, there are marked trails of various lengths that can be taken from several parking areas.

The Auto Tour route returns you to the Visitor Center, adjacent to which is the:

GETTYSBURG NATIONAL CEMETERY (5). *Open daily. Free. ૯, paved paths, no motorized vehicles allowed.*

It was at the dedication of this cemetery on November 19, 1863, that President Lincoln delivered his famous *Gettysburg Address*, a brief 272-word speech that has become a part of American history. Several thousand Union soldiers, many unknown, are buried here, along with veterans of other conflicts from the Spanish-American War to Vietnam. Confederate soldiers were re-interred in the South after the war.

Return to the Visitor Center for a trip to the:

EISENHOWER NATIONAL HISTORIC SITE (6), Gettysburg, PA 17325, ☎ 717-338-9114. *Accessible only by bus from the Eisenhower Tour office along the north side of the Visitor Center (1). Usually open daily from April through Oct., and Wed.–Sun. from Nov. to early Jan. and early Feb. through March, but schedule may vary; phone ahead. Closed Thanksgiving, Christmas, New Year's, and January. Buses operate 9–4. Bus fees: Adults $5.25, youths (13–16) $3.25, children (6–12) $2.25. Tickets may be ordered in advance,* ☎ *877-438-8929. ♿, arrangements can be made to drive there if unable to board the bus; first floor of house is accessible.*

Purchase your bus ticket and, if time permits, watch the short video on the life of the 34th President given in the tour office before departure. Allow at least one hour for the complete trip.

General Eisenhower bought this old dairy farm in 1950 as a weekend retreat, and as his first permanent home. Before that, he and his wife Mamie had lived in temporary housing all around the world ever since their marriage in 1916. Completed in 1955, during his first term as President, the **main house** incorporates parts of a 200-year-old farmhouse. Your tour begins in the rarely-used formal living room, then proceeds to the casual enclosed porch, where the Eisenhowers spent most of their time. After seeing the dining room, visitors can climb upstairs to the sitting room, bedrooms, and guest rooms before descending to a typical 1950's kitchen and homey den. The adjacent office, with a desk made from boards from the White House, was used for both farm and presidential business.

From here you can take a short walk around the grounds, stopping at the 1887 **barn** for a peek at Ike's golf carts. A free map is available for a self-guided **farm walking tour** that explores the working parts of the farm, following in the footsteps of the many world leaders who were always taken here by the President.

Return by bus to the Visitor Center.

In addition to official sites operated by the National Park Service, Gettysburg has a number of commercial attractions that might interest you. The most noticeable of these is the **National Tower** (7), just behind the cemetery, which offers bird's-eye views along with a sight-and-sound program describing the battle. Its indoor and outdoor observation levels, some 300 feet above the ground, are reached by elevator. ☎ *717-334-6754. Open daily Apr.–Oct. and Fri.–Sun. in Nov. Adults $5, seniors (62+) $4.50, children (6–12) $3. Gift shop. ♿.*

The **National Civil War Wax Museum** (8) features some 200 life-size figures in 30 tableaux along with a re-creation of Pickett's Charge and an animated figure of President Lincoln delivering his *Gettysburg Address*. Cassette tape tours of the battlefield may be rented or purchased here.

297 Steinwehr Ave., ☎ *717-334-6245. Open daily Mar.–Dec., weekends Jan.–Feb. Adults $4.50, ages 13–17 $2.50, ages 6–12 $1.75.* Nearby, the **Lincoln Train Museum** (9) offers a simulated "ride" with the President to Gettysburg, and a large collection of model trains. ☎ *717-334-5678. Open daily, closed Dec.–Feb. Adults $5.75, children (6–11) $3.25.*

Other commercial places to check out include the **Hall of Presidents and First Ladies,** the **Jennie Wade House,** the **Soldier's National Museum,** the **Lincoln Room Museum, General Lee's Headquarters,** the **Gettysburg Railroad Steam Train,** the **Magic Town of Gettysburg,** the **Samuel Colt Heritage Museum,** the **Confederate States Armory,** The **Conflict Theater,** and the **Land of Little Horses.** The tourist office in the center of town will happily load you down with brochures describing them all.

Lancaster

I f Lancaster had remained the capital of the United States, its most famous resident would not have had to travel to Washington when he became President. But, alas, it didn't, so James Buchanan left his grand mansion to take up residence in the White House just before the Civil War. America's largest inland Colonial town has retained much of its historic ambiance, and is still the hub of the prosperous and abundant Pennsylvania Dutch countryside. Its compact downtown is easily explored on foot, whether on a guided tour or on your own.

First settled in 1721, Lancaster became a major manufacturing center, specializing in armaments for the French and Indian War as well as for the Revolution. It was the capital of the United States for just one day, September 27, 1777, when the wandering Congress halted after being chased out of Philadelphia by the British. The next day Congress moved safely across the Susquehanna River to York; an unnecessary precaution as Lancaster was never invaded. The city was also the capital of Pennsylvania from 1799 until 1812.

This trip can easily be combined with Trip 46, exploring the Pennsylvania Dutch countryside; and with Trip 47, a railfan's journey to Paradise. You'll need to stay at least overnight to do this, but that's no problem as the region has plenty of accommodations ranging from fancy hotels to inexpensive B & Bs. Just ask at the Visitor Center for details. If you have still more time, you can drive about 70 miles east to Philadelphia and the Brandywine Valley, described on pages 328 through 359.

GETTING THERE:

By car, Lancaster is about 110 miles northeast of Washington. Take Route **I-95** north through Baltimore and cross the Susquehanna River at Havre de Grace. From Exit 93 turn north on **US-222**, which becomes Queen Street in Lancaster.

If you also want to visit Columbia, leave Lancaster by heading west on **PA-23** and **US-30** for about 12 miles. From there, the easiest way back to Washington is to go west on US-30 to York, then south on **I-83**. Skirt Baltimore by going southwest on **I-695**, then follow **I-95** into

Washington.

PRACTICALITIES:

Many of the attractions are seasonal, usually open from April or May through October, November, or December. Quite a few of them close on Sundays and/or Mondays, and also on major holidays. Check the individual listings carefully, and play safe by calling ahead. The colorful Central Market is open on Tuesdays, Fridays, and Saturdays.

For further information, contact the **Lancaster Chamber of Commerce** at South Queen and Vine streets, ☎ 717-392-1776. Regional information is available from the **Pennsylvania Dutch Convention & Visitors Bureau**, just east of the city at 501 Greenfield Road (at US-30), Lancaster, PA 17601, ☎ 717-299-8901 or 800-723-8824, fax 717-299-0470, Internet: www.800padutch.com.

FOOD AND DRINK:

Some choice restaurants in the historic center of downtown Lancaster are:

Market Fare (Grant & Market streets, by the Central Market) Creative American cuisine in a traditional dining room resembling a private club. Reservations suggested. Sunday brunch. Lighter fare in the upstairs café. ☎ 717-299-7090. $$ and $$$

Stockyard Inn (1147 Lititz Pike, PA-501 and US-222, 1.5 miles north of the Central Market, just east of Amtrak station) American/Continental cuisine in an historic home. ☎ 717-394-7975. X: Sat. lunch, Mon. lunch. $$ and $$$

The Pressroom (26 W. King St. at Market) American cuisine is served at this smart bistro in an historic center city building. X: Sun., Mon. ☎ 717-399-5400. $ and $$

Issac's Restaurant & Deli (Central Market Mall, 44 N. Queen St., by the market) Wonderful soups, sandwiches, salads, and other light fare. ☎ 717-394-5544. $

LOCAL ATTRACTIONS:

Numbers in parentheses correspond to numbers on the map.

Begin your daytrip with a stroll through the historic core at Lancaster's **Downtown Visitor Center**, home of the:

HISTORIC LANCASTER WALKING TOUR (1), 100 South Queen St., ☎ 717-392-1776. *Operates daily from April through October; tours Sun.–Mon. & Wed.–Thurs. at 1, Tues. & Fri.–Sat. at 10 and 1. Fee: $7.50.*

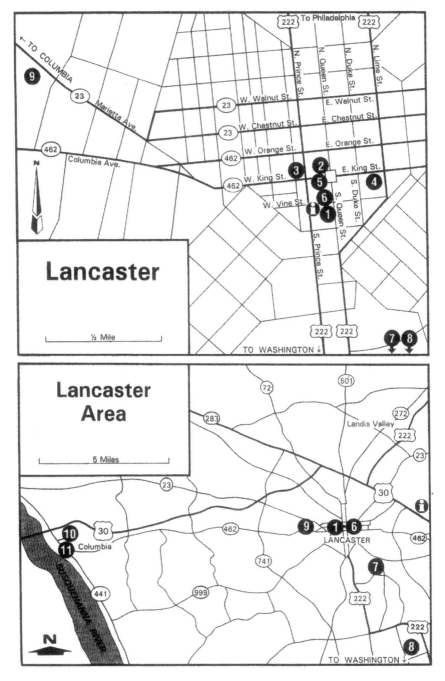

Run by a non-profit organization, these 90-minute tours are led by volunteer guides in period costume. You'll begin with a short audio-visual presentation of the town's history, then take a stroll around its historic core. Stops are made at whichever sites are open, and the entire tour is enlivened with colorful stories and anecdotes. Along the nearly-two-mile route you'll wander through back alleys and visit hidden courtyards, getting a more intimate view of Lancaster than you would on your own.

Even if you don't take the walking tour, you can get information about the town at the Visitor Center. Be sure to see the **Central Market** (2), where farmers from around the region sell their fresh produce directly to consumers. Built in 1889 on a site used for the same purpose since the 1730s, this marvelously Victorian red-brick structure is the oldest publicly-owned, continuously-operating farmers' market in America. Some of the local delicacies to try include sweet bologna and shoofly pie, the latter so tasty that you'll have to "shoo" the flies away. *Open Tues. and Fri. 6–4, Sat. 6–2.*

Just a block west of the market stands the **Fulton Opera House** (3) of 1852, built on the foundations of a Colonial jail where the last of the Conestoga Indians were massacred in 1763. Its lush Victorian interior is allegedly haunted by ghosts. Many of the greatest stars of the late 19th and early 20th centuries performed here, including Mark Twain, Buffalo Bill, Wild Bill Hickok, John Phillip Sousa, Ethel Barrymore, W.C. Fields, Sarah Bernhardt, Sophie Tucker, Al Jolson, Alfred Lunt, Irene Dunne, Busby Berkely, and Anna Pavlova. Completely renovated in 1969, the Opera House is now a National Historic Landmark and serves as the community's performing arts center. *12 N. Price St.,* ☎ *717- 397-7425.*

The noted American artist, Charles Demuth (1883–1935), had his studio in the 18th-century **Demuth House and Tobacco Shop** (4), which has been restored. You can visit the studio, art gallery, home, and courtyard garden; as well as the adjacent shop. The latter, still in business, was opened around 1770 and is the oldest tobacco shop in America. *114–120 E. King St. (rear),* ☎ *717-299-9940. Open Tues.–Sat. 10–4, Sun. 1–4. Closed Mon., holidays, Dec. 24, Jan. Free.*

Penn Square, at the intersection of King and Queen streets, is the very heart of historic Lancaster. Near its northwest corner stands the:

HERITAGE CENTER MUSEUM (5), Penn Square, ☎ 717-299-6440. *Open Apr.–Dec., Tues.–Sat. 10–5. Closed Sun., Mon., holidays. Donation. Gift shop.* ♿.

Three centuries of Lancaster County history are explored in this

Old City Hall structure from the 1790s. Among the regional fine and decorative arts on display are paintings, furniture, weathervanes, toys, clocks, Pennsylvania long rifles, fraktur, pewter, silver, copperware, quilts, and samplers.

Walk a block south to the:

LANCASTER NEWSPAPERS NEWSEUM (6), 28 S. Queen St., ☎ 717-291-8600. *Always open. Free.* &.

Lancaster Newspapers, Inc., has combined the words *newspaper* and *museum* to describe their window displays on the evolution of local newspapers from 1794 to the present. You'll see, directly from the sidewalk, the changing styles of newspapers, early presses, wooden type, a Linotype machine, historical headlines, distribution methods, and their modern presses of today. Explanatory panels tell the whole story.

Return to your car and drive to the next destinations. About a mile and a half to the southeast, in Lancaster County Park, is the:

ROCK FORD PLANTATION & KAUFFMAN MUSEUM (7), 881 Rock Ford Rd., ☎ 717-392-7223. *Open Apr.–Oct., Tues.–Fri. 10–4, Sun. noon–4. Adults $4.50, seniors $3.50, children (6–12) $2. Tours. Gift shop.*

George Washington's adjutant, General Edward Hand, lived in this elegant 18th-century Georgian mansion from 1793 until his death in 1802. Standing on the wooded banks of the Conestoga River, the house is remarkably well-preserved and essentially unchanged. It is furnished with period antiques, some of which once belonged to General Hand. The reconstructed barn now houses the Kauffman Museum of Pennsylvania Folk Arts and Crafts, featuring works of fraktur, pewter, copper, brass, tin, wood carvings, firearms, and furniture from the 18th and 19th centuries.

Five miles south of Lancaster, just off Route US-222, stands the oldest structure in Lancaster County:

HANS HERR HOUSE (8), 1849 Hans Herr Drive, Willow Street, PA 17584, ☎ 717-464-4438. *Open Apr. through Nov., Mon.–Sat. 9–4, closed Sun., Thanksgiving, Dec. to March. Adults $3.50, children (7–12) $1. Picnic facilities. Gift shop.*

America's oldest Mennonite meetinghouse was built by Hans Herr and his family as a wilderness home in 1719. This simple stone structure is considered to be one of the finest examples of medieval Germanic architecture in the country. Today both it, the outbuildings, and the extensive grounds have been restored to their original appearance, and

offer a fascinating glimpse into the lives of the early Mennonites.
Return to Lancaster and turn west on PA-23 to:

*WHEATLAND (9), 1120 Marietta Ave., Lancaster, PA 17603, ☎ 717-392-
8721. *Open Apr.–Nov., daily, 10–4, closed Easter and Thanksgiving.
Special candlelight tours in early Dec. Adults: $5.50, seniors $4.50, students $3.50, children (6–11) $1.75. Tours. Gift shop. &, partial access.*

James Buchanan, the 15th President of the United States, purchased
this estate in 1848 while he was still Secretary of State, and continued to
use it for the rest of his life. He died here in 1868, still defending what
most people regarded as a disastrous presidency (1857–61) that failed to
prevent the Civil War. Buchanan was the only President to have come
from Pennsylvania, and the only one to have remained unmarried.
Always politically active, he was a member of the House of
Representatives, a U.S. Senator, minister to both Russia and Great
Britain, and Secretary of State under President James Polk.

The mansion, built in the Federal style in 1828 by a wealthy lawyer
and banker, was named "The Wheatlands" after its then-rural location
near fields of wheat. It is furnished much as it would have been during
Buchanan's life, with many of his own treasures gathered from around
the world. His niece, Harriet Lane, also lived here and added an elegant
domestic touch to the decor. She served as First Lady during Buchanan's
stay in the White House.

A visit to Wheatland begins with a video show in the carriage
house, and continues with a thorough tour of the mansion, led by
knowledgeable guides in period costume.

If you have time for a few more sights, you can return to
Washington by way of Columbia and Route I-83. To do this, continue
west on PA-23 (Marietta Avenue), soon turning north at Rohrerstown to
US-30. This leads west into Columbia on the Susquehanna River, where
you'll find the:

NATIONAL WATCH & CLOCK MUSEUM (10), 514 Poplar St., Columbia,
PA 17512, ☎ 717-684-8261. *Open Tues.–Sat. 9–4. Closed major holidays.
Adults $6, seniors $5, children (6–12) $4. Gift shop. &.*

Operated by the National Association of Watch and Clock
Collectors, this intriguing and newly expanded museum celebrates the
history of timekeeping with over 10,000 items, including clocks dating
from the 17th century to the present. Some of them are quite amazing
in the intricate and unexpected ways they have of counting the minutes.

Try to be there on the hour, when the whole place comes alive with wondrous sounds.

Also in town is the:

WRIGHT'S FERRY MANSION (11), 38 S. 2nd St., Columbia, PA 17512, ☎ 717-684-4325. *Open May–Oct., Tues., Wed., Fri., Sat. 10–3. Closed July 4. Adults $5, students (6–18) $2.50.*

Back in 1726, a refined, well-educated Quaker lady left the comforts of Philadelphia to live in what was then a wilderness. Here she set up a thriving silkworm industry and maintained correspondence with some of the leading intellects of Colonial America, including Benjamin Franklin. Successful at business, she had this mansion built in 1738 in a typical English style with Pennsylvania-Dutch overtones. Beautifully restored, the house now contains one of the best collections of early-18th-century Pennsylvania furnishings to be found anywhere.

The Pennsylvania Dutch Country

Exploring the Pennsylvania Dutch Country can be a highly rewarding experience—or a day wasted on shameless tourist traps. The key is to know what you're looking for. This daytrip concentrates on the less-commercialized sites, including a fine introduction into the lifestyles of the "Plain People," makes stops at some old-time farms, and visits an 18th-century religious retreat.

What sets Lancaster County's lovely, fertile countryside apart from other lovely, fertile countrysides is the culture of the folks who live there. Their collective name, the Pennsylvania Dutch, is a misnomer. Actually, the correct term is *Deutsch*, meaning German. During the early 18th century many non-conformist religious sects from Europe found refuge in William Penn's "Holy Experiment," his tolerant colony of Pennsylvania. Among those who settled in Lancaster County are the various orders of "Plain People," who to differing degrees reject much of the modern world and still live more or less as their ancestors did. These include the Amish, the Mennonites, the Hutterites, and the Brethren.

The Old Order Amish are the most conservative of the religious groups, and easily the most unusual. They shun the use of electricity from power lines (but not from private generators), telephones in their homes (but not in barns), ownership of automobiles (but not riding in them), farm tractors, and marriage to non-Amish. The most prevalent symbol of the Amish, at least to outsiders, is their horse-drawn buggies that snarl motor traffic on local roads. Actually, some of the other Plain People also use these slow-moving vehicles, as do several tour operators. Both the Amish and other conservative sects are usually trilingual, speaking German, "Pennsylvania Dutch," and English quite fluently. Far from being a dying breed, the Amish population is growing rapidly; faster than the ability of the land to support them, so that many now operate small businesses or have moved to farmland in other areas. Their amazing ability to come to terms with the modern world without becoming a part of it has made their order prosper to the point where they now number over 130,000 members in the United States and Canada; with some 18,000 in Lancaster County alone.

The colorful lifestyles, combined with idyllic scenery, tasty food, and proximity to major urban areas, attracts travelers by the millions. That in turn has encouraged more than a few tacky tourist traps to open along the main roads. However, there are still far more genuinely worthwhile attractions than you can see in a day, or possibly a week. You'll have to pick and choose carefully, stay overnight, or plan on coming back another time. Those able to stay longer can easily combine this trip with the ones to Lancaster and Strasburg, or even the trips to Philadelphia and the Brandywine Valley.

GETTING THERE:

By car, Intercourse is about 118 miles northeast of Washington. Take Route I-95 north through Baltimore and cross the Susquehanna River at Havre de Grace. From Exit 93 turn north on US-222, heading towards Lancaster. Just south of that city, turn right (east) on PA-741, following it through Strasburg and continuing for about another three miles, then turning north on Belmont Road to the village of Intercourse.

PRACTICALITIES:

Many of the sites on this trip are closed on Sundays and a few major holidays. Avoid weekends in summer, when traffic on the two-lane roads is bumper-to-bumper.

Taking photographs of Amish people in which they can be recognized is a violation of their religious beliefs and is highly offensive. *Please respect their privacy and honor the Biblical command to make no graven images.*

For further information, contact or visit the **Pennsylvania Dutch Convention & Visitors Bureau** at 501 Greenfield Road, Lancaster, PA 17601, ☎ 717-299-8901 or 800-723-8824, 717-fax 299-0470, Internet: www.800padutch.com. Their information center is located just east of Lancaster, on Greenfield Road at the intersection with US-30.

FOOD AND DRINK:

Pennsylvania Dutch cuisine means hearty servings of "comfort" foods like great-grandmother used to make, often in large restaurants with communal seating and frequently no menus. This "family style" dining is just that—you sit with strangers, pass around the overflowing dishes, take all you want of whatever you want, and generally have a good time. Some establishments offer buffet or à la carte service at private tables instead. Be sure to try the shoofly pie— "just this once." Most restaurants do not serve liquor, and some are closed on Sundays.

Among the better choices are:

The Restaurant at Doneckers (333 N. State St. in Ephrata, near the Cloisters) French and American cuisine, an extensive wine list, and a pleasant country atmosphere with both indoor and outdoor dining makes this place a favorite. Reservations advised, ☎ 717-738-9501. X: Sun., Wed., major holidays. $$ and $$$

Miller's Smorgasbord (US-30, east of the intersection with N. Ronks Rd.) A fixed-price buffet with all you can eat. Special price for children. In business since 1929. ☎ 717-687-6621. $$

Plain & Fancy Farm (PA-340, 2 miles east of Bird-in-Hand) Fixed-price PA-Dutch meals served family-style in a large barn. Special meals for children. No menu. ☎ 717-768-4400. $ and $$

Good 'N Plenty (PA-896, a half-mile south of PA 340, at Smoketown) An enormous family-style restaurant with copious servings of PA-Dutch favorites. ☎ 717-394-7111. X: Sun. $ and $$

Amish Barn Restaurant (PA-340, a mile east of Bird-in- Hand) Abundant PA-Dutch dishes are offered either à la carte or family-style. ☎ 717-768-8886. X: Jan.-Mar. $ and $$

Bird-in-Hand Family Restaurant (PA-340 near Ronks Rd., Bird-in-Hand) PA-Dutch home cooking, served à la carte or from a buffet. X: Sun. ☎ 717-768-8266. $ and $$

For other local selections, check the listings for trips in neighboring Lancaster and Strasburg. Fast-food addicts will find their fill along Route US-30 just east of Lancaster.

LOCAL ATTRACTIONS:

Numbers in parentheses correspond to numbers on the map.

Begin your journey in the curiously-named village of **Intercourse**, located just north of Paradise and east of Bird-in-Hand. No puns, please—they've been done to death. Once a delightful Amish settlement, Intercourse is today overrun with quainte gifte shoppes and olde countrie stores, but it does have one compelling sight that will help you understand the rest of the area's attractions, namely:

THE PEOPLE'S PLACE, Route 340, Intercourse, PA 17534, ☎ 717-768-7171. *Open Mon.–Sat., 9:30 a.m.–8 p.m., closing at 5 after Labor Day and before Memorial Day. Closed Sun., New Year's, Thanksgiving, Christmas. Show: Adults $4, children (5–11) $2. Museum: Adults $4, children $2. Combination tickets available. Bookstore. Craft shop.*

The world of the Plain People is skillfully explained in this cultural

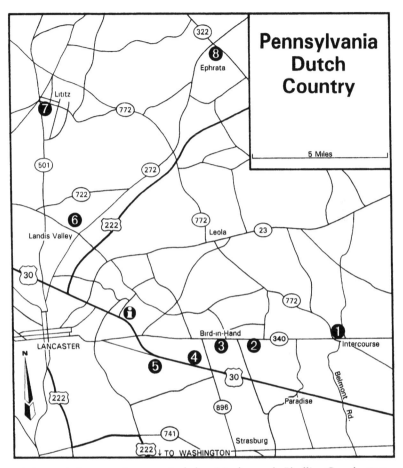

Pennsylvania
Dutch
Country

5 Miles

322

8 Ephrata

Lititz

7

772

501

272

722

6

222

Landis Valley

772

Leola

23

30

772

i

Bird-in-Hand

3

2

340

1

Intercourse

5

4

30

Belmont Rd.

222

896

Paradise

741

Strasburg

222 ↓ TO WASHINGTON

LANCASTER

N

interpretation center created by Merle and Phyllis Good, two Mennonites who set out to promote a better understanding of the Amish, Mennonite, and Hutterite ways of life. They do this through a 25-minute audio-visual presentation entitled *Who Are the Amish?* (shown continuously from 9:30 to 6:45, 4:30 in winter), a hands-on museum called **Twenty Questions** that you can experience at your own pace, and exhibits of local arts and crafts.

After exploring Intercourse, head west on PA-340, the old "King's Highway" of the early 18th century, possibly stopping at the **Weavertown One-Room Schoolhouse** (2). This was a real country schoolhouse from 1877 until 1969, after which the teacher and students were replaced with realistic animated figures who put on an entertaining show. ☎ *717-768-3976, Internet: www.800padutch.com/wvrtown.html. Open Apr.–Oct. daily 10–5, 9–5 from Memorial Day to Labor Day, and weekends 10–5 in Mar. and Nov. Adults $2.95, seniors $2.50, children (5–11) $2.*

Bird-in-Hand, which got its name from the sign of an early inn, is the next village. Just west of it is **Abe's Buggy Rides** (3), a concession that has been offering short two-mile rides in Amish horse-drawn buggies for over 29 years. ☎ *717-392-1794, Internet: www.800padutch. com/abes.html. Open Mon.–Sat., 8:30–dusk; shorter hours Nov. to March. Adults $10, children (3–12) $5.*

At Smoketown, turn south on PA-896 and west on US-30, the main tourist drag, to the:

AMISH FARM AND HOUSE (12), 2395 Lincoln Hwy. East (US-30), Lancaster, PA 17602, ☎ 717-394-6185, Internet: www.amishfarmand house.com. *Open daily all year, 8:30–6 in summer, until 5 in spring and fall, and closing at 4 in winter. Closed Christmas. Adults $5.95, seniors $5.25, children (5–11) $3.25. Gift shop. Snacks. Ꮠ.*

You won't meet any Amish at this commercial attraction, but otherwise it's a quite authentic presentation of their rural ways of life. Visits begin with a lecture and tour of the ten-room **farmhouse**, built around 1805 and simply furnished in the Old- Order Amish tradition. You can then explore the 25-acre **farm** with its barn, windmill, waterwheels, spring house, chicken coop, corn crib, lime kiln, blacksmith shop, and more. Live animals and growing crops add to the interest, as does the small museum.

Although it's incongruously stuck behind a maze of factory-outlet stores and fast-food eateries, the **Mennonite Information Center** (5) is a worthwhile stop where you can learn more about the Amish and Mennonite ways of life. The center also offers a short film about the Mennonites, and tour guides who can lead you (in your car) to many out-of-the-way places not spoiled by commercialism. Adjacent to the center is the **Hebrew Tabernacle Reproduction**, an actual-size model of the ancient Tabernacle of Jerusalem described in the Bible, including the golden Ark of the Covenant. *2209 Mill Stream Rd., Lancaster, PA 17602, ☎ 717-299-0954, Internet: www.mennoniteinfoctr.com. Open Mon.–Sat., 8–5. Center free, tabernacle tours: Adults $5, seniors $4, children (7–12) $2.50. Tour guides $9.50 per hour plus a flat charge of $7 per car. Ꮠ.*

Return to Route US-30, the old Lincoln Highway that was first built in 1792 as the Lancaster Turnpike, a toll road for stagecoaches. Follow it to the northwest past the **Pennsylvania Dutch Tourist Information Center**, then turn north on PA-272, the Oregon Pike, to the:

*LANDIS VALLEY MUSEUM (1), 2451 Kissel Hill Rd., Lancaster, PA 17601, ☎ 717-569-0401. *Open March–Dec., Mon.–Sat. 9–5, Sun. noon–5. Closed holidays except Memorial Day, July 4, and Labor Day. Craft demonstrations Apr.–Oct., guided tours available. Adults $7, seniors (60+) $6.50, youths (6–12) $5, under 6 free. Reduced rates in March, Nov., and Dec. Gift shop. Snacks in summer. Picnic facilities. ♿, partial access.*

You can really step back into the past in this reconstructed country village of 18th- and 19th-century buildings, where the old ways of life are kept alive by craftspeople and guides in period costumes. The largest outdoor museum of Pennsylvania German rural heritage anywhere, it was begun in the 1920s by George and Henry Landis, two local brothers whose German ancestors came to Lancaster County in the early 1700s. The Commonwealth of Pennsylvania acquired the museum in 1953, and has since added many historic buildings from the area, and re-created others that had been lost. Some of the highlights include a functioning **log farm** of the 1700s, a **Mennonite farmstead** of 1820, an early **tavern**, a **country store** filled with period merchandise, a **firehouse**, and a beautifully-decorated **Victorian house** of the 1870s. About 18 buildings may be visited, several of which feature traditional craft demonstrations from May through October.

Just about five miles north of the museum is the small town of **Lititz** (7), an as-yet unspoiled survivor in the endless battle against touristy ticky-tack that pervades so much of the county. Named after a village in Bohemia (now the Czech Republic) where the Moravian Church had its origins in 1467, Lititz was founded in 1756 by immigrant Moravians as a refuge from "worldly connections." Their religion, a Protestant denomination that predates the Reformation by some 60 years, stresses simple, honest living, and places great importance on the role of music in daily life.

Main Street is lined with a remarkable collection of 18th-century houses, along with a smattering of more "modern" structures from the 1800s. To appreciate the unusual history of this most extraordinary village, head east a few blocks to the **Johannes Mueller House** of 1792, which now houses the Lititz Historical Foundation and its adjacent museum. A rare collection of early artifacts may be seen in the log portion of the house, while the stone section is authentically furnished. There are also items associated with General Johann Augustus Sutter (1803–80), surely the most famous—or infamous—resident of Lititz.

Sutter was born in Germany, moved to the West Coast in 1835, founded the colony of Nueva Helvetia at was is now Sacramento, California, became a Mexican citizen, and started his own empire in central California. It was there that gold was discovered in 1848. A womanizer, an adventurer, and a heavy drinker, Sutter was unfortunately not very adept at business, and soon went bankrupt. At the age of 70 he moved to Lititz after hearing rumors of the alleged healing powers of the local spring water. He died there in 1880, and is buried across the street, in the graveyard behind the Moravian Church. *Johannes Mueller House, 137 East Main St.,* ☎ *717-626-7958. Open May 1 to Memorial Day, Mon.–Sat. 10–4; day after Memorial Day to Dec., Sat.–Mon. 10-4. Adults $3, children (6–18) $1.50. A walking tour map of the village is available.*

Walk across the street to the **Moravian Church Square**, most of whose buildings date from the 18th century. The oldest is the Gemeinhaus of 1762, now the parsonage. To its right is the Church of 1787, which has a small museum featuring period musical instruments. *Tours by appointment, Memorial Day through Labor Day.* ☎ *717-626-8515.*

Nearby, in an old factory on North Water Street, is the fascinating **Heritage Map Museum** with its fabulous collection of 15th- through 19th-century maps from around the world. You could spend hours here discovering how man's concept of the world has changed over the centuries as nations came and went, and as new lands were explored. *55 N. Water St.,* ☎ *717-626-5002. Open daily 10–5. Adults $4, children (6–12) $3.*

Maybe by now you're hungry. How about a pretzel? America's first pretzel bakery, the **Sturgis Pretzel House**, is just down Main Street, and children from 2 to 100 are invited to come in and twist their own, earning a diploma after mastering the art. You can see the original ovens in action, along with their modern counterparts in the factory. And, of course, there's a pretzel store. *219 East Main St.,* ☎ *717-626-4354, Internet: www.sturgispretzel.com. Open Mon.–Sat. 9:30–4:30, closed New Year's, Easter, Thanksgiving, Christmas. Admission $2.*

Return along Main Street and turn north a block on Broad Street (PA-501). Follow your nose to the **Candy Americana Museum** in the Wilbur Chocolate factory, home of Wilbur Buds. Here you can examine antique confectionery equipment and watch hand-dipped candies being made in the adjoining factory. To the profit of dentists everywhere, the delicious products can be purchased in the outlet store. ☎ *717-626-3249, Internet: www.800padutch.com/wilbur.html. Open Mon.–Sat. 10–5, closed Jan. 1–2, Labor Day, Thanksgiving, and Christmas. Free.*

Saving the most extraordinary sight for last, follow PA-772 (Main St. in Lititz) east to PA-272, then continue north to PA-322. A right turn here brings you to the:

*EPHRATA CLOISTER (8), 632 W. Main St., Ephrata, PA 17522, ☎ 717-733-6600. *Open Mon.–Sat. 9–5, Sun. noon–5. Closed holidays except Memorial Day, July 4, and Labor Day, also Mon. in Jan. and Feb.. Adults $5, seniors (60+) $4.50, youths (6–17) $3. Gift shop. Special events. ♿, partial access.*

One of America's first communal societies, Ephrata was founded in 1732 by Conrad Beissel (1690–1768), a German Pietist who sought spiritual regeneration through an ascetic lifestyle and ancient mystical rites. Preaching among the Mennonites and Dunkards of Lancaster County, this charismatic leader attracted a following to his monastic community, and there developed a substantial economy that thrived until after the Revolutionary War. By that time the celibate orders had died out, and in 1814 the remaining married order formed the Seventh Day Baptist Church. Their descendants continued to use the Cloister until 1934. In 1941 it was taken over by the Pennsylvania Historical and Museum Commission.

The ten surviving buildings of the original Cloister have been restored, and a few others re-created in the distinctive medieval Germanic style that Ephrata is famous for. Visits begin with an audio-visual show, followed by a tour led by a robed guide through rooms of the main structures. After that, you can explore the other buildings, including the print shop, where one of the society's major economic functions was carried out.

Trip 47

Strasburg

Railfans (and normal folk, too) will literally be in Paradise when they take this daytrip into America's railroading past. That's the name of the village to which the antique steam train takes you as you ride across the Pennsylvania Dutch countryside, and that's the feeling you'll get as you marvel at the workings of these hissing black beasts.

Strasburg has become quite a center for train enthusiasts ever since the once-defunct Strasburg Rail Road, founded in 1832, came back to life in 1959. No mere tourist attraction, this is a real, standard-gauge working railroad that operates all year round. You've probably already seen its meticulously-restored trains in movies and TV commercials.

Just across the street from the station is the fabulous Railroad Museum of Pennsylvania, one of the largest and most comprehensive of its kind in the world. You can easily spend hours here examining dozens of locomotives and cars dating from the 1820s to the near-present, both inside the museum and out in the yards.

Having two major attractions so close together has naturally brought on other related sights to help make your day even more enjoyable. The village of Strasburg itself is of more than passing historic interest, with houses dating back as far as 1764 and a Main Street that was once part of the first route leading from Philadelphia to the booming West.

Although it's in the heart of the delightful Pennsylvania Dutch country, this trip sticks to a railroading theme. Other, more rural aspects of the area are explored on Trip 46.

GETTING THERE:

By car, Strasburg is about 110 miles northeast of Washington. Take Route I-95 north through Baltimore and cross the Susquehanna River at Havre de Grace. From Exit 93 turn north on **US-222** past Conowingo, heading towards Lancaster. Just south of that city, turn right (east) on **PA-741**, which soon becomes Strasburg's Main Street.

PRACTICALITIES:

The Strasburg Rail Road operates daily from April through September, and on weekends the rest of the year. The Railroad Museum of Pennsylvania is open daily from April through October, and daily except Mondays the rest of the year, closing on some holidays. Most of the other attractions are open on a similar schedule. Strasburg can get quite crowded on summer weekends.

For further information on this region, contact the **Pennsylvania Dutch Convention & Visitors Bureau** at 501 Greenfield Road, Lancaster, PA 17601, ☎ 717-299-8901 or 800-723-8824, fax 717-299-0470, Internet: www.800padutch.com. Another source is the **Strasburg Visitors Information Center** on PA-896, at the Historic Strasburg Inn, ☎ 717-687-7922.

The Strasburg Rail Road runs **special event trains** around Easter, Halloween, and before Christmas. Call them for current details and reservations.

Throughout this area you will encounter many of Lancaster County's "Plain People," especially members of the Amish faith, who choose to reject the trappings of modern life. *Please respect their privacy and religious beliefs by not taking any photographs of them in which faces may be recognizable, a violation of the Biblical command to make no graven images.* Drivers must keep an eye out for slow-moving horse-drawn buggies.

FOOD AND DRINK:

Some good restaurants in and around Strasburg are:

Historic Revere Tavern (3063 Lincoln Highway/US-30, in Paradise, about 5 miles northeast of Strasburg) Steak and seafood in a 1740 inn; lighter fare at lunch. ☎ 717-687-8601. $$ and $$$

Washington House (in the Historic Strasburg Inn on Route 896, in town) Colonial-style dining in a re-created 1793 inn. ☎ 717-687-7691 or 800-872-0201. $$

Red Caboose (312 Paradise Lane/ PA-741, just northeast of the R.R. Museum) Railfans will love having lunch in a dining car surrounded by rolling stock, now part of a motel. Nothing fancy, but it's fun. ☎ 717-687-5001. $ and $$

Isaac's Restaurant & Deli (Route 741 in town, at the Shops of Traintown) Soups, salads, sandwiches, and the like in a friendly atmosphere. ☎ 717-687-7699. X: major holidays. $

Alternatively, you might bring a **picnic lunch** to eat at Groff's Grove, a stop on the steam railroad. Box lunches may be purchased at the station, or you can get the makings of a picnic at the Country Store in Strasburg. The **Dining Car Restaurant** at the station features burgers and other simple dishes ($).

LOCAL ATTRACTIONS:
Numbers in parentheses correspond to numbers on the map.

Since its ticket may be used repeatedly all day long and since it opens first, has a huge parking lot, and is just across the street from the station, you'll probably find it most convenient to start with the Railroad Museum.

*RAILROAD MUSEUM OF PENNSYLVANIA (1), Route 741, Strasburg, PA 17579, ☎ 717-687-8628. *Open Mon.–Sat. 9–5, Sun. noon–5; closed Mondays from Nov.–Apr. and some holidays. Adults $6, seniors $5.50, children $4. Tickets valid for multiple entries throughout the day. Gift shop. Largely ఉ.*

This modern, state-operated museum has one of the very best collections of historic motive power, rolling stock, and railroading artifacts to be found anywhere on Earth. At last count there were over 30 locomotives and about 40 passenger, freight, and service cars on display inside the hall and out in the yards. Two of these are exact replicas of pioneer locomotives from the 1820s, and at least one of the electrics is of recent enough vintage to bear the Amtrak logo. But mostly there is a lot of steam. You can stand in the cab of one engine, climb into the pit beneath another, and peer into all kinds of passenger cars.

Along with the trains are displays on the rich history of Pennsylvania's railroads and a vast collection of old-time memorabilia. Don't miss the 20-minute film shown continuously inside a period station, or the view from the upper balcony. Near the exit is a gift shop with an enticing selection of railroading books, videos, and related matter.

*STRASBURG RAIL ROAD (2), Route 741, Strasburg, PA 17579, ☎ 717-687-7522, Internet www.strasburgrailroad.com. *Open daily Apr.–Sept., weekends the rest of the year. Train schedule varies, usually hourly 10–7 in peak season, hourly noon–3 in off-season. Ride takes 45 minutes round trip. Layover stop may be made at Groff's Grove. Basic fares: Adults $8.25, children (3–11) $4, all day fare with unlimited rides $16.50. $1 extra for reserved seats, premium for parlor and dining cars. Gift shop. Bookstore. Restaurant, snack bar, picnic tables. Partially ఉ, inquire for details.*

America's oldest short-line railroad has been hauling passengers and freight from Strasburg to the Main Line of the Pennsylvania Railroad, a 4.5-mile distance, ever since 1832. Decreasing revenues and destruction caused by violent storms forced it to file for abandonment

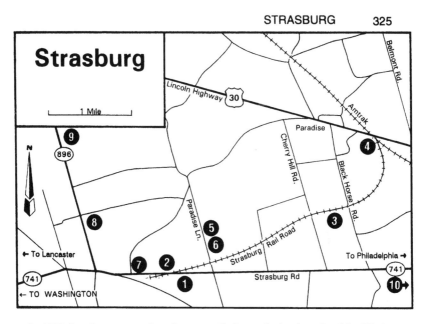

in 1957, but it was saved and eventually brought back to healthy life by a group of local railfans in 1958. Money for this endeavor was raised by the simple gimmick of making every investor a vice-president! In addition to its considerable tourist trade, the Strasburg Rail Road still carries occasional freight to the main line at Paradise, PA, where it connects with ConRail as Amtrak trains speed by.

A steam locomotive was acquired in 1960 (the line had switched to gasoline power as early as 1926), and some ancient coaches were discovered on a remote siding in New Hampshire, brought here, and restored. Also hauled in pieces to this spot was the Victorian station of 1882, where the tickets are now sold. Over the years since, additional old locomotives and cars were found and refurbished, so that today the railroad boasts one of the finest stables of vintage rolling stock in the nation. In addition to six steam locomotives, these include both open and closed coaches, a fantastic open observation car used in the film *Hello Dolly*, and a parlor car of palatial luxury. On a siding sits the elegant private car built in 1916 for the president of the Reading Railroad, which may be boarded for inspection.

One of the delights of riding the Strasburg Rail Road is the bucolic countryside through which it travels. Small farms, mostly owned by Amish families who still rely on animal power, line the right-of-way. The few small roads that cross the tracks are just as likely to be used by horse-drawn buggies as by automobiles, so you may truly feel that the clock has been turned back nearly a century.

Your ride on the steam train takes you from the **East Strasburg**

Station (2) to **Groff's Grove** (3), where you have the option of getting off for a picnic and taking a later train back. While there, you might want to get lost in the **Amazing Maize Maze**, a 10-acre corn field arranged as a challenging maze. In addition, a petting zoo, hay ride, and other treats are featured. *Open July to Labor Day, Tues.–Sat., and mid-Sept. through Oct. on Fri. and Sat.; 10–dusk. Adults $7, children (5–11) $4.* ☎ *717-687-6843, Internet: www.amazingmaze.com.* The end of the line is at **Leaman Place** (4) by the village of **Paradise**, where the tracks join Amtrak's main line and the engine is run around for the return journey.

NATIONAL TOY TRAIN MUSEUM (5), Paradise Lane, Box 248, Strasburg, PA 17579, ☎ 717-687-8976, Internet: www.traincollectors.org. *Open daily 10–5, May–Oct; weekends in April, Nov. to mid-Dec.; plus Good Friday, Easter Mon., Thanksgiving Fri., and Dec. 26–31. Adults $3, seniors $2.75, children (5–12) $1.50. Gift shop.* ᵹ.

Not just another commercial enterprise, this is actually the national headquarters of the non-profit Train Collectors Association, an organization devoted to the preservation and history of toy trains. Don't confuse these delights with the more serious model trains that stress authentic detail in scaled miniature. Toy trains are the stuff of childhood dreams, and bear such famous brand names as Lionel and American Flyer.

The vast collections exhibited here include examples dating from 1880 to the present. There are five huge operating layouts in O, S, G, HO, and Standard gauges, all of which respond to the buttons you push. A continuous video show both entertains and educates visitors about the joys that adults (and even children) can have playing with toys.

Almost next door to the Toy Train Museum is the **Red Caboose Motel** (6), ☎ *717-687-5000,* which houses its guests in a yard full of real cabooses! This is the perfect overnight stop for dedicated railfans, who might also want to take on fuel at the motel's Dining Car restaurant.

CHOO CHOO BARN (7), Route 741, Strasburg, PA 17579, ☎ 717-687-7911, Internet: www.choochoobarn.com. *Open daily Apr.–Dec., 10–4:30, closing at 5:30 in summer. Adults $4, children (5–12) $2. Model train shop.* ᵹ.

Many of Lancaster County's charms have been re-created in O-gauge scale in this 1,700-square-foot model train layout. Thirteen trains whiz around while some 135 animated scenes depict barn-raisings, a circus, a parade, an amusement park, and even a house on fire. Days are compressed, too, as the lights periodically dim and a nightime scene appears.

GAST CLASSIC MOTORCARS EXHIBIT (8), 421 Hartman Bridge Road, Route 896, Strasburg, PA 17579, ☎ 717-687-9500. *Open daily 9–5. Closed Jan 1, Easter, Thanksgiving, Christmas. Adults $8, children (7–12) $4. Gift shop.* ♿.

It's not such a great leap from trains to automobiles, and you'll find plenty of the latter in this exhibition. More than 50 cars are on display at any time, including rare antiques, high-performance sports cars, celebrity specials, and even "wheels" you may have owned yourself at one time.

THE AMISH VILLAGE (9), Route PA-896 a mile south of US-30, Strasburg, PA 17579, ☎ 717-687-8511, Internet: www.800padutch.com/avillage.html. *Open daily 9–6 mid-March to Labor Day, 9–4 day after Labor Day through Oct., 10–4 Nov. and Dec.; and weekends 10–4 the rest of the year. Closed Thanksgiving week, Christmas. Adults $5.50, children 6–12 $1.50. Picnic area. Gift shop.* ♿.

Almost as far removed from railroading as you can get, the nearby Amish Village makes a nice contrast to all those mechanical goings-on. Visitors are treated to a half-hour tour into the world of the Old Order Amish, with stops at an authentically-furnished farm house of 1840, a spring house, an Amish village store, an operating smokehouse, a blacksmith's shop, a windmill, and a waterwheel. The schoolhouse was built by Amish craftsmen, and is typical of those in use today. And, of course, there are live farm animals, including pigs, goats, horses, and others.

Pennsylvania's Brandywine Valley

I t's hard to know where to begin when you're exploring the historic Brandywine Valley. In fact, there are so many attractions that it takes two separate daytrips to touch just the highlights. Trip 43 covers the southern part of the valley in Delaware, while this excursion visits the sights in Pennsylvania. Since they are only a few miles apart, you could, of course, combine elements of each into your own custom itinerary.

The Brandywine is a special river, both in history and in natural beauty. Not very large, or long, it rises in the Welsh hills of southeastern Pennsylvania and flows some 60 miles south into the Delaware at Wilmington. Its waters powered the mills of early industry, created vast fortunes, and provided the setting for one of the pivotal battles of the American Revolution.

Artists have long been attracted to the valley, capturing its moods in what was to become a uniquely American style of illustration. One of its leading practitioners, Howard Pyle (1853–1911), worked here and helped develop the talents of such younger artists as Maxfield Parrish and N.C. Wyeth. Two succeeding generations of the Wyeth family, Andrew and Jamie, have continued the artistic heritage of the Brandywine Valley, which is best represented at the delightful Brandywine River Museum in Chadds Ford.

Along with art, history, and scenic splendor, the valley features what many regard as America's finest horticultural gardens, a must-see for anyone who appreciates the beauty of flowers and plants.

GETTING THERE:

By car, the first attraction on this trip is about 100 miles northeast of Washington. Take route I-95 as far as Exit 93, just across the Susquehanna River. From there head north on **MD-275** and **MD-276** to the intersection with **US-1**, turn right, and follow it northeast to Kennett Square, PA. The location of each site is clearly shown on the accompanying map.

PRACTICALITIES:

Most of the major attractions are open daily, with some closing on Christmas or on a few holidays. The Brandywine Battlefield closes on Mondays and holidays (except Memorial Day, July 4, and Labor Day). For some of the minor sights, however, you'll have to come on a weekend between May and September. Each listing gives specific details.

For further information contact the **Delaware County Convention & Visitors Bureau**, 200 E. State St., Media, PA 19063, ☎ 610-565-3679 or 800-343-3983., Internet: www.delcocvb.org. Another good source is the **Chester County Tourist Bureau**, 601 Westtown Rd., Suite 170, P.O. Box 2747, West Chester PA 19380, ☎ 610-344-6365 or 800-228-9933, fax 610-344-6999, Internet: www.brandywinevalley.com. They have a handy **Tourist Information Center** on US-1 at Kennett Square, in an historic Quaker Meeting House of 1885 located next to the entrance to Longwood Gardens.

FOOD AND DRINK:

With so many visitors throughout the year, the valley has no shortage of inns and restaurants. Among the better choices are:

Crier in the Country (US-1 at PA-261, Glen Mills) Renowned Continental cuisine in a Victorian mansion Reserve, ☎ 610-358-2411. X: Mon., weekend lunch. $$$

Chadds Ford Inn (US-1 at PA-100, near the Brandywine River Museum) An historic 18th-century inn noted for its American and Continental cuisine, and Colonial atmosphere. Reservations are advised, ☎ 610-388-7361. X: Fri. and Sat. lunch; brunch on Sun. $$ and $$$

The Terrace (in Longwood Gardens) Both a cafeteria and a full-service restaurant, this delightful spot has both indoor and outdoor tables for garden visitors. Reservations are accepted for the restaurant. ☎ 610-388-6771. Restaurant X: Jan., Feb. $ and $$

Taqueria Moroleon (15 New Garden Shopping Center, Baltimore Pike, Kennett Square) Authentic Mexican food in an unprepossessing setting. ☎ 610-444-1210. $ and $$

Hank's Place (US-1 at PA-100, near the Brandywine River Museum) Everyone in Wyeth Country comes to Hank's for its simple, homestyle cooking. Nothing fancy here. ☎ 610-388-7061. $

Brandywine River Museum Restaurant (inside the museum) A small and exceptionally pleasant cafeteria overlooking the river, reserved for museum visitors. ☎ 610-388-2700. X: Mon. & Tues. from Jan.–March. $

Alternatively, there are several good spots for a **picnic** in this area. The most romantic is along the banks of the Brandywine, either just behind the museum or on the trail that starts there. The Brandywine Battlefield has picnic tables high on a ridge overlooking the countryside.

LOCAL ATTRACTIONS:
Numbers in parentheses correspond to numbers on the map.

The Brandywine Valley sites in Pennsylvania are all conveniently located on or near Route US-1, and are listed in the order that you will pass them in.

PHILLIPS MUSHROOM MUSEUM (1), Route 1, Kennett Square, PA 19348, ☎ 610-388-6082. *Open daily except New Year's, Easter, Thanksgiving, and Christmas, 10–6. Adults $1.25, seniors 75¢, children 7–12 50¢, children 6 and under free. Gift shop. ♿.*

A museum for a fungus? Yes, indeed. Kennett Square is the center of America's mushroom industry, so it's the best place to find out more about these delicious edibles. Their history, folklore, and culinary mystique are explained through films, dioramas, and exhibits before watching the real things grow. The gift shop sells exotic species that you may never have seen before, along with all manner of items with mushroom motifs.

*LONGWOOD GARDENS (2), Route 1, Kennett Square, PA 19348-0501, ☎ 610-388-1000 or 800-737-5500, Internet: www.longwoodgardens.org. *Open every day of the year, 9–6, closing at 5 from Nov.–March. Conservatories open at 10. Both are frequently open late into the evening for fountain displays and special events. General admission: Adults $12, $8 on Tues.; youths (16–20) $6; children (6–15) $2; children under 6 free. Inquire about prices for special events. Gift shop. Cafeteria and restaurant. ♿ wheelchairs available free of charge.*

You'd have to travel all the way to Europe to experience the likes of Longwood, since nowhere else in America will you find such a magnificent horticultural estate. Some 350 of its 1,050 manicured acres are open to the public, offering 11,000 different kinds of plants in exquisite settings. Among the highlights is a complex of enormous ***conservatories** where the weather is perfect all year-round, an outdoor ***Italian water garden** right out of a Florentine dream, the estate house of Pierre S. duPont, spectacular fountains, waterfalls, a topiary garden of whimsical shapes, a secluded forest walk, formal rose gardens, and an "idea garden" where you can pick up hints on starting your very own Longwood.

William Penn originally sold Longwood to a Quaker family named Peirce in 1700 for agricultural use. Handed down from generation to generation, it slowly became more of a garden and less of a farm. In 1906 the estate was purchased by a wealthy industrialist, Pierre S. duPont, who created the present gardens and set up an endowment to maintain them.

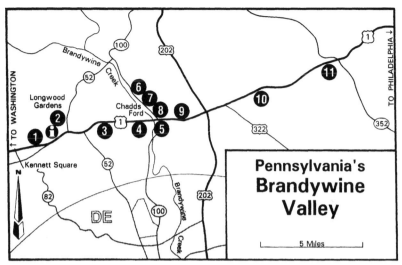

Pennsylvania's
**Brandywine
Valley**

5 Miles

As you enter through the Visitor Center, be sure to pick up a free map of the estate, which shows where everything is and also indicates an easy route suitable for wheelchairs. Allow a minimum of two hours for this visit—you could easily spend the whole day here.

CHADDSFORD WINERY (3), Route 1, Chadds Ford, PA 19317, ☎ 610-388-6221, Internet: www.chaddsford.com. *Open daily, noon–6. Entry free, fee for tasting. Wine shop. Special events.* &.

Tasting the local country wines is always interesting, and these are well worth the sampling. You can watch the entire process of making wine, from the crushing of the grapes to the final bottling. Then, after tasting them, you can purchase a bottle or so right from the winemakers.

BARNS-BRINTON HOUSE (4), Route 1, Chadds Ford, PA 19317, ☎ 610-388-7376. *Open May–Sept., weekends only, noon–5; otherwise by appointment. Adults $3, children $1. Crafts demonstrations.*

Guides in Colonial dress will take you through this brick tavern of 1714, restored and authentically furnished by the Chadds Ford Historical Society. Listed on the National Register of Historic Places, the structure is noted for its fine interior woodwork and exterior brickwork.

*BRANDYWINE RIVER MUSEUM (5), Route US-1, Chadds Ford, PA 19317, ☎ 610-388-2700, fax 610-388-1197, Internet: www.brandy winemuseum.org. *Open daily except Christmas, 9:30–4:30. Adults $5,* *seniors, students, and children 6–12 $2.50, under 6 free. Inquire about tours to nearby N.C. Wyeth Studio, offered Apr.–Oct. Gift shop. Cafeteria, closed Mon.–Tues. from Jan.–March. &, use entrance on river side near reserved parking.*

Whether you're an art fan or not, you'll almost certainly enjoy a visit to the Brandywine River Museum. This is the best place to see works of the Brandywine River School, a quintessential American style that bridges the gap between fine art and popular illustration. From the local landscape paintings of the 19th century to the fantasy worlds created by Maxfield Parrish and N.C. Wyeth in the early 20th, the works shown here appeal to a wide range of tastes. Andrew Wyeth, the latter's son, was born in Chadds Ford in 1917 and became one of America's leading fine artists, a tradition continued by his son Jamie. Both are well represented with major works in this museum, as are other artistic members of the Wyeth family.

The museum, founded in 1971, is housed in a restored gristmill of 1864 set on the banks of the Brandywine. Complementing the original structure is a large, modern wing of 1984, with glass towers that enable visitors to take in the local scenery along with the art. The self-service restaurant is a great place for either lunch or light refreshments.

Be sure to stroll in the riverside garden adjacent to the museum. The **River Trail** is a mile-long nature path leading from here along the water's edge, under Route 1, and on a boardwalk over a marsh to the next attraction, John Chads House. This can also be reached by car.

JOHN CHADS HOUSE (6), Route 100, a quarter-mile north of Route 1, Chadds Ford, PA 19317, ☎ 610-388-7376. *Open May–Sept., weekends only, noon–5; otherwise by appointment. Adults $3, children $1.*

Eighteenth-century life in the hamlet of Chadds Ford is described by guides in Colonial dress as they show visitors through this stone farmhouse of 1725. You may also get to see baking in the beehive oven. Just across the road is an 18th-century springhouse, used as a schoolhouse in the 1840s. Related material is shown nearby at:

THE BARN (7), Route 100, a quarter-mile north of Route 1, Chadds Ford, PA 19317, ☎ 610-388-7376. <u>Open May–Sept., weekends only, noon–6. Adults $1.</u>

Headquarters of the Chadds Ford Historical Society, this museum displays local furniture and furnishings from the 18th century. Just to the south is the:

CHRISTIAN C. SANDERSON MUSEUM (8), Route 100, 100 yards north of Route 1, Chadds Ford, PA 19317, ☎ 610-388-6545. *Open weekends, Memorial Day, July 4, and Labor Day; 1–4:30; and by appointment. Donation requested.*

Chris Sanderson was a close friend of the Wyeths, an all-around Renaissance man, and an incurable collector. The latter trait resulted in a house full of all sorts of treasures including works by the Wyeths, but mostly with the strangest mementos that you can possibly imagine. A sample of these includes melted ice from the South Pole, sand from digging the Panama Canal, Easter eggs from 1886, and a piece of the bandage used on President Lincoln after he was shot.

BRANDYWINE BATTLEFIELD STATE PARK (9), Route 1, Chadds Ford, PA 19317, ☎ 610-459-3342, Internet: www.libertynet.org/iha/brandywine/index.html. *Open Tues.–Sat. 9–5, Sun. noon–5, grounds remain open until 8 from Memorial Day through Labor Day. Closed Mon. and non-summer holidays. Visitor Center, museum, and grounds free. Tours: Adults $3.50, seniors $2.50, children 6–17 $1.50, under 6 free. Museum. Gift shop. Picnic facilities. ♿ for Visitor Center & museum. Grounds are hilly with gravel paths.*

General Washington and his Colonial troops may have lost the Battle of Brandywine on September 11, 1777, but they inflicted such damage on the British that the French were convinced into joining the fray and helping to bring about final victory. The whole story is told in an interesting slide show given frequently in the Visitor Center. There's also a museum of artifacts and dioramas that brings the story to life.

Elsewhere in the 50-acre park are the restored **headquarters** of General Washington and the Marquis de Lafayette, looking much as they did in 1777. Their interiors may be explored on guided tours that begin at the Visitor Center, or you can just walk around outside and enjoy the views. This is a fine place for a picnic.

If you're game for even more, continue about six miles father east on Route 1 to the:

NEWLIN MILL PARK (10), 219 South Cheyney Rd., Glen Mills, PA 19342, ☎ 610-459-2359. *Open daily 8–dusk. Gristmill times and fees vary. Picnic facilities & fishing by reservation, hiking trails.*

An operating stone gristmill of 1704 is the highlight of this reconstructed Colonial village, operated by a non-profit foundation. There's also a furnished miller's house of 1739, a springhouse, a blacksmith's shop, and a log cabin—all set in 150 acres of land and forest.

In another three miles you'll come to:

THE FRANKLIN MINT MUSEUM (11), Franklin Center, PA 19091, ☎ 610-459-6168. *Open Mon.–Sat., 9:30–4:30, Sun. 1–4:30. Closed major holidays. Free. Gift shop.* ♿.

You've seen their ads—now see their treasures. Prized as collectibles by many (and considered high-class kitsch by others), the future heirlooms offered by the Franklin Mint are hard to categorize, but always interesting. There are original works of art by Andrew Wyeth and Norman Rockwell, along with sculptures in porcelain, crystal, pewter, and bronze. Dolls, miniature cars, classic books, coins, philatelics, jewelry, and much, much more round out the collection.

*Philadelphia's Historic Area

A walk back in time through the beautifully-restored neighborhoods of Colonial Philadelphia is easily one of the most rewarding daytrips that can be made from the Washington area, and an experience no American should miss. The sights along the way are varied enough to appeal to everyone from school-age children to the most sophisticated of adults.

Philadelphia, the birthplace of American freedom, was founded in 1682 by an Englishman, William Penn. A rich Quaker from a prominent family, Penn was a constant irritant to King Charles II, who once even had him thrown into the Tower of London. To rid himself of Penn and his followers, and to satisfy a debt owed the family, the king granted William the large tract of land in the New World that later became Pennsylvania. There Penn named his new settlement after the Greek words for "Brotherly Love."

From the beginning, Penn's colony was noted for its religious tolerance, a quality all too lacking in other parts of Colonial America. This naturally attracted talented, open-minded persons such as Benjamin Franklin (1706–90), who became a leading citizen, statesman, scientist, inventor, and philosopher. A signer of the Declaration of Independence, Franklin was also a member of the Constitutional Convention of 1787. These two events in effect created the United States, and Philadelphia remained its capital until 1800. Much of that late-18th-century city has survived in the Historic Area that is the focus of this daytrip.

The suggested walking tour shown on the map is only about two miles long and level all the way, not including the highly recommended side trip to Penn's Landing. Still, there are more attractions here than you can comfortably digest in one day, so you'll have to pick and choose according to your interests. If going to Philadelphia seems a bit far for a one-day excursion, why not make it a weekend trip, or even a mini-vacation? By staying for two or more days you can explore more of the city's attractions on Trip 50, the Brandywine Valley, or the nearby Pennsylvania Dutch country.

GETTING THERE:

By car, Philadelphia is about 147 miles northeast of Washington via Route I-95 all the way. Just beyond the Ben Franklin Bridge turn west onto I-676, and in a few blocks south on 6th Street to the underground parking facility at Independence Mall. There are also several other parking lots in the vicinity. Cars parked illegally along the streets are soon ticketed and even towed away!

Trains operated by **Amtrak** provide frequent service between Washington's Union Station, points in Maryland, and Philadelphia's 30th Street Station. The run takes between 90 minutes and 2 hours, with a premium fare and reservations required for the new high-speed Acela Express trains. Round-trip excursion fares cut costs considerably but have some restrictions on use during peak travel periods. For current schedules and fare information ☎ 800-USA-RAIL, Internet: www.amtrak.com.

The best way to get from Philadelphia's 30th Street Station to the Historic Area is to take any **SEPTA** commuter train from the upper suburban level going in the direction of the city (you can see this from the platform). Your Amtrak ticket stub covers the fare to Center City, where you get off at the second stop, **Market East Station.** From there it's a short walk to the Liberty Bell. Alternatively, you can take the Market-Frankford subway from just outside 30th Street Station east to 5th Street, or a taxi to the Liberty Bell Pavilion (under two miles).

PRACTICALITIES:

Although it can be taken at any time of the year, consider making this daytrip during the off-season, after Labor Day and before May, when there are no waiting lines for the sights. Most of the attractions are open daily, but a few minor ones operate on an irregular schedule. See the individual listings for details.

For further information, contact the **Philadelphia Visitors Center** at 16th Street & John F. Kennedy Blvd., Philadelphia, PA 19102, ☎ 215-636-1666 or 800-537-7676, TDD 215-636-3403, Internet: www/libertynet.org/phila-visitor; or the Superintendent, **Independence National Historical Park**, 313 Walnut St., Philadelphia, PA 19106, ☎ 215-597-8974, TTY 215-597-1785, Internet: www.nps.gov/inde.

FOOD AND DRINK:

Philadelphia's Historic Area offers a wide selection of restaurants. Some of the best choices, all open for lunch, are:

City Tavern (2nd & Walnut streets, a block southeast of the Visitor Center) Traditional American cuisine in a reconstructed 18th-century tavern, served by staff in period costume. Indoor/outdoor dining. For reservations ☎ 215-413-1443. $$$

Old Original Bookbinders (125 Walnut St. at 2nd St.) A landmark restaurant since 1865, serving seafood and meats. ☎ 215-925-7027 for reservations. X: weekend lunch. $$$

New Mexico Grille (50 South 2nd St., between Chestnut and Market) A good value in Southwestern and Mexican cuisine. ☎ 215-922-7061. $$

DiNardo's (312 Race St., a block northwest of Elfreth's Alley) Famous for its steamed hard-shell crabs, also serves other seafood and meat dishes. ☎ 215-925-5115. X: Sun. lunch, holidays. $$

Society Hill (301 Chestnut at 3rd St.) Burgers, sandwiches, omelettes, salads, and the like at the outdoor café or indoor pub. ☎ 215-925-1919. $ and $$

Sassafras (48 South 2nd St., a block east of the Visitor Center) Fancy burgers, salads, omelettes, and the like. ☎ 215-925-2317. $ and $$

The Bourse Food Court (215 North 5th St., across from the Liberty Bell) A variety of fast-food outlets in a beautifully restored 19th-century commodities exchange, the nation's first. ☎ 215-625-0300. X: Sun. in winter. $

If the weather's fine, you can save time and money by purchasing a sandwich or salad from one of the many **sidewalk vendors** between the Liberty Bell and Independence Hall, and eating in the adjacent park.

SUGGESTED TOUR:

Numbers in parentheses correspond to numbers on the map. Begin your walk at the:

*LIBERTY BELL PAVILION (1), Market St. between 5th & 6th streets, on Independence Mall. *Open daily 9–5; early July to early Sept. 9–8. Free.* &.

Housed in its own glass pavilion, the very symbol of American freedom is silhouetted against Independence Hall. There, on July 8, 1776, it was tolled to announce the first public reading of the Declaration of Independence, signed just four days earlier. The bell was originally cast in England in 1751 to commemorate the 50th anniversary of William Penn's Charter of Privileges guaranteeing certain freedoms for Pennsylvania residents. Recast in Philadelphia in 1753 after a defect was discovered, it carries the Biblical quotation "Proclaim liberty throughout all the land, unto all the inhabitants thereof" (Leviticus 25:10). Its famous crack appeared well after the Revolution, and the bell has remained silent since 1846. *NOTE: There are plans to move the Liberty Bell closer to Independence Hall, below, and house it in a more appropriate structure.*

Stroll south on Independence Mall to the:

*INDEPENDENCE HALL (2), Chestnut St. between 5th & 6th streets.

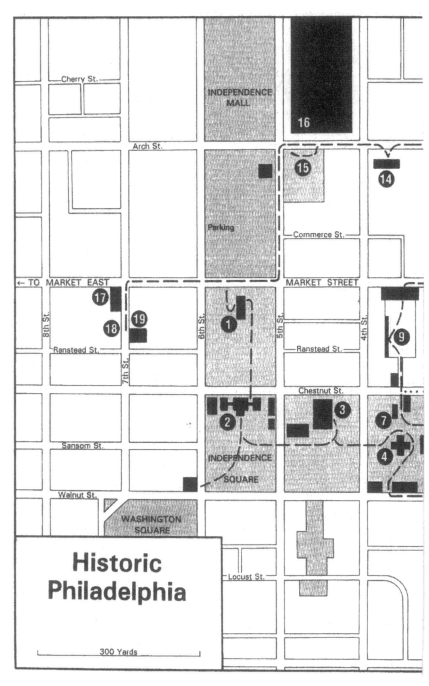

Historic
Philadelphia

300 Yards

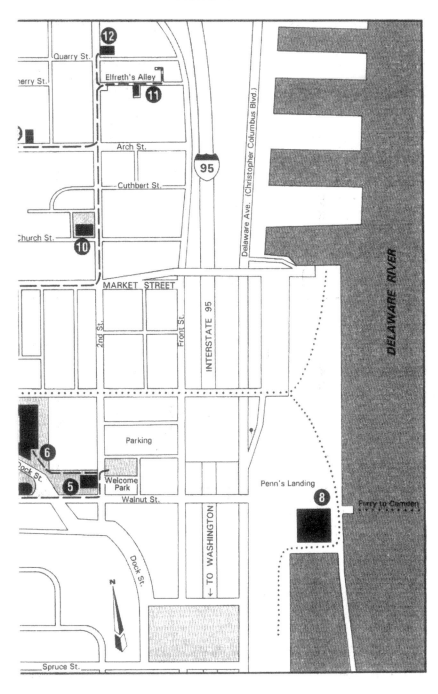

Open daily 9–5; early June to early Sept. 9–8. Visit by free guided tours only. &.

Built between 1732 and 1756 as the Pennsylvania State House, this elegant structure is where the Declaration of Independence was adopted in 1776, the Articles of Confederation were ratified in 1781, and the Constitution of the United States framed in 1787. Tours through its beautifully-restored interior take you first to the old **Pennsylvania Supreme Court Chamber**, arranged in the British manner with a bench for the judges, two jury boxes, and a prisoner's dock. The state coat of arms above the judges replaced that of King George III, which was dragged through the streets and burned following the public reading of the Declaration of Independence.

You will then visit the ***Assembly Room**, where those momentous events of American history actually took place. Most of the original furnishings, both here and throughout the building, were destroyed by the occupying British in 1777; what you see today are authentic antiques similar to what would have been here. One of the few original pieces is the "Rising Sun" chair used by George Washington during the Constitutional Convention in 1787, which Benjamin Franklin said depicted a rising, not a setting, sun—surely a good omen for the new nation. The lovely silver inkstand in front of it was the one actually used to sign both the Declaration and the Constitution.

On the second floor is the **Long Gallery**, an enormous light- filled room that served in Colonial days as a banqueting hall, during the British occupation as a prison for captured American officers, and later as an art gallery.

Flanking Independence Hall are, to the west, the **Congress Hall** where the U.S. Congress met from 1790 to 1800 (House of Representatives on the first floor, Senate upstairs) and, to the east, the **Old City Hall** that housed both local government and the U.S. Supreme Court until the latter moved to Washington in 1800. *Both buildings open daily 9–5. Free.* &.

Independence Square, the park behind the hall, is where the Declaration of Independence was first read in public. Near its northeast corner is **Philosophical Hall**, headquarters of the American Philosophical Society, a scholarly organization founded in 1743 by Benjamin Franklin. *Not open to the public.*

Walk east past the reconstructed **Library Hall** *(open to scholars only)* and turn left to the:

SECOND BANK OF THE UNITED STATES (3), 420 Chestnut St. *Open on* *varying schedule. Adults $2, under 17 free.*

Built between 1819 and 1824 to house the government's central bank, this handsome Greek Revival structure was modeled after the Parthenon in Athens. From 1845 until 1935 it served as a customs house, and in 1974 was restored as an art gallery. Step inside to see some 90 portraits of the founders of the United States, both the famous and the obscure, and be sure to examine the life-size wooden statue of George Washington by William Rush.

Just across 4th Street is:

CARPENTERS' HALL (4), 320 Chestnut St., ☎ 215-925-0167. *Open Tues.–Sun. 10–4, closed Mon. and also Tues. in Jan.–Feb. Closed New Year's Day, Easter, Thanksgiving, Christmas. Free.*

Still owned and operated by the Carpenters' Company, a trade guild founded in 1724 to promote construction skills, this Georgian structure was the setting for the First Continental Congress in 1774. It was here that the colonists' grievances against the king were first aired and a declaration of rights sent to him, and it was here that the boycott against English goods began. Today, the hall houses changing exhibitions, models, period furniture, and a display of Colonial carpenters' tools.

Follow the map south through the 18th-century garden. Next to this, at the corner of 4th and Walnut streets, is the **Todd House**. This typical 18th-century middle-class home was the residence of Dolley Todd, who after her husband's death became the wife of James Madison, the fourth President of the United States. *Ask at the Visitor Center, below, about a tour ($2) that includes this house.* A few steps east on Walnut Street brings you to another row of modest 18th-century houses, including the **Bishop White House** of 1787, an ornate, upper-class residence where many of the nation's leaders were entertained. *Ask at the Visitor Center, below, about a tour ($2) that includes this house.*

The large Greek Revival structure at the corner of 3rd and Walnut streets is the former **Philadelphia Merchants' Exchange**, a center of commerce in the 19th century. It now houses offices of the National Park Service. *Not open to the public.* Continue on to the:

CITY TAVERN (5), 2nd and Walnut streets, ☎ 215-413-1443. *Open for patrons, daily 11:30 a.m.–10 p.m., closing at 11 on Fri. and Sat. and 8 on Sun.*

This was the favorite eating and drinking place for the nation's Founding Fathers during the 18th century. First built in 1773, it was demolished in 1854 and completely reconstructed in 1975. Once again operating as a restaurant, it is furnished with period reproductions and features mostly Colonial dishes served by staff in 18th-century dress. Reservations are suggested.

Catercorner from the tavern is **Welcome Park**, the site of William Penn's home and the spot where in 1701 he granted the famous Charter of Privileges to Pennsylvania residents. It is now arranged as a rather unattractive outdoor museum that describes the founding of Pennsylvania. From here follow the map to the:

VISITOR CENTER (6), 3rd and Chestnut streets, ☎ 215-597-8974, Internet: www.nps.gov/inde. *Open daily 9–5. Free.* ♿.

A large, modern structure operated by the National Park Service, the center features a free 28-minute film entitled *Independence*, on the founding of the nation. There is a self-operated interactive computer exhibit, information desks for both the park and the City of Philadelphia, free brochures and maps, convenient restrooms, and a bookstore. The Bicentennial Bell in the center's 130-foot tower was presented to the American people in July, 1976, by Britain's Queen Elizabeth II.

Follow the map past the **First Bank of the United States**, which from 1797 until 1811 was the central bank of the new nation. The pediment decorations above the Corinthian columns are carved in mahogany, and are among the very few such outdoor wooden sculptures to have survived from the 18th century. *Not open to the public.* Just beyond this, a right turn leads to the:

NEW HALL MILITARY MUSEUM (7), Carpenters' Court. *Open daily, 9–5. Free.*

This reconstruction of a 1791 building once used by the War Department now houses a museum devoted to the history of the U.S. Army, Navy, and Marine Corps from 1775 to 1805. Opposite this is the **Pemberton House**, another Colonial reconstruction that is currently home to the National Parks Museum Shop.

*At this point you may want to make a **side trip** to Penn's Landing on the Delaware River, which adds a little over a mile to the total walking-tour distance.*

Penn's Landing is Philadelphia's revitalized waterfront area, where William Penn first landed to found his colony in 1682. For a long time this had been a derelict neighborhood, but modern development since 1967 has overcome decades of neglect and an awkward location, squeezed between Route I-95 and the Delaware River. In recent years it has played a much more prominent role in the city's cultural and tourist life, with frequent concerts and festivals along with the maritime attractions, including the fascinating Independence Seaport Museum. Besides the great river views, there are some really worthwhile places to visit here:

*INDEPENDENCE SEAPORT MUSEUM** (8), 211 S. Columbus Blvd. at Walnut St., ☎ 215-925-5439, Internet: www.libertynet.org/seaport. *Open daily 10–5, closed New Year's, Thanksgiving, Christmas. Admission to museum and historic ships, adults $7.50, seniors $6, children 4–12 $3.50. Museum only: Adults $5, seniors $4, children $2.50. Museum, historic ships, NJ State Aquarium, and ferry to the aquarium: Adults $15, seniors $12, children $10. Gift shop.* ♿.

The former Philadelphia Maritime Museum has changed its name and moved into much larger quarters, right on the waterfront. Walk beneath a three-story replica of the Benjamin Franklin Bridge as you enter **Home Port: Philadelphia**, an exciting interactive exhibit that explores the events shaping one of America's most historic urban ports. Unload a giant container ship, experience a general quarters drill aboard the bridge of a naval destroyer, try your hand at welding, hop in a simulated scull and row along the Schuylkill River, and then have an undersea adventure in **Divers of the Deep**. You can even watch boats being built in the **Workshop on the Water**. Lots of fun for all, especially kids, and you'll even learn something.

Just outside, and associated with the Seaport Museum, are two historic naval vessels that may be boarded:

U.S.S. *OLYMPIA* and U.S.S. *BECUNA*, Penn's Landing, ☎ 215-922-1898. *Open daily except Christmas and New Year's, 10–4:30. Admission to both vessels: Adults $3.50, children under 12 $1.75. Joint admission with Seaport Museum available. Ship's store.*

The cruiser *Olympia* was Commodore Dewey's flagship in the Philippines during the Spanish-American War in 1898. Fully restored and open to your inspection, it is the only surviving capital ship from that era. Docked next to it is a World War II submarine, the U.S.S. *Becuna*, whose interior may be explored.

If time permits, you might want to take the Riverbus ferry across the Delaware River to visit the outstanding **New Jersey State Aquarium at Camden**, ☎ *609-365-3300 or 800-616-5297, Internet: www.njaquarium.org.*

Penn's Landing has other attractions and activities, enough in fact to finish off your day here. When it's in port, the *Gazela of Philadelphia*, a square-rigger built in Portugal in 1883, welcomes visitors aboard to explore the oldest and largest vessel of its kind that still puts out to sea. *For information,* ☎ *215-923-9030.* Other historic boats make appearances here, and some may be boarded. There are also a variety of special events, concerts, festivals, and exhibitions throughout the year. ☎ *215-629-3200 for current programs.* Other attractions include the **Columbus Monument and International Sculpture Garden**, and the **Philadelphia Vietnam Veterans' Memorial.** *NOTE: Expect major construction in this area as new attractions are added.*

Return to Chestnut Street at Carpenters' Court to continue with the main tour.

*FRANKLIN COURT (9), 316 Market St. *Open daily 9–5. Free. Museum* ৬.

Little is known about the exact design of Benjamin Franklin's last Philadelphia home, which was torn down in 1812. Its foundation has, however, been unearthed and today a simple steel frame represents the house in its original setting. Adjacent to this a ramp leads down to the **Underground Museum**, where Franklin's amazingly varied achievements are celebrated through a collection of antiques, reproductions, and documents. A room full of high-tech gadgetry allows you to access opinions about the man, and a 20-minute film on his life is shown at frequent intervals.

The adjoining **row of houses** along Market Street were either built by or owned by Franklin. At number 322 is the restored office of *The Aurora*, a newspaper published by his grandson. Next door to this is an exhibit on Franklin's early career as a printer, followed by architectural and archaeological exhibitions. The **U.S. Post Office** at number 316 commemorates his role as postmaster by canceling stamps with the old postmark "B. Free Franklin." Authentically restored in the Colonial style, it is the only post office in the nation that does not display the U.S. flag.

Now follow the map and turn left on 2nd Street to:

CHRIST CHURCH (10), 2nd St. between Market and Arch streets. ☎ 215-922-1695. *Open for tourists Mon.–Sat. 9–5, Sun. 1–5. Closed New Year's, Thanksgiving, Christmas, Mon.–Tues. in Jan. & Feb. Donation.* ৬.

Fifteen signers of the Declaration of Independence worshiped at this Georgian-style church, as did many prominent citizens. President George Washington had his own entrance door and box pew, and other pews were reserved for the Penn family, Benjamin Franklin, and other notables. Fully restored, the church serves an Episcopal congregation with Sunday services at 9 and 11, and a Communion service on Wednesdays at noon.

Continue up 2nd Street to:

ELFRETH'S ALLEY (11), 2nd St. between Arch and Race streets. ☎ 215-574-0560. *Alley always open, museum open March through Dec. Tues.–Sat. 10–4, Sun. noon–4. Alley is free; museum $2, children 5–14 $1.*

Dating from 1702, this is thought to be the oldest continuously-occupied residential street in America. Its 30 small houses were built between 1728 and 1836, and are today highly desirable city residences. The one at number 126, open to the public as a museum, is furnished in the Colonial style. Don't miss tiny Bladens Court, off to the left near the east end of the alley.

Just north of this is:

FIREMAN'S HALL (12) 149 N. 2nd St., ☎ 215-923-1438. *Open Tues.–Sat., 9–4:30. Closed holidays. Free. Gift shop. ♿.*

The Philadelphia Fire department has restored an authentic 1876 firehouse and turned it into a marvelous museum of firefighting, complete with an 1815 hand pumper and a horse-drawn steamer from 1907. You can see how the firemen lived, board the wheelhouse of an actual fireboat, and watch a film on the history of firefighting.

Now follow the map to the:

BETSY ROSS HOUSE (13), 239 Arch St., ☎ 215-627-5343. *Open Tues.–Sun., 10–5. Donation.*

According to tradition, Betsy Ross, a seamstress who probably lived in this house, is credited with sewing the first American flag. However accurate the story, the house is certainly filled with interesting memorabilia that makes it worth a visit.

Continue down Arch Street to the:

FRIENDS' MEETING HOUSE (14), Arch and 4th streets, ☎ 215-627-2667. *Open Mon.–Sat., 10–4. Donation. ♿.*

Built in 1804 to accommodate an annual meeting of the Society of

Friends, this Quaker meeting house still serves its original purpose. There is a small exhibition and a slide show recalling the life of William Penn.

CHRIST CHURCH BURIAL GROUND (15), Arch and 5th streets. *Open by appointment, but Franklin's grave is visible from Arch St.*

Benjamin Franklin and four other signers of the Declaration of Independence are buried in this oasis of quiet in the middle of town. Toss a penny on his grave for good luck.

While you're thinking of pennies, you might cross Arch Street to visit the:

UNITED STATES MINT (16). 5th and Arch streets, ☎ 215-408-0114. *Open July–Aug., daily 9–4:30; May–June, Mon.–Sat. 9–4:30; Sept.–April, Mon.–Fri. 9–4:30. Closed major holidays. Coin-making machines do not usually operate on weekends, nor from just before Christmas until after New Year's. Free. ﹠.*

Here, in the world's largest mint, visitors can view the activities from an enclosed gallery, and examine rare coins in a museum. Don't expect free samples, though, and don't try to enter carrying a camera or video gear.

If time permits, you may want to finish off this walk with the next three attractions:

GRAFF HOUSE (17), Market and 7th streets. *Opening times vary. Free. ﹠.*

In May, 1776, Thomas Jefferson rented two furnished rooms here in what was then the outskirts of Philadelphia. It was here that he drafted the Declaration of Independence, adopted with only a few changes on July 4th. The house you visit today is a total re-creation as the original was demolished in 1883. Jefferson's historic role is portrayed in a short film, and his rooms have been re-created with both period and reproduction furnishings.

Almost next door is the:

BALCH INSTITUTE FOR ETHNIC STUDIES (18), 18 South 7th Street, ☎ 215-925-8090. *Open Mon.–Sat. 10–4. Adults $3; seniors, students & children under 12 $1.50. ﹠.*

Philadelphia is nothing if not ethnically diverse, so it's perfectly fitting that America's immigrant heritage should be celebrated here. A multicultural museum, library, archive, and educational center focuses on the national ethnic, racial, and immigration experiences from both the historical and contemporary perspective.

Directly across the street is the:

ATWATER KENT MUSEUM (19), 15 South 7th Street, ☎ 215-922-3031. *Open Wed.–Mon., 10–5. Closed holidays. Adults $3, children 3–12 $1.50.*

This is the museum of Philadelphia's history from the earliest days to the present. Filled with an enormous collection of artifacts, it is especially noted for its temporary exhibitions. The museum is named for its benefactor, the famous early manufacturer of radios.

Philadelphia's Center City and the Parkway

T here's a whole lot more to Philly than just its historic core. This walk explores the most interesting parts of Center City, an area that has changed dramatically in the past few years and is now one of the liveliest, most sophisticated urban scenes in America. No longer do the old jokes apply, no longer can anyone get away with such wisecracks as the famous one by native son W.C. Fields: "Last week I went to Philadelphia, but it was closed." Stereotypes like that might once have had a grain of truth to them, but a tour of today's Center City quickly shows just how far things have changed.

Along the route you can gaze down from City Hall's tower, stroll the length of America's Champs-Élysées, visit some of the finest museums on Earth, relax in a most elegant park, shop at world-class emporiums, and enjoy taste delights that exist nowhere else. Above all, you can mingle with the fascinating mix of cultures that make up Philadelphia's diverse population.

If time permits, why not stay overnight or longer and also discover the Historic Area, the attractions of the nearby Brandywine Valley, or the Pennsylvania Dutch Country?

GETTING THERE:

By car, Philadelphia is about 147 miles northeast of Washington via Route I-95 all the way. Just beyond the Ben Franklin Bridge turn west on I-676, exiting at 15th Street and grabbing the first available parking place or lot. Cars parked illegally here are quickly ticketed and towed away!

Trains operated by **Amtrak** provide frequent service between Washington's Union Station, points in Maryland, and Philadelphia's 30th Street Station. The run takes between 90 minutes and 2 hours, with a premium fare and reservations required for the new high-speed Acela Express trains. Round-trip excursion fares cut costs considerably but have some restrictions on use during peak travel periods. For current schedules and fare information ☎ 800-USA-RAIL, Internet:

www.amtrak.com.

The best way to get from Philadelphia's 30th Street Station to the Center City is to take any **SEPTA** commuter train from the upper suburban level, going in the direction of the city (you can see this from the platform). Your Amtrak ticket stub covers the fare to **Suburban Station**, the first stop, which is right in front of City Hall.

PRACTICALITIES:

The Rodin Museum and the Philadelphia Museum of Art are closed on Mondays and certain holidays, while City Hall is closed on weekends and holidays. To see *everything*, try to make this tour on a Tuesday, Wednesday, Thursday, or Friday. The street life is at its liveliest on workdays.

The suggested walk is slightly over three miles long, level all the way. If you get tired, buses operate frequently along the Parkway and other midtown thoroughfares.

For further information, stop by the friendly **Philadelphia Visitors Center** at 16th Street & John F. Kennedy Blvd., Philadelphia, PA 19102, ☎ 215-636-1666 or 800-537-7676, Internet: www/libertynet.org/phila-visitor.

FOOD AND DRINK:

Philadelphia's Center City is amazingly rich in good restaurants, most of which are geared to the business crowd. Those listed below are particularly suitable for tourists following this walking route.

Swann Lounge & Café (Four Seasons Hotel, Ben Franklin Parkway at 18th St.) Light, contemporary American cuisine in luxurious surroundings overlooking the Parkway. ☎ 215-963-1500. $$$

Jack's Firehouse (2130 Fairmount Ave., 5 blocks north of the Rodin Museum) An adventure in creative, even daring, American cuisine; including unusual game dishes. The setting is dramatic, too—it's an old firehouse. Reservations suggested. ☎ 215-232-9000. $$$

Museum Restaurant (in the Art Museum) This delightful full-service museum restaurant serves light American cuisine. ☎ 215-684-7990. $$

Dock Street Brewery (2 Logan Sq., 18th & Cherry streets) Beer mavens will savor the tasty brews made fresh on the premises, served along with an eclectic menu of innovative dishes. ☎ 215-496-0413. $ and $$

Marathon Grill (1617 J.F.K. Blvd., near the Visitors Center) Great burgers, salads, and the like. A cut above fast-food places. ☎ 215-564-4745. $

Reading Terminal Market (3 blocks northeast of City Hall, by the Convention Center) You haven't been to Philly if you haven't visited the old market under the former Reading Railroad train shed, now part of the new Convention Center. Dozens of ethnic lunch counters offer a cornucopia of eating experiences, mostly good and mostly cheap. ☎

215-922-2317. X: evenings, Sun. $

In addition, you might try **Ben's Restaurant** in the Franklin Institute (accessible without paying museum entrance), the **Skyline Cafeteria** in the Free Library, or the **Art Museum Cafeteria**. All are inexpensive. There are many **street vendors** near the Visitors Center, an area featuring plenty of park benches for an enjoyable alfresco lunch. For the most part, these stands serve sandwiches, sausages, cheesesteaks, and fruit salads, but if you look around you can find more exotic fare at both locations, including Chinese, vegetarian, and Middle Eastern specialties. Prices are quite low.

SUGGESTED TOUR:
Numbers in parentheses correspond to numbers on the map.

Where better to begin your walk than at **City Hall** (1)? This extraordinary structure stands at the center of nearly everything in Philadelphia and is visible for miles around. The largest (and most elaborate) city hall in the United States, it is also the world's tallest self-supporting masonry structure, built completely without a steel frame. Until 1987, an unwritten gentleman's agreement prohibited any other building in town from exceeding its 548-foot height, but during that pivotal year Philadelphia finally entered the Skyscraper Age—and with a vengeance!

Construction on City Hall began in 1871 and was not completed until the turn of the century. It was then topped off with a 37-foot-high statue of *William Penn* by Alexander Milne Calder, whose son and grandson were both born in Philadelphia and were also destined to become renowned sculptors. While you're at the base, swing around to see an entirely different kind of carving, Claes Oldenburg's pop-art masterpiece *Clothespin*—a 45-foot-high 1976 rendering in steel of just that.

For a fabulous ***view** of Center City and way beyond, enter City Hall from the north side and take any elevator to the seventh floor, then follow arrows and take an escalator to the ninth floor, where you'll board a tiny elevator for the **Tower** and **Observation Deck**. You can make reservations for later if necessary, as the tower can only accommodate a few people at a time. ☎ *215-686-9074. Open weekdays except certain holidays, 10–3. Free. An interior tour is also offered on the same days at 12:30.*

Just opposite the northeast corner of City Hall stands another fantastic structure, the **Masonic Temple** (2) of 1873. Its seven lavishly-decorated interior lodge halls each represent a different architectural style— Oriental, Egyptian, Ionic, Corinthian, Norman, Gothic, and Renaissance. They may be seen on guided tours that also include Masonic treasures once owned by George Washington, Benjamin Franklin, Andrew Jackson, the Marquis de Lafayette, and other notables. ☎ *215-988-1917. Tours on weekdays at 10, 11, 1, 2, and 3; on Sat. at 10 and 11. Closed Sun.,*

Sat. in July and Aug., and major holidays. Free. &.

If you have a special interest in art, you might want to go two blocks out of your way to the:

*PENNSYLVANIA ACADEMY OF THE FINE ARTS (3), 118 North Broad St., Philadelphia, PA 19102, ☎ 215-972-7600, Internet: www.pafa.org. *Open Mon.–Sat. 10–5, Sun. 11–5. Free Sun. 3–5. Closed New Year's, Thanksgiving, Christmas. During May, most galleries are devoted to the Annual Student Exhibition. Adults $5.95, seniors & students with ID $4.95, children under 12 $3.95. Higher admission for special exhibitions. Gift shop. Café. Tours on weekends at 12:30 and 2.* &.

Before entering, cross Broad Street and take a good look at the fabulous **Pennsylvania Academy of the Fine Arts**, home of both the museum and a renowned art school. The building itself is a gem, a true masterpiece of the exotic High Victorian Gothic style and long a Philadelphia landmark. Designed by the noted architect Frank Furness (1838–1912), it was completed in 1876, the year of the great Centennial Exhibition. Passers-by have been stunned by its appearance ever since.

Inside, visitors are treated to a sweeping survey of major works by American artists from Colonial times right up to today's latest trends. Founded in 1805 and modeled after Britain's Royal Academy, this is the oldest museum and school of art in the nation, and remains one of the most important—a "must-see" for any art lover.

Now follow the map to **John F. Kennedy Plaza** (4), a large open area commanding vast urban vistas. In its southwest corner is the circular **Philadelphia Visitors Center** whose friendly staff will patiently answer your questions while loading you down with free maps and brochures. ☎ *215-636-1666. Open daily except Thanksgiving and Christmas, 9–5, closing at 6 in summer. Gift shop.*

Just west of this stands **Suburban Station**, once the headquarters of the Pennsylvania Railroad and now a busy stop for all SEPTA commuter trains. With its sidewalk vendors and plentiful park benches, J.F.K. Plaza is a great place for an outdoor lunch or snack. Don't miss Robert Indiana's often-copied sculpture, *Love*, a 1976 piece of typography-as-art framing the glorious view down the Parkway.

Cross 16th Street and head northwest on ***Benjamin Franklin Parkway**, a magnificent boulevard in the tradition of Europe's most elegant cities. Surely America's answer to the Champs-Élysées, it was laid out in 1918 as relief from the rigid grid pattern imposed on the town by William Penn in the 17th century. Running nearly a mile northwest from City Hall, the Parkway provides a grand entrance to the world's largest

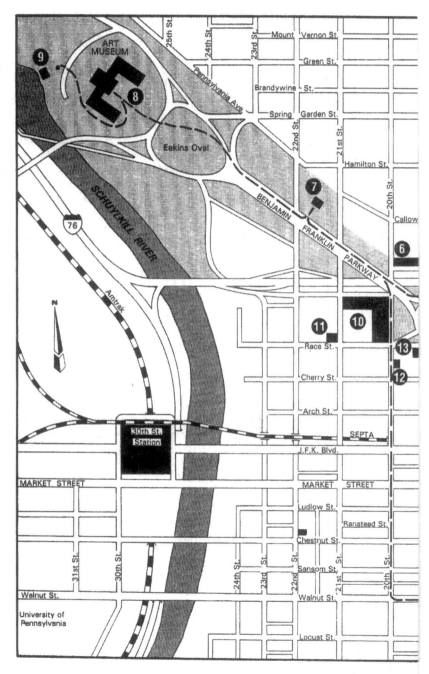

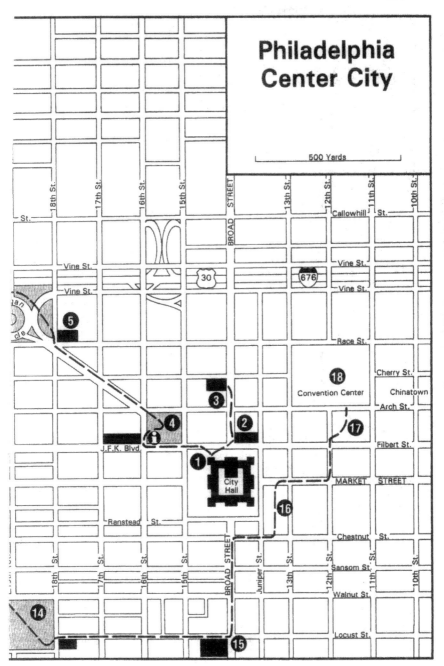

Philadelphia Center City

500 Yards

municipal park.

Passing numerous hotels and cafés, you will soon come to **Logan Circle**. In the center of this lovely open area is the **Swann Memorial Fountain**, whose waters spout some 50 feet into the air from a centerpiece enlivened with three reclining nude statues representing the three great rivers of Philadelphia—the Delaware, the Schuylkill, and the Wissahickon (the latter is really only a creek). The figures were sculpted by Alexander Stirling Calder, son of the creator of the William Penn statue atop City hall and father of Alexander Calder of mobile statuary fame, whose works are well represented in the Art Museum.

Adjoining the Circle on the east is **Sister Cities Plaza**, which celebrates Philadelphia's links to Florence and Tel Aviv, as well as to Tianjin (China), Inchon (South Korea), Douala (Cameroon), and Tourn (Poland). Overlooking the entire scene is the old **Cathedral of Saints Peter and Paul** (5), begun in 1846 when this was still the boondocks. It is the head church of the Philadelphia Archdiocese, seats nearly 2,000 worshipers, and was designated a Basilica in 1976. ☎ *215-561-1313. Open to visitors daily 9–3:30. Weekday masses at 7:15, 8, 12:05, and 12:35; Sundays at 8, 9:30, 12:15, and 5. Use side entrance.*

Just north of the Circle stands the **Free Library of Philadelphia** (6), one of a pair of matching neoclassical buildings modeled after the famous twin palaces on the Place de la Concorde in Paris. The library has millions and millions of books and other reference materials, and also features changing exhibitions on many subjects. Its Rare Book Department, shown on daily tours, is among the finest on Earth. And for a great view of the Parkway, visit the library's rooftop **Skyline Cafeteria** for lunch or just a snack. ☎ *215-686-5322. Open daily with the exception of Sun. in summer. Free. Gift shop. Tours. ♿, ramp entrance at 20th and Wood streets.*

Continue up the Parkway to the:

*RODIN MUSEUM (7), 22nd St. and Ben. Franklin Parkway, ☎ 215-763-8100. *Open Tues.–Sun. 10–5. Donation requested. Gift shop. ♿, use rear driveway and buzz.*

You don't have to travel to Paris to examine the works of Auguste Rodin (1840–1917), one of the greatest artists of all time. His powerful sculptures transcend style, bridging the gap between Romanticism and modern art while capturing the most fleeting, ephemeral moments of life. Because several casts were made of his greatest works, each as much an original as the others, they can be seen in Paris, London, and a few other places besides Philadelphia—but this is the largest collection to be found outside of France.

A cast of **The Thinker* beckons visitors into the tranquil gardens, at the end of which is a 1929 reproduction of the château that Rodin had built for himself outside Paris. Just before the entrance is the fabulous *Gate of Hell* with over a hundred sculpted figures emerging from its 21-foot height. Inside, you'll see the renowned *Burghers of Calais* as well as nearly 200 sculptures and other works of art by the master.

Keep heading northwest on the Parkway until you come to **Eakins Oval**, beyond which is the old rise of "Faire Mount," a low hill once topped by the city's reservoir. Today a broad set of steps—made famous by the film *Rocky*—leads up to the neoclassical pile of the:

*PHILADELPHIA MUSEUM OF ART (8), 26th St. and Ben Franklin Parkway, ☎ 215-763-8100, Internet: www.philamuseum.org. *Open Tues.–Sun., 10–5, until 8:45 on Wed. Closed Mon. and legal holidays. Adults $8; seniors, students, and children 5–17 $5. Additional charge for special shows. Free to everyone on Sun. 10–1. Gift shop. Tours. Cafeteria and restaurant. ♿, ramp entrance on south side by special parking places.*

Even if you detest art museums, you should at least walk around the outside of this 1920's complex to admire the superb ***views** of Philadelphia, the Schuylkill River, and Fairmount Park that it offers.

Inside, you'll be treated to one of the greatest art collections on Earth. More than 200 galleries cover some 10 acres, but it's not necessary (or possible) to see them all in order to uncover those treasures that appeal to you most. Just pick up a diagram of the museum at the entrance and head off towards such masterpieces as Poussin's *Birth of Venus*, Van Eyck's *St. Francis Receiving the Stigmata*, Ruben's *Prometheus Bound*, Renoir's *The Bathers*, Van Gogh's *Sunflowers*, Charles Willson Peale's *Staircase Group*, Benjamin West's *Benjamin Franklin Drawing Electricity from the Sky*, Picasso's *Three Musicians*, and Claes Oldenburg's *Giant Three-Way Plug*. And that's just for starters. There's also the most extensive collection of works by Marcel Duchamp anywhere, weapons, tapestries, a medieval French cloister, a stone Hindu temple from India, a Japanese Buddhist temple and ceremonial teahouse, a 17th-century Chinese palace hall, and much, much more. Visit the period room settings from France, England, and early America. And, if you get tired, you can always relax over lunch or snacks in the cafeteria or restaurant.

Amble around to the rear of the museum (or exit from its west entrance) for some truly glorious views. From the gazebo just beyond the parking lot you can gaze down on the marvelous **Fairmount**

Waterworks (9) of 1812, looking for all the world like a group of mis-placed Greek temples. A National Historic Engineering Landmark, this fantastic complex on the edge of the Schuylkill River once used steam power to pump water up to a reservoir on the site of the present Museum of Art. Several outbreaks of typhoid caused the city to lose confidence in the river's water, so pumping stopped in 1911. Until 1962 the waterworks were used as an aquarium.

From here on stretches **Fairmount Park**, the largest landscaped city park on Earth. Over 100 miles of trails snake through its more than 8,700 acres, with a multitude of historic, cultural, and recreational attractions along the way. Even a quick probe of the park will take an entire day. If you're interested, the Visitors Center back at J.F.K. Plaza will give you free maps and information.

Return to the front of the Museum of Art and head back down the Parkway to 20th Street. Here you might want to stop at the world-renowned:

*FRANKLIN INSTITUTE (10), 20th St. and Ben Franklin Parkway, ☎ 215-448-1200, Internet: www.fi.edu. *Open daily 9:30–5, with the Tuttleman Omniverse Theater remaining open on Fri.–Sat. until 9. Closed July 4, Thanksgiving, Dec. 24, Christmas, and New Year's. Basic admission: Adults $9.75, seniors and children 4–11 $8.50, under 4 free. Additional charges for Omniverse Theater and Fels Planetarium. Combination tickets available. Gift shops. Parking garage. Cafeteria and restaurant. ♿, use ramp at Winter St. entrance.*

Step from the past into the 21st Century in this hands-on science museum, considered by many to be the best of its kind in the world. Here you can learn all about the fundamentals of science, then explore the possibilities of tomorrow through state-of-the-art exhibits that you manipulate yourself. These attractions are contained in the **Science Center**, while the ***Omniverse Theater** surrounds its audience with enormous wraparound images of thrilling scientific escapades. The **Fels Planetarium** uses its Digistar projector to simulate time travel throughout the Universe.

You can easily spend days at the Franklin Institute, but even a short visit of an hour or two will prove to be both entertaining and enlightening. And, if you only have a few moments, at least pop into the **Benjamin Franklin National Memorial** *(free admission from the 20th Street entrance)* for a look at scientific artifacts and personal mementos of the great man in a hall dominated by his huge statue.

Needless to say, a visit to the Franklin Institute is a delight for the younger set and an enjoyable one for the young-at-heart of all ages. Don't miss it.

Turn south on 20th Street. If you happen to have any small kids (age 7 or younger) in tow, you might want to treat them to the **Please Touch Museum** (11) where everything from Nature's Nursery to a TV studio can be climbed over, played on, tried out, or otherwise explored. SuperMarket Science allows kids to experiment in a child-size grocery store and kitchen, while Sendak is an interactive exhibit of characters from the children's books by illustrator Maurice Sendak. *210 North 21st St. ☎ 215-963-0667, Internet: www.libertynet.org/~pleastch. Open daily 9–4:30. Admission $6.95, under 1 free. ᕗ.*

Another nearby attraction is the **Goldie Paley Gallery** of the **Moore College of Art and Design** (12), which features changing exhibitions of art, architecture, crafts, photography, and design. Sometimes the works of yet-to-be-discovered artists, these shows are often provocative and always worthwhile for those with an interest in art. *20th St. and Ben Franklin Parkway, ☎ 215-568-4515. Open Tues.–Fri. 10–5, Thurs. until 7, weekends noon–4, closed weekends in summer, and holidays. Free.*

Dinosaur fans and other nature lovers can saunter a block east to the:

ACADEMY OF NATURAL SCIENCES (13), 19th St. and Ben Franklin Parkway, ☎ 215-299-1000, Internet: www.acnatsci.org. *Open weekdays 10–4:30, weekends and holidays 10–5. Closed Thanksgiving, Christmas, New Year's. Adults $8.50, seniors $7.75, children 3–12 $7.50, under 3 free. Gift shop. ᕗ, level entrance on 19th St.*

America's oldest museum of natural history has been greatly modernized in recent years, and of late has been focusing its attention on everyone's favorite monsters, the dinosaurs. More than a dozen of these awesome creatures, or at least their bones, inhabit a hall that re-creates their prehistoric world and uses the latest technology to answer your questions. In addition, there's a hands-on nature center, mummies, gem exhibitions, stuffed animals in realistic dioramas, and everything else you'd expect to find in a leading natural history museum.

Continue south on 20th Street. Just before J.F.K. Boulevard you'll have a grand view of the recently-restored **30th Street Station** off in the distance. Opened in 1933, this opulent depot is a major stop for Amtrak trains—and also for all SEPTA commuter trains, NJT trains to Atlantic City, subways, trolleys, and local buses.

Until the 1950s, the south side of J.F.K. Boulevard was the site of the infamous "Chinese Wall," an elevated railroad viaduct that rained soot and cinders down upon the city ever since the late and hardly-lamented Broad Street Station opened next to City Hall in 1882. This neighborhood is now home to the new Philadelphia, an area of strikingly Postmodern skyscrapers that rivals even Manhattan.

In a few blocks you'll come to **Rittenhouse Square** (14), one of the most urbane of urban parks anywhere. This is Philadelphia at its most gracious—a corner of civility where the ideals of William Penn's "Greene Country Towne" still survive, despite the shops and high-rise apartment buildings surrounding it. If you haven't had lunch yet, why not get something to eat from one of the nearby sidewalk vendors and enjoy an alfresco snack at a park bench? And if **shopping** is your thing, you'll find a great selection of intriguing stores on most of the streets between here and Broad Street.

Head east on Locust Street, passing the highly-respected **Curtis Institute of Music**, whose graduates include such luminaries as Leonard Bernstein, Gian-Carlo Menotti, and Samuel Barber. Free concerts are given every Monday, Wednesday, and Friday evening during the school year. ☎ *215-893-7902*. Continuing on the same note, the **Academy of Music** (15), at the corner of Broad Street, is home to the Philadelphia Orchestra, the Opera Company of Philadelphia, the Philly Pops, and other musical organizations. Opened in 1857, it is the oldest concert hall in the nation to remain in use today.

Turn left on Broad Street, now called the **Avenue of the Arts**—a work-in-progress with a great future—and head back towards City Hall. A right turn on Chestnut Street soon brings you to one of the world's grandest shopping emporiums, **Lord & Taylor's** (formerly the John Wanamaker Department Store) (16). Decorated with a gigantic bronze eagle, its towering **Grand Court** has been a Philadelphia landmark and meeting place for over 80 years. The world's largest pipe organ, complete with 30,000 pipes, still provides free concerts every shopping day at 11:15 and 5:15, as it has since its installation in 1911. Those lucky enough to come around Christmas time can witness a fabulous sound-and-light show.

Follow the map across Market Street and enter another old Philadelphia tradition, the **Reading Terminal Market** (17). When the now-defunct Reading Railroad opened its great station in 1892, it leased out the space beneath the then-world's-largest train shed to a variety of food vendors as a sort of farmers' market for city folk. In 1984 the trains, now operated by SEPTA, moved underground to the new Market East Station, but the food merchants remained as the train shed above them became part of the new Pennsylvania Convention Center. Heroic efforts were made to insure that the market would not deteriorate into yet another sterile "food court," so that today it is still a bustling, boisterous nosher's heaven where you can sample wonderful delicacies from around the world while basking in its friendly (and ever so slightly seedy) ambiance. Don't miss this special Philly treat, and be sure to stop at Bassett's to sample America's best ice cream. ☎ *215-922-2317. Open*

Mon.–Sat. 8–6. &.

Adjoining—and above—the market place is the impressive **Pennsylvania Convention Center** (18), opened in 1993. Actually a rather nice piece of architecture, this is among the largest facilities of its type in the nation. Its location in the heart of Center City and its wide-open design successfully integrate conventions into the daily life of the city itself, making visitors feel right at home. *Free tours on Tues. & Thurs. at 11:30, 12:30, 1:30, and 2:15, depart from northwest corner of 12th and Arch streets. Call first to confirm,* ☎ *215-418-4728.*

Index

Special interest attractions are also listed under their category headings.

OTHER DAYTRIPS
TRAVEL GUIDES INCLUDE:

- Florida • France • Germany • Hawaii •
- Holland, Belgium & Luxembourg • Ireland •
- Israel • Italy • London • New England • New York • Pennsylvania Dutch Country & Philadelphia • San Francisco & Northern California • Spain & Portugal • Switzerland •

ABOUT THE AUTHOR:

EARL STEINBICKER is a born tourist who believes that travel should be a joy, not an endurance test. For over 30 years he has been refining his carefree style of daytripping while working in New York, London, Paris, and other cities; first as head of a firm specializing in promotional photography and later as a professional writer. Whether by public transportation or private car, he has thoroughly probed the most delightful aspects of countries around the world — while always returning to the comforts of city life at night. A strong desire to share these experiences has led him to develop the "Daytrips" series of guides, which he continues to expand and revise. Recently, he has been assisting other authors in developing additional "Daytrips" books, further expanding the series. He presently lives in the Philadelphia suburbs.

Made in the USA
San Bernardino, CA
13 December 2012